D1126390

AIA GUIDE TO THE ARCHITECTURE OF WASHINGTON, D.C.

AIA GUIDE TO THE ARCHITECTURE OF Washing

FIFTH EDITION

G. MARTIN MOELLER, JR., ASSOC. AIA

for the Washington Chapter of the American Institute of Architects

with an Introduction by **FRANCIS D. LETHBRIDGE, FAIA**

BORIS FELDBLYUM, photo editor

THE JOHNS HOPKINS UNIVERSITY PRESS Baltimore

ton, D.C.

Printed in Canada on acid-free paper

9 8 7 6 5 4 3 2 1

The Johns Hopkins University Press
2715 North Charles Street
Baltimore, Maryland 21218-4363
www.press.jhu.edu

Library of Congress Cataloging-
in-Publication Data
Moeller, Gerard Martin.
AIA guide to the architecture of Washington, D.C. / by G. Martin Moeller, Jr. for the Washington Chapter of the American Institute of Architects ; with an introduction by Francis D. Lethbridge ; Boris Feldblyum, photo editor. — 5th ed.
p. cm.
Includes index.
ISBN-13: 978-1-4214-0269-7 (hardback : alk. paper)
ISBN-13: 978-1-4214-0270-3 (pbk. : alk. paper)
ISBN-13: 978-1-4214-0626-8 (electronic)
ISBN-10: 1-4214-0269-6 (hardback : alk. paper)
ISBN-10: 1-4214-0270-x (pbk. : alk. paper)
ISBN-10: 1-4214-0626-8 (electronic)
1. Architecture—Washington (D.C.)—Guidebooks. 2. Washington (D.C.)—Buildings, structures, etc.—Guidebooks. 3. Washington (D.C.)—Guidebooks. I. Feldblyum, Boris, 1951– II. American Institute of Architects. III. Title.
NA735.W3M64 2012
720.9753—dc23 2011042880

A catalog record for this book is available from the British Library.

Special discounts are available for bulk purchases of this book. For more information, please contact Special Sales at 410-516-6936 or specialsales@press.jhu.edu.

The Johns Hopkins University Press uses environmentally friendly book materials, including recycled text paper that is composed of at least 30 percent post-consumer waste, whenever possible.

Contents

Preface

In the mid-1960s, a quartet of Washington architects—Warren J. Cox, Hugh Newell Jacobsen, Francis D. Lethbridge, and David R. Rosenthal—accepted the daunting challenge of producing a handy but thorough guide to the architecture of the capital. Written and published for what was then called the Washington Metropolitan Chapter of the American Institute of Architects (AIA), the book, which contained brief descriptions of buildings in the District of Columbia, northern Virginia, and suburban Maryland, appeared in 1965. A second edition, incorporating modest revisions and additions, was published in 1974.

During the 1980s, the Washington area grew rapidly, and dozens of major new buildings were added to the cityscape. By the end of the decade, many members of the Chapter—by then named the Washington Chapter / AIA—were clamoring for an updated guidebook. The original four authors had become well established in their careers and were in no position to take on the third edition, which would have required substantial new research and writing, so the Chapter engaged Maryland-based writer Christopher Weeks to produce an updated and expanded guide. Given the tremendous increase in the number of potential entries since the previous edition, the Chapter's leadership decided to narrow the scope of the book to the District of Columbia proper (an exception was made for Arlington National Cemetery, which was deemed a crucial component of the capital's monumental core). The third edition hit the bookstores in 1994.

In the decade that followed, Washington experienced yet another impressive construction boom, and benefited from a nationwide resurgence of interest in urban living. By the early 2000s, it was becoming clear that a new version of the popular guidebook was needed. Initially, I was asked to "revise and update" the Weeks edition, but the Chapter and I soon came to agree that a wholesale rewriting was in order because the architectural culture and identity of the city had changed so dramatically during the intervening years. I reinvestigated factual data appearing in the previous book, rewrote all of the existing entries (not counting a small number of deletions), and researched newly added buildings, writing the corresponding entries. The result was an almost entirely new text that was published as the fourth edition in 2006.

The current edition—the fifth—is based on the previous one, though many entries have been rewritten once again for various reasons. In some cases, the buildings have been altered, requiring updated descriptions; in others, continuing research has unearthed interesting facts about the buildings that warranted revisions to the text. And in some instances my opinions about the buildings have simply changed. The Chapter asked a group of experts—consisting of architects Heather Cass, FAIA, Mary Oehrlein, FAIA, and Marshall Purnell, FAIA, and historians Richard Longstreth and Judith Robinson—to advise on which new buildings to include and which of the old entries to delete. The final list totaled 407 entries, of which 44 are new. These include recently built and recently renovated structures along with a few older buildings that seemed worthy of inclusion. Meanwhile, 27 entries from the previous edition were either deleted or incorporated into other listings.

Writing guidebooks is a tricky business. Accuracy and currency can be elusive goals, as buildings are constantly being built, renovated, enlarged, demolished, renamed, or sold. Even seemingly pedigreed landmarks can pose challenges, as historians sometimes disagree about basic "facts" such as dates of construction (throughout this book, the years listed in the credits are intended to represent the years in which the corresponding projects were *completed*—a range of dates is given in cases involving unusually drawn-out design or construction periods). In preparing this guide,

I sought credible sources for all data, relying heavily on the documents of the Historic American Buildings Survey, specific institutional archives, local governmental agencies, and authoritative articles and books. To the extent possible, all essential information in a given entry was verified with the building's owner or architect, or in the case of a historic building, a person presumed to have relevant knowledge such as a curator, archivist, or historian. If, despite this diligence, an error has slipped through, I would welcome a correction, which may be submitted through AIA | DC.

This guide is not intended to serve as a purely factual historical record; much of the content, in fact, is subjective, and often includes positive or negative criticism. The reader should remember that the opinions expressed herein are just that—opinions—and are solely those of the author. Reasonable people may disagree as to whether a given work of architecture is good, bad, gorgeous, or hideous—a negative comment about a particular building is not intended to give offense to the architects or any others involved in its creation.

It is unfortunate, but perhaps inevitable, that architecture guidebooks tend to emphasize prominent public, institutional, and commercial buildings at the expense of smaller, privately owned structures, especially single-family residences. The reasons are simple: first, there are limits on the number of entries that may be included in such books without compromising readability and portability; second, the vast quantity of distinct houses makes selection of representative examples difficult; and third, privacy concerns can complicate research into the history of residential buildings. I am acutely aware that row houses, in particular, are underrepresented in this book. Row houses—in all their variations—collectively constitute one of the most important building types in the nation's capital, and contribute a great deal to the architectural and urban character of the city. Of course, Washington also boasts many beautiful streets lined with detached houses of various scales and styles.

Even if you faithfully complete every tour in this guidebook, there is much more architecture to see in Washington. Take some time to stroll through the city's residential areas. Note the characteristic scale and texture of the houses, consider the varied relationships of the buildings to yards and sidewalks, and observe the vital role of trees and other plants in defining the streetscape. Enjoy the quotidian details that make these distinct and culturally rich neighborhoods the true heart of Washington, overlooked though they may be by the typical tourist. Then perhaps you can head back to the Lincoln Memorial, gaze down the Mall toward the Capitol, and contemplate the broader course of civilization.

Acknowledgments

The Chapter is extremely grateful to all the people who helped to prepare this fifth edition. First and foremost G. Martin Moeller, Jr., Assoc. AIA, who worked under an impossible deadline to produce an even better book than the last. Although this volume is set up in distinct tours, I read it cover to cover and it's a delightful read. I encourage you to read the chapters in full. Martin's clever turns of phrase (the FBI building as a "swaggering bully" is my favorite) will give you fresh perspective on the architecture of our city whether you see it every day or only occasionally as a visitor here.

Second, I want to thank our photo editor, Boris Feldblyum, who carefully organized all of the images. His spreadsheet is really a thing of beauty and will help future editions of this guide enormously. Boris also took many of the photos in this and the previous edition and we are very grateful that this talented photographer has become such a good friend of the Chapter.

And while we are at it, let's thank all the photographers in this guide: Alan Karchmer, Assoc. AIA, and Boris Feldblyum, with additional photography by Peter Aaron, Wolfgang Hoyt, and Ezra Stoller of Esto, Nic Lehoux, Michael Andrade, Shalom Baranes, Bryan Becker, CORE Group, George Cott, Robert Creamer, Devrouax & Purnell, Dumbarton Oaks, Debi Fox, Richard Greenhouse, Carol Highsmith, Dan Cunningham, Fred Sons Photography, Julia Heine, Bill Lebovich, Larry M. Levine, Jon Miller, Donald Paine, Robert Polidori, Dan Poyourow, Paúl Rivera, Ken Wyner, Michael Dersin, Michael Houlahan, Paul Warchol, Prakash Patel, Ron Solomon, Timothy Hursley, Arthur Cotton Moore, Alex Jamison, Max MacKenzie, Anice Hoachlander, the late Robert Lautman, Hon. AIA, and Ronald O'Rourke.

Thanks also to KUBE Architecture for working hard to make sure the maps are as accurate as they are handsome and to Robert J. Brugger and his team at the Johns Hopkins University Press.

Our author, Martin, adds his thanks to the many architectural historians, architects, and others who reviewed all or part of the draft text and provided comments and corrections, including Richard Longstreth, Judith Robinson, and most notably Steven K. Dickens, AIA.

And last, we are very grateful to Microdesk for sponsoring additional research and also to the members of the Washington Chapter of the American Institute of Architects, who not only underwrote a substantial part of the production of this publication but also are its real stars.

Mary Fitch, AICP, Hon. AIA
Executive Director
AIA | DC

AIA GUIDE TO THE ARCHITECTURE OF WASHINGTON, D.C.

The Architecture of Washington, D.C., 1791–1965

FRANCIS D. LETHBRIDGE, FAIA

This introduction is reprinted from the 1965 edition of A Guide to the Architecture of Washington, D.C., *with minor revisions for stylistic consistency or clarity and historical updates where appropriate.*

The selection of a site for the federal capital was finally settled in New York City one evening in the summer of 1790, when Thomas Jefferson and Alexander Hamilton dined together and concluded what might be described as a political deal. Bitter political enemies though they were, Jefferson and Hamilton each wanted something that only their combined influence in Congress could bring about. And so it came to pass that sufficient southern votes were cast for the Funding Bill; that the Pennsylvanians, wooed by the prospect of removal of the federal capital to Philadelphia for the next ten years, cast their votes for the Residence Bill; and that, to the accompaniment of cries of rage from New York and New England, the federal government assumed the debts of the states and made plans to set up its home on the shores of the Potomac River.[1]

The planning of the city of Washington is a familiar tale, yet one that bears repeating, for the quality, durability, and persistent effect of that plan upon the city must always be a central theme in the story of its architecture. We must first, however, go somewhat farther back in time, for long before the construction of the federal city began, there was a flourishing colonial society on the shores of the Potomac near the place where the tidewater country ends. The fall line—that abrupt rise from the eastern coastal plain that marks the end of navigable water—may be traced as an uneven line from New England southward and westward. The cities of Trenton and Richmond, for example, lie at the falls of the Delaware and the James, and if the capital had never been established on the Potomac, the ports of Georgetown and Alexandria would doubtless have prospered and grown into thriving cities by virtue of their location at this crossroads of travel by land and river.

The Chesapeake Bay had been explored by the Spanish before the end of the 16th century, but not until 1608, when Captain John Smith sailed up the Potomac River, quite possibly as far as the Little Falls, north of the present site of Georgetown, was very much known of the area that became the capital of the New World. Smith's *General Historie of Virginia, New England and the Summer Isles,* published in England in 1627, was accompanied by a remarkable map that was the basis for all cartography of the Chesapeake region for nearly 100 years. His description of the river is still a vivid one:

> The fourth river is called Patawomeke, 6 or 7 myles in breadth. It is navigable 140 myles, and fed as the rest with many sweet rivers and springs, which fall from the bordering hills. These hills many of them are planted, and yeeld no lesse plentie and varietie of fruit, then the river exceedeth with abundance of fish. It is inhabited on both sides. . . . The river above this place maketh his passage downe a low pleasant valley overshaddowed in many places with high rocky mountaines; from whence distill innumerable sweet and pleasant springs.

In the next 25 years the Potomac became a scene of increasing activity on the part of traders, who began to tap a rich supply of furs, not from the adjacent country alone, but from the lands beyond the Alleghenies, from which they were carried by the Indians to the headwaters of the river. These adventurers were necessarily a hardy and resourceful lot, who plied their trade, in small shallops, from the lower reaches of

Chesapeake Bay; and some of them, such as Henry Spelman and Henry Fleete, knew the Algonquin language well from having lived with the Indians as hostages or captives.

In March 1634, Leonard Calvert arrived upon this Potomac scene in two ships, the *Ark* and the *Dove,* with a cargo of Protestant and Roman Catholic settlers, the Catholics seeking their fortunes but also haven from English religious persecution. Near the mouth of the river they founded St. Mary's City, which served as the capital of Maryland until a Protestant revolt late in the century. While St. Mary's City has been engaged in an ambitious reconstruction program on the site of the old capital, there are, in fact, very few remaining examples of 17th-century construction on either the Maryland or the Virginia shores of the river. You must travel farther south, to the banks of the James River, to the sites of the Thomas Rolfe House (1651); the Allen House, or "Bacon's Castle" (1655); and St. Luke's Church (c. 1650), to see the only recognizable survivals of Jacobean architecture in the tidewater country. It is ironic that the most famous example of the period, Governor William Berkeley's mansion "Greenspring" (1642), which Thomas Tileston Waterman terms "probably the greatest Virginia house of the Century," was destroyed in 1806 to make way for Benjamin Henry Latrobe's house for William Ludwell Lee, which in its turn was demolished during the Civil War.[2]

Despite recurring troubles with the dwindling Indian tribes up until the beginning of the 18th century, settlement along the Potomac continued steadily. Large land grants were taken up in both Virginia and Maryland, and estates of many thousands of acres were not unusual. Compared to the lands of Robert Carter of Nomini Hall, who owned 63,093 acres, and William Fitzhugh of Bedford, who had acquired more than 45,000 acres, the 8,000-acre holdings of George Washington at Mount Vernon and George Mason's combined holdings of about 15,000 acres along the river seem modest in size. Cheap land, abundant labor, easy transportation from private landings to ships, and a ready market for tobacco in England made possible the development of the great plantations of the tidewater country.

At least for the planters who prospered, the country offered a gracious life, which flourished in the early and mid-18th century and resulted in some handsome houses. Within a relatively few miles of Washington you can see many noble examples of these country mansions,[3] and a short trip to Williamsburg, Virginia, will help you to imagine what life was like in a provincial capital of that period.

The prosperity of the plantations and the settlements of tracts beyond the borders of the river and its navigable tributaries stimulated the founding of the ports of Alexandria (1748) and Georgetown (1751). Another earlier port, Garrison's Landing, known later as Bladensburg (1742), on the Eastern Branch, or Anacostia River, sank into commercial obscurity at the end of the 18th century, when the river silted up beyond that point. Two of these Potomac ports were the scene of an important event in colonial history not long after they had been established. In the year 1755, General Edward Braddock embarked with his army from Alexandria, landed near the foot of Rock Creek, and marched up the path of what is now Wisconsin Avenue, on the ill-fated expedition against the French and Indians that ended in disaster near Fort Duquesne. One of the few provincial officers to return unscathed from the campaign was a young Virginian who had been spared to play a greater role in history.

Georgetown and Alexandria still retain some of the atmosphere and much of the scale and texture of colonial river port towns. From the accounts of travelers it would seem that by the latter part of the century they were thriving, pleasant places. Thomas Twining, after a rough all-day wagon journey from Baltimore in 1795, described Georgetown as "a small but neat town . . . the road from Virginia and the Southern States, crossing the Potomac here, already gives an air of prosperity to this little town, and assures its future importance, whatever may be the fate of the

"Plan of the City of Washington, in the Territory of Columbia ceded by the States of Virginia and Maryland to the United States of America," by Andrew Ellicott, published in The Universal Asylum, and Columbian Magazine, *March 1792. This was the first published plan of the proposed city, and while at first glance it appears to be a replica of L'Enfant's original plan, in fact there are many subtle differences between the two.*

projected metropolis."[4] The fate of the future "metropolis" was, in fact, frequently in doubt during the succeeding 75 years.

At George Washington's request, the act of 1790 specifying the location of a federal district of "ten miles square" to be located at any point *above* the Eastern Branch, was modified to include the town of Alexandria, several miles below that point. (Alexandria was ceded back to Virginia in 1846.) Congress enacted this change on March 3, 1791, and by the ninth of that month Major Pierre Charles L'Enfant (who went by the name Peter) had arrived in Georgetown to commence the planning of the capital city. Andrew Ellicott and Benjamin Banneker had already been employed to survey and map the federal territory, and they proceeded without delay to carry out as much of this work as they could before Washington's arrival at the site.

On the evening of March 29, a crucial meeting took place after dinner at the home of General Uriah Forrest,[5] at which the president, the newly appointed commissioners, and the principal landowners of the federal district were present. The next day Washington recorded in his diary:

> The parties to whom I addressed myself yesterday evening, having taken the matter into consideration, saw the propriety of my observations; and whilst they were contending for the shadow they might lose the substance; and therefore mutually agreed and entered into articles to surrender for public purposes, one half the land they severally possessed within the bounds which were designated as necessary for the city to stand.
>
> This business being thus happily finished and some directions given to the Commissioners, the Surveyor and Engineer with respect to the mode of laying out the district—Surveying the grounds for the City and forming them into lots—I left Georgetown, dined in Alexandria and reached Mount Vernon in the evening.[6]

Philip Hart proposed this design for the new Capitol, which would have had a rather collegiate character were it not for the cartoonish finials.

It was only fitting that the commissioners agreed in September that the federal district be called "The Territory of Columbia" and the federal city "The City of Washington"!

L'Enfant had less than a year to prepare the plan of the capital city before he was dismissed for his failure—or his temperamental inability—to acknowledge the authority of the commissioners over his work. To the end, he maintained that he was responsible to the president alone, and when Washington himself reluctantly denied that this was so, L'Enfant's dismissal was inevitable. He had sufficient time, nevertheless, to set the mold into which the city would be formed, and with the sole exception of Washington himself, no one's influence upon its conception and development was greater.

The architecture of the area from 1791 to the 1960s may be conveniently divided into four major phases. The first, which extended to the middle of the 19th century, is generally characterized by work in the Late Georgian and Classic Revival styles. Some designs in the Gothic Revival style also appeared in this period, but they were limited principally to small examples of ecclesiastical architecture. The second phase, in a variety of styles that might be grouped under the term Romantic Revival, dominated from about 1850 to the end of the century. The third period, Classic Eclecticism, was to a large degree an outgrowth of the Columbian Exposition of 1893 and the McMillan Plan for Washington of 1901. The fourth and last phase can be said to extend from about the beginning of World War II to the present [that period, the heyday of modernism in Washington, continued into the early 1980s].

From the first, the federal capital attracted the talents of many of the most gifted designers of the period. They included architect-builders, or "undertakers," such as William Lovering; self-taught gentleman-architects like Dr. William Thornton; and trained professional architect-engineers, of whom Benjamin Henry Latrobe was the most notable example. Some, like James Hoban, architect of the White House, and Charles Bulfinch, who succeeded Latrobe as Architect of the Capitol in 1818, do not fit neatly into any of these categories.

In an era that was not distinguished by temperance of speech and writing in the political arena, architects frequently indulged in bitter personal invective. Architects have been inclined to disagree with one another since the beginning of time and will probably continue to do so until the end, but they have seldom expressed themselves so forcefully in writing as in the case of:

(a) Thornton versus Latrobe:
This Dutchman in taste, this monument builder,
This planner of grand steps and walls,
This falling-arch maker, this blunder-roof gilder,
Himself still an architect calls.

(b) Latrobe versus Hoban:
. . . the style [Jefferson] proposes is exactly consistent with Hoban's pile—a litter of pigs worthy of the great sow it surrounds, and of the wild Irish boar, the father of her.

(c) Hadfield versus Thornton et al.:
This premium [for the best design of the Capitol] was offered at a period when scarcely a professional architect was to be found in any of the United States; which is plainly to be seen in the pile of trash presented as designs for [the Capitol] building.[7]

Paradoxically, the men who hurled such violent criticism at one another lived in an age of harmonious urban architecture, for, despite personal animosities and professional jealousies, they were all working within the limits of generally accepted standards of taste, and perhaps just as important, within fairly narrow limits of available construction materials and techniques.[8]

Although work on the first major public buildings, the White House and the Capitol, had begun in 1793—seven years before the government moved to Washington—they were virtually built anew after British troops sacked and burned Washington in 1814. The rout of the hastily assembled militia at the Battle of Bladensburg (known

Published in London, this engraving marks the day the British took Washington in the War of 1812 and, according to the original caption, the invading army "burnt and destroyed their Dock Yard, . . . Senate House, President's Palace, War Office, Treasury, and the Great Bridge."

The C&O Canal was popular with early 20th-century schoolchildren but not with merchants, who preferred the speed and reliability of the B&O Railroad out of Baltimore. The canal was closed to commercial traffic in 1923.

thereafter as "The Bladensburg Races") caused President James Madison, Madame Madison, and the rest of official Washington to beat a hasty retreat to the suburbs. The president returned to take up temporary residence in Colonel John Tayloe's town house, the Octagon; the Treaty of Ghent, which ended the War of 1812, was signed in the round room on the second floor.

In the early 1830s, the commercial leaders of Washington City thought its future lay in the success of the Chesapeake and Ohio Canal, which was supposed to connect the Potomac with the headwaters of the Ohio River. After 1850, the canal did tie Washington to Cumberland, Maryland, and it continued in operation until 1923. But it was never a profitable investment, because the more successful Baltimore and Ohio Railroad, following much the same route and with its eastern terminus at Baltimore, had been begun at exactly the same time (a remarkable act of optimism, since steam locomotives had not yet been tried on such a scale). The canal today provides a valuable recreational area—an attractive stretch for hiking, cycling, and canoeing.

When Robert Mills served as Architect of Public Buildings in 1841, he supplemented his modest income by producing the *Guide to the National Executive Offices and the Capitol of the United States,* a slim paperbound volume of only 50 pages that is of interest today chiefly because within those covers he was able to include plans of the Capitol and of all the executive buildings, to list the names and room numbers of all federal employees, and to have room left over to print the menu for the congressional dining room, or "Refectory for Members of Congress."[9]

Mills (who had been a pupil of Latrobe), Ammi Young, and Thomas U. Walter were probably the last federal architects of the period to design work in the Classic Revival style. In 1849, Robert Dale Owen, son of Robert Owen, who was the leader of the utopian colony of New Harmony, published *Hints on Public Architecture.* A former representative from Indiana, the younger Owen served as chairman of the building committee of the Smithsonian Institution, and his book supplied an elaborate presentation of, and argument for, the honest functional qualities of James Renwick's design, "exemplifying the style of the 12th century," as contrasted with the false qualities of the Greek and Roman manners of other public buildings in Washington. The book

This engraving, published c. 1854, exaggerates the scale of the almost-completed Smithsonian Castle but vividly conveys the building's picturesque composition.

and the design appear to have been strongly influenced by the writings of A. Welby Pugin and Andrew Jackson Downing. Some of the text gives one the impression that, though time may pass and styles may change, architectural jargon remains usable for any occasion: "to reach an Architecture suited to our own country and our own time . . . an actual example, at the Seat of Government, the architect of which seems to me to have struck into the right road, to have made a step in advance, and to have given us, in his design, not a little of what may be fitting and appropriate in any manner . . . that shall deserve to be named as a National Style of Architecture for America."[10]

Not many architects chose to follow Renwick's new "national style" (Renwick himself, when he designed the old Corcoran Gallery [now the Renwick Gallery] some years later, adopted the style of the French Renaissance), but most architects thereafter seemed determined to submit their own candidates for that honor.

Before his death in a Hudson riverboat explosion in 1852, Downing had laid out the grounds of the Smithsonian and the White House in the romantic, meandering style of the period. His popular books on landscape design and rural architecture publicized residential designs by A. J. Davis, Richard Upjohn, and Downing's own partner, Calvert Vaux, who planned houses for some of the fashionable and wealthy citizens of Georgetown. Vaux's houses show, in an interesting way, the transition of residential design from the late Classic Revival through the relatively chaste Italianate or Tuscan Villa style to the heavily ornamented, mansard-roofed houses of the latter part of the 19th century.

The Civil War turned the city of Washington into an armed camp. The location of the capital, selected so carefully to be near the line between the North and South, became a position at the edge of the battlefront. A ring of defensive forts was constructed on the hills surrounding the city, and although in 1864 a Confederate army

Georgetown merchant Francis Dodge built this "suburban villa," designed by A. J. Downing and Calvert Vaux, at 1517 30th Street, NW. From the glass-enclosed tower, Francis, whose brother Robert commissioned his own house nearby based on the same design, could watch over the family's warehouse near the C&O Canal.

led by Jubal Early reached the outskirts of the federal district at Fort Stevens, the city's defenses were never penetrated.[11]

Apart from the completion of the new Capitol wings and dome, work on which continued despite the war, little construction of a permanent nature went on in the city until the end of hostilities. A significant aftermath, however, was the increased influence and activity of the U.S. Army Corps of Engineers—not restricted to works of engineering alone, but extending to the design or supervision of construction of major public buildings such as the Pension Building [now the National Building Museum] and the old State, War, and Navy Building [now the Eisenhower Executive Office Building]. Most prominent in the corps at that time was General Montgomery C. Meigs, the talented officer who had earlier challenged Thomas U. Walter's authority as Architect of the Capitol. Meigs designed the astonishing post–Civil War Pension Building but left what may be his most enduring monument in the Washington aqueduct system, extending to the city from above the Little Falls of the Potomac. Two of the bridges along its route are especially notable—the Cabin John Aqueduct Bridge, which for many years was the longest stone arch in the world (220 feet), and the Rock Creek Aqueduct Bridge, where the road was carried on the arched tubular metal pipes of the water supply system.

Construction of the old State, War, and Navy Building after the Civil War was considered by many to be an act signifying the permanence of Washington, D.C., as the site of the national capital. If cost of construction and permanence of materials were any measure of that intent, it must have served admirably to make the intention clear. Alfred B. Mullett was not an architect whose work rested lightly upon the earth (the Post Office Building in St. Louis is another good example of his work). Like MacArthur's Philadelphia City Hall, his buildings were as much an expression of civic confidence as of architectural diligence.

The Smithsonian's Arts and Industries Building, designed by Cluss and Schulze, is an interesting survivor from the exhibition architecture of the 1876 Philadelphia Centennial Exposition. The Oriental flavor of its form and polychrome decorations was echoed in some of the city's market buildings, schools, railroad stations, and residences of the 1880s, of which relatively few remain. The influence of H. H. Richardson and the Romanesque Revival made an impression on Washington architecture from about 1880 to 1900, and although Richardson's Hay and Adams houses were de-

The Franklin School, designed by Adolf Cluss and completed in 1869, as depicted in Joseph West Moore's Picturesque Washington *(1886). A model of the school building, which still stands at 13th and K streets, NW, was featured in the 1873 World Exposition in Vienna, Austria, and earned for the Washington public school system a Medal for Progress.*

stroyed to build the hotel that bears their names, the Tuckerman House, built the year of his death, 1886, on an adjoining site, was carried out by Hornblower and Marshall in a direct continuity of style and exterior detailing. The Presbyterian Church of the Covenant, designed by J. C. Cady, architect of the Museum of Natural History in New York, and the old Post Office on Pennsylvania Avenue, are other important examples of the period.[12]

The Washington firm of Smithmeyer and Pelz was prominent on the architectural scene toward the end of the 19th century, with buildings to its credit as widely different as Georgetown's Healy Hall, a Victorian neo-Gothic college building, and the Library of Congress, a competition-winning design in the Renaissance style. Some of the more startling designs of this versatile firm were never built, including a Gothic multi-towered bridge across the Potomac and a new White House spanning 16th Street at Meridian Hill.

The lack of any effective controls over its rapid and haphazard growth was gradually destroying any evidence of the capital as a uniquely planned city, but in the year 1901 the American Institute of Architects played a central role in the initiation of the McMillan Plan, which modified, enlarged, and reestablished L'Enfant's plan of Washington. Glenn Brown, an architect whose deep interest in the history of the Capitol later produced a monumental two-volume account of its development, had been appointed secretary of the institute in 1899, and it was largely through his efforts that the program for the AIA convention of 1900 was prepared. The meeting convened in Washington on the centennial of the establishment of the federal city, and the papers delivered at that meeting inspired Senator James McMillan, chairman of the Senate District Committee, to appoint a commission to study the planning of the city. He asked the institute to suggest who would be most qualified to serve, and the names of Daniel H. Burnham and Frederick Law Olmsted Jr. emerged by common consent. The Chicago Columbian Exposition of 1893 was still fresh in the minds of all, and Burnham, having headed the group of architects and artists who planned the exhibition, was a logical choice, as was Olmsted, son and successor of the famous landscape architect who had designed the grounds and terraces of the Capitol. Burnham and Olmsted, in turn, asked for the appointment of architect Charles Follen McKim and sculptor Augustus Saint-Gaudens, both of whom had worked intimately with Burnham during the Columbian Exposition. The report of this group, officially named the Senate Park Commission, was published in 1902 and was a remarkable document. These talented men—bound together by friendship, respect, and common purpose—made the most of the opportunity to describe and delineate a vision of what the city might become.

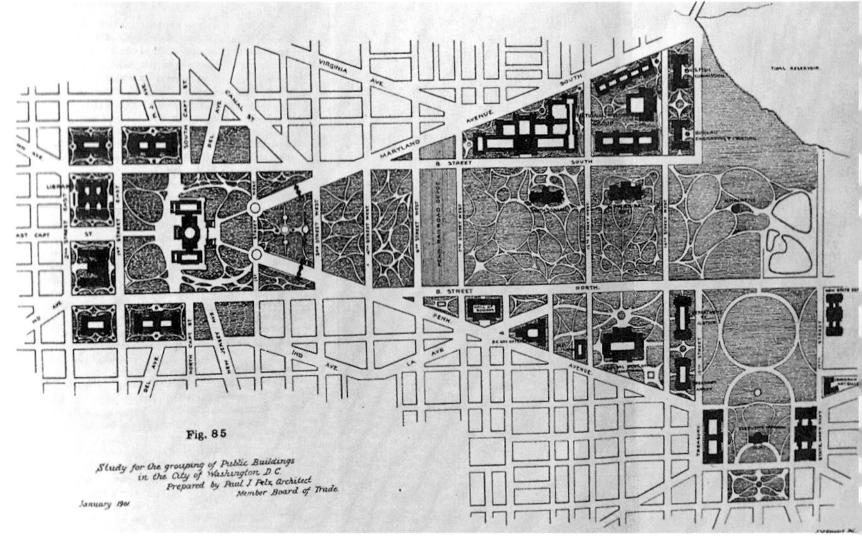

"Study for the grouping of Public Buildings in the City of Washington, D.C.," prepared by architect Paul Pelz in 1901. Pelz's efforts to tidy up the unkempt Mall did not go nearly as far as those of the Senate Park Commission, which released its ambitious plan the following year.

Some of the Senate Park Commission's recommendations were never carried out—among them ideas that could be profitably restudied today—but many of them were, and the effect upon Washington's architectural style was just as pronounced as the effects upon its plan. The formality of L'Enfant's plan was restored, and the argument that an architecture derived from classical antecedents was the only suitable style for such a plan was persuasively presented in visual terms. Whatever weight or merit this argument may have had, it is undeniably true that some of the finest buildings in Washington date from the early decades of the 20th century quite simply because the best architects in the country designed them.

It was a time of great optimism, clients wanted and would pay for the best, and Art was respectable enough to sit at the table when the money was being served. Not only were prominent architects of the period, such as Burnham, the firm of McKim, Mead and White, Henry Bacon, Paul Cret, and Cass Gilbert, given important commissions in the capital, but their buildings were embellished by the work of sculptors such as Saint-Gaudens, Daniel Chester French, and Lorado Taft.

The spirit pervading the best work of that period seems gradually to have been lost. Whether it was dried up by the Depression, squeezed out by the weight of bureaucracy, or simply enfeebled by lack of conviction and talent would be hard to say. Whatever the cause, work in the style of academic classicism, with few exceptions, seemed to become progressively larger, more sterile, and less graceful in conception and execution.

It is difficult to view architecture in Washington since 1940 in any clear historical perspective. Dating a new phase of architectural development from a period at the beginning of World War II is in itself a somewhat arbitrary decision, but the Saarinen competition-winning design for the Smithsonian Gallery of Art in 1939 [which was never constructed] and William Lescaze's Longfellow Building in 1940 [later modified beyond recognition] probably mark as distinct a point of change as any that might be named. Since that time, certain other isolated examples, such as the Dulles Airport Terminal building, loom as important and serious works of architecture, but a leveling influence of sorts has been at work. The majority of contemporary commercial and

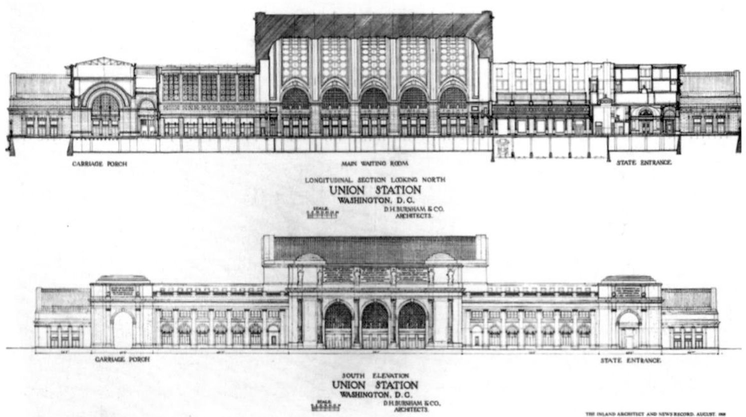

Cross-section and main elevation of the new Union Station, designed by D. H. Burnham & Co., the first building to be executed in the spirit of the Senate Park Commission's plan of 1901–2.

governmental office buildings tended to become larger and more standardized to the point where they were virtually indistinguishable in form. This was perhaps inevitable, since the functions of these structures were very nearly the same. The great variety of industrially produced materials and building components that became available after World War II, along with the economies of modern curtain wall construction, created a new element in the cityscape that was both monotonous and distracting: monotonous because many of the newer buildings were wrapped, like packages, in an overall pattern of windows and spandrels; distracting because there seemed no limit to the number of unsuitable patterns that one could place in juxtaposition to one another.

Washington is a horizontal city. The maximum building heights Congress established in 1910 to prevent our principal federal monuments from being overshadowed by commercial construction are in general still considered to be a desirable limitation. But these height limits, coupled with building programs calling for hundreds of thousands of square feet of construction, have created architectural and planning problems within the city that remain unresolved.

The urban renewal area in Southwest Washington will probably remain interesting to architects and planners for many years, not only as one of the first large-scale applications of the powers of urban renewal, but also as an architectural sampler of the mid-20th century. Rarely may one view such a variety of architectural solutions to essentially the same problem, constructed in such a relatively concentrated area, over such a short period of time. Some examples of planned communities near Washington—ranging from Greenbelt, Maryland, the most famous of the government-sponsored resettlement housing projects of the 1930s, and Hollin Hills in Virginia, a pioneer example of postwar contemporary development planning, to Reston, conceived as a New Town, in nearby Fairfax County—also are of particular interest.

NOTES

1. See Kenneth R. Bowling and Helen E. Veit, eds., *The Diary of William Maclay and Other Notes on the Senate Debates*, vol. 9 of the *Documentary History of the First Federal Congress of the United States of America, March 4, 1789–March 3, 1791* (Baltimore, 1988), pp. 307–8. Maclay, a senator from Pennsylvania, had no illusions. His journal entry for June 30, 1790, reports: "I am fully convinced Pennsylvania could do no better. The Matter could not be longer delayed. It is in fact the Interest of the President of the United States, that pushes the Potowmack, he by means of Jefferson Madison Carroll & others Urges the Business,

and if We had not closed with these Terms a bargain would have been made, for the Temporary Residence in New York."

2. Thomas Tileston Waterman, *The Mansions of Virginia, 1706–1776* (Chapel Hill, 1946).

3. Gunston Hall, Virginia (1753); Mount Vernon, Virginia (1757–87); Montpelier, Laurel, Maryland (1770). See also Mills Lane, *Architecture of the Old South: Virginia* (New York, 1987) and *Architecture of the Old South: Maryland* (New York, 1991) for other examples.

4. Thomas Twining, *Travels in America 100 Years Ago* (New York: Harper & Bros., 1893), pp. 98–99.

5. The building that was Forrest's home, 2550 M Street, though much altered, remains standing.

6. Donald Jackson and Dorothy Toohig, eds., *The Diaries of George Washington* (Charlottesville: University Press of Virginia, 1979), vol. 6.

7. Talbot Hamlin, *Benjamin Henry Latrobe* (New York: Oxford University Press, 1955), pp. 285, 294; George Hadfield, *The Washington Guide* (Washington, D.C.: S. A. Elliott, 1826), p. 22.

8. See, for example, Thornton's Tudor Place and the Octagon; Latrobe's Decatur House and St. John's Church, Lafayette Square; The White House's central façade by Hoban and Latrobe; and Hadfield's Arlington House and Old City Hall (now the Superior Court of the District of Columbia).

9. Some of the fixed prices were: venison steak, 37½ cents; beefsteak, 25 cents; pork steak, 25 cents; mutton chop, 25 cents; veal cutlet, 25 cents; one dozen raw oysters, 12½ cents; ham and eggs, 37½ cents; one plate of common turtle soup, 25 cents; one plate of green turtle soup, 50 cents; wine and water, and malt liquor, per tumbler, 6¼ cents.

10. Robert Dale Owen, *Hints on Public Architecture* (New York: G. P. Putnam, 1849), pp. 104, 109.

11. See John G. Barnard, *A Report on the Defenses of Washington* (Washington, D.C.: Government Printing Office, 1871). The remains of this chain of earthwork defenses are now under the jurisdiction of the National Park Service. Fort Stevens, at the head of Georgia Avenue, NW, is probably the most interesting, historically if not topographically.

12. Of these three buildings, only the old Post Office remains, the Tuckerman House and Church of the Covenant having been demolished in the late 1960s to make way for new speculative office buildings.

The Architecture of Washington, D.C., 1965–2012

G. MARTIN MOELLER, JR., ASSOC. AIA

As Francis D. Lethbridge, FAIA, was writing the introduction to the first edition of this guide, published in 1965, Washington was in the early stages of an unusually fertile period in its architectural history. During the 1960s and 1970s, internationally recognized architects, including Marcel Breuer, I. M. Pei, Philip Johnson, and Gordon Bunshaft, were designing prominent governmental and institutional buildings in what might be called a "High Modernist" vein that celebrated pure, abstract geometry. Nathaniel Owings was leading a presidentially appointed advisory council that proposed an audacious, if flawed, plan for the redevelopment of Pennsylvania Avenue. Talented local firms, such as Chloethiel Woodard Smith & Associated Architects and Keyes Lethbridge & Condon, were producing in Southwest Washington some of the most convincingly livable "urban renewal" projects in the country. At the same time, years before the preservation movement took root, the nation's capital seemed ahead of the curve in this regard, as John Carl Warnecke was devising a scheme that saved Lafayette Square from demolition and Arthur Cotton Moore was finding a way to turn an old industrial facility in Georgetown into a model of architectural recycling known as Canal Square.

Although Washington was still a small city compared to New York, Chicago, and the great European capitals, and was not exactly a mecca for newly minted architects, the city's architectural scene during this period certainly seemed to be emerging from its reactionary past. Particularly during the early 1960s, when the Kennedy administration infused the city with an air of youthful exuberance, the capital was viewed by many architects as an up-and-coming, modern metropolis.

Even so, the city's population at that point was already declining steadily as suburban development, here as elsewhere in the country, was exploding. When the last D.C. streetcar disappeared from the tracks on January 27, 1962, longstanding assumptions about civic scale, neighborhood viability, and urban density evaporated. The prevalence of the private automobile, which both government and industry went to great lengths to accommodate, dictated subsequent urban planning and development. Downtown retailers were already struggling to hold their own against new suburban shopping malls when riots in the wake of the 1968 assassination of Martin Luther King Jr. laid waste to once-thriving commercial thoroughfares along 14th

In 1966, Chloethiel Woodard Smith proposed the Washington Channel Bridge, a modern version of Florence's Ponte Vecchio, containing a mix of shops and restaurants. It would have stretched between the Southwest urban renewal area and East Potomac Park.

Street, NW, and H Street, NE. Urban emigration accelerated into the 1970s and even the 1980s amid a classic vicious cycle of crime, poverty, poor schools, and deteriorating infrastructure.

In this increasingly desperate urban context, the bold and sometimes heroic architectural gestures that had made Washington a poster city for High Modernism began to look stale and barren to many designers and clients alike. Of course, a reaction to the purism of the modern movement was not unique to Washington, nor was it a new phenomenon—Robert Venturi had published his *Complexity and Contradiction in Architecture* in 1966, and the two most widely heralded (and derided) early works of postmodern architecture were not in Washington but in Portland, Oregon (Michael Graves's Public Services Building), and in New York (Philip Johnson's AT&T—now Sony—Building). But by the mid-1980s, local architects were firmly on board with the counter-revolution, creating buildings such as 1300 New York Avenue (now the Inter-American Development Bank), which moved away from modern abstraction in favor of a more traditional hierarchy of forms, articulated windows, and allusions to historical architectural motifs.

The postmodern movement essentially developed as two different, if sometimes overlapping, strains: a playful, "Mannerist," often jokey school, as exemplified by Charles Moore's Piazza d'Italia in New Orleans, and a quite serious, unabashedly historicist school that celebrated specific "styles," traditional materials, and contextualism. In Washington especially, the former strain never took hold, but the latter quickly became predominant. The ideals of the City Beautiful movement, of course, had never really fallen out of favor here. In retrospect, even during the heyday of modernism, most of the capital's official and commercial architecture had always adhered to a monumental purity that never seriously challenged the fundamental precepts of Daniel Burnham and his cohort, even though the strictly classical vocabulary they favored had been abandoned. So a return to historicism—especially but not exclusively a kind of classicism—was an easy transition for many Washington architects. Soon, downtown was becoming filled with polite buildings, each with a clearly articulated base, middle, and top, typically with punched windows, and ever-respectful of the street line. The better ones had well controlled proportions and carefully conceived ornament, while the poorer ones were ponderous, formulaic, and ultimately quite dreary.

Washington may have avoided most of the postmodern excesses that now tend to engender embarrassed throat-clearing at cocktail parties, but it also turned into something of a caricature of itself. In the late 1980s, one Washington architect quipped that his local colleagues constituted "the avant-garde of the rear guard." Another, more cynically, dubbed Washington in the early 1990s "Stepford, D.C.," alluding to the fictional Connecticut town populated by what seem to be attractive, happy, but soulless housewives. His comment reflected a profound ambivalence about the architecture of the day: on the one hand, he relished how buildings seemed to work together to form coherent and pleasant streetscapes, but on the other, he missed the excitement, the exuberant inventiveness, and even the occasional bold mistakes that made other large cities so interesting.

Around the turn of the 21st century, several events suggested that this circumstance might be about to change . . . or not. In 1999 came the news that Frank Gehry had been selected to design the addition to the Corcoran Gallery of Art, and thus to bring his signature metallic squiggles to the city of marble and limestone. Washington skeptics cheered the prospect of a bona fide piece of trendy design to help put the city on some unspecified map presumably carried by members of the cultural elite. After half a decade of trying to raise the money for the addition, however, the Corcoran announced that it was abandoning the project. The skeptics threw their hands

The sleekly remodeled interior of this house in downtown Washington was the work of Robert M. Gurney, FAIA.

in the air and said that they had always known that staid old Washington could not pull it off. Largely missing from the public debate was the point that, even by the time the new wing was proposed, Gehry's basic architectural vocabulary had already become something of a cliché. Had the structure gone ahead, the same skeptics might well have scoffed "it's been done," and dismissed the city as a cultural backwater anyway.

Much more important than this one aborted project by a famous architect from California is the recent emergence of a new generation of local architectural talent that is producing world-class work, albeit often at a small scale. The Washington metropolitan area now boasts dozens of innovative, boldly modern houses, apartments, restaurants, stores, and office interiors designed by local architects who are just beginning to attract overdue national attention. Several of these architects—including Robert Gurney, David Jameson, and Mark McInturff, to name a few—are little represented in this book (and in some cases not at all) because most of their projects either are residential interiors or are outside the District of Columbia. Nonetheless, they are contributing to a significant transformation of Washington's architectural culture. It is noteworthy that in a survey of readers of *ArchitectureDC,* the magazine of the AIA | DC, more than 80 percent of the respondents indicated that they were interested in coverage of modern design. Clearly, the image of Washington as a city of almost exclusively traditional tastes is no longer an accurate one, and it has not been for some time.

L'Enfant, the Senate Park Commission, and many of the individual architects and firms that have practiced here over the last two centuries have actively worked to manufacture a coherent urbanism for Washington, and by doing so, to give it a sense of place. Their efforts speak for themselves. Compare Washington to most any other "artificial" city in relatively recent history and the superiority of its design quickly becomes evident. Canberra? Beyond a handful of monumental structures, one could search in vain for any landmark or memorable streetscape. Brasilia? Home to several absolutely brilliant buildings, the place is otherwise an unmitigated horror—a beautiful plan on paper rendered vacuous in three dimensions. In contrast, Washington works quite well in urbanistic terms. The famous building height limit has had the (presumably) coincidental effect of keeping the urban core reasonably dense, as developers have sought to fill their maximum allowable building envelopes. Washington has thus avoided the hodgepodge land use patterns of many American cities, in which skyscrapers alternate with surface parking lots, creating haphazard and inhospitable streetscapes. A 2007 Brookings Institution report ranked Washington as the most walkable major metropolitan area in the country, and a recently launched local bike-sharing system has greatly surpassed expectations. Meanwhile, Washington's famous row house neighborhoods continue to provide block after block of rich urban texture, intermingled with flourishing commercial nodes. And an abundance of green spaces yields a good balance between the natural and the human-made environments.

In 1842, Charles Dickens snidely labeled Washington the "City of Magnificent Intentions." Today many of those intentions have been realized in stone, steel, and concrete. What the city may lack in sheer quantity of cutting-edge works of architecture, it makes up in thriving neighborhoods, cohesive streetscapes, and surpassing civic order. Given such a solid urbanistic foundation, coupled with a growing pool of design talent, perhaps Washington is poised to enter a golden age, in which a reasoned respect for the historic urban fabric, combined with thoughtful but ambitious planning and innovative, exciting architecture, will yield a city that is both a civic model and a source of national pride.

A classic view of a row of attached houses in one of Washington's residential neighborhoods, exhibiting great variety in materials, colors, and details but creating a consistent and unified streetscape.

TOUR A

Governmental Capitol Hill

The Washington Monument may be taller, and the White House the more potent symbol of political power, but the primary architectural icon of Washington, D.C.—and, by extension, of American democracy—is undoubtedly the Capitol. Standing at the intersection of L'Enfant's cardinal axes, it is both the conceptual center of the city and the majestic terminus of the Mall. Refined and, in some places, lavish in its materials and details, and surrounded by well-landscaped grounds, the Capitol is simultaneously urbane and bucolic, making it the perfect emblem of a capital city forged out of a compromise between northern urban and southern agrarian interests.

Its primacy notwithstanding, the Capitol today is just one element of a sizeable complex accommodating the U.S. Congress and related functions. The jurisdiction of the Architect of the Capitol, in fact, extends to the House and Senate office buildings that bracket the Capitol grounds, the three major buildings of the Library of Congress, the Supreme Court Building, and the U.S. Botanic Garden, among other structures. Various private institutions, such as the Folger Shakespeare Library, are interspersed among these landmarks.

This chapter explores the public and private buildings at the core of the Capitol Hill neighborhood, the site of so many workings of the national government, from the petty and mundane to the noble and momentous.

An aerial view, c. 1920, of Capitol Hill, with Union Station in the left background and the Library of Congress in the right middle ground.

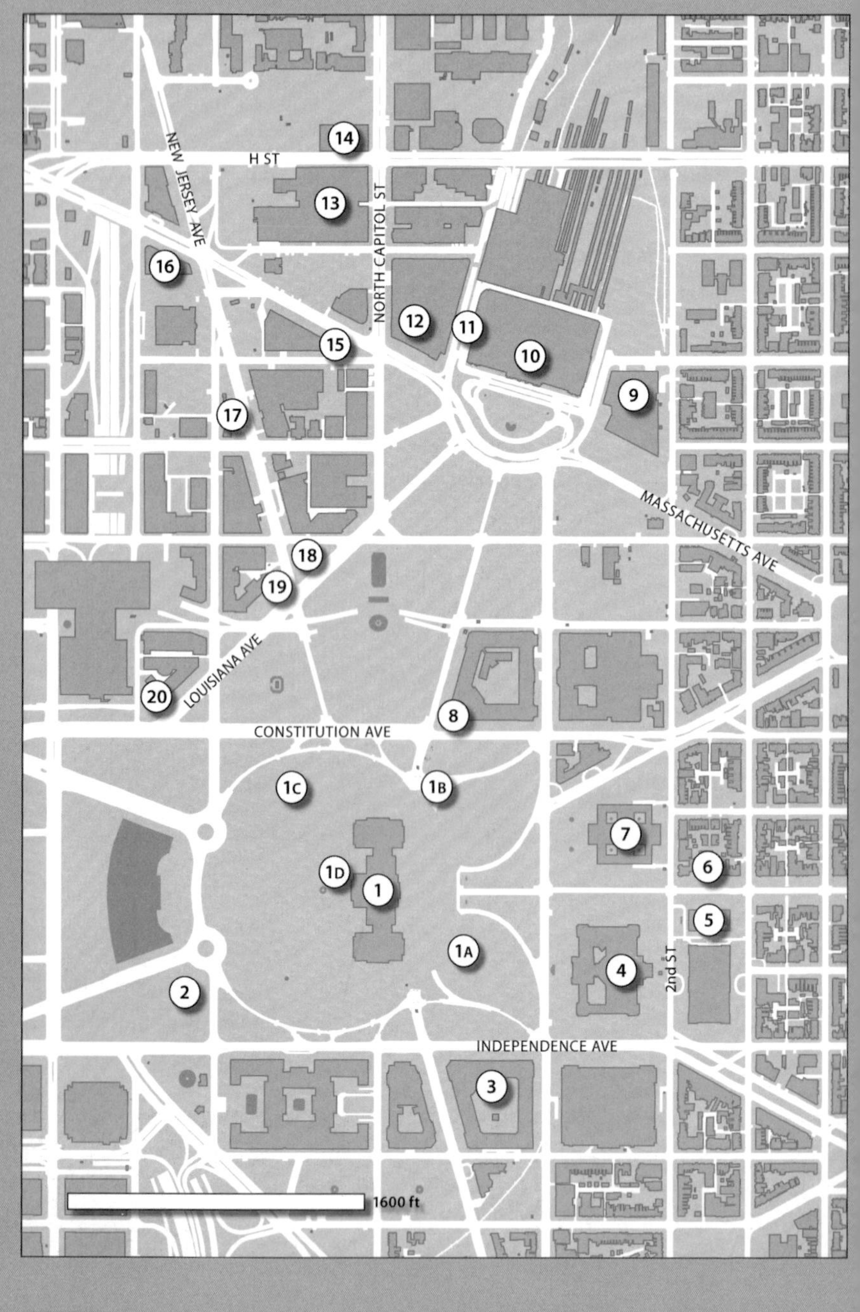
H ST
NEW JERSEY AVE
NORTH CAPITOL ST
MASSACHUSETTS AVE
LOUISIANA AVE
CONSTITUTION AVE
INDEPENDENCE AVE
2nd ST
14
13
16
12
11
10
15
9
17
18
19
20
8
1C
1B
7
6
1D
1
5
1A
4
2
3
1600 ft

A1 The Capitol

1793–1802—WILLIAM THORNTON, WITH STEPHEN HALLET, GEORGE HADFIELD, AND JAMES HOBAN
1803–17—BENJAMIN HENRY LATROBE
1818–29—CHARLES BULFINCH
1836–51—Various modifications: ROBERT MILLS ET AL.
1851–65—Extensions and new dome: THOMAS U. WALTER, WITH MONTGOMERY C. MEIGS
1949–50—Remodeling of House and Senate chambers: Associate architect: FRANCIS P. SULLIVAN; Consulting architects: HARBESON, HOUGH, LIVINGSTON & LARSON
1958–62—East Front extension: J. GEORGE STEWART; Advisory architects: ROSCOE DEWITT & FRED L. HARDISON; Associate architects: ALFRED POOR & ALBERT SWANKE
1976—Restoration of old Senate and Supreme Court chambers: GEORGE WHITE; Design architects: DEWITT, POOR & SHELTON
1987—West Front restoration: GEORGE WHITE; AMMANN & WHITNEY
1993—New structures in West Terrace courtyards: GEORGE WHITE; Design architect: HUGH NEWELL JACOBSEN
2008—Capitol Visitor Center: ALAN HANTMAN; Design architects: RTKL ASSOCIATES

Tel: (202) 226-8000
www.visitthecapitol.gov

Now that it is surrounded by a 21st-century metropolis, Capitol "Hill" seems little more than a mound. But in 1791, the 88-foot rise then known as Jenkins Hill (or Jenkins Heights) impressed L'Enfant, who described it in a letter to George Washington as "a pedestal waiting for a superstructure." For him, this was the most logical site for the principal building of the new capital city, and the rest of his plan was organized around the placement of the "Congress house" there.

The original design for the Capitol was the result of a competition, albeit only indirectly. None of the submissions received by the deadline in July 1792 fully pleased either President Washington or Secretary of State Jefferson. They therefore decided not to select a winner but instead to invite one entrant, a professional builder named Stephen Hallet, to redevelop his proposal for further consideration. After the deadline had passed, William Thornton, a physician from the West Indies, submitted another proposal, which impressed the president, who recommended the design to the city commissioners. The design by Thornton was ultimately selected. Although architecture as a true profession was virtually unknown in 18th-century America, Thornton's amateurism worried Washington and Jefferson, so they hired Hallet to supervise the construction of Thornton's design.

William R. Birch's 1800 drawing of the Capitol's north (Senate) wing shows an idealized Executive Mansion floating in the misty distance.

When Congress fired Latrobe in 1817, the House and Senate wings were connected by only a wooden walkway, as shown in this c. 1819 watercolor.

On September 18, 1793, President Washington, following Masonic ritual, laid the cornerstone using a silver trowel and a marble-headed gavel. The spirit of optimism that prevailed on that auspicious day soon faded, however, as conflicts arose among the project's principal players. Hallet was fired and replaced by George Hadfield, who was replaced in turn by James Hoban, who already had won the design competition for the President's House. Construction of the Capitol proceeded very slowly due to fiscal limitations and political bickering. As Irish journalist Isaac Weld noted in 1799, "numbers of people . . . particularly in Philadelphia" tried to sabotage work on the Capitol by withholding funds. Given this penny-pinching and intrigue-filled atmosphere, Jefferson and Washington wisely had laborers concentrate their efforts on the north wing alone, which they managed to finish in 1800, just in time for the government's official move to the new city. Congress met there for the first time that November. Looking at the present building from the east, one can see a small dome (to the right) that crowns the earliest part of the structure.

Detail of one of Latrobe's acclaimed corncob columns. He replaced the traditional acanthus leaves in the capital with indigenous maize and made the shaft a bundle of corn stalks.

The small dome to the left, atop the House of Representatives wing, dates to a section completed in 1807 under architect Benjamin Henry Latrobe, whom then-President Jefferson had appointed surveyor of public buildings in 1803. Latrobe refined Thornton's design, introducing elements that brought a uniquely American flavor to a building that, like most prominent buildings in the young nation, was obviously based on European precedents. His signature "corncob" column capitals, for example, were conceived as a truly American successor to the acanthus-leafed capitals of ancient Greece and Rome. Frances Trollope wrote in 1832 that "the beautiful capitals . . . composed of the ears and leaves of Indian corn" were "the only instance I saw in which America has ventured to attempt national originality; the success is perfect. A sense of fitness always enhances the effect of beauty." Latrobe later added column capitals featuring tobacco leaves, continuing the decorative theme based on Native American plants. Another of Latrobe's contributions was the masonry vault structural system, a rare American example of such a system at the time.

The War of 1812 brought the British to Washington, with devastating results for the Capitol. On August 24, 1814, British admiral Sir George Cockburn torched "this harbor of Yankee democracy," leaving what Latrobe called "a most magnificent ruin." After the war, Congress moved temporarily to the "Old Brick Capitol," on the site of the present-day Supreme Court, and Latrobe was brought back to reconstruct the original building. When he resigned in 1817 over a contract dispute, Latrobe left behind a curious structure on Jenkins Hill—the Senate and House wings were complete, but with only a walkway connecting them, creating a fragile U in plan. President James Monroe then brought in Boston architect Charles Bulfinch to continue work on the building, and specifically to fill the void between the wings. Bulfinch's link was topped by a copper-clad dome of wood, stone, and brick, modeled on the one he had designed for the Massachusetts State

Bulfinch added the center section and dome to Latrobe's wings, as depicted in this 1849 engraving of what most everyone assumed was the finished Capitol.

House in the 1790s. Under his supervision, the Capitol finally reached what everyone assumed was completion in 1829.

As the government and the nation grew, however, the Capitol began to bulge, so in 1850 Congress authorized an expansion and launched another competition. Once again, this competition produced no clear winner, but President Millard Fillmore selected entrant Thomas U. Walter, a Philadelphia architect, to undertake the work. Walter designed the huge south and north extensions—the outermost elements of the building today—to accommodate new House and Senate chambers, which were spanned with state-of-the-art iron trusses. The House extension was finished in time for that body to convene there on December 16, 1857. The Senate moved into its completed quarters on January 4, 1859.

Walter's tour-de-force, however, was the enlargement of the Capitol's dome. The 1850s extensions had more than doubled the building's length to 751 feet, thus reducing Bulfinch's dome to visual insignificance. So in 1855 Walter designed a soaring replacement consisting of two trussed cast iron shells, one inside the other, painted to resemble the marble of the extensions. The dome was still under construction as the Civil War began, and, according to a legend, President Lincoln directed that the work continue because he believed that "if people see the Capitol going on . . . it is a sign we intend the Union shall go on." The construction came to a climax on December 2, 1863, when Thomas Crawford's 19-foot statue, *Freedom*—cast using slave labor, incredibly enough—was lifted into place at the peak of the cast iron dome.

Predictably, given the building's complex history, the Capitol's interiors are a hodgepodge, reflecting the tastes of the various eras during which major work was undertaken. The principal ceremonial space is the Rotunda beneath the great dome, which is 180 feet high and profusely decorated. At its apex is Constantino Brumidi's fresco, *The Apotheosis of Washington,* in which the Father of Our Country hobnobs with various allegorical figures. Because the fresco is applied to the inside of the *outer dome,* it appears to float above a hole at the top of the *inner dome,* creating the illusion that the figures in the fresco are hovering in the sky. Closer to eye level, the Rotunda's walls are embellished with eight large, historical paintings, including four by John Trumbull, known as the "Artist of the Revolution," which were installed between 1819 and 1824, and four others by different artists depicting great moments in exploration, which were added between 1840 and 1855.

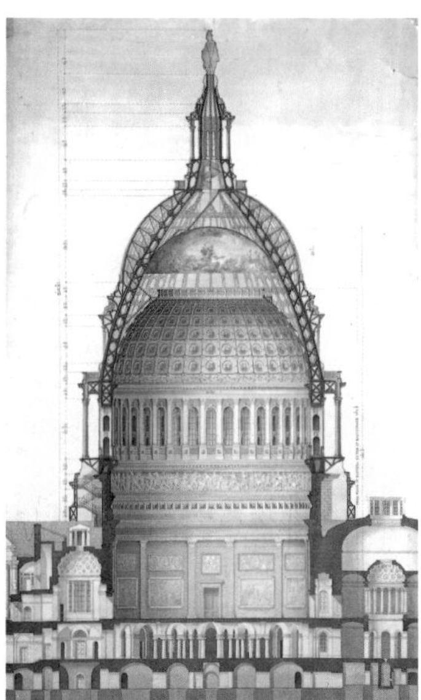

Sectional drawing, from 1859, of the new Capitol dome by Thomas U. Walter.

Beyond the Rotunda, the building contains a dizzying warren of rooms, punctuated by three major semicircular spaces: the Old Hall of the House (now the sculpture-choked National Statuary Hall), the Old Senate chamber (surprisingly intimate in scale), and the Old Supreme Court chamber (the judicial branch did not have its own separate quarters until 1935). The sprawling extensions are full of delightfully excessive Victorian elements, from elaborate fireplaces to intricate cast iron grilles. While most of these are in suites that are not accessible to the general public, several of the corridors in the Senate wing boast extravagant frescos and other paintings by Brumidi and his associates, as well as richly colored and patterned encaustic floor tiles. The current House and Senate chambers are rather bland by comparison, having been stripped of their original grandeur in 1949–51.

Between 1958 and 1962, the center of the East Front was extended outward roughly 32 feet. This single stroke added 102 rooms and provided a deeper base for the dome. The stonework was changed from fragile Aquia Creek sandstone to Georgia marble in the process, but the old sandstone columns were preserved and now stand starkly and rather hauntingly on an open lawn at the National Arboretum [see S23]. Although wildly controversial at the time, such an extension had actually been proposed by Thomas U. Walter and others a century earlier. A similar expansion scheme for the West Front arose in the 1970s, but this time public outcry was so great that Congress scrapped the plans and voted to restore rather than extend it. Accordingly, the façade was stripped of dozens of layers of paint and reinforced with steel rods, while roughly 40 percent of the crumbling sandstone was replaced with limestone and the entirety repainted.

The most recent major change to the Capitol was the addition of the underground Capitol Visitor Center, which was conceived to help manage the flow of visitors and assumed new urgency after the terrorist attacks of September 11, 2001. The architects had the unenviable job of responding to the conflicting demands of 535 members of Congress (not to mention the numerous other appointed officials and staffers with a say in the matter), coupled with changing security expectations, substantial increases in space requirements, and concomitant escalations in the budget. Completed and opened to the public in 2008, the 580,000-square-foot facility, which includes space for congressional offices and meeting rooms, has a generic, convention center quality in some areas, but it does seem to fulfill its function and offers a few exhilarating moments, such as the glimpse of the Capitol dome through one of the center's huge skylights. At any rate, experience dictates that it is only a matter of time before another major construction project comes along, ensuring that the Capitol can continue to serve the needs of an ever-growing nation.

A1a Capitol Grounds

Primary grounds: 1st Street, NE, to 1st Street, NW, between Constitution and Independence avenues

1874–92—FREDERICK LAW OLMSTED

It was perhaps inevitable that Frederick Law Olmsted, whose name is virtually synonymous with the profession of landscape architecture in America, would be called on to redesign the Capitol grounds. Congress commissioned him to

do so in 1874, and the plan he devised was bold and comprehensive, addressing elements at all scales, from tree-lined walkways to cast iron planters. A surprising amount of Olmsted's original street furniture, such as the lampstands at the East Capitol Street entrance, endures *in situ* on the leafy grounds. A parking lot that had marred the East Front of the Capitol was removed during the construction of the new Capitol Visitor Center and replaced by landscaping more in keeping with Olmsted's design.

A1b Waiting Stations

Near the East Front of the Capitol

C. 1876—FREDERICK LAW OLMSTED

These two stations testify to the thoroughness and consistency of Olmsted's design for the grounds surrounding the Capitol. The stations were once known as "Herdics," after the Herdic Phaeton Company, whose line of horse-drawn, plushly upholstered trolleys they served.

A1c Summerhouse

Near the West Front of the Capitol

1881—FREDERICK LAW OLMSTED

Olmsted envisioned this sheltered spring as a "cool retreat during hot summer." The hexagonal grotto, with brick and terra cotta walls and a red tile roof, still serves its intended purpose, although it now flows with city water, since the original spring soured and had to be diverted. The nearby stone tower, also designed by Olmsted, initially served both aesthetic and functional purposes: its upward thrust balanced the declivity of the grotto, while a now-closed vent within carried fresh, cooled air into the Capitol through a series of underground tunnels.

A1d West Terrace

1884–92—FREDERICK LAW OLMSTED
1993—HUGH NEWELL JACOBSEN

Following the completion of the new wings and larger dome in the 1860s, the Capitol had evolved into an enormous building. Seen from the Mall side, it had come to appear somewhat precarious—a heavy, imposing structure perched atop a scruffy hill, with no clear connection to the landscape below.

To resolve these issues, Olmsted designed an elaborate system of terraces and walkways to provide a more substantial visual base for the west façade and to ease the transition between the grand building and the then-informally landscaped Mall. These changes made the Capitol seem less like a citadel and more like a truly *public* building. Standing on the West Terrace and admiring the view, visitors can almost imagine themselves on the patio of a luxurious resort hotel, but here the vista is of museums and monuments rather than mountains or the sea.

A 1990s renovation of the terraces designed by Hugh Newell Jacobsen filled in courtyards to create additional meeting space and offices. Glass panels at the base of the Capitol's west façade serve as skylights for the new spaces below.

At the bottom of the hill is a memorial to Ulysses S. Grant, which was completed in 1922. The central sculpture of Grant atop his beloved horse, Cincinnati, is one of the largest equestrian statues in the world. It is the work of Henry M. Schrady, with a base designed by Edward Pearce Casey, the architect responsible for the original interiors of the Jefferson Building of the Library of Congress [see A4].

A2 U.S. Botanic Garden

1st Street, Maryland Avenue, and Independence Avenue

1933—BENNETT, PARSONS & FROST
2001—Restoration: DMJM DESIGN
2006—National Garden: SMITHGROUP IN ASSOCIATION WITH EDAW

Tel: (202) 225-8333
www.usbg.gov

For much of its history, the U.S. Botanic Garden, established in 1820, occupied a site at the foot of Capitol Hill, not far off the centerline of the Mall. The Senate Park Commission Plan of 1901–2, however, demanded a clear vista along the Mall's central swath, and the garden's facilities were in the way. Although it took several decades, the government eventually demolished the fanciful Victorian structure that had housed the institution since 1850, and built this new Beaux-Arts conservatory at the edge of the Mall.

The rusticated north façade, evocative of a 17th-century French *orangerie,* relates the Botanic Garden to the predominantly neoclassical buildings of Capitol Hill. Behind this formal front stands an exuberant conservatory, now restored and incorporating sophisticated systems to maintain humidity and temperature levels. The structure's tall ribcage, manufactured by the venerable greenhouse firm of Lord & Burnham, is made of non-corroding aluminum, and when built was the largest such structure in the world.

The Botanic Garden complex also includes the adjacent National Garden and a small, triangular park across Independence Avenue, which features a fountain created for the Philadelphia Centennial Exhibition of 1876 by Frédéric Auguste Bartholdi (who later sculpted the Statue of Liberty). The fountain audaciously juxtaposed fire and water in a single work, with gas flames flickering amid spouting jets of water. When the ex-

hibition closed, the federal government bought the fountain and moved it to Washington, where it has occupied two different sites. Electric lights eventually replaced the gas flames.

A3 Cannon House Office Building

New Jersey and Independence avenues, SE

1908—CARRÈRE & HASTINGS
1913—Addition: ARCHITECT OF THE CAPITOL, WITH CARRÈRE & HASTINGS
1932—Renovation: ARCHITECT OF THE CAPITOL, WITH ALLIED ARCHITECTS

The commission to erect freestanding office buildings for the Senate and the House was divided between the two principals of one architectural firm. Thomas Hastings was responsible for the House Office Building (pictured here), later named for Speaker Joseph Cannon; John Carrère took the lead on the design of its Senate counterpart [see A8]. The result was a set of fraternal Beaux-Arts twins that, with their giant columns and gleaming Vermont marble, visually merged to form a unified backdrop for the Capitol, at least until the more sober Longworth Building and the irredeemably hideous Rayburn Building came along and spoiled the view.

A4 Library of Congress (Thomas Jefferson Building)

1st Street and Independence Avenue, SE

1888–97—JOHN L. SMITHMEYER & PAUL J. PELZ; Interiors: EDWARD PEARCE CASEY
1910–65—Renovations and additions: VARIOUS ARCHITECTS
1986–97—Restoration: ARTHUR COTTON MOORE / ASSOCIATES

Tel: (202) 707-5458
www.loc.gov

As the government was preparing to move to the new federal city in 1800, Congress approved an expenditure of $5,000 to buy books and create a library for its own use. Housed within the Capitol, these original tomes were destroyed during the British invasion of 1814. To replace them, former president Thomas Jefferson, who declared that "there is, in fact, no subject to which a Member of Congress may not have occasion to refer," sold his remarkably broad-based private library of precisely 6,487 volumes to the government. From this core, the Library of Congress has evolved into the largest and best-equipped library in the world, containing more than 144 million items.

The institution's growth was slow and steady until Congress passed the Copyright Act of 1870, which required that the library receive two copies of every book, drawing, photograph, map, or

other item submitted to the government for copyright protection. The legislation immediately resulted in a flood of new acquisitions—some 20,000 in the first year alone—exceeding the capacity of the library space inside the Capitol, so in 1873, Congress authorized a competition for a new, stand-alone facility. The team of John L. Smithmeyer and Paul Pelz won first place with a sedate, Italian Renaissance Revival design that did not inspire much enthusiasm. Over the following 13 years, Smithmeyer and Pelz continued to tinker with the design like teenagers trying on different outfits before a date, exploring a wide variety of styles including French Renaissance, German Renaissance, and "Victorian Gothic." Congress finally agreed to a specific proposal and authorized construction in 1886, but there were more delays, and the library was not completed until 1897, 24 years after the original competition.

The executed design is, at least on the exterior, a rather stodgy Beaux-Arts affair that combines aspects of the architects' French and Italian schemes but ultimately is pervaded by a baronial, Germanic aura. The entrance pavilion, nonetheless, was almost certainly inspired by the elegant Paris Opera House designed by Charles Garnier. The key similarities include the arched doorways on the main level; the five central bays above, framed by paired columns, with circular openings above the windows; and the projecting bays on either side, topped by arched pediments. While Garnier's original conveys a kind of delicate grandeur, however, Smithmeyer & Pelz's interpretation seems overwrought and bombastic. One significant difference is that the Opera House is set right at street level, while the Library of Congress is raised on a podium, contributing to a sense of aloofness. The architect and critic Russell Sturgis lambasted the library's entrance as representing "that false idea of grandeur which consists mainly in hoisting a building up from a reasonable level of the ground, mainly in order to secure for it a monstrous flight of steps which must be surmounted before the main door can be reached."

The library's exterior may be awkward, but once inside, even the most skeptical visitor is likely to be dazzled. The principal interior spaces, which were overseen by Edward Pearce Casey after both Smithmeyer and Pelz were dismissed from the project, are among the most regal rooms in Washington. Casey led a team of more than 50 sculptors and painters, who brought the architecture to life through an artistic program of appropriately encyclopedic proportions. The heroic great hall is replete with mosaics and statuary set amid a sea of marble, stained glass, and bronze. Paired columns support arches that seem to spring effortlessly into the air.

The main reading room, topped by a 160-foot-high dome, is the grand finale. The room's octagonal shape was dictated by Ainsworth Spofford, the librarian of Congress during the building's construction, to reflect a new system for organizing books into eight categories. A mind-boggling assortment of allegorical sculptures and paintings provides intellectual inspiration for the reader, should any be needed. Here, the opening of a book becomes a noble rite.

A5 Folger Shakespeare Library

201 East Capitol Street, SE

1932—PAUL PHILIPPE CRET; Consulting architect: ALEXANDER B. TROWBRIDGE
1983—Additions and renovations: HARTMAN-COX ARCHITECTS

Tel: (202) 544-4600
www.folger.edu

When he wasn't raking in money as an oil tycoon, Henry Clay Folger and his wife, Emily Jordan Folger, were busy amassing the world's largest collection of Shakespeare's printed works and related material. Once Henry retired as chairman of the Standard Oil Company of New York in 1928, he turned his full attention to establishing a library to house their collection. Emily saw the project to completion following her husband's death in 1930.

The building they commissioned, designed by Paul Philippe Cret, is one of the city's premier examples of the modernist-classical hybrid sometimes called "stripped classicism," "Greco-Deco," or, more wittily, "Stark Deco." This severe yet elegant style was popular in Depression-era Washington, as architects and clients tried to have things both ways: formal and hierarchical, in keeping with the city's conservative traditions, but also simple and spartan, perhaps in recognition of the economic crisis that had permeated the country's psyche, but also reflecting the influence of the burgeoning modern movement. The exterior of the building is a tightly controlled composition, with only minimal recesses and projections from the principal planes of the façades. Tall windows on the north and west façades are divided by fluted pilasters—hints of pilasters, really, since the fluting is the only remnant of the traditional form. Sculptural panels below the windows on the main façade depict scenes from Shakespeare's plays.

Cret's design appears to be a perfectly exemplary building of the period until one ventures inside. Within that fashionable 1930s envelope is an astounding neo-Elizabethan fantasy in dark, heavy wood. Cret explained the sharp difference thus: "The reason is quite simple. Mr. and Mrs. Folger desired surroundings . . . reminiscent of England. . . . On the other hand, the architect . . . could readily see that the site selected, facing a wide, straight avenue in one of the most classical of cities . . . would be inappropriate for an Elizabethan building." In short, the outside was a direct response to the architectural and cultural context of Washington, while the interior was designed to evoke the spirit of the era during which the Bard wrote his plays.

The new reading room, added by Hartman-Cox, is a modern reinterpretation of the great hall that runs along the front of the original building, but also suggests the inspiration of French visionary architect Étienne-Louis Boullée's hypothetical Bibliothèque nationale, with its semicircular-vaulted ceiling. While examining original drawings by Cret's office for the building, the architects of the addition noticed that several of the documents bore the initials "LK." It is safe to assume that these drawings were produced by none other than Louis Kahn, the great modernist architect who had worked for Cret during the period that this project was on the boards.

A6 Lutheran Church of the Reformation

212 East Capitol Street, NE

1934—IRWIN S. PORTER

Like the roughly contemporary Folger Shakespeare Library across the street, the Lutheran Church of the Reformation has something of a split personality. In this case, a Greco-Deco façade contrasts with an Arts-and-Crafts interior, replete with oak paneling and heavy wood beams connected by king posts. The design of the sanctuary reflects the influence of Scandinavian ecclesiastical traditions, which favored a simple, column-free "hall" for the congregation with a modest, rectangular chancel. While far from ornate, the church does have a rich decorative program, including depictions of *fleurs-de-lis*, the tree of life, and at least 15 different versions of the Christian cross.

A7 Supreme Court Building

1st and East Capitol streets, NE

1935—CASS GILBERT; COMPLETED BY CASS GILBERT JR. AND JOHN R. ROCKART
2010—Modernization: HILLIER ARCHITECTURE

Tel: (202) 479-3030
www.supremecourtus.gov

Generations of American schoolchildren have been taught that the judiciary is one of the three branches of the federal government, of equal importance to the executive and legislative components. Many people are therefore surprised to learn that the Supreme Court did not have a home of its own until 1935. Before that year, the Court had occupied a succession of chambers within the Capitol, an arrangement that not only muddled the separation of powers envisioned by the country's founders, but also caused a good deal of harrumphing among jurists who had to compete for space with members of Congress and their staffs.

In 1929, Chief Justice (and former president) William Howard Taft convinced Congress to commission a new building exclusively for the Court. The government selected a site occupied by the remnants of the "Old Brick Capitol," which had served as the temporary seat of Congress while the Capitol itself was being rebuilt following the British invasion of 1814. The property, then owned by the National Woman's Party (NWP), was acquired through eminent domain and razed (the NWP received compensation and moved its headquarters to the Sewall-Belmont House at 144 Massachusetts Avenue, NE). Cass Gilbert, architect of the Woolworth Building in New York, which had reigned as the world's tallest building since 1913, was hired to design the Court's new seat.

Gilbert's design was one of the last major works of academic classicism in Washington. Conceived as a temple of justice, the building draws heavily on Roman precedents. The entire structure is raised on a plinth, which extends to the front of the building proper to create a broad entry plaza. A central spine, bracketed by porticoes with sculpted pediments, contains the principal interior spaces—including the Court Chamber at the east end—and completely dominates the two side wings. Four courtyards within the wings bring natural light into adjacent offices and other spaces.

The great, bronze entrance doors, which weigh a total of thirteen tons and open not by swinging but by sliding into pockets in the adjacent walls, were sculpted by John Donnelly Jr. Eight panels within the doors depict important moments in legal and judicial history, with ancient examples on the left and Anglo-American ones on the right. (Sadly, the doors are currently closed indefinitely in the name of security.) Above the doors is the west pediment, by sculptor Robert Aitken, with a central figure representing Liberty, attended by two Roman soldiers. Architect Gilbert appears immediately to the left of this trio, followed by statesman Elihu Root. At the far left is an image of Chief Justice Taft, rendered for some odd reason as a youth, which explains his improbably trim figure. Depicted on the right side are Chief Justice Charles Evans Hughes, followed by sculptor Aitken's own image, and finally, a young John Marshall.

A8 Russell Senate Office Building

Delaware and Constitution avenues, NE

1909—CARRÈRE & HASTINGS
1933—Addition: ARCHITECT OF THE CAPITOL, WITH NATHAN C. WYETH AND FRANCIS P. SULLIVAN

This is the companion piece to the Cannon House Office Building [see A3].

A9 Thurgood Marshall Federal Judiciary Building

Massachusetts Avenue at Columbus Circle, NE

1992—EDWARD LARABEE BARNES ASSOCIATES

Edward Larabee Barnes's attempt to reinterpret the Beaux-Arts splendor of Union Station in a modern governmental office building next door is half-hearted and unsatisfying. The arches on the judiciary building and the sculpturally impoverished pilasters that bracket them are anemic in contrast to their richly detailed and finely crafted antecedents. The new building's most successful element is its unapologetically modern atrium, which is quite inviting, particularly at night when brightly lit, although it does look more like the centerpiece of a shopping mall or entertainment center than the entry to a judicial office building.

A10 Union Station and Plaza

Massachusetts and Louisiana avenues, NE

1908—DANIEL H. BURNHAM; Sculptor: LOUIS SAINT-GAUDENS
1912—Columbus Fountain: DANIEL H. BURNHAM; Sculptor: LORADO TAFT; Landscape architect: FREDERICK LAW OLMSTED JR.
1988—Renovation and new retail facilities: HARRY WEESE & ASSOCIATES; BENJAMIN THOMPSON & ASSOCIATES

To the Senate Park Commission of 1901–2, one of the most vexing nuisances in Washington's monumental core was the train station that straddled the eastern end of the Mall, drawing smoke-belching trains directly across the primary vista from the Capitol. The commission recommended that a new station be built at the confluence of Massachusetts and Louisiana avenues, in a style conforming to the City Beautiful principles that the group espoused. Having settled on this location, commission member Daniel Burnham then went directly to President A. J. Cassatt of the Pennsylvania Railroad and persuaded him to re-lay the company's tracks to this site, making the grand new station possible and freeing the Mall of a sooty eyesore.

The new Union Station thus became the first building erected in conformance with the Senate Park Commission's recommendations. Sheathed in white Vermont granite (not marble), the station was inspired by ancient Roman precedents. The central pavilion of the main façade, for instance, is a reinterpretation of a tripartite Roman triumphal arch. While the Roman version typically would have had one tall arch in the middle flanked by two shorter ones, here Burnham made all three arches the same height, while taking other liberties with proportions and decorative devices. Running transversely through the central pavilion and continuing along the entire length of this façade is an open-air loggia, composed of a row of vaulted bays with suspended light fixtures. The view from one end of the loggia to the other is among the most beautiful in Washington.

The station's primary interior spaces create just what the Senate Park Com-

mission had in mind—a triumphant gateway to the capital of an increasingly powerful nation. The waiting room, an homage to the Roman Baths of Diocletian, measures 219 feet by 120 feet, and lies beneath a gilded, coffered, barrel-vaulted ceiling. Visitors to this space may notice adolescents amusing themselves by attempting to determine whether the scantily clad statues along the upper levels are anatomically correct behind their shields (they were designed to be, but supposedly only one of them ended up that way). Behind the waiting room is the 760-foot-long grand concourse, which, in its day, was among the largest uninterrupted interior public spaces in the United States.

After a period of neglect and an abortive, misguided scheme to turn the facility into a visitors' center for the city, the station underwent a comprehensive restoration and was reopened in 1988. Today, the clothing stores, souvenir shops, and fast-food joints have turned Union Station into something of a mini-mall, yet these intrusions have not destroyed the grandeur of the building, which once again superbly fills its role as a ceremonial gateway to the nation's capital.

In front of the station is a D-shaped plaza organized around a fountain honoring Christopher Columbus. As an urban space, the plaza is a bit nebulous, with its curving side lacking architectural definition and its center crossed by a tangle of driveways. The fountain and the street furniture in the plaza are nonetheless engaging, with the Columbian theme carried through to such smaller elements as the light standards, which bear appendages designed to suggest the prows of Spanish galleons.

A11 Bikestation Washington, D.C.

1st Street, NE, adjacent to Union Station

2009—KGP DESIGN STUDIO

This bicycle transit center is an unabashedly modern structure that fits comfortably among its neoclassical neighbors. The gentle arc alludes to the barrel vaults in the train station while also abstractly suggesting other imagery—a cyclist's helmet, perhaps, or even a bicycle wheel emerging from the ground. Incorporating

storage spaces for more than 100 bikes, a changing area, rental and repair services, and a small retail operation, the facility primarily serves commuters who take the train to Union Station and then switch to their bicycles to get the rest of the way to work. The louvered glass enclosure provides protection from the elements while allowing fresh air to circulate freely.

A12 Postal Square / National Postal Museum

(City Post Office Building)
Massachusetts Avenue and North Capitol Street, NE

1914—GRAHAM, BURNHAM & COMPANY
1935—Addition: GRAHAM, ANDERSON, PROBST AND WHITE
1959—Interior alterations: TURPIN, WACHTER AND ASSOCIATES
1992—Renovation and addition: SHALOM BARANES ASSOCIATES; Preservation architects: OEHRLEIN & ASSOCIATES ARCHITECTS
1993—Postal Museum: FLORANCE EICHBAUM ESOCOFF KING

Tel: (202) 633-5555
www.postalmuseum.si.edu

Designed by the successor firm to D. H. Burnham & Co., the old City Post Office, with its Ionic colonnade and projecting entrance pavilions, harmonizes with, but defers to, Burnham's Union Station across the street. The architects continued the Ionic order inside in the former main service room, marked by opulent decorative details that were largely destroyed in a disastrous 1959 remodeling but have now been restored. The 1992 renovation entailed an almost invisible expansion of the building's floor space by 50 percent, which was achieved by filling in the courtyard, adding a mezzanine, and capturing unused space in the attic. The building now incorporates a mix of uses, including the Smithsonian's National Postal Museum, while still accommodating a working post office.

A13 U.S. Government Printing Office (GPO)

North Capitol Street between G and H streets, NW

1903—710 N. Capitol Street: JAMES G. HILL
1930—45 G Street: J. J. MCMAHON
1940—732 N. Capitol Street: LOUIS A. SIMON (SUPERVISING ARCHITECT), WITH VICTOR D. ABEL AND WILLIAM DEWEY FOSTER

> Early Irish settlers . . . gave to this locality the picturesque, if inelegant, nickname of "Swampoodle," more on account of the swamps, however, than the poodles. . . . Perhaps Swampoodle was a corruption of "swamp-puddle." Certainly there were both swamps and puddles galore in the shadow of the GPO and the Capitol.
>
> —*Washington, a not too serious history,* George Rothwell Brown, 1930

The Government Printing Office (GPO) first put ink to paper on March 4, 1861, the day of President Lincoln's inauguration. The agency set up shop in a group of existing, low-rise buildings on the same block it occupies today, and almost immediately began pleading with Congress for more space. Several stopgap expansions in the late 19th century proved inadequate given the burgeoning demands on the printing operation. It was not until 1903 that the GPO finally got a large, new facility, which is now the "old" building at the corner of North Capitol and G streets. This massive structure was clearly inspired by the muscular commercial architecture of post-fire Chicago, particularly the Auditorium Building by Louis Sullivan and the Marshall Field store by H. H. Richardson, both of which share the GPO's blocky massing and multi-story, arch-topped window bays.

A small addition along G Street from 1930 closely matches the 1903 building, while the 1940 structure, at the corner of North Capitol and H streets, is a slightly stripped-down version of the original, reflecting the Depression-era penchant for reducing historical architectural forms to their essence. Across North Capitol Street, along G Place, NE, is the GPO's warehouse, completed in 1938, which has a dedicated rail line coming into the building for the delivery of large quantities of paper.

A14 800 North Capitol Street, NW

1991—HARTMAN-COX ARCHITECTS

Obviously inspired by the old GPO building down the street, this commercial office building remains one of Hartman-Cox's most faithfully historicist works. Despite its apparent heft, it was built on a relatively modest budget using brick and cast stone, a refined concrete masonry product.

A15 SunTrust Bank

(Childs Restaurant Building)
2 Massachusetts Avenue, NW

1926—WILLIAM VAN ALEN

Yes, *that* William Van Alen—architect of the Chrysler Building, one of the most beloved landmarks in the United States. He designed this sliver of a building for the Childs brothers, who ran a successful chain of lunchroom-style restaurants based in New York. The entire ground floor, expensively finished in travertine, marble, and bronze, was originally devoted to dining space (the kitchen was in the basement). The building is sheathed in an unusual stone that is obviously quite soft—note the heavily weathered, circular medallions between the arched windows, now barely visible. Just above the cornice on each of the two façades is the faint inscription "Capitoline," a reference to the famous Roman hill, site of the ancient temple that gave us the word *Capitol.*

A16 Edward Bennett Williams Law Library, Georgetown University Law Center

Massachusetts and New Jersey avenues, NW

1989—HARTMAN-COX ARCHITECTS

For two decades, Georgetown University's Law School was relegated to a dreary, if monumental, box of a building designed by Edward Durell Stone, located in what was then a rather dodgy

part of town. This library was the first of several new structures that Hartman-Cox designed for the Law School, all of which now work together to create a compact but credible campus (meanwhile, the neighborhood has become livelier and safer). The exterior of the library recalls the stripped classicism of the 1930s, which tended toward austerity—here, subtle ornamental bands, deeply set windows, and delicate railings help to keep things interesting. The south façade, facing into the campus, is the most animated, with an asymmetrically placed, projecting rotunda marking the main entrance and a trellis sheltering one end of the terrace. Inside, the wood-paneled main reading room is a quintessential collegiate library space.

A17 National Association of Realtors Building

500 New Jersey Avenue, NW

2004—Design architects: GUND PARTNERSHIP; Architects of record: SMB ARCHITECTS

This was the first newly constructed building in the District of Columbia to earn certification under the U.S. Green Building Council's Leadership in Energy and Environmental Design (LEED) rating system. The architects achieved this through such measures as high-efficiency ventilation systems, a sophisticated curtain wall that minimizes thermal transfer, and the copious use of recycled materials in the construction of the building. The land was previously occupied by a service station, requiring substantial site cleanup before the National Association of Realtors could begin construction. Views of the slender

building are particularly dramatic from the north—the tower at the apex reads rather like a ship's mast, with the sleek, sail-like curtain walls billowing behind it.

A18 National Japanese American Memorial

Louisiana and New Jersey avenues at D Street, NW

2001—DAVIS BUCKLEY ARCHITECTS AND PLANNERS; Sculptors: NINA AKAMU, PAUL MATISSE

This monument, officially known as the National Japanese American Memorial to Patriotism During World War II, recognizes both the service of Japanese American veterans and the U.S. government's internment of more than 100,000 people of Japanese descent during the war. The most compelling feature of the memorial is a long, tubular bell created by sculptor Paul Matisse (grandson of Henri, the famous painter), which may be rung by pumping a lever to lift and release a clapper. The bell emits a profound and sustained tone—actually a pair of tones that gradually merge, symbolizing the healing of emotional wounds.

A19 Acacia Building/ 300 New Jersey Avenue

51 Louisiana Avenue, NW and
300 New Jersey Avenue, NW

1936—SHREVE, LAMB & HARMON; Sculptor: EDMOND ROMULUS AMATEIS
1953—Addition: SHREVE, LAMB & HARMON
1999—Interior and exterior restoration: HARTMAN-COX ARCHITECTS
2009—300 New Jersey Avenue: ROGERS STIRK HARBOUR + PARTNERS; Architects of record: HKS; Associated architects for lobby interior: LEHMAN SMITH MCLEISH

The Depression-era Acacia Building, built for an insurance company that was headquartered here until 1997, was designed by the architects of the Empire State Building and shares a stripped classical aesthetic with its much more famous cousin. The façades of the Washington building are undeniably severe, relieved only by a projecting central doorway with a hint of a scroll above it, simple fluting on the tall pilasters, and a few medallions below the primary cornice. Most passersby barely even glance at the building, however, as they are too entranced by the pair of limestone griffins that fiercely guard its entrance.

The insurance company's absorption by another firm and subsequent move opened an opportunity to rethink this property. A local developer hired the firm of Richard Rogers, one of the architects of the famed Pompidou Center in Paris, to design an addition and integrate it into the original building and a wing dating from the 1950s. The design team's solution involved placing a simple, curtain-walled block at the northwest corner of the site, and turning the irregularly shaped space between the three buildings into an atrium. To tie the disparate structures together, the architects created the "Tree"—a bright yellow mast that supports a web of bridges, stairs, and an elevator. A very large branch of the Tree, resting on a secondary mast outside the atrium, extends toward

Louisiana Avenue to support a louvered, triangular canopy that marks the primary entrance to the complex.

Curiously, while the atrium space, with its colorful Tree, myriad bridges, and intricate details, recalls the sometimes startlingly high-tech work of Rogers's early career, the new office block itself is rather staid. This portion of the project was originally designed to be taller, but representatives of the Architect of the Capitol complained that a higher "tower" would pose a security threat to the Capitol complex by providing a perch for potential snipers. Never mind the fact that there seem to be several other buildings nearby that already provide equally good vantage points.

A20 101 Constitution Avenue, NW

2002—SHALOM BARANES ASSOCIATES

If real estate is all about location, then this commercial property—one of the closest private buildings to the Capitol—was destined for success. Fortunately, the design of the structure befits its prominent setting. The cylindrical tower serves as a minor landmark in an area that is otherwise rather nebulous in urban design terms, with ill-defined park spaces to the east and south and the monstrously banal U.S. Department of Labor building to the west (the tower also works in concert with the similarly shaped element of the Prettyman Courthouse annex [see F1] to provide a visual frame for the Labor building when seen from the Mall). The long, Louisiana Avenue façade is composed of two basic forms: a tall slab with a shallow curve in plan, and a rectilinear, gridded block that holds the line of the street. An open colonnade at the street level creates a pleasant, quasi-public space and helps to shade the all-glass walls of the adjacent restaurant.

At the rear of this new building, along 2nd Street, is a surprising little enclave of surviving 19th-century buildings, reminders of how this part of town looked before the Senate Park Commission of 1901–2 imposed its will on the city's core.

TOUR B

Residential Capitol Hill

Capitol Hill is synonymous with the legislative branch of the U.S. government, but in local parlance, the term also refers to the adjacent neighborhood to the east of the Capitol, which is home to a diverse collection of institutional, commercial, and residential buildings. The juncture between the two faces of Capitol Hill can be strikingly abrupt, as along the unit block of Second Street, NE, where modest, privately owned row houses stand directly across from the seat of the highest court in the nation.

The city's founders assumed that this area would become the primary locus of nongovernmental development, since it was convenient to both the "Congress house" and the port facilities along the Anacostia River (then known as the Eastern Branch). Perhaps, however, they underestimated the attraction of executive authority, because over time the White House, rather than the Capitol, became the center of gravity for Washington real estate. Ultimately, the city's commercial and residential development surged in the Northwest quadrant, leaving the residential part of Capitol Hill a surprisingly quiet enclave despite its proximity to many of the nation's most important institutions.

Although the neighborhood suffered a disheartening period of high crime rates and other urban ills in the mid- to late 20th century, Capitol Hill never lost its sense of community. For decades it has been beloved by residents for its ethnic diversity. Today, despite rising housing prices and demographic homogenization, "the Hill" remains a vibrant and highly sought-after place to live.

This 1992 aerial view of Stanton Park looking toward the northwest shows the dense texture of the Capitol Hill neighborhood.

C ST
EAST CAPITOL ST
A ST
NORTH CAROLINA AVE
INDEPENDENCE AVE
6th ST
PENNSYLVANIA AVE
11th ST
8th ST
1200 ft
1
2
3
4
5
6
7
8
9
10
14

13
12
17th ST
19th ST
13th ST
E ST
11
G ST

B1 518 C Street, NW

1990—WEINSTEIN ASSOCIATES ARCHITECTS

Amy Weinstein reintroduced Washington to brick polychromy—the use of several colors of masonry forming decorative patterns—which she viewed as an economical means of lending visual texture to projects such as this small, speculative office building. The primary façade, with its implied tower (the tower is not actually a discrete element in plan), has a civic—even church-like—character, while the projecting bays along 6th Street clearly relate to the rhythm of row houses on that block and throughout the neighborhood.

The building faces Stanton Park, one of several squares that lend a small-town quality to the residential part of Capitol Hill. The peripheral buildings are notably diverse, and include a historic school, small commercial structures, and single-family residences.

B2 St. Mark's Episcopal Church

3rd and A streets, SE

1889—T. BUCKLER GHEQUIER
1894, 1930—Additions: ARCHITECTS UNKNOWN
1926—Addition: DELOS SMITH
1965—Interior alterations: KENT COOPER & ASSOCIATES
1991—Undercroft and interior alterations: MUSE-WIEDEMANN ARCHITECTS

From 1896 to 1902, this church served as the "pro-cathedral"—in effect, an acting cathedral—for the Episcopal Diocese of Washington. It is ostensibly in the Romanesque Revival style, but not

as bulky and stern as that label might suggest. Inside the sanctuary, abundant stained glass windows and slender cast iron columns contribute to a sense of lightness. The glass in the main baptistery window came from the studio of Louis Comfort Tiffany, while most of the other stained glass windows were created by Mayer of Munich. Fixed pews were removed in the 1960s in favor of flexible seating in the round, better to accommodate the parish's progressive style of services, as well as its ambitious arts programming.

B3 Eastern Market

7th and C streets, SE

1873—South Hall: ADOLF CLUSS
1908—North Hall: SNOWDEN ASHFORD
2009—Rehabilitation: QUINN EVANS ARCHITECTS

Washington once boasted several of these airy markets offering fresh produce, flowers, and other goods. The Georgetown Market [see K17] still exists, but has been gussied up as a branch of a high-end retail food chain, while the former O Street Market in Northwest Washington is, as of this writing, a shell awaiting reuse as part of a modern grocery store. Eastern Market is the only survivor still functioning as a municipal market in the traditional sense. Many Capitol Hill residents consider it to be the unofficial center of their neighborhood.

The oldest part of this building was designed by the German-born Adolf Cluss, one of Washington's most prolific mid-19th-century architects. An avid Communist and close friend of Karl Marx (until they had a falling out in 1853), Cluss later was chided by his fellow travelers for becoming an "America-enthusiast," especially after he attained U.S. citizenship in 1855 and received a substantial inheritance in 1857. He went on to hold several appointed positions with the federal government and the District of Columbia "territorial" government, and designed or renovated at least 67 buildings, including schools, churches, hospitals, office buildings, and houses.

The façades of the Cluss-designed portion of the market are animated by a distinctive pattern of alternating arched and bull's-eye windows that provide light for the stalls inside. A corbelled brick cornice lends a Moorish quality to the structure while casting sharp, dramatic shadows on a bright day. The 1908 addition at the north end continues the arched-window motif, but in a more regular and subdued fashion. A cast iron shed, intended to shelter vendors, runs along the 7th Street edge of the site and visually ties the two wings together.

Eastern Market was heavily damaged by a fire in April 2007, causing great distress among area residents, who feared that it might be too difficult or too expensive to restore the building properly. Civic leaders assured citizens that they need not worry, however, and in 2009, the market reopened following an extensive rehabilitation. By virtually all accounts from vendors and patrons, this local landmark is now more efficient, pleasant, and sustainable than ever.

B4 The Penn Theater Project

650 Pennsylvania Avenue, SE

1935—JOHN EBERSON
1986—DAVID M. SCHWARZ / ARCHITECTURAL SERVICES

In this project, a rather small remnant of an Art Moderne theater served as the centerpiece for a mixed-use development. The new structure fronting Pennsylvania Avenue employs Moderne-inspired motifs that are appropriately modest (the old theater was built during the Depression, after all, when the lavish ornament common to earlier Art Deco buildings had given way to a simpler, streamlined aesthetic). The building shares a courtyard with the red brick apartment house at 649 C Street, which was part of the same redevelopment project but completely different in architectural expression.

B5 660 Pennsylvania Avenue, SE

1939—ARCHITECT UNKNOWN
1943—Addition: ARCHITECT UNKNOWN
1991—Renovation and addition: WEINSTEIN ASSOCIATES ARCHITECTS

A one-story, Art Moderne, former Kresge store was the foundation for a 1991 development that included rebuilding the old storefront and adding three stories of speculative office space. Both the distinctive decorative panels, executed in fiber-reinforced concrete, and the pattern of glazed and unglazed bricks were inspired by textile designs of the era in which the original store was built. The office entrance lobby on 7th Street elegantly continues this decorative program and is worth a special look.

B6 The Maples

619 D Street, SE

1796—WILLIAM LOVERING, ARCHITECT-BUILDER
1858, 1871—Additions: ARCHITECT UNKNOWN
1936—Restoration and additions: HORACE W. PEASLEE

"This fine house in the woods between Capitol Hill and the Navy Yard," as George Washington is said to have described it, has been expanded several times, has been used for a variety of purposes (including a hospital), and has a lengthy list of owners, yet still manages to retain a modicum of its 18th-century character. William Lovering, one of early Washington's best-known master craftsmen, built the place for William Mayne Duncanson, a rich planter who made and lost a fortune in District real estate, though according to *The WPA Guide to Washington, D.C.,* it was not poor investments but "Lavish entertainment [that] brought Duncanson to poverty." Later owners included Francis Scott Key.

Until recently the headquarters of a social services organization, the property is, as of this writing, being converted into a condominium under the direction of Cunningham | Quill Architects. The project entails the restoration of the original house, renovations of the 1930s structures, and the addition of several town houses. The plan preserves most of the open yard.

B7 Christ Church Washington Parish

620 G Street, SE

1807—ROBERT ALEXANDER
1824, 1849, 1874, 1891—Additions and renovations: ARCHITECTS UNKNOWN
1878—Renovation: WILLIAM H. HOFFMAN
1921—Interior alterations: DELOS SMITH
1954—Interior alterations: HORACE W. PEASLEE
1996—Interior renovation: ARCHITECTNIQUE, EDWARD S. FLEMMING JR. AND BENNY N. HINTZ

The myriad expansions, renovations, and reversals of previous alterations that mark the history of this Gothic Revival church are typical of the changes that venerable buildings tend to undergo over time. The original church was a simple brick box designed by Robert Alexander, a builder who worked with architect Benjamin Henry Latrobe on the Washington Navy Yard (and Latrobe may have overseen aspects of the church's design and construction). In 1824 came a small expansion at the rear, and in 1849, the narthex and the bell tower were appended to the front. The 1870s brought an interior renovation intended to make the church more fashionably Victorian, and then in 1891, the tower was enlarged and a new entry vestibule added. In the 1950s, Horace Peaslee set out to undo the fussy Victorian interiors and return the sanctuary to its more restrained origins. After all that, the little stucco building still stands serenely in its modest churchyard, looking only slightly weary from two centuries of tinkering.

B8 Townhomes on Capitol Hill

(Ellen Wilson Complex)
I Street and Ellen Wilson Place, between 6th and 7th streets, SE

2000—WEINSTEIN ASSOCIATES ARCHITECTS

A product of the U.S. Department of Housing and Urban Development's HOPE VI program, which was conceived to convert failed public housing projects into healthy, mixed-income communities, this complex replaced the dilapidated Ellen Wilson Dwellings. The new development consists solely of row houses, each with its own direct entry from the street, in keeping with the predominant housing type in the Capitol Hill neighborhood. Given a predictably modest budget, the architect chose to concentrate funds on creating a wide range of different façades, using a kit of parts to produce varied effects (these elements included an inexpensive but versatile bracket of an uncertain material that architect Amy Weinstein jokingly calls "mystery meat"). The result looks a bit like a stage set, thanks in part to the thin, vertical extensions of many of the façades that are evident from certain angles, but certainly yields a strong sense of place and communal identity.

Ellen Wilson Place, a newly created street in the middle of the block, harks back to the alleys of Capitol Hill that were once lined with working-class housing—some of it quite squalid—surrounded by higher-quality housing on the main streets. There is no such distinction in quality here, of course, but the contrasting house styles and distinct spatial character of the mid-block street hint at this historical difference. Ellen Wilson, by the way, was the first wife of President Woodrow Wilson. She actively advocated improvements to the living conditions of African Americans. When she was on her deathbed in 1914, Congress approved a bill in her honor banning substandard dwellings in alleys, but the law was later declared unconstitutional.

B9 Marine Barracks Washington and the Home of the Commandants

8th and I streets, SE

1806—Home of the Commandants: GEORGE HADFIELD
1840, 1891, 1934—Additions: VARIOUS ARCHITECTS
1906—Barracks, officers' housing, and Band Hall: HORNBLOWER & MARSHALL
2004—Annex and band facility, renovation of southern part of complex: BBG-BBGM

Tel: (202) 433-4073
www.marines.mil/unit/barracks/pages/welcome.aspx

Commonly called "8th and I," after two of its four surrounding streets, Marine Barracks Washington is the oldest continuously occupied Marine Corps base in the country, and served as the Corps' administrative headquarters from 1801 to 1901. In plan the base is a simple rectangle, with a perimeter of relatively narrow buildings surrounding an expansive drill field. The 8th Street side is lined with a tidy row of duplex residences for officers, while the 9th Street edge consists mostly of a single, continuous structure housing enlisted men and women. At the northern end of the site, on G Street, is the Home of the Commandants, which has served as the official residence of every Marine Corps chief since 1806, and has been remodeled many times, bearing witness to the shifting tastes of successive generations. Ancillary facilities form the southern edge of the complex.

On Fridays in the summer, the public may enter to watch the Evening Parade, featuring precision marching and musical performances by groups including the U.S. Marine Band, "The President's Own," which is based here. Reservations are suggested.

B10 Old Naval Hospital

921 Pennsylvania Avenue, SE

1866—ARCHITECT UNKNOWN; Executive architect: ATTRIBUTED TO AMMI B. YOUNG
2011—Restoration: BELL ARCHITECTS

The Old Naval Hospital served that function until 1906, when a new medical center was built along 23rd Street, NW, near the Mall. After that, the old hospital was used by the navy as a training facility before being converted into a short-term dormitory for veterans visiting Washington to obtain federal benefits. Control of the building was transferred to the District of Columbia government in 1965, and over the next couple of decades it was used mostly by local, nonprofit social services organizations. In 2007, the D.C. government issued a request for proposals for the reuse of the building, which by then had been effectively abandoned for years. The winner was the Hill Center, an organization of neighborhood citizens that converted the property into an educational center and community gathering space.

Ostensibly designed in the Second Empire style, with a mansard roof and pronounced quoins, the building is more subdued than that label might suggest, probably because it was being planned while the Civil War was still raging. It eschewed the heavy window surrounds and other lavish ornament more typically associated with Second Empire architecture, resulting in a relatively chaste structure that was nonetheless distinguished by its pleasing proportions. The iron fence that surrounds the property was almost lost when a military official proposed melting it down to make bullets during World War II—fortunately it survived (if only barely and with some missing sections) long enough to be restored as part of the recent renovation project.

B11 Congressional Cemetery

18th and E streets, SE
Established in 1807

1816–76—Cenotaphs: BENJAMIN HENRY LATROBE
1903—Chapel: ARTHUR M. POYNTON

Tel: (202) 543-0539
www.congressionalcemetery.org

Established by a group of private citizens who later donated the property to the nearby Christ Church [see B7], the Washington Parish Burial Ground soon earned its more common moniker—Congressional Cemetery—after becoming the semiofficial repository for members of Congress and other dignitaries whose remains could not be returned to their places of origin in the days before modern embalming techniques. Architects William Thornton, George Hadfield, and Robert Mills managed to squeeze their way in among the politicians, as did John Philip Sousa, Push-Ma-Ta-Ha (a Choctaw chief who died while in Washington negotiating a treaty), Marion Kahlert (killed at age 10 in 1904, the city's first automobile accident victim), and photographer Mathew Brady. Government officials interred here include longtime FBI director J. Edgar Hoover and Elbridge Gerry, a signer of the Declaration of Independence and vice president under James Madison, but probably best known as the inspiration for the word *gerrymander.*

Many politicians buried elsewhere are also commemorated here in more than 80 official cenotaphs. Use of the cenotaphs, designed by Benjamin Henry Latrobe and paid for by Congress, began around 1816 but abruptly ended in 1876 (with one 20th-century exception for Louisiana Representative Thomas Hale Boggs Sr.), when Representative George Hoar of Massachusetts remarked on the floor of the House that the ungainly structures added "new terrors to death." The sandstone cenotaphs were recently restored under the direction of the National Park Service's Historic Preservation Training Center. The cemetery is still owned by Christ Church, but currently is leased to a private foundation dedicated to preserving the grounds.

B12 St. Coletta of Greater Washington

1901 Independence Avenue, SE

2006—MICHAEL GRAVES

Michael Graves's best work in Washington, St. Coletta is an educational facility for children and adults with cognitive disabilities. Here, the architect's signature forms—boldly colored pavilions composed of basic geometric shapes reminiscent of children's building blocks—serve practical purposes. The distinct shapes and colors assist students in orienting themselves within the building and, taken together, create a unique visual identity and a strong sense of place. One mark of the success of the architecture is the institution's logo, which incorporates the "skyline" of the building itself.

The pavilions along Independence Avenue, covered in colorful glazed tiles, contain the entrance and common facilities. Running along 19th Street is a series of gabled classroom pavilions, decorated with super-scale masonry patterns, which are intended to relate to the row houses that are typical of the adjacent neighborhood. The classrooms are linked by the "Village Green," a wide corridor that serves not only as a circulation spine but also as a gathering place. The result is a clear, hierarchical sequence of spaces yielding a memorable experience for all users.

B13 East Capitol Street Car Barn

1400 East Capitol Street, NE

1896—WADDY B. WOOD
1983—Renovation and additions: MARTIN AND JONES

Like the Car Barn in Georgetown [see K10], the original complex here was built as an administrative, storage, and repair facility for electric streetcars. The long, low structure facing East Capitol Street housed offices; the storage and repair sheds were located at the northern side of the block. In the early 1980s, when this part of Capitol Hill was terra incognita to most real estate agents, a developer saw the potential of the old car barn to become a residential complex of unique character. The office wing was largely preserved, while only a few remnants of the other structures were kept and incorporated into new apartments.

B14 Philadelphia Row

132–154 11th Street, SE

1867—GEORGE GESSFORD

According to oral tradition, George Gessford built these side hall-plan row houses to assuage the homesickness of his Philadelphia-born wife. The style is clearly evocative of the Federal-period houses in that city, with their flat, chaste brick façades, arched doors, and simple stone sills and lintels, though Victorian brackets and unusual window patterns betray the houses' anachronism.

TOUR C

Capitol South

Once the site of the new capital city had been selected, land speculators flocked to the banks of the Anacostia River, hoping to cash in on the development potential along what was then a readily navigable waterway. John Greenleaf, who gave his name to the point of land at the convergence of the Anacostia and the Potomac, struck a particularly advantageous deal with Congress: he was allowed to purchase 3,000 city lots on the cheap, in exchange for lending the municipal government funds to be used for public improvements. Wheat Row resulted from this cozy arrangement, but little else did, since Greenleaf went bankrupt in 1797. Other developers active in the area included William Duncanson, whose mansion has been incorporated into the Harbour Square complex, and Thomas Law, whose house still stands at 6th and N streets, SW.

The initial burst of development along the Anacostia never turned into a sustained boom, partially because the river silted up and was heavily polluted by the late 19th century. Conditions in the near Southwest quadrant, in particular, deteriorated rapidly in the early 20th century—by World War II, it had degenerated into the city's most notorious slum, in which half the dwellings lacked plumbing. In the 1950s,

The Navy Yard along the Anacostia River figures prominently in this 1837 engraving by Louis Clover. The White House and Capitol, in the left and right background, respectively, appear isolated from the bustle of the waterfront. The large flag in the right middle ground marks the Marine Barracks just beyond the Navy Yard.

INDEPENDENCE AVE
C ST
12th ST
3rd ST
D ST
I-395
G ST
7th ST
4th ST
P ST
1
2
3
4
5
6
7
8
9
10
11
12
13
14
2400 ft

8th ST
11th ST
I-295
M ST
16
N ST
SOUTH CAPITOL ST
15

the District and federal governments took action, embarking on a vast campaign resulting in the demolition of more than 6,000 dwellings.

"Urban renewal" was a national buzz phrase during that period, as America's struggling cities went under the knife for experimental surgery intended to cure a variety of social maladies. Decades later, many cities are still recuperating from these generally well-intentioned initiatives, and that once-optimistic term—urban *renewal*—has come to symbolize indiscriminate destruction of neighborhoods (squalid though they may have been) in favor of drab, soulless superblocks. Fortunately for Washington, however, much of the redevelopment in the Southwest quadrant was of unusually high quality, avoiding the pitfalls that plagued many such projects elsewhere. Notwithstanding the sensitive social issues surrounding such endeavors, several of the housing developments in Southwest Washington are among the best works of large-scale urban architecture of their era.

In 2000, the District of Columbia government launched the Anacostia Waterfront Initiative, intended to spur the revitalization of areas on both sides of the river. A semi-independent, government-owned corporation was established to oversee the project, but was disbanded in 2007 and its functions absorbed by the Office of the Deputy Mayor for Planning and Economic Development. Despite that setback, several of the initiative's key elements have been realized, including Waterfront Station, a mixed-use development that replaced a forbidding, enclosed shopping center, and the Yards Park, one of the first sections of a planned riverfront walkway. Other major projects seem poised to begin soon, providing reasons for optimism about the future of a section of the city that has yet to fulfill its potential.

C1 L'Enfant Plaza

10th Street and Independence Avenue, SW

1968—I. M. PEI & PARTNERS (ARALDO COSSUTTA, PARTNER IN CHARGE OF DESIGN FOR OFFICE BUILDINGS); Landscape architect for Banneker Circle: DAN KILEY
1970—Forrestal Building: CURTIS AND DAVIS ARCHITECTS AND PLANNERS; FORDYCE & HAMBY ASSOCIATES; FRANK GRAD AND SONS
1973—Hotel and west office building: VLASTIMIL KOUBEK
1987—370 L'Enfant Promenade: EISENMAN ROBERTSON

L'Enfant Plaza was designed during an era in which heroically scaled, monumental buildings were in vogue, and governmental authorities commanded wholesale reconstruction of large urban areas without a quiver of doubt about the wisdom of such initiatives. The grand intentions for the complex are evident not only in its lofty name, honoring the city's creator, but also in its enormous scale and the knot of Metro lines that meet below it. Conceived as a cultural center of a vibrant new Southwest Washington, it is instead a hopelessly sterile precinct and, ironically, a blatant violation of L'Enfant's plan in its disregard for the street pattern he so thoughtfully devised.

The hollowness of the development is most evident in the barren swath running down the middle of the 10th Street spine and leading to Banneker Circle, named for the 18th-century African American surveyor of the District of Columbia, which terminates the axis. Intended as a belvedere, but in reality a place offering no amenity to reward the pedestrian (or motorist) other than a lonely fountain and some spindly trees, the cul-de-sac is not worth the trek across the freeway overpass that separates it from the main complex.

For what it's worth, the individual buildings in L'Enfant Plaza, though bombastic, are generally well composed and constructed. The least successful from an aesthetic standpoint is the Forrestal Building, which houses the U.S. Department of Energy. Its primary component is a bulky bar that spans 10th Street, thereby creating a grudging gateway to the complex. Every so often, someone proposes tearing down the whole building, or at least removing the section that bridges the street. That would be a step in the right direction.

C2 Central Heating Plant

13th and C streets, SW

1934—PAUL PHILIPPE CRET

Although it cannot compete with, say, London's Battersea Power Station for awesome industrial beauty, Cret's Art Deco-inspired heating plant is remarkably elegant considering its mundane purpose. The facility, which supplies heat to all of the federal buildings along the Mall, bears sculptural limestone panels depicting the machinery of power production.

C3 Robert C. Weaver Federal Building

(U.S. Department of Housing and Urban Development [HUD])
451 7th Street, SW

1968—MARCEL BREUER AND ASSOCIATES (MARCEL BREUER AND HERBERT BECKHARD); Architects of record: NOLEN-SWINBURNE & ASSOCIATES
1998—Plaza landscape: MARTHA SCHWARTZ

The word *Brutalism* derives from the French term *béton brut,* meaning "raw concrete," but you can't tell that to the movement's many detractors, for whom the term aptly describes what they consider to be the inhumanity of buildings in this style. Nonetheless, Brutalism could be done well or badly, and Marcel Breuer was certainly among its most skillful exponents.

Breuer's design for the HUD building was immediately newsworthy as a departure from the plain, boxy structures that had become standard for mid-20th-century government offices. In plan, the HUD building is a giant X (Breuer's UNESCO Headquarters complex in Paris is its Y-shaped counterpart), with a long spine and four bilaterally symmetrical, gently curving appendages. The muscular columns at the base of the building provide an angular counterpoint to the sweeping curves. The ends of the wings are sheathed in dark stone to contrast with the lighter concrete of the main façades.

The spaces between the arms of the X are exterior plazas. In the 1990s, HUD commissioned Martha Schwartz to make the primary plaza more attractive as an urban space. The solution is only partially successful. While the hovering translucent doughnuts are jaunty at first glance, they are disengaged from the seating areas, rendering them almost useless as shading devices in warm weather. The landscape architect had originally planned to introduce bright colors into the composition, which would have helped to give it life, but sadly that aspect of the proposal was abandoned.

C4 Washington Design Center

300 D Street, SW

1920s—Original structure: ARCHITECT UNKNOWN
1983—Renovation: KEYES CONDON FLORANCE ARCHITECTS; Associated architects: BRYANT & BRYANT ARCHITECTS
1994—Office addition: KEYES CONDON FLORANCE ARCHITECTS

Originally a refrigerated warehouse, this building was adapted to house the Washington Design Center, the first branch of Chicago's Merchandise Mart outside that city. One of the big questions in the minds of the architects during the renovation was what would happen to the old building's structure as it thawed. The answer: nothing.

C5 Capitol Park

Between 1st and 4th and G and I streets, SW

1958–63—SATTERLEE & SMITH; CHLOETHIEL WOODARD SMITH AND ASSOCIATES; Landscape architect: DAN KILEY

The first of the major modern housing developments in Southwest Washington, Capitol Park is a complex of apartment towers and town houses, creating a community that is typologically diverse but aesthetically cohesive. While the

apartment blocks are unusually varied in texture, it is the town house clusters that make this project extraordinary, thanks to their intricate networks of courtyards, pathways, and gardens. Although thoroughly modern in their materials and architectural expression, these buildings and spaces evoke the mysterious qualities typical of streetscapes in medieval European towns—quiet and modestly scaled, but richly layered and full of small surprises.

This project is also noteworthy as one of the earliest major American urban-scale projects designed by a woman. Chloethiel Woodard Smith was a pioneer not just by virtue of her sex but also in the inventiveness and finesse of her work.

C6 Mead Center for American Theater / Arena Stage

6th and M streets, SW

1961—Fichandler Stage: HARRY WEESE & ASSOCIATES
1970—Kreeger Theater: HARRY WEESE & ASSOCIATES
2010—Mead Center, including renovation of existing theaters: BING THOM ARCHITECTS

Arena Stage, according to the organization's mission statement, "produces huge plays of all that is passionate, exuberant, profound, deep and dangerous in the American spirit." It might seem surprising that a nonprofit cultural institution would court danger so brazenly, but Arena Stage has a history of taking risks. Founded in 1950, it was one of the first private, nonprofit theaters in the country, and *the* first theater in Washington to be racially integrated. Its original home, a former burlesque house downtown, was notable for its innovative, theater-in-the-round layout.

In 1961, Arena moved to a custom-built facility, designed by Chicago architect Harry Weese, in the Southwest urban renewal area. The building was monumental, abstract, and rather forbidding, but it maintained the theater-in-the-round format that had become an Arena hallmark. Weese later designed an addition including a second auditorium, using the same architectural vocabulary.

By the late 1990s, Arena Stage was desperate for more and better space, and hired Vancouver architect Bing Thom to oversee an expansion. Because the complex was a locally designated Historic Site, key elements—namely, the two main theater spaces—had to be preserved. Thom's solution was to demolish the administrative wing of the Weese-designed complex, renovate the two existing auditoriums, and encapsulate them within a larger structure lined with soaring, glass walls and topped by a vast but seemingly weightless roof. Supporting the roof are canted, wood-composite columns with struts that brace the sinuously curved curtain wall. Nestled between the older structures is a small new theater called the Cradle, for both its oval shape and the fact that it is intended as an incubator for future plays. Curving stairs lead to an upper-level café and an outdoor terrace shielded by an acutely angled, 90-foot cantilever pointing toward the Washington Monument in the distance.

The design of the enlarged complex is certainly idiosyncratic, and some elements, such as the tilted, wood-composite columns, look like they might be more at home in Washington State than in Washington, D.C., but the building is a lively and urbane presence in a neighborhood that sorely needed a jolt of architectural energy.

C7 The View at Waterfront Apartments / Town Center Plaza

1000 and 1100 6th Street, SW, and 1000 and 1100 3rd Street, SW

1962—I. M. PEI & PARTNERS
2008—Renovation of 6th Street towers: ESOCOFF & ASSOCIATES | ARCHITECTS

Pei designed four identical towers—two on 3rd Street and two on 6th Street—which were divided by the now-demolished Waterside Mall. Unlike most other apartment complexes in the area, these included neither town houses nor balconies. The façades exhibit a subtle balance of horizontal and vertical lines: recessed bands between floors emphasize the former, while the slender columns, split into pairs above the ground floor with operable windows between them, provide the vertical counterpoint.

In renovating the two towers on 6th Street, Esocoff & Associates went to great lengths to preserve Pei's original design intent while modernizing the buildings and making them more energy-efficient. Rather than patching or painting over the inevitable age-related cracks in the concrete, the architects specified a clear sealant, thus preserving the surface's consistent texture and patina. Upgrading the single-pane, seven-by-seven-foot windows required clever visual tricks to ensure that the larger frames supporting double-pane glass were not too prominent. The renovation also included the addition of green roofs on both towers.

C8 Waterfront Station

1100 and 1101 4th Street, SW

2010—SHALOM BARANES ASSOCIATES

This complex is noteworthy because of the damage it *undid.* It replaced the bunker-like Waterside Mall, which previously filled most of the block bounded by M, I, 3rd, and 6th streets, SW, and was perhaps the single greatest error of the Southwest urban renewal campaign of the mid-20th century. The new development allowed 4th Street—which had been blocked by the old mall—to be reopened, a move that instantly improved both pedestrian and vehicular traffic flow throughout the neighborhood (the Metro station entrance at 4th and M had already been built on axis with the old mall, so the reopened street had to swerve to bypass it). The two buildings completed so far represent the first phase of a larger master plan. Their designs are complementary, using similar materials—mostly glass and terra cotta tiles—in completely different compositions.

C9 Law House

6th and N streets, SW

C. 1796—ATTRIBUTED TO WILLIAM LOVERING
C. 1938—Addition: ARCHITECT UNKNOWN
1964—Restoration: KEYES, LETHBRIDGE & CONDON; CHLOETHIEL WOODARD SMITH & ASSOCIATES

Congressional authorization of the new federal city in 1790 set off a spate of speculative building, especially near the rivers. Thomas Law, an influential businessman who had made a fortune in the East India trade, was among the major speculators. He commissioned this center-hall, *piano nobile* house for himself and his bride, *née* Elizabeth Parke Custis, the wealthy grand-

daughter of Martha Washington and her first husband, Daniel Parke Custis. The generously sized house has inset, arched windows on the first floor—a motif favored by designer-builder William Lovering—and an elegant, asymmetrical, iron staircase. In 1797, Law optimistically built a sugar refinery nearby, the city's first heavy industry, but he overextended himself and, notwithstanding his rich wife, promptly went bankrupt. The Law House now serves as a meeting and event venue for the Tiber Island Cooperative complex.

C10 Tiber Island Cooperative Homes / Carrollsburg Square Condominium

M and N streets, SW, between Delaware Avenue and the Waterfront

1965—KEYES, LETHBRIDGE & CONDON
1993—Concrete restoration: ARCHITRAVE, P.C., ARCHITECTS

The design for this complex by Keyes, Lethbridge & Condon was selected in a competition conducted by the Redevelopment Land Agency. In several respects, such as the inclusion of both towers and town houses and the incorporation of a web of small outdoor spaces, these projects are similar to Capitol Park [see C5]. These buildings have a very different character, though, especially evident in the brick-and-precast concrete town houses, which draw more directly from the local domestic vernacular than does the relatively abstract Capitol Park.

C11 River Park

Between 4th Street and Delaware Avenue and N and O streets, SW

1963—CHARLES M. GOODMAN ASSOCIATES

Quietly sitting in Southwest Washington is one of the most innovative modernist urban developments anywhere in the country—an enclave of apartment towers and town houses in which aluminum is featured as a structural and ornamental material. Most notable are the town houses, many of which are improbably and entertainingly capped with wafer-thin barrel vaults. The use of aluminum in such structures was highly unusual, but was no mere whim on the part of the architect. Rather, it reflects the role of the developer—none other than the Reynolds Aluminum Service Corporation—eager to promote the use of its parent company's products in the many urban redevelopment projects then under way across the country.

Charles Goodman helped pioneer modernist architecture in Washington, but his national reputation was limited, probably because aspects of his work—such as those rather whimsical barrel vaults—did not always fit comfortably with International Style orthodoxy. His greatest work is arguably Hollin Hills, an entire neighborhood of sleek, single-family houses in suburban Virginia.

C12 Harbour Square / Wheat Row

500 N Street, SW and 1313–1321 4th Street, SW

c. 1794—Wheat Row: ATTRIBUTED TO WILLIAM LOVERING
1966—Harbour Square and renovation of Wheat Row: CHLOETHIEL WOODARD SMITH & ASSOCIATES; Landscape architect: DAN KILEY

Wheat Row is an example of the speculative housing ventures that were common early in Washington's history. This development, named for John Wheat (who lived at 1315) and financed by wheeler-dealer John Greenleaf, may be the oldest surviving set of row houses in the city. Saved and renovated when most of the neighborhood was destroyed during the urban renewal era, these Federal-style houses (along with a couple of other historic houses around the corner of N Street) were incorporated into the new Harbour Square complex, the centerpiece of which is a large reflecting pool with a causeway-like pedestrian bridge. From certain vantage points, passing pedestrians can see little hexagonal pavilions atop several of the towers, which provide access to private roof decks for upper-level apartments.

C13 National War College

(Theodore Roosevelt Hall)
Fort Lesley J. McNair, 4th and P streets, SW

1907—MCKIM, MEAD & WHITE
2000—Renovation: ELLERBE BECKET

Fort McNair, established in 1791, is the third oldest military reservation in the country, after West Point in New York and Carlisle Barracks in Pennsylvania. The fort (which acquired its current name after World War II) was damaged by the British in 1814, but was rebuilt shortly thereafter. It was later the site of the District's federal penitentiary, where four people convicted of conspiracy in the Lincoln assassination were hanged.

In 1901, President Theodore Roosevelt and Secretary of War Elihu Root established the Army (now National) War College as part of an initiative to modernize the nation's military in the wake of the Spanish-American War, and in 1907, the institution moved into its permanent home here at the apex of Greenleaf Point. The domed college building itself, solidly executed in brick with granite trim, presides at the end of a grand lawn, much like Thomas Jefferson's library at the University of Virginia. In this case, the sides of the lawn are lined with houses for officers (on the water side) and noncommissioned officers (opposite), surely among the most genteel military housing anywhere in the country. The National War College is now one constituent of the National Defense University, which has facilities at Fort McNair and in Norfolk, Virginia.

C14 King Greenleaf Recreation Center

201 N Street, SW

2005—DEVROUAX + PURNELL ARCHITECTS

The curving and angled forms of this public recreation center contrast with the rectilinearity that was typical of the mid-20th-century modern architecture in the Southwest urban renewal area. Glass walls allow views from the park into the basketball court and other interior spaces; in the evenings, the glow emanating from the building advertises its role as a gathering place for the neighborhood.

C15 Nationals Park

1500 South Capitol Street, SE

2008—HOK / POPULOUS / DEVROUAX + PURNELL ARCHITECTS, A JOINT VENTURE; Associated architects for interiors: BOWIE GRIDLEY ARCHITECTS

When Baltimore's Oriole Park at Camden Yards opened in 1992, people of diverse architectural tastes praised the stadium—largely for not looking like a wayward UFO as had so many of its modernist predecessors. Its success as a catalyst for urban redevelopment inspired a generation of historicist ballparks and stadiums in cities across the country. By the time Washington finally got a professional baseball team again in 2005, however, the retro stadium trend seemed to be running its course. Following a great deal of public debate about whether the city should pay for a new stadium, and if so, where it should be built, the team's owners and D.C. officials finally agreed to build a modern, publicly financed ballpark on this site.

Nationals Park was not only the first major professional sports stadium to be LEED certified, but actually achieved Silver status, thanks in part to a large green roof area over concession structures, energy-efficient field lighting, and substantial use of recycled materials in the construction of the facility. To maintain the more intimate feel of some of the retro ballparks, Nationals Park was conceived as a series of "neighborhoods," each with a distinct layout and unique sightlines. The main concourse, rather than being raised as in many earlier modernist stadiums, is at roughly the same level as the sidewalk outside, so a large percentage of fans do not have to climb ramps or stairs to get to their seating area.

It is too early to assess the urbanistic impact of Nationals Park, which clearly inspired a good deal of other redevelopment in the immediate area, but much of that activity was interrupted during the recession that began in 2007. The most unfortunate aspect of the development is the pair of aboveground parking garages that bracket the principal entry gate. Perhaps as the area continues to develop and mass transit options increase, these structures can eventually be converted to a livelier use.

C16 Washington Navy Yard

8th and M streets, SE

c. 1801—Quarters B: ATTRIBUTED TO LOVERING AND DYER
1804—Commandant's House (Tingey House): ATTRIBUTED TO LOVERING AND DYER
1806—Latrobe Gate: BENJAMIN HENRY LATROBE
1838—Middendorf Building and Historic Commandant's Office: ARCHITECT UNKNOWN
Numerous other buildings, additions, and renovations: VARIOUS ARCHITECTS

Established in 1799, this is America's oldest extant naval base. It was a major shipbuilding center until the 1830s and remained Washington's most significant manufacturing facility throughout the 19th century. Early construction on the base was spotty until 1803, when Benjamin Henry Latrobe assumed supervision of its development in his new capacity as surveyor of public buildings. Shortly after his appointment, Latrobe designed the yard's brick entrance gate at the base of 8th Street, one of the earliest works of Greek Revival architecture in the United States. The gate was altered many times, most notably in the 1880s, when a three-story, Victorian structure was built around and over it. Sometime later, the entire structure was covered in stucco and painted white. Even after all that, one can still get a sense of Latrobe's original work in the center of the structure on the ground level.

Two officers' quarters, including the Commandant's House (commonly called Tingey House), are the only other substantial survivors of the Latrobe era at the Navy Yard, which the commandant ordered burned in order to keep it out of the hands of the British invaders in 1814. One later building of note is the former Commandant's office, originally a symmetrical, two-story structure surrounded by verandas on both levels. All of these buildings have undergone extensive changes.

TOUR D

The Mall

The Mall is both the oldest federal park in the nation and the most ambitious single gesture in the plan of Washington, D.C. L'Enfant conceived it as a grand, axial sweep running from the Capitol to a large equestrian statue of George Washington, but for most of the city's history the space fell far short of his vision. In the mid- to late 19th century, trains chugged in and out of a railroad station near the center of the Mall, generating smoke that frequently obscured the view of the Capitol. An open sewer, built as a canal, crossed the Mall, while the marshy Potomac end was prone to flooding. Some of the leftover space was landscaped in a "romantic" manner, with winding paths and what A. J. Downing intended as a "public museum of living trees and shrubs," but this picturesque layout contributed to the perception of disorder. The ruddy turrets of the Smithsonian Castle, then starkly isolated in the middle of the Mall, added a somber touch, and for a considerable interval, the incomplete shaft of the Washington Monument loomed near the Mall's western terminus, as if to mock the chaos of it all.

In 1901, the Senate Park Commission, often called the McMillan Commission after the Michigan senator who formed it, launched a campaign to change the Mall from a civic embarrassment to a national treasure. The commissioners sought inspiration in L'Enfant's original design, but their plan was no mere revival—rather, it reflected the spirit of the time, and in particular, the tenets of the City Beautiful movement that

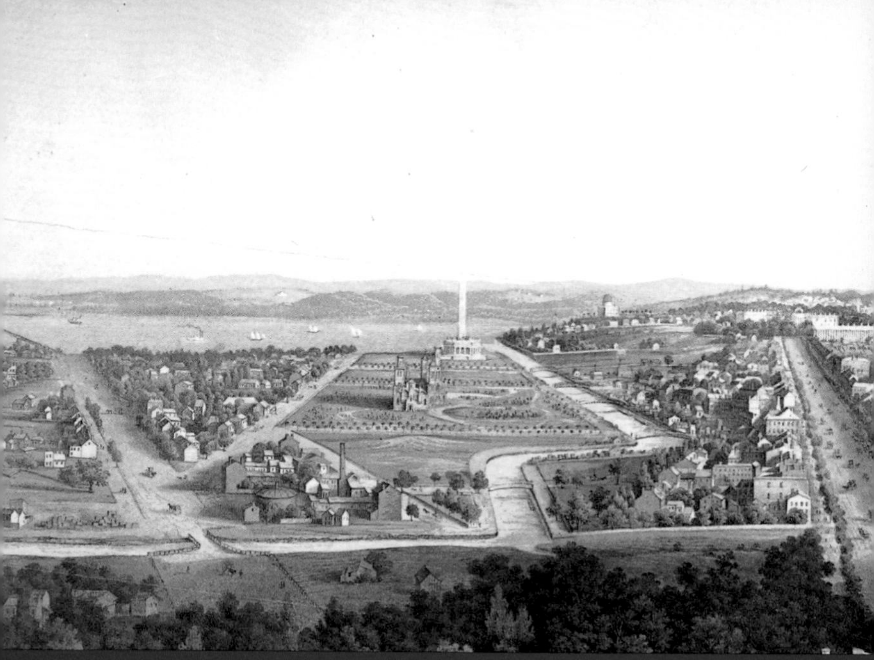

Although titled View of Washington, *this engraving published by Baltimore's E. Sachse & Co. in 1852 mostly conveyed wishful thinking. The Mall is inaccurately depicted as a clean, grassy swath, and in the distance the Washington Monument, which at this time was nowhere near finished, is shown full height, surrounded by the circular temple-like base that was never built.*

CONSTITUTION AVE
23rd ST
20
19
17
16
15
18
21
14
13
12
11
2000 ft

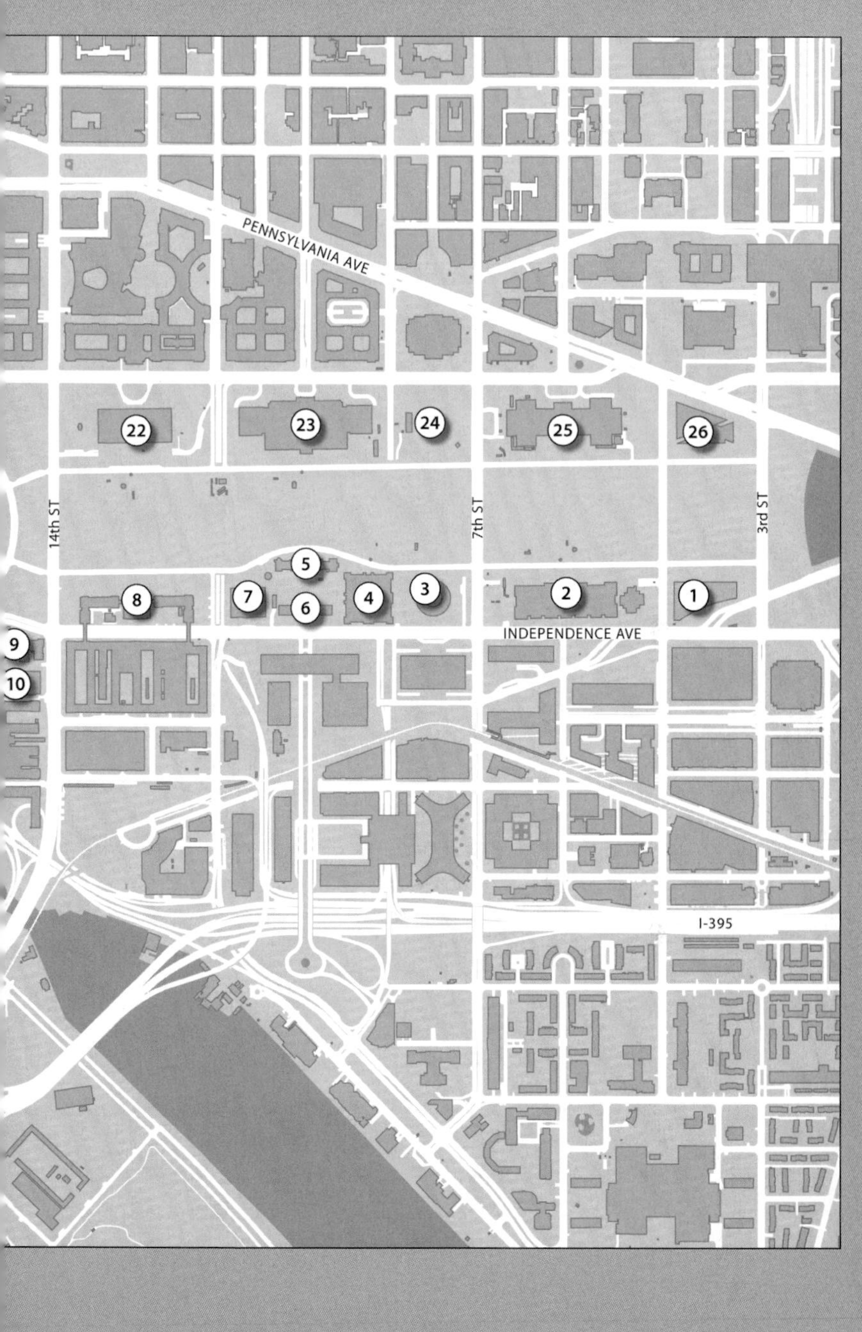

PENNSYLVANIA AVE
14th ST
7th ST
3rd ST
INDEPENDENCE AVE
I-395
22
23
24
25
26
5
7
8
6
4
3
2
1
9
10

was largely inspired by the 1893 World's Columbian Exposition in Chicago. Following much deliberation (and a lengthy tour of European capitals offering models for outstanding urban design), the commission produced a majestic, classically inspired plan for Washington's monumental core. Over time, the railroad agreed to relocate (and received the new Union Station for being so public-spirited), the marshes and canals were drained and filled in, and the Lincoln and Jefferson memorials rose in marble splendor in the reclaimed marshlands. The commission's imperially scaled plan was never fully realized—the decidedly non-classical Smithsonian Castle successfully held its ground, for instance, and the broad, imposing terrace proposed for the base of the Washington Monument was not built—but the essence of the 1902 plan has largely come to fruition.

The present two-mile-long Mall is almost incomprehensibly grand; it is also one of the most audacious urban landscapes in the world, an impressive rebuke to the *horror vacui* that has engendered so many overwrought public and quasi-public spaces in America (think Disney). Christopher Knight of the *Los Angeles Times* praised the Mall's "sublime emptiness," which he defended as an important symbol of the nation's democratic, open society. Interestingly, his comments appeared in an article decrying a great threat to this important space—a proliferation of new monuments and memorials, with countless other groups already clamoring for their own causes to be recognized on this highly symbolic tract. The Mall is thus in danger of becoming a victim of its own civic success. At the same time, the space is notably lacking in many of the amenities typically associated with an urban park, such as outdoor cafés, children's play areas, and locally oriented programming. As the capital's various design review agencies work to address these issues, for now the Mall can safely be enjoyed for its myriad museums, its often inspiring monuments, and, above all, its gloriously improbable openness.

D1 National Museum of the American Indian

4th Street and Independence Avenue, SW

2004—Architect and project designer: DOUGLAS CARDINAL; Design architects: GBQC ARCHITECTS AND JOHNPAUL JONES; Project architects: JONES & JONES ARCHITECTS AND LANDSCAPE ARCHITECTS, AND SMITHGROUP, IN ASSOCIATION WITH LOU WELLER AND THE NATIVE AMERICAN DESIGN COLLABORATIVE, AND POLSHEK PARTNERSHIP ARCHITECTS; Landscape architects: JONES & JONES ARCHITECTS AND LANDSCAPE ARCHITECTS, AND EDAW

Tel: (202) 633-1000
www.nmai.si.edu

The first new museum on the Mall proper in nearly two decades, the National Museum of the American Indian (NMAI) stands out for its organic form and its overt symbolism. The museum's curvilinear façades, covered in rough-hewn Kasota limestone, were designed so as to suggest natural rock formations sculpted by wind and rain over millennia—an allusion to the importance of the natural landscape in Native American cultures. The curves also establish a dramatic contrast to the intensely angular, impeccably honed East Building of the National Gallery of Art directly across the Mall. The landscape immediately surrounding the building captures a portion of the vast and largely undifferentiated Mall, gently appropriating it for the museum's own identity and programmatic purposes. The informal arrangement of indigenous plants in the garden is another nod to naturalism; the garden also shelters several paved outdoor areas designed to accommodate Native American rituals and ceremonies.

The original design for the building was by Douglas Cardinal, a Native North American (he is Canadian) whose substantial portfolio contains many equally sculptural buildings. Cardinal was removed from the project, however, following a dispute with the Smithsonian administration. Polshek Partnership then took over, working with many of the original team members, but not without controversy. Cardinal claimed that his design was hijacked, though the exterior as executed seems generally true to his intentions. The interior is less successful—the domed atrium space, called simply "the Potomac," is vacuous and a little disorienting, while the galleries and peripheral spaces are generally unmemorable.

D2 National Air and Space Museum

Between Jefferson Drive and Independence Avenue and 4th and 7th streets, SW

1976—HELLMUTH, OBATA + KASSABAUM
1988—Addition: HELLMUTH, OBATA + KASSABAUM

Tel: (202) 633-1000
www.nasm.si.edu

This blandly monumental building is laudable mostly for staying out of the way and allowing the museum's awe-inspiring artifacts to speak for themselves. From the Wright Brothers' "Flyer" of 1903, to Charles Lindbergh's *Spirit of St. Louis*, to the *Apollo 11* command module, the hangar-like halls brim with historic airplanes, spacecraft, and related objects filling more than 160,000 square feet of exhibition space. The idea of hanging many of the airplanes from the trusses now seems obvious, but it was an innovative design move when employed here for the first time at a significant scale.

The museum's exterior subtly plays off of nearby buildings. For example, architect Gyo Obata designed the north façade as a series of projecting and recessed bays, geometrically complementing the pattern of bays on the National Gallery of Art's south façade across the Mall—a kind of abstracted version of the yin and yang. The two buildings also share a distinctive, pinkish Tennessee marble. Meanwhile, the dark, horizontal recesses near the tops of the Air and Space Museum's stone-faced blocks recall the similar slit in the Hirshhorn next door.

In 1988, a glassy restaurant was appended to the east end of the building, with a sloping, stepped roof that offsets the chunky quality of the main structure. In 2003, the Smithsonian opened a branch of the museum—if "branch" is the right word, since it is large enough to swallow the "home" museum whole—adjacent to Dulles airport. Named the Steven F. Udvar-Hazy Center, the new facility holds some of the institution's largest items, including a space shuttle and the eerily beautiful SR-71 Blackbird spy plane.

D3 Hirshhorn Museum and Sculpture Garden

Independence Avenue at 7th Street, SW

1974—SKIDMORE, OWINGS & MERRILL
1981—Redesign of Sculpture Garden: LESTER COLLINS
1993—Redesign of plaza: JAMES URBAN
2005—Restoration of fountain and conversion of tunnel to program space: ARCHITRAVE, P.C., ARCHITECTS

Tel: (202) 633-1000
hirshhorn.si.edu

At the opening of the Hirshhorn Museum, the legendary S. Dillon Ripley, secretary of the Smithsonian, declared that if the building "were not controversial in almost every way, it would hardly qualify as a place to house contemporary art." If that was Ripley's wish, it certainly came true. For decades, Washingtonians and visitors alike have scoffed at the museum's blank façade and its disregard for the Mall's prevailing, rectilinear classicism. Indeed, it is easy to dismiss the Hirshhorn as a glorified bunker—especially considering the dark, horizontal slit on the Mall side that looks as though it might produce 16-inch gun barrels at any moment—but a more careful consideration of the building reveals a number of things to like.

Designed by Skidmore, Owings & Merrill partner Gordon Bunshaft, the Hirshhorn is actually a doughnut in plan, with a central courtyard focused on an eccentrically placed bronze fountain. In contrast to the almost completely solid perimeter, the internal façade is a grid of windows behind which are corridor-like galleries—mostly for sculpture—that hug the inside of the doughnut on the second and third levels. This arrangement makes for a circulation pattern that is both clear (since visitors easily return to where they started) and pleasant (since the corridors are naturally lit and punctuated by art). The windowless perimeter galleries are well suited to paintings and other artworks that are sensitive to light. While the gently curving walls can be awkward for hanging large works, the upside is that they lend a subtle panoramic quality to art installations.

Across Jefferson Drive is the Hirshhorn's sunken garden for large-scale modern sculptures, one of the finest such collections in the United States. The garden was originally designed to span the Mall, but was scaled back following a public outcry. As reworked by Lester Collins, it is a pleasant enclave

in which the landscape design and the sculptures complement each other.

As of this writing, the Hirshhorn is developing an exciting scheme for an inflatable structure—dubbed, inevitably, "the Balloon"—that would create a temporary pavilion within the courtyard and a satellite pod just outside the museum's perimeter. Designed by Diller Scofidio + Renfro, this structure would be deployed seasonally for special programming and events. S. Dillon Ripley would not be surprised to learn that, so far, the idea appears to be controversial in almost every way.

D4 Arts and Industries Building

900 Jefferson Drive, SW

1881—ADOLF CLUSS AND PAUL SCHULZE, WITH MONTGOMERY C. MEIGS; Sculptor: CASPAR BUBERL
1897-1903—Modifications: HORNBLOWER & MARSHALL
1976—Restoration: HUGH NEWELL JACOBSEN
1985—Exterior restoration: OEHRLEIN & ASSOCIATES ARCHITECTS

Covering more than two acres, the Arts and Industries Building is one of the largest extant Victorian-era structures in Washington. Initially known as the National Museum Building (not to be confused with the National *Building Museum* [see E2], especially since Montgomery Meigs played a role in the design of both buildings), it was built to house the Smithsonian's growing collection, which had recently expanded with the addition of artifacts from the 1876 Centennial Exposition in Philadelphia.

Meigs prepared a conceptual plan for the building, calling for a large square structure with a central rotunda. Cluss and Schulze subsequently won a competition for the actual commission. Their plan was similar to Meigs's, but with an overlay of a Greek cross that divided the building into quadrants, which were in turn subdivided into smaller spaces. Both schemes were likely inspired by a well-known ideal museum plan developed in the early 1800s by J.-N.-L. Durand, a teacher of architecture at the École polytechnique in Paris. Meigs served as a consultant to Cluss and Schulze during the construction.

The polychrome brick building was touted as the least expensive major structure erected by the federal government up to that time, costing less than $3 per square foot (though this figure ignored the costs of mechanical systems and marble floors that were pushed into the following year's budget). Work began in April 1879, some offices were occupied by the end of 1880, and the building was sufficiently finished to host President James Garfield's inaugural ball in March 1881, though temporary floors and furniture had to be installed for the occasion.

Inside, the great trusses, meandering iron balconies, and complex roofing system have a character that is simultaneously industrial and old-timey. Cluss had a seemingly limitless faith in the possibilities of technology, which may help to explain why so many aspects of the building suggest settings from a Jules Verne novel. As of this writing, the building is undergoing renovation—its reopening date and ultimate use remain uncertain.

D5 The Smithsonian Institution Building ("The Castle")

1000 Jefferson Drive, SW

1855—JAMES RENWICK JR.
1867, 1884, 1888—Reconstruction and alterations: ADOLF CLUSS
1970—Restoration: CHATELAIN, SAMPERTON AND NOLAN ARCHITECTS
1999—Exterior masonry restoration and window replacement: OEHRLEIN & ASSOCIATES ARCHITECTS

Tel: (202) 633-1000
www.si.edu/Museums/smithsonian-institution-building

When James Smithson, a British scientist and illegitimate son of the first Duke of Northumberland, died in 1829, he left his estate to his nephew. Smithson's will, however, included an odd stipulation: if the nephew should die without heirs, which he did in 1835, then the bulk of the fortune would go instead to the United States of America—a country Smithson had never visited—for the purpose of founding in Washington "an Establishment for the increase & diffusion of knowledge among men."

In some respects, the bequest should not have been so surprising, since Smithson was something of a political radical, who had dismissed the British monarchy as a "contemptible encumbrance" and publicly declared that the future lay with the new democracy across the Atlantic. Nonetheless, American politicians were not only surprised by Smithson's gift, but also highly suspicious of it. After a good deal of debate and anti-British posturing, Congress finally accepted Smithson's posthumous largesse in 1836, and in 1838, the government received funds totaling more than $500,000, an enormous sum at the time. The Smithsonian Institution—the exact name was also stipulated in the benefactor's will—was formally established in 1846.

The young James Renwick was soon chosen over more established architects in a competition for the design of the new institution's home. Renwick produced a picturesque, "Norman"-style structure with a dramatically asymmetrical skyline that belies its balanced, orderly plan. The Castle, as it came to be called for obvious reasons, originally contained the entire institution, including the residence of the secretary, the Smithsonian's chief executive. It now houses administrative offices and an information center, along with long-term and rotating exhibitions. Notable interior spaces include the airy Great Hall, with its neo-Romanesque, faux-stone columns; the elegant Commons, with soaring groin vaults and diamond-shaped skylights; and a small chamber holding the sarcophagus of Smithson himself, whose corporal remains belatedly followed his money to the New World in 1904.

Like many of its stylistic siblings, the Castle almost fell victim to changing tastes when the Senate Park Commission proposed its plan for the Mall in 1902. The plan called for both the Castle and the neighboring Arts and Industries Building to be razed in favor of Beaux-Arts classical buildings that would toe a rigid line in terms of both architectural style and the physical boundaries of the Mall. Both survived, though, and are now beloved for their exceptional (in the true sense of the word) character—bastions of the old brick Washington that survived the marble, classical onslaught.

D6 Quadrangle Museums Project

(Arthur M. Sackler Gallery, National Museum of African Art, Enid A. Haupt Garden, and S. Dillon Ripley Center)
Independence Avenue between the Arts and Industries Building and the Freer Gallery of Art

1987—SHEPLEY, BULFINCH, RICHARDSON & ABBOTT, BASED ON INITIAL CONCEPT BY JUNZO YOSHIMURA; Landscape architect: LESTER COLLINS

Tel: (202) 633-1000
www.asia.si.edu
www.nmafa.si.edu

Designing a new museum complex adjacent to the revered Smithsonian Castle and nestled between the Victorian Arts and Industries Building and the neo-classical Freer Gallery of Art would be a challenge under any circumstances. Given that the project also had to accommodate three quite distinct programmatic components, including new galleries for Asian and African art, this was surely one of the most difficult architectural commissions of the late 20th century.

The conceptual design, by Japanese architect Junzo Yoshimura, understandably called for placing the bulk of the new facilities underground. After Yoshimura suffered a stroke, the venerable Boston firm of Shepley, Bulfinch, Richardson & Abbott, which had initially served in an associate role, assumed full control of the project. For the aboveground structures, lead architect Jean-Paul Carlhian responded to the blizzard of competing styles and functions he faced by using a kind of generic, classically inspired vocabulary. Unfortunately, as executed, these elements seem stiff and self-conscious. Blocky granite trim, awkwardly large spherical finials, and a profusion of pyramidal and domed roofs yield buildings that appear comparatively crude on such a star-studded stage, though the garden itself succeeds as a pleasant public space thanks to its changing flora, elegant fountains, and a few relatively engaging works of sculpture.

The most intriguing architectural elements of the complex are the two vertiginous atria, with spiraling stairs, which connect the ground-level pavilions to the facilities below. Once inside the bowels of the museums, however, the visitor is likely to feel a bit claustrophobic and disoriented, faced with a labyrinth of corridors, galleries, and shops. To add to the confusion, the Sackler Gallery is connected underground to the Freer, as the two museums share a single administrative structure.

D7 Freer Gallery of Art

Between Independence Avenue and Jefferson Drive at 12th Street, SW

1923—CHARLES ADAMS PLATT
1990—Interior renovations: SHEPLEY, BULFINCH, RICHARDSON & ABBOTT; E. VERNER JOHNSON AND ASSOCIATES; SMITHSONIAN STAFF ARCHITECTS
1993—Renovations of interiors and courtyard: COLE & DENNY / BVH

Tel: (202) 633-1000
www.asia.si.edu

Charles Lang Freer made a fortune manufacturing railroad cars, but his real interest always lay in art. In fact, one fellow Detroit industrialist complained that Freer "would rather discuss the tariffs on early Italian art than the price of pig iron." Freer's collecting focused on the work of contemporary Americans, such as James McNeill Whistler, and on the ancient painting and sculpture of Asia. Once he had assembled his collection, he donated it to the Smithsonian, along with money to build a museum to house it. Freer personally hired Charles Adams Platt to cre-

ate the building and worked closely with him throughout the design process.

Freer's art may have been mostly American and Asian, but Platt's building is unapologetically European—not surprising, given that he was an accomplished classicist and served on the Beaux-Arts-oriented Commission of Fine Arts while designing this museum. Firmly committed to the precepts of the Senate Park Commission Plan, Platt produced an infallibly polite, low-rise *palazzo* sited along Independence Avenue (he surely shared the common assumption that the Smithsonian Castle, which intruded into the central swath of the Mall declared sacrosanct by the commission, would eventually be demolished). The building's heavy rustication, arches, and pronounced balustrade reflect Platt's interest in Italian Mannerism, most notably the work of the 16th-century Venetian architect Michele Sanmicheli. The Freer is, in fact, the most faithfully derivative of all the buildings on the Mall.

At the core of the museum is a rather intimate courtyard, surrounded by an open loggia. Most of the gallery spaces are austere, though well proportioned and perfectly suited to the display of Freer's art. During the design process, Platt built a full-scale mockup of one of the galleries and borrowed some of Freer's paintings in order to assess the quality of the artificial and natural lighting in the space. A highlight of the museum is the Peacock Room, an interior designed by architect Thomas Jeckyll and decorated by Whistler for the London house of shipbuilder Frederick Leyland. The room was dismantled and reconstructed in Freer's Detroit mansion, and later moved again to its current location in the museum.

D8 Jamie L. Whitten Federal Building

(U.S. Department of Agriculture)
14th Street and Independence Avenue, SW

1908—WINGS: RANKIN, KELLOGG & CRANE
1930—Central section: RANKIN, KELLOGG & CRANE

This federal office building was the first project designed for the south side of the Mall in accordance with the Senate Park

Commission Plan of 1901–2. It superseded the earlier Agriculture Department headquarters, designed by Adolf Cluss, which was a brick building that stood closer to the Mall's central axis, aligned more or less with the Smithsonian Castle. Controversy raged as to the best location for the new building—it took the direct intervention of President Theodore Roosevelt to stop the department from putting it smack in the middle of the Mall—but the cornerstone was eventually laid here in 1905, on a site previously occupied by greenhouses. As with the Capitol, the wings were built first, with the central section finished much later. On the side facing the Mall, within the four pediments on the wings, are rather odd sculptures depicting pairs of naked youths holding escutcheons labeled "Forests," "Cereals," "Flowers," and "Fruits."

D9 Sidney R. Yates Federal Building

(Auditors Main Building)
201 14th Street, SW, at Independence Avenue

1880—JAMES G. HILL
1902—Addition: JAMES KNOX TAYLOR
1915—Renovation: ARCHITECT UNKNOWN
1989—Renovation: NOTTER FINEGOLD + ALEXANDER INC. / MARIANI, ARCHITECTS

Along with the Smithsonian Castle, the Arts and Industries Building, and the National Building Museum, this is one of the major remnants of the red brick era in federal architecture. Like its few remaining siblings, the building survived even though its craggy, asymmetrical forms soon fell out of favor with the advent of the City Beautiful movement. Built for the Bureau of Engraving and Printing, it now houses offices of the Department of Agriculture.

D10 U.S. Holocaust Memorial Museum

Raoul Wallenberg Place (between 14th and 15th streets, SW)

1993—PEI COBB FREED & PARTNERS; Associated architects: NOTTER FINEGOLD + ALEXANDER

Tel: (202) 488-0400
www.ushmm.org

This haunting structure is America's living memorial to the millions of Jews, homosexuals, prisoners of war, and others murdered by the Nazis in the 1930s and 1940s. The brilliance of the architecture lies in its evocation of the veneer of normalcy that cloaked so many aspects of the Holocaust. The exterior of the museum, by virtue of its materials, scale, and simple forms, is disarmingly harmonious with the governmental buildings surrounding it, as if to remind visitors of the insidious integration of the Holocaust's administrative mechanisms into broader society. The interior is more strongly referential, with blank brick walls, steel bridges, and stark lighting suggesting the mundane industrial architecture of concentration camps. Beneath the ostensible banality there lurks a sinister quality that powerfully frames some of the most affecting exhibitions to be found in any museum.

"You cannot deal with the Holocaust as a reasonable thing," explained architect James Ingo Freed; this "wholly un-American subject" can only be treated in "an emotional dimension." In designing this building, he successfully created an environment in which visitors are inexorably drawn into the personal stories of Holocaust victims and engaged in an intensely emotional experience from which few emerge unmoved.

D11 Thomas Jefferson Memorial

The Tidal Basin

1938–43—JOHN RUSSELL POPE / EGGERS & HIGGINS; SCULPTOR: RUDULPH EVANS
1995–2000—Restoration: EINHORN YAFFEE PRESCOTT; HARTMAN-COX ARCHITECTS
2006—Security upgrades and stone restoration: MCKISSACK & MCKISSACK; Preservation consultants: JOHN MILNER ASSOCIATES

Perhaps the culmination of City Beautiful classicism in official Washington, finished 50 years after the World's Columbian Exposition in Chicago launched the movement, the Jefferson Memorial was the subject of bitter debate after John Russell Pope's plans were revealed in late 1936. Frank Lloyd Wright and other prominent architects were scandalized by the retrograde design, and argued that the famously erudite and progressive Jefferson would have preferred a memorial that reflected the technology and ethos of its era. Meanwhile, non-architects were upset about the memorial's siting, which would require the removal of many of the famous Japanese cherry trees surrounding the Tidal Basin. Political and cultural journalists decried the expenditure of vast sums on an "imperial" monument while the country was mired in the Great Depression. In response, Congress revoked the funding for the project, but President Franklin D. Roosevelt eventually pushed it through, and by the time the memorial was nearing completion in 1943, few Americans were worried about the loss of a few trees donated by a country with which they were at war.

Pope's design was based, of course, on the ancient Roman Pantheon—which had also inspired Jefferson's rotunda at the University of Virginia—but Pope took many liberties with the prototype. The Pantheon's two principal forms are a solid, masonry-and-concrete cylinder and a very deep, Corinthian portico articulated as a distinct though complementary form. Similarly, the rotunda at Virginia consists of a mostly solid masonry cylinder (with punched windows) and a deep, all-white Corinthian portico that contrasts with the red brick of the principal structure. The Jefferson Memorial, while relying on the same basic forms, is quite different in several ways. First, the cylinder is expressed as an open, peristyle colonnade, giving the structure a much lighter, more permeable character than that of its predecessors. Second, the portico is relatively shallow, and is seamlessly joined to the cylinder by virtue of their consistent color, shared column heights, and common entablature. Finally, Pope used the Ionic order rather than the Corinthian, thus making the building slightly less formal and giving it a more horizontal aspect (since, under classical precepts, Ionic columns have a lower height-to-width ratio than Corinthian ones).

The result, while undeniably anachronistic, has proved to be popular with tourists despite being stranded on the far shore of the Tidal Basin, cut off from the core of the Mall. The best aspect of the memorial is its setting at the edge of the water, especially when the nearby cherry trees—of which the vast majority remain—are in bloom. The second best may be the glimpse of Jefferson's statue through one of the side openings, silhouetted against the sky.

Pope died of cancer long before the memorial was finished, and the design was subsequently modified and executed by his successor firm, Eggers & Higgins.

D12 Franklin Delano Roosevelt Memorial

West Potomac Park

1997 (based on design of 1974)—LAWRENCE HALPRIN; Sculptors: LEONARD BASKIN, NEIL ESTERN, ROBERT GRAHAM, THOMAS HARDY, GEORGE SEGAL

www.nps.gov/frde

Franklin Delano Roosevelt supposedly once told Supreme Court Justice Felix Frankfurter that if the nation ever wished to erect a monument to him, it should be no larger than his desk. He got that—a simple, marble block that stands on the Pennsylvania Avenue side of the National Archives—but his admirers found that inadequate, and in 1955, a special commission was established to bring about a larger memorial on a site near the Mall. An open design competition in 1960 produced a winning project by the New York firm of Pedersen and Tilney, consisting of towering pylons inscribed with quotations from FDR's speeches. It was widely ridiculed as an "instant Stonehenge," however, and rejected by the Commission of Fine Arts. A revised version of the design was shelved after the Roosevelt family expressed opposition to it. The FDR Memorial Commission then conducted another, more limited competition, selecting a proposal by Marcel Breuer and Herbert Beckhard, but their design, featuring a pinwheel of granite-clad, triangular shards, fared no better.

The third time was a charm—and maybe a curse. Administered by the U.S.

Department of the Interior, yet another competition culminated in 1974 with the selection of a design by landscape architect Lawrence Halprin. His winning proposal was soon revised, yielding a scheme that was perhaps the opposite of what FDR wanted—an expansive composition of four outdoor "rooms," one for each of Roosevelt's terms as president, spreading across some seven-and-a-half acres. Although this design received all necessary governmental approvals, its scale and estimated cost engendered bitter criticism that raged off and on for fully 16 years. It was not until 1991 that construction finally began on a scaled-back version of that design. The memorial was dedicated in 1997, more than four decades after Congress formed the special commission charged with creating it.

Considering the time that elapsed between the design and its execution, the project turned out surprisingly well. Yes, it's over-scaled and heavy-handed—most of the symbolism is about as subtle as a surprise attack on Pearl Harbor—but the memorial as *landscape* is pleasant, with varied water features, abundant trees, and a balance of material textures. The memorial is also greatly enlivened by an engaging sculptural program. Examples include the timeless, all-white George Segal piece representing a breadline during the Depression. One particularly clever work is the sculpture that shows Roosevelt seated in what appears to be a simple wooden chair, but just beneath his cape one can see the small casters on the chair's legs—an accurate depiction of one of the disabled president's preferred mobility devices. Unfortunately, some vocal detractors decried the fact that the president's disability was not portrayed overtly, and an uninspiring sculpture of Roosevelt in a wheelchair was added as an obvious afterthought.

Between the FDR Memorial and the District of Columbia War Memorial [see following entry] is the new memorial to Martin Luther King Jr., not yet complete at the time of this writing.

D13 District of Columbia War Memorial

West Potomac Park between the Reflecting Pool and Independence Avenue, SE

1931—FREDERICK H. BROOKE; Associated architects: NATHAN C. WYETH AND HORACE W. PEASLEE
2011—Restoration: NATIONAL PARK SERVICE, NATIONAL MALL & MEMORIAL PARKS, WITH PRIMARY ARCHITECTS HCM AND VITETTA

Easily overlooked amid the much larger and more famous memorials that line the Mall, this neoclassical *tempietto* honors the citizens of the District of Columbia who served in what the inscription calls simply "the World War," that is, World War I. Designed to double as a stand for commemorative performances by the U.S. Marine Band, it was the first memorial on the Mall to list the names of African Americans and women alongside those of white men.

D14 Korean War Veterans Memorial

The Mall, near Independence Avenue, SW

1995—COOPER-LECKY ARCHITECTS; Sculptor: FRANK GAYLORD

www.nps.gov/kowa

The Korean War Veterans Memorial is based on a competition-winning design by a team of faculty members from Pennsylvania State University, but due to controversies that arose during the de-

sign review process, it was actually executed without their direct involvement. The memorial seems to be derivative of several more famous projects, and suffers by comparison. The black granite wall, for instance, obviously evokes the Vietnam Veterans Memorial across the Mall, but is used to lesser effect here. Meanwhile, the bland literalness of the over-scaled statues, which are deliberately antiheroic depictions of soldiers on a routine march, inadvertently trivializes the subject matter.

D15 Lincoln Memorial

West Potomac Park (west end of the Mall)

1922—HENRY BACON; Sculptor: DANIEL CHESTER FRENCH; Muralist: JULES GUERIN
1995–2000—Restoration: EINHORN YAFFEE PRESCOTT; HARTMAN-COX ARCHITECTS
2006—Security upgrades and stone restoration: MCKISSACK & MCKISSACK; Preservation consultants: JOHN MILNER ASSOCIATES

www.nps.gov/linc

Built on land that did not exist when L'Enfant devised his plan for Washington—or even when Lincoln was president—the Lincoln Memorial is a worthy counterpoint to the Capitol at the other end of the Mall. To some extent, the memorial's dignity defies analysis, but probably relates as much to Americans' continuing reverence for Lincoln and the structure's incomparable site as it does to the architecture itself.

A movement to erect some sort of monument to Lincoln began almost immediately after his assassination, but there were no significant developments until the Senate Park Commission of 1901–2 proposed a site at the western end of the Mall, which by then had been extended through landfill. The proposal was controversial: Illinois Congressman (and later Speaker of the House) Joseph Cannon bellowed, "I'll never let a memorial to Abraham Lincoln be erected in that God-damned swamp," and pressed for a site on the high ground across the Potomac. The idea of building a memorial to Lincoln on Robert E. Lee's former turf did not seem quite right, however, so the debate continued to simmer. Around 1908, Daniel Burnham, despite having served on the commission that recommended the Mall site, sketched designs for memorial colonnades in front of Union Station and along Delaware Avenue. A few years later, John Russell Pope produced at least seven different proposals, including Greek-inspired temples on Meridian Hill and at the Old Soldier's

Home, and several bizarre schemes for stepped pyramids on the Mall.

In the end, the commission went to Henry Bacon, whose final design was loosely based on the Parthenon, but different in two key respects: first, he replaced the gabled roof with a flattened and recessed attic, and second, he rotated the plan 90 degrees, abandoning the traditional longitudinal orientation in favor of a transverse position (consequently, he also moved the entrance from the short side to the long side). Bacon gave the memorial 36 columns, the number of states in the Union when Lincoln was elected president, and 48 festoons, the number when the memorial was completed. Much of the memorial's emotional power derives from Daniel Chester French's iconic statue of the seated Lincoln, which compellingly portrays the president's anguished resolve. The lateral walls on either side of the sculpture are engraved with the text of two of Lincoln's most eloquent speeches: the Gettysburg Address and his second inaugural address. Light enters the space from above through panels made not of glass but of marble soaked in beeswax in order to enhance its translucence (to understand the rationale for this technique, think of a piece of paper stained with oil, and imagine how much more light passes through the greasy spot—the concept behind the beeswax bath is essentially the same). Beneath the memorial is a fascinating, crypt-like space where visitors could once examine the memorial's foundations and substructure, but which is now closed to the public.

The memorial, like Lincoln himself, is a symbol of freedom, and has therefore become a popular place for public demonstrations in favor of civil rights and related causes. It was here that Marian Anderson sang after she was turned away from Constitution Hall [see I7], and it was on the steps in front of the memorial that Martin Luther King Jr. matched Lincoln's eloquence with his "I Have a Dream" speech.

D16 Vietnam Veterans Memorial

The Mall, near 21st Street, NW

1982—Designer: MAYA YING LIN; Architects of record: COOPER-LECKY PARTNERSHIP

One of the most beautiful and moving memorials anywhere, this black granite slash in the Mall is inscribed with the names of Americans killed or missing in the undeclared war in Southeast Asia. Maya Lin, who was still an architecture student when she won the international competition for the memorial, envisioned it as a symbol of regeneration: "Take a knife and cut open the earth," she explained, "and with time the grass will heal it."

Lin's design was revolutionary not only in its simplicity, but also in the way that it directly engages visitors. The egalitarian listing of casualties, arranged chronologically by the dates they were wounded or reported missing rather than alphabetically or by rank, instantly personalizes the message of the memorial. The texture of the inscribed names compels most visitors to touch the wall, while the reflectivity of the black granite turns each visitor's own image into a virtual part of the surface. (The two wings of the memorial are aligned with the Washington Monument and the Lincoln Memorial, respectively, and from certain vantage points, the reflections of those two white structures can be seen in the black stone.) The procession from one end to the other—approaching with the top of the wall at one's feet, then descending to a point where the wall is over one's head, and then gradually ascending again to ground level—serves as a poignant metaphor for so many aspects of war, grief, and remembrance.

The wall's brilliant minimalism confounded many critics after the design was revealed, and even after it was completed. Various proposals to "hero-ify" the memorial with more traditional sculptural installations were, fortunately, either dismissed or relegated to a nearby spot out of immediate view. So far, the original has survived intact.

D17 Constitution Gardens / 56 Signers of the Declaration of Independence Memorial

The Mall, near 19th Street, NW

1976—Constitution Gardens: SKIDMORE, OWINGS & MERRILL
1982—Memorial: EDAW

The elements used in this landscape—a free-form pond, meadows, clumps of trees, and serpentine paths—are remarkably like what A. J. Downing had planned for the entire Mall some 120 years earlier and precisely what the classically inclined Senate Park Commission Plan swept away. During World War I, this area of the Mall was filled with dozens of "temporary" government office buildings. The "tempos" lingered (causing some to remark that nothing is so permanent in Washington as a temporary building), until they were finally removed in the late 1960s and early 1970s to make way for these gardens.

Built on a little island in the pond is Washington's only monument to the signers of the Declaration of Independence. Each signer is represented by a block of red marble incised with an enlarged replica of his signature. EDAW (now a part of the mega-firm AECOM) arranged the blocks in a semicircle to suggest the composition of figures in John Trumbull's famous painting of the signing.

D18 World War II Memorial

17th Street between Constitution and Independence avenues

2004—FRIEDRICH ST. FLORIAN; Architects of record: LEO A DALY; Associated architect: GEORGE HARTMAN; Landscape architects: OEHME, VAN SWEDEN & ASSOCIATES; Sculptor: RAY KASKEY

The World War II Memorial was mired in controversy as soon as it was proposed for this location. Many people argued that no new structure of any kind should go here and risk interrupting the views between the Washington Monument and the Lincoln Memorial; others felt that an appropriate memorial was possible on this site, but that the competition-winning design by Friedrich St. Florian was not it. After the winner was selected, federal design review agencies insisted that the scope of the project be reduced—eliminating, for example, interior exhibition spaces that had been included in the original program. Now that the pared-down project is completed, it seems that the fears about compromising views were largely, if not wholly, unjustified. The center of the memorial is a void—a rebuilt version of the shallow "Rainbow Pool" that was already there—and the most prominent structures are kept well off of the main axis. Thus, the view corridor is essentially preserved.

The lingering questions now are ones of architectural expression. The stele-like piers, arranged in two opposing semicircles, hark back to the severe classical architecture popular in various countries—including both the United States and Germany—in the 1930s and 1940s. To some critics, there is a particularly strong association with the work of Hitler's architect, Albert Speer. St. Florian presumably had no intention of evoking fascist architecture in this memorial, but such reactions underscore the difficulties that can arise from the use of forms and motifs that are so strongly rooted in a particular historical era.

Then there is the problem of the memorial's iconography. The names of individual states are called out on separate piers, for instance, and each pier stands in a hemicycle labeled either "Atlantic" or "Pacific." This scheme not only suggests an inaccurate connection between each state and a particular theater of war, but also implies that state identity was especially prominent in the public consciousness during a period that was in fact marked by remarkable national unity. Meanwhile, at the western side of the memorial stands the "Freedom Wall," which bears 4,048 gold stars. Why 4,048? Because each represents 100 American military deaths during the war. But why does each star stand for 100 people? Wouldn't a field of more than 400,000 smaller stars, each representing an individual casualty, have been more moving and potentially more beautiful?

Ultimately, in its stiff classicism, its arbitrary symbolism, and its lack of compelling expressive gestures, the World War II Memorial's impression is not so much fascist as it is merely generic.

D19 Old Canal Lockkeeper's House

Southwest corner of Constitution Avenue and 17th Street, NW

c. 1833—ARCHITECT UNKNOWN

This small building is a reminder that, for much of the 19th century, the north side of the Mall was lined not by Constitution Avenue but by a canal (which became a de facto open sewer in its later years). Like many canals, it had locks allowing boats to negotiate changes in level. This structure was the residence of the lockkeeper, who collected tolls and operated machinery while the canal was still navigable. The fieldstone house used to be one story taller, but when the canal and the surrounding area were filled in during the 1870s, it lost its lowest level. In the 1930s, the structure was moved about forty feet when 17th Street was widened. Historic photographs reveal that at some point in the early 20th century the house was occupied by squatters. It is now used by the National Park Service for equipment storage.

D20 Capitol Gatehouses

Constitution Avenue at 15th and 17th streets, NW

c. 1828—CHARLES BULFINCH
1874—Dismantled
1880—Installed in current location
1939—Restoration: ARCHITECT UNKNOWN

The observant reader will notice that these are the *Capitol,* not *Capital,* Gatehouses. That is because they formerly guarded the Capitol itself, and are made of the same soft sandstone found in that building. They were dismantled in 1874 and moved here in 1880.

D21 The Washington Monument

The Mall

1848–56—ROBERT MILLS
1876–84—Completion, with modifications to original design: THOMAS L. CASEY
1962—Exterior restoration: DON MYER / NATIONAL PARK SERVICE
2000—Preservation architects for exterior restoration and interior renovation: OEHRLEIN & ASSOCIATES ARCHITECTS; Interior renovation: MICHAEL GRAVES & ASSOCIATES
2005—Landscape perimeter security improvements: OLIN PARTNERSHIP

Tel: (202) 426-6841
www.nps.gov/wamo

At 555 feet, 5⅛ inches, the Washington Monument was the tallest structure in the world when completed, and remains the tallest made of stone. It now seems so obvious, so perfect, so timeless, that it is hard to imagine when this symbol of Washington—both the president and the city—was far from a certainty.

The monument's tumultuous history goes back to 1783, when the Continental Congress voted to build a statue of General Washington on horseback "at the place where the residence of Congress shall be established." When Pierre L'Enfant created his plan for the capital city, he proposed placing the equestrian statue on the Mall, at the point where the axes of the Capitol and the President's House crossed. Washington died in 1799 before that sculpture was executed, however, and in 1800, congressional leaders jettisoned the original plan in favor of a "mausoleum of American granite and marble, in pyramidal form," to be built inside the Capitol (meanwhile, Benjamin Henry Latrobe proposed a freestanding memorial, also in the shape of a pyramid). The Senate failed to approve funds for this scheme, however, and several subsequent plans faced opposition from Washington's family and others.

In 1832, the centenary of Washington's birth sparked renewed interest in creating some sort of memorial to him. The Washington National Monument Society was formed in 1833, and in 1836 its members launched a national design competition, which was won by architect Robert Mills. His design called for an obelisk slightly taller (at 600 feet) and blunter than the present shaft, with a circular, Greek-inspired, peristyle temple at the base. Lack of funds caused more delay, but ground was finally broken for this design on July 4, 1848.

The site for the construction was not exactly where L'Enfant had intended. Soil tests indicated that the planned position, forming a right triangle with the President's House and the Capitol, was too marshy, so the foundation was instead placed well east, and slightly south, of the original spot. This decision had major ramifications for the Mall, forcing a slight southward kink in the axis emanating from the west portico of the Capitol, and leaving its obvious intersection with the cross-axis through the White House strangely vacant.

Construction sputtered along for eight years despite a near-farcical series of delays and complications. Members of the anti-immigrant, anti-Catholic Know-Nothing Party stole a stone donated by Pope Pius IX, and then wrested control of the Washington National Monument Society in a rigged election, effectively bringing construction to a halt in 1856. The Know-Nothings eventually relented, but by then the country was at the brink of the Civil War, and finishing the monument was not a priority. A slight shift in the color of the marble about one-third of the way up indicates the point of the hiatus in construction, which ultimately lasted nearly two decades.

Ostensibly showing the construction of the Washington Monument, this drawing actually depicts how the perpetually unfinished monument looked for much of the 19th century.

One of the many fanciful proposals from the 1870s for a redesign of the incomplete Washington Monument. This one is attributed to Arthur Mathews.

During the 1870s, amid a growing clamor to do *something* about the mammoth stone stump on the Mall, a spate of revisionism nearly derailed the whole effort. Architects and artists submitted various proposals for the completion of the monument, ranging from Montgomery Meigs's design for an Italian campanile to several bizarre and exotic schemes, including one modeled after "the better Hindu pagodas." Each proposal was given due (or excessive) consideration, but after heated discussion, all were tossed aside, and the simple shaft continued its fitful rise, following a revised design that omitted the circular colonnade at the base. On December 6, 1884, the aluminum capstone was finally set and the monument was dedicated in February of the following year. The result, despite all the drama, is one of the noblest memorials ever erected.

D22 National Museum of American History, Behring Center

Between Constitution Avenue and Madison Drive and 12th and 14th streets, NW

1964—STEINMAN, CAIN & WHITE (SUCCESSOR TO MCKIM, MEAD & WHITE); Associated architects: MILLS, PETTICORD & MILLS
2008—Renovation: SKIDMORE, OWINGS & MERRILL

Tel: (202) 633-1000
www.americanhistory.si.edu

If the Smithsonian is "the nation's attic," then the National Museum of American History is the hulking chest in the attic, stuffed with America's collective mementos—some precious, some odd, some a

bit embarrassing. These artifacts range from Judy Garland's ruby slippers, to the trite but irresistible collection of First Ladies' gowns, to cars, locomotives, and even a substantial chunk of a suspension bridge (the latter few items serving as reminders that this was initially the Museum of History and Technology before it was renamed in 1980).

If only the building erected for the display of these curious objects were equally intriguing. Designed by the professional heirs of McKim, Mead & White and conceived as a modern reinterpretation of the classical temples that inspired many Washington landmarks, it is neither convincingly modern nor credibly neoclassical. It's just a box. After the museum opened, columnist Russell Baker lamented, "Our own generation is unable to build a shelter worthy of housing what the old people left us."

Upon entering the museum, visitors may feel as if they are, in fact, inside a giant storage chest. The interior is a befuddling warren of exhibition galleries, corridors, and support functions, making orientation difficult and exhaustion easy. Fortunately, a recent renovation brought much-needed hierarchy to the principal spaces and clarified the building's confusing circulation patterns, but more remains to be done. This is among the most visited museums in the country, and it would be worth spending serious money in an effort to make it one of the most beautiful and functional, too.

D23 National Museum of Natural History

Between Constitution Avenue and Madison Drive and 9th and 12th streets, NW

1911—HORNBLOWER & MARSHALL (WITH DANIEL BURNHAM AND CHARLES MCKIM)
1964, 1965—Additions: MILLS, PETTICORD & MILLS
1990—Upgrades: HSMM
1994—Enclosure of east court: MARIANI & ASSOCIATES
1995—Enclosure of west court: DESIGNTECH EAST
1999—Renovations (including new Discovery Center, theater, and restaurant): HAMMEL, GREEN AND ABRAHAMSON (HGA) WITH SMITHGROUP
2000—Renovations: ARCHITRAVE, P.C., ARCHITECTS
2003—Restoration of West Exhibit Hall (Kenneth E. Behring Family Hall of Mammals): HSMM
2009—Renovation of Sant Ocean Hall: QUINN EVANS ARCHITECTS

Tel: (202) 633-1000
www.mnh.si.edu

The U.S. Department of Agriculture's main building was the first one on the south side of the Mall erected in accordance with the Senate Park Commission Plan, and this rather academic-looking Beaux-Arts building was the first on the north. Part of the Smithsonian, the National Museum of Natural History contains a hodgepodge of artifacts that might be regarded as a microcosm of the parent institution. Highlights include the "striding" bull elephant that greets visitors in the building's octagonal rotunda, countless other stuffed critters of varied size and ferocity, and a pretty little hunk of rock known as the Hope Diamond.

The early designs for the museum, by the local firm of Hornblower & Marshall, were sumptuous compositions inspired by ornate, turn-of-the-century Parisian buildings such as the Petit Palais. Unfortunately, the continuing conservative influence of former Senate Park Commission members Daniel Burnham and Charles McKim doomed these flights of fancy. An impatient McKim ultimately sent the local architects a sketch of a more modest, Roman-inspired design, along with a directive saying, in effect, "Just do it this way." It's a pity. The result, while dignified, is much less interesting than it could have been, at least on the exterior. Hornblower & Marshall were largely left to their own devices for the design of the interior.

Recent enclosures of the two courtyards on either side of what is now the Sant Ocean Hall have introduced some airy, modern spaces to the building. Of particular note is the new staircase in the west court, the design of which was allegedly inspired by the anatomy of vertebrate animals. The façades of the symmetrical office wings, added in the 1960s, are dumbed-down versions of the original.

D24 National Gallery of Art Sculpture Garden

Between Constitution Avenue and Madison Drive and 7th and 9th streets, NW

1988—Pavilion: SKIDMORE, OWINGS & MERRILL
1999—Sculpture Garden: OLIN PARTNERSHIP
2000—Renovation of pavilion: SMITHGROUP

Tel: (202) 737-4215
www.nga.gov

A national sculpture garden was first formally proposed for this site in 1966. In 1974, an ice skating rink was built here, and then in 1988 came the little green pavilion—a modern take on Art Nouveau motifs, and the main reason the garden warrants inclusion in this book—that now houses a delightful café. The full Sculpture Garden finally came to fruition in 1999, when the original skating rink was removed and reconstructed. The somewhat staid landscape design, incorporating cast iron and steel fences, as well as the same marble used on the National Gallery's two buildings, is offset by a dynamic fountain (in warm weather) and some very entertaining modern sculptures. Standing near Claes Oldenburg's huge rendition of a typewriter eraser, one may often hear adults attempting to explain to their computer-oriented children and grandchildren just what it represents.

D25 National Gallery of Art (West Building)

Between Constitution Avenue and Madison Drive and 4th and 7th streets, NW

1941—JOHN RUSSELL POPE / EGGERS & HIGGINS
1983—Reorganization and renovation: KEYES CONDON FLORANCE ARCHITECTS
2002—Renovation of sculpture gallery: HSMM

Tel: (202) 737-4215
www.nga.gov

Founded in 1937, the National Gallery of Art owes its existence to Andrew Mellon, who donated both his own collection of Old Master paintings and a sizeable pile of cash to establish the institution. Mellon directly engaged John Russell Pope, an unapologetic classicist, to design a home for the collection on a site set aside by Congress. Visitors unaware of the late date of the gallery's construction generally assume that the building is much older than it is. While the large blank areas on the façade and the general restraint in ornamentation may suggest the influence of modern minimalism, for the most part, Pope's museum is a pure homage to classical antiquity and the Renaissance. As with the Jefferson Memorial [see D11] completed a few years later, the historicist design vexed many contemporary critics. Joseph Hudnut, dean of the School of Architecture at Harvard, called it "the final disaster on the Mall," while architect Philip Goodwin dismissed it as "a costly mummy."

Conservative though the building may be, it incorporates some subtle gestures that add interest. Note, for instance, the very shallow pilasters, barely articulated against the apparently blank walls near the central portico of the north façade. Also, look closely at the color of the pink Tennessee marble—in just the right light, one can see that it is not monochromatic, but graduated from a somewhat darker color at the bottom of the façade to a lighter shade at the top.

Regardless of one's opinion about the building's historicism, there is little debate about the high quality of its execution, particularly on the interior. The rotunda, which so easily could have been just another cold, formal, neoclassical Washington chamber, is instead a warm, visually rich space, thanks to its dark green marble columns, its elegant floor patterns, and the perfectly scaled fountain. Major corridors are well proportioned and beautifully skylit, and some of the grand staircases are outstanding works of sculpture in their own right. A 1980s reorganization, prompted by the addition of the new East Building, vastly improved how the entire gallery works, both for museum staff and for the visiting public.

D26 National Gallery of Art (East Building)

Constitution Avenue and 4th Street, NW

1978—I. M. PEI & PARTNERS; Landscape architect: DAN KILEY

Tel: (202) 737-4215
www.nga.gov

The East Building of the National Gallery of Art is widely regarded as the pinnacle of what might be termed "high modernist" architecture in Washington, and arguably one of the finest such works anywhere in the country, despite its slavish reliance on a geometrical regimen that may have caused as many problems as it solved. Pei's planning strategy was to split the potentially awkward, trapezoidal site into two triangles, with a larger, isosceles triangle along 4th Street and Pennsylvania Avenue containing gallery space, and a smaller, right triangle on the Mall side accommodating offices and a study center. Vertical and horizontal slivers have been excised from these two basic forms, creating voids that reduce the structure's bulk and introduce dramatic shadows (while also yielding some obviously orphaned nooks and crannies on the interior). At the core of the building is a brightly skylit atrium, which appears in plan as a second isosceles triangle slightly offset from the main block. The triangular theme is carried through obsessively at various scales, including the shape of the floor tiles in the atrium. A huge, colorful mobile by Alexander Calder—the artist's last major work—rotates languidly in this space, providing a sensuous counterpoint to the prevailing geometrical precision.

Pei carefully related the building to its neighbors without stooping to imitation. The East Building's main forms are of two quite different heights, the lower blocks corresponding to the scale of the West Building and the towers addressing the more bureaucratic structures across Pennsylvania and Constitution avenues. The new building is clad in the same pink marble as the original gallery, and is physically connected to its sibling by an underground tunnel whose design now seems dated, though in a rather amusing, 1970s, space-age way (a recent light installation by Leo Villareal enhances the effect). At the western end of the tunnel awaits a classically modern cafeteria, fronting a glass wall improbably holding back a torrential, cascading fountain.

TOUR E

Judiciary Square / Gallery Place

The name *Judiciary Square* technically describes a multi-block area spanning from D to G Street, NW, and from 4th to 5th Street, NW. In the late 19th century, the full square was easily perceived as such, since it was a cohesively landscaped park containing just two discrete, though monumental, structures—the City Hall (now the Superior Court) and the Pension Building (now the National Building Museum). Several other structures were added in the early 20th century to house various judicial functions, and today, with E and F streets continuing straight through the site and miscellaneous parking lots lining its edges, the larger historic square is illegible in person, though it is still evident on most maps.

Judiciary Square figured prominently in L'Enfant's plan—it is one of the few spots where a specific building shape is indicated—yet strangely, he did not call it out in the key, so there is no direct explanation of its intended purpose. Evidence suggests, however, that he envisioned it as a site for judiciary functions. Early in the city's history, homeowners, innkeepers, and merchants were drawn to the neighborhood by a powerful stream that began at a spring near 5th and L streets and raced southward to join the Tiber Creek near the Mall (sometimes, according to the *Evening Star,* the water in the canal was "deep enough for canoeing," but more often it was simply a fast-moving sewer). Italian, Jewish, and Chinese enclaves emerged at different times in the vicinity. The construction of the City Hall in 1820 established the square as a municipal hub, and that has remained the case ever since, even after the principal city government offices moved to the new District Building (now the John Wilson Building) on Pennsylvania Avenue in 1908.

A few blocks west of Judiciary Square, the area now known as Gallery Place *was* called out on L'Enfant's plan as the site of a nondenominational church and shrine to national heroes. Instead, it gradually developed into a nucleus of federal offices,

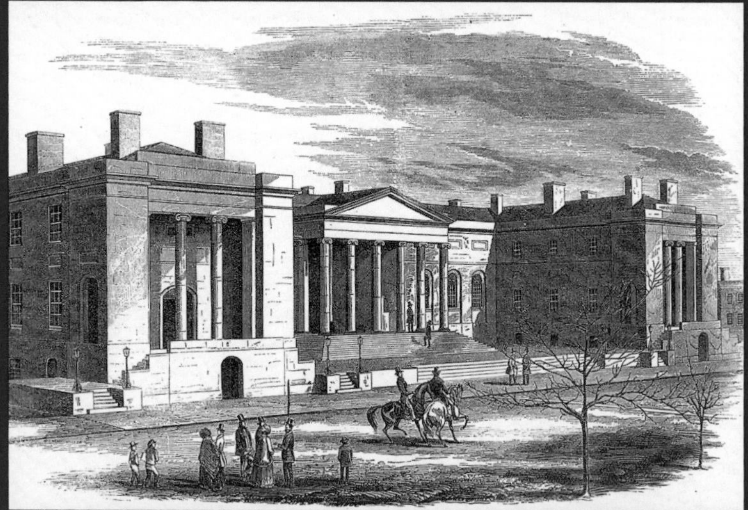

View of the Old City Hall (now part of the Superior Court of the District of Columbia), c. 1853, when the building had a much more immediate relationship to the street than it does today.

RIDGE ST
M ST
K ST
5th ST
MASSACHUSETTS AVE
I ST
9th ST
7th ST
6th ST
H ST
3rd ST
F ST
E ST
1200 ft
1
2
3
4
5
6
7
8
9
10
11
12
13
14
15
16
17
18
19
20
21
22
23

including the Patent Office and the Tariff Commission. The broader neighborhood declined in the mid-20th century as commercial investment became focused on the area northwest of the White House. Since the 1990s, however, substantial new commercial and residential development has brought life to the Gallery Place and Judiciary Square areas and especially to the 7th Street corridor, which is now a vibrant spine of restaurants, cultural institutions, and nightlife.

E1 National Law Enforcement Officers Memorial

Between E and F streets, NW, across from the National Building Museum

1991—DAVIS BUCKLEY, ARCHITECTS AND PLANNERS; Sculptor: RAY KASKEY

The public space at the heart of Judiciary Square is now occupied by a memorial to law enforcement officers killed in the line of duty, whose names are inscribed in the low marble walls that trace broad arcs at the east and west sides of the site. The memorial is organized around an open plaza with a distinctive paving pattern inspired by that of Michelangelo's Campidoglio in Rome. The plaza has a subtle camber, with a medallion at the center marking the crown.

The site presented a design challenge in the form of two pre-existing Metro elevator structures set at an angle reflecting the diagonal path of the station below. The architect cleverly restored symmetry by using the elevators as the compositional anchors for two complementary, curving pergolas. Because the pergolas stand directly over the Metro tunnel, they were constructed of aluminum to minimize their weight.

E2 National Building Museum

(Pension Building)
4th and F streets, NW

1887—MONTGOMERY C. MEIGS; Sculptor: CASPAR BUBERL
1985—Renovation: KEYES CONDON FLORANCE ARCHITECTS; Associated architect: GIORGIO CAVAGLIERI
1991–2003—Various alterations: KARN CHARUHAS CHAPMAN & TWOHEY

Tel: (202) 272-2448
www.nbm.org

Built, improbably enough, as a government office building, and now serving as the home of the world's most-visited museum of architecture and engineering, this is one of Washington's largest, quirkiest, and most beloved landmarks. Supposedly built of 15½ million bricks, the imposing structure was designed by Montgomery C. Meigs, who had served as quartermaster general of the Union Army during the Civil War. Meigs, an inventive and multitalented engineer, is credited by author David Miller as having been "second only to Grant" in terms of his importance to the Union victory. Before and after the war, he was involved in several major Washington building projects, including the expansion of the Capitol.

This building was constructed for the federal Bureau of Pensions, which needed a large new facility to process payments to Civil War veterans, widows, and orphans (at one point, nearly one-quarter of the entire federal budget was administered here). Meigs was a logical choice as architect, given his army background and substantial engineering experience, but his design was not well received at first. Many politicians derided the building as "Meigs's Old Red Barn," and William Tecumseh Sherman supposedly scoffed, "The worst of it is, it is fireproof," or words to that effect. After the Pension Bureau moved out in the early 20th century, the building was occupied by various federal agencies and even served as a courthouse. In 1980, a group of avid preservationists successfully lobbied Congress to save the structure, which had come to be regarded as a white elephant, and set it aside for use as a private, nonprofit museum of the building arts. Following extensive reno-

A photograph of Teddy Roosevelt's 1901 inaugural ball in what was then known as the Pension Building.

vations, the museum opened to the public in 1985.

The exterior of the building owes a debt to the 16th-century Palazzo Farnese, designed by Antonio da Sangallo the Younger and later modified by Michelangelo, which Meigs had admired while visiting Rome. The comparison goes only so far, however—the principal façade of the museum is much longer than that of its Renaissance counterpart, it is rendered in red brick rather than buff brick and stone, and it is crowned by a pedimented roof structure set back from the perimeter walls, while the Palazzo Farnese ends with a flat cornice. Also, the window surrounds on Meigs's structure are of red brick, rather than contrasting stone, making the building appear almost as if it were carved out of a single block of clay.

The relentless "brickiness" is relieved by the building's most remarkable exterior feature—a three-foot-tall, terra cotta sculptural band between the first and second floors, depicting scenes of Union military forces. Spanning the entire perimeter of the 400-by-200-foot structure, the frieze is thus nearly a quarter of a mile in total length. The sculptor, Caspar Buberl, was a Bohemian—back when that was a geographical term rather than a comment on his lifestyle—who immigrated to the United States in 1854. Buberl's other works include the sculptures over the entry to the Smithsonian's Arts and Industries Building and numerous commemorative statues of soldiers, firemen, and other heroic figures in cities across the country.

Impressive as the exterior is, it pales in comparison to the building's big surprise—the main interior space known as the Great Hall, which is larger than a football field and soars to 159 feet at its highest point. This space—in effect, an early version of the modern atrium—was partially inspired by the courtyard of the Palazzo della Cancelleria, not far from the Palazzo Farnese in Rome. The Great Hall is divided into three courts by two rows of colossal Corinthian columns—among the tallest such columns in the world—which are made of some 70,000 bricks each, covered in plaster, and painted to look like solid blocks of marble. Surrounding the hall is a double arcade with terra cotta columns on the first floor and cast iron columns above. The cast iron-trussed roof, reminiscent of a Victorian train shed, contrasts sharply with the space's predominant classicism. The hall has been the site of presidential inaugural balls going back to Grover Cleveland's in 1885 (before the building was even finished), and now provides a place for the museum's educational programs, special events, and occasional exhibitions. The primary exhibition galleries are in the perimeter rooms on the first and second floors.

The building is also noteworthy for its incorporation of what would now be called "green" design strategies. Originally, small openings under each window allowed fresh air to enter the perimeter office spaces. Warmed during the winter over radiators along the exterior walls, the air then passed through the arched openings into the Great Hall. Clerestory windows at the crest of the roof vented the space, resulting in a remarkably efficient ventilation system that Meigs later claimed had dramatically reduced absenteeism among Pension Bureau employees. Now, of course, the building is air-conditioned to museum standards and the exterior openings are sealed off, but the "Old Red Barn" survives as a testament to Meigs's ingenuity and as a handsome venue for exhibitions and educational programs about architecture, engineering, and construction.

E3 Lillian and Albert Small Jewish Museum / Jewish Historical Society of Greater Washington

(Adas Israel Synagogue)
701 3rd Street, NW

1876—ARCHITECT UNKNOWN; Draftsman: MAX KLEINMAN
1969—Moved to present site

Tel: (202) 789-0900
www.jhsgw.org

The Adas Israel congregation was established in 1869 by roughly 35 conservative Jewish families who broke off from the reform-minded Washington Hebrew Congregation (founded in 1852). The design of their new building, constructed in 1876, reflected the immigrant congregation's more orthodox bent and limited financial resources. Exterior decoration was restricted to simple wooden fans over the windows and doors, while inside, a second-floor women's gallery allowed segregation of the sexes during services.

Most, but not all, of this building originally stood at the southeast corner of 6th and G streets, NW. Adas Israel left in 1908 for new quarters [see E5] and the structure fell into a succession of uses, including four churches, a grocery, and, ironically enough, a pork barbeque carryout. With demolition looming in the 1960s, the Jewish Historical Society of Greater Washington worked with local and federal agencies to move the building to a new location for conversion into a museum. In 1969, the upper portion of the old synagogue was sheared off and moved in one piece to the current site, where it was carefully placed atop newly constructed base walls. Subtle differences in the color and proportions of the brick and mortar reveal the juncture between the original structure and the new base.

As of this writing, there is a possibility that the historic little building may be moved yet again. A major real estate developer has secured air rights to build a mixed-use complex over the "Center Leg" freeway just east of the Small Museum, which would be relocated as part of the project.

E4 400 Massachusetts Avenue, NW

2005—ESOCOFF & ASSOCIATES | ARCHITECTS

By the late 20th century, the stretch of Massachusetts Avenue between Union Station and Mount Vernon Square had deteriorated into a civic embarrassment, lined with weedy, vacant lots and—most appallingly—the shell of one apartment building that was missing its entire front façade (infamously employed as a set in the wretched 1996 movie *Mars Attacks!*). The subsequent real estate boom brought new development to this portion of the avenue and today, though it still has many missing teeth, the corridor is gradually being filled in with large-scale residential and commercial buildings. Among the most interesting of these is the condominium at 400 Massachusetts Avenue, distinguished by its undulating façades, striated brick patterns, and animated roofline. The project had to wrap around a historic firehouse, yielding an unusual floor plan with long, skinny apartments in the tall wing at the northwest corner of the site. The residential buildings at 401 and 425 Massachusetts, directly across the street, are by the same architecture firm—together, the three buildings form a set piece that brings a sense of place to a generally nondescript part of town.

E5 6th & I Historic Synagogue

1908—LOUIS LEVI
1979—Addition: ARCHITECT UNKNOWN
2004—Restoration: SHALOM BARANES ASSOCIATES

This synagogue was built for the Adas Israel congregation after it outgrew its original home [see E3], which then stood at 6th and G streets. With the dedication of this building in 1908, all of the city's oldest Jewish congregations were located within three blocks of each other: the Orthodox Ohev Sholom at 5th and I, the Conservative Adas Israel here, and the Reform Washington Hebrew Congregation near the corner of 8th and I.

In 1951, Adas Israel moved to a still larger synagogue in Cleveland Park, and sold this building to the Turner Memorial A.M.E. Church, which promptly replaced most of the Jewish symbols with Christian ones. Turner occupied the building for more than 50 years, but in 2002, it, too, moved to the suburbs. At that point, one developer expressed interest in converting this structure into a nightclub. Ultimately, three Jewish developers bought the building, and in 2004, it reopened as the home of a decidedly progressive institution—a nondenominational synagogue with no fixed membership, offering dynamic cultural programming in addition to religious services.

The architecture of the building incorporates Byzantine, Moorish, and Romanesque elements. As with many Byzantine churches, it has a square plan organized around a large, central dome supported by pendentives, with smaller domes at the corners (except that, in this case, there is no dome at the southwest corner). Balcony seating—originally reserved for women—occupies the upper level behind three of the four arches supporting the pendentives. The fourth niche is the site of the *bimah,* which serves as a platform for readings from the Torah or a stage for performances and lectures.

The interior was originally quite plain, but during the renovation, the architects and clients agreed that a more decorative approach was in order. The ceiling of the dome now bears a vibrant composition in gold leaf, red, and sky blue, with a Star of David at the center. The walls behind the arched niches are also richly colored. Stained glass windows have been restored or re-created, as have elaborate light fixtures and other decorative details.

E6 Metropolitan Community Church of Washington, D.C.

474 Ridge Street, NW

1992—SUZANNE REATIG ARCHITECTURE

One of the first entirely new structures in the country built expressly for a gay and lesbian religious congregation, the Metropolitan Community Church of Washington, D.C., was a harbinger of gentrification in this rapidly changing neighborhood. The church's auxiliary functions are housed in an L-shaped band along the two street façades, sheathed in split-face concrete block that relates to the texture of nearby masonry row houses. These wings shield a bright and airy sanctuary of steel and glass, which is covered with a shallow barrel vault supported by delicate bowstring trusses. From the inside, at certain times of day, the sanctuary appears to be twice as long as it really is thanks to the use of reflective glass.

E7 Walter E. Washington Convention Center

801 Mount Vernon Place, NW

2003—THOMPSON, VENTULETT, STAINBACK & ASSOCIATES; DEVROUAX + PURNELL ARCHITECTS; MARIANI ARCHITECTS-ENGINEERS

Washington's 2.3-million-square-foot convention center is a rhapsody in beige—dauntingly monochromatic, but skillfully chiseled, tucked, and squeezed to fit *relatively* unobtrusively into a low-rise residential and commercial context. To preserve as much of the existing street pattern as possible, the architects placed the primary exhibit hall underground, with various secondary halls, ballrooms, meeting rooms, and other spaces above ground, connected by wide bridges spanning L and M streets. Although this unusual arrangement results in a rather confusing and inconvenient internal circulation pattern, the tradeoff seems worthwhile.

The best features of the building are the lounge spaces cantilevered over the sidewalks along 7th and 9th streets, near the southern end of the building, which suggest lookout platforms projecting from the bridge of a giant cruise ship. Also noteworthy are the tall pylons bracketing the main entrance on Mount Vernon Square, which incorporate stacks of flat glass strips—modern totem poles welcoming the hordes of badge-bedecked conventioneers, while also marking the corners where 8th Street originally met the square.

E8 Historical Society of Washington, D.C.

(Central Library)
Mount Vernon Square (8th and K streets, NW)

1903—ACKERMAN & ROSS
1980—Partial renovation: ARCHITECTS UNKNOWN
2003—Renovation: DEVROUAX + PURNELL ARCHITECTS, WITH RKK&G MUSEUM AND CULTURAL FACILITIES CONSULTANTS

One of scores of library buildings across the nation built with funds donated by Andrew Carnegie, this was the District's central public library for nearly 70 years, until it was replaced by its own aesthetic foil—the Mies van der Rohe-designed, dark steel-and-glass Martin Luther King Library at 9th and G streets, NW.

The exterior of this Beaux-Arts building is distinctive in several respects. The main entrance is marked by a pair of gracious, curving benches leading to a lavishly ornamented central pavilion. The two flanking wings, while more sedate, are intriguing because of the large, arched windows set into rectangular niches, with an *aedicula*—a small, shrine-like temple form—at the base of each window. The north side of the central pavilion has a dramatically different fenestration pattern, with narrow, vertical slits indicating the original location of the library stacks.

After nearly a decade of disuse, the old Carnegie building was partially renovated and turned over to the University of the District of Columbia. Then, in 1999, the Historical Society of Washington, D.C., proposed that the building be converted into a museum dedicated to the civic history of the capital. The District government granted the Historical Society a long-term lease on the building for $1 per year, and in May 2003, the City Museum of Washington, D.C., opened to the public. Alas, the enterprise was short-lived. Projections for income and visitorship proved to be overly optimistic, and the museum was forced to cease operations in late 2004. Following several abortive efforts to find other cultural uses for the building, for now it remains the headquarters of the Historical Society, which continues to offer exhibitions and programs there.

E9 PEPCO Headquarters

701 9th Street, NW

2001—DEVROUAX + PURNELL ARCHITECTS

For the pedestrian or driver approaching along 9th Street from the north, the curving glass curtain wall of the headquarters for the city's electrical utility gradually reveals views of the historic Old Patent Office building across G Street. The bold gesture of this broad, curving wall is offset by a simple, delicate trellis that simultaneously reinforces the street edge and lends a human scale to the building's base. Amazingly, given how recently it was built, this was the first major building in downtown Washington designed by an African American-owned architecture firm.

E10 Smithsonian Institution Donald W. Reynolds Center for American Art and Portraiture, home of the National Portrait Gallery and the Smithsonian American Art Museum

(Old Patent Office)
Between 7th, 9th, F, and G streets, NW

1836-42—South wing: ROBERT MILLS, BASED ON DESIGN BY WILLIAM P. ELLIOT JR. AND ITHIEL TOWN
1849-55—East wing: ROBERT MILLS, SUCCEEDED BY THOMAS U. WALTER
1852-68—West and north wings: THOMAS U. WALTER AND EDWARD CLARK
1878-85—Renovations: CLUSS & SCHULZE
1936—Removal of south portico steps
1968—Renovation: FAULKNER, KINGSBURY & STENHOUSE / FAULKNER, FRYER & FAULKNER; BAYARD UNDERWOOD
2006—Renovation and restoration: HARTMAN-COX ARCHITECTS; Preservation architects: OEHRLEIN & ASSOCIATES ARCHITECTS
2007—Kogod Courtyard enclosure: FOSTER + PARTNERS; Architects of record: SMITHGROUP; Landscape architect: KATHRYN GUSTAFSON

Tel: (202) 633-1000
www.npg.si.edu
www.americanart.si.edu

L'Enfant's plan reserved this site for a national, nonsectarian church and shrine to "heroes who fell in the cause of liberty, and for such others as may hereafter be decreed by the voice of a grateful Nation," but it was never used for that purpose. After the government's first Patent Office burned, this largely vacant lot was selected as the site for its fireproof replacement. Another of Washington's innumerable design competitions ensued and was won by a young local architect, William Elliot, working in association with Ithiel Town, who was based in New York at the time. The construction of their design was supervised, however, by Robert Mills, whom President Andrew Jackson appointed as the official architect of federal buildings in 1836. Unfortunately, he and Elliot later ended up in a highly public dispute regarding credit for specific aspects of the Patent Office's design, making a clear assessment of authorship difficult.

It was probably Mills who designed the building's quintessential south portico, supported by eight beefy Doric columns rendered in fragile Aquia sandstone (the steps leading to the portico were removed in 1936 when F Street was widened, and the entrance was moved to the ground floor). Mills was also the lead architect for the expansion of the building beginning in 1849, and here he switched to sturdier marble as the finish material for the new wings. Mills was ousted from the job in 1851 and replaced by Thomas U. Walter, who worked with Edward Clark to complete what Mills had begun. When work on the last wing was finally finished, the result was the largest office building in Washington. It was a busy place; over the years clerks here issued 500,000 patents to the likes of Alexander Graham Bell, Cyrus McCormick, and Thomas Edison. During the Civil War, the building served as a hospital; one of the ministering nurses was Walt Whitman, who based his poem "The Wound Dresser" on his experiences here. Whitman returned to the building in 1865, working as a clerk for the Indian Bureau, which, like the Patent Office at the time, was a division of the U.S. Department of the Interior. A puritanical new secretary of the interior soon discovered a copy of *Leaves of Grass* in Whitman's desk, however, and immediately fired him, declaring, "I will not have the author of that book in this department."

A fire in 1877 seriously damaged the west and north wings of the building, leading to a major reconstruction and subsequent renovations by Cluss & Schulze that included several of the most important interior spaces, such as the third-floor display halls for models of inventions submitted for patents. Executed in a style that author E. J. Applewhite called "Victorian Psychedelic," with encaustic tile floors, stained glass skylights, and iron balcony railings, these fantastically ornate rooms contrast dramatically with the building's severe exterior.

The Patent Office moved out in 1932, and the Civil Service Commission occupied the building until 1963. By the 1950s, however, the elderly structure was already considered thoroughly obsolete for governmental offices, and demolition loomed as a possibility. President Eisenhower intervened in 1955 and offered the building to the Smithsonian, which eventually assumed control and adapted it to museum use. Now known as the Donald W. Reynolds Center for American Art and Portraiture, the building actually houses two separate institutions: the National Portrait Gallery and the Smithsonian American Art Museum.

The most recent changes to the building included a comprehensive renovation by Hartman-Cox, which freshened the gallery spaces and added art storage and conservation facilities that are visible to the public. In a separate, controversial project, the building's courtyard was enclosed and covered with an undulating glass roof by the British firm of Foster + Partners. The canopy was originally designed to be somewhat higher, but review agencies were concerned that it would be too visible from nearby streets, so the height was reduced, which is unfortunate, since now the roof seems a bit too constrained at the points where it meets the existing building. On a cloudy day, the space appears washed out—all beige and gray—but on sunny days, when the shadows from the roof's structure create lively patterns on the walls and floor, or at night, when dramatic lighting emphasizes the geometry of the canopy, the courtyard can be spectacular.

E11 International Spy Museum

8th and F streets, NW

1875—LeDroit Building (800–810 F Street): JAMES H. MCGILL
1875–81—Adams Building and adjacent structures: ARCHITECTS UNKNOWN (POSSIBLY BY JAMES H. MCGILL)
1892—Warder Building: NICHOLAS T. HALLER
2003—Renovation of existing buildings and addition: SHALOM BARANES ASSOCIATES; Museum interiors: SMITHGROUP; Visitor experience: GALLAGHER & ASSOCIATES; Restaurant and meeting space interiors: ADAMSTEIN & DEMETRIOU; Shop interior: FRCH DESIGN WORLDWIDE

The historic block that is now part of the International Spy Museum is a rare surviving example of the kind of late-19th-century commercial architecture that was once common in Washington's central business district. The Victorian buildings, with their ornamental brackets and distinctive tripartite windows, still seem more likely to hold shoe repair shops and milliners than a for-profit museum of espionage. The modern addition, including some museum facilities as well as leasable office space, is designed to be compatible with, but clearly different from, the existing structures.

E12 Hotel Monaco

(General Post Office / Tariff Commission)
7th and 8th streets between E and F streets, NW

1839–44—ROBERT MILLS
1855–66—North wing: THOMAS U. WALTER, WITH EDWARD CLARK; Superintendent of construction: MONTGOMERY C. MEIGS
2002—Rehabilitation: MICHAEL STANTON ARCHITECTS; Preservation architects: OEHRLEIN & ASSOCIATES ARCHITECTS; Restaurant: ADAMSTEIN & DEMETRIOU

There are three extant office buildings by Robert Mills in Washington: the Patent Office, the Treasury, and this former General Post Office, later occupied by the Tariff Commission, which gave the building its common name. (If one stands at the southeast corner of 7th and F streets and faces west, one can simultaneously see all three buildings, which employ each of the three basic Greek orders—Doric on the Patent Office, Ionic on the Treasury, and Corinthian on the Tariff Building.)

Perhaps the least known of the trio, the Tariff Building occupies the former site of Blodget's Hotel (c. 1793), which burned to the ground in 1836. The fate of the hotel helped make fire prevention a paramount concern as the design of the new post office developed, and Mills therefore gave the building masonry vaults and thick walls—a structural system also used in his sections of the Treasury and Patent Office. The Tariff Building is well proportioned and, though more ornate than its cousin across the street, still reflects the restrained aesthetic that Mills developed in response to the budgetary limitations he faced.

Like so many of the city's large, early structures, the Tariff Building fell on hard times when the East End of downtown grew unfashionable, and its highly compartmentalized floor plan proved inimical to modern governmental office use. In 1997, the General Services Administration issued a request for proposals seeking the best possible use for the building. The winning idea was a hotel, which made sense because the relentless march of vaulted structural bays around the perimeter could be relatively easily converted into discrete guest rooms, requiring no significant modifications to the historic building fabric. The Kimpton Group, a hospitality chain known for its boutique hostelries, took a 60-year lease on the building, and oversaw conversion into a surprisingly nontraditional hotel. The former mail-sorting room, occupying a peninsular structure in the central courtyard, was converted into a restaurant. The slick glass addition, which is structurally independent of the historic building, serves as a beacon when lit at night, drawing patrons through the carriageway off of 8th Street.

E13 The Lansburgh

420–424 7th Street, NW and 425 8th Street, NW

1890–1918—Original buildings: VARIOUS ARCHITECTS
1991—Renovations and additions: GRAHAM GUND ARCHITECTS (NOW GUND PARTNERSHIP); Associated architects: BRYANT & BRYANT; Preservation architects: OEHRLEIN & ASSOCIATES ARCHITECTS

The Lansburgh complex, which gets its name from a venerable department store that once occupied part of this block, is a quilt of many patterns. Incorporating the rescued shells of several adjacent structures, including Kresge's (the corner of 7th and E streets) and the Busch Building (710 E Street), the development includes commercial, retail, and residential uses, as well as one of two theaters used by Washington's Shakespeare Theatre Company, renowned for its resident actors and inventive reinterpretations of plays by Shakespeare and others [see also E18]. A raised, open courtyard occupies the center of the block and serves the complex's residents.

E14 Gallery Row

401–417 7th Street, NW

1877—Original buildings at 401–407: J. A. MICHIELS
1883—Original building at what is now 413: JOHN G. MEYER (OR POSSIBLY MEYERS)
1986—New building at 409: HARTMAN-COX ARCHITECTS; Preservation architects: OEHRLEIN & ASSOCIATES ARCHITECTS

In the 19th century, this part of town was a vibrant mix of commercial and residential buildings. Architect Thomas U. Walter lived at 614 F Street; the *National Era* (an abolitionist newspaper) was published at 427 F Street; the improbably named Mr. Croissant led the city's temperance drive from his Holly Tree Hotel at 518 9th Street; and Samuel F. B. Morse tinkered with his new-fangled telegraph in a since-demolished building that stood on 7th Street between E and F.

During the 1980s, the area was rediscovered—like countless other rundown urban neighborhoods with "good bones"—by artists. Hartman-Cox and Oehrlein & Associates were hired to tie together this row of buildings into an art gallery complex. The older buildings appear to have been restored in place, but in fact, they were in such bad shape that they had to be completely dismantled and reassembled. Hartman-Cox filled in the gap at 409 7th Street (which had been the site of a small, unexceptional structure) with a new building whose four-story rotunda acts as a lobby and a pivot for the entire project. The Mannerist façade literally bends the rules of classical composition in order to mediate between the divergent floor levels of the adjacent buildings.

E15 District Architecture Center
421 7th Street, NW

1917—W. S. PLAGER
2011—Interior of District Architecture Center: HICKOK COLE ARCHITECTS

After operating out of a large row house in the Dupont Circle neighborhood for more than 40 years, the Washington Chapter of the American Institute of Architects (AIA|DC) moved to the new District Architecture Center (DAC) in 2011. Occupying the first floor and basement of the Independent Order of Odd Fellows temple—no jokes about the appropriateness of that location, please—the DAC accommodates the Chapter's offices, meeting space, and an exhibition gallery. The primary organizing element of the interior is the "Glass Box," a two-story volume, offset by openings in the first-floor slab, containing classrooms on both levels.

E16 Terrell Place
(Old Hecht Company Building)
575 7th Street, NW

1924—JARVIS HUNT
2003—Renovation and addition: SMITHGROUP; Preservation architects: OEHRLEIN & ASSOCIATES ARCHITECTS

The former Hecht's department store at the southeast corner of 7th and F streets was designed by a nephew of Richard Morris Hunt, architect of the Biltmore House in Asheville, North Carolina, and other opulent works of the Gilded Age. With white, glazed terra cotta façades, intricate iron detailing, and an ornate clock suspended above the street corner, the building exudes a subdued elegance that evokes the heyday of urban retail in the early 20th century.

After Hecht's moved to a new flagship store in the 1980s, the old structure sat idle for many years until it was adapted for office use during the renaissance of the East End of downtown. Much of the exterior ornament had been removed but preserved inside the building, and was put back in place during the renovation. The project also involved weaving together parts of several smaller structures on the same block of 7th Street (three of which were even earlier Hecht Company properties), plus an entirely new structure immediately to the east on F Street.

E17 Verizon Center
F Street between 6th and 7th streets, NW

1997—ELLERBE BECKET; Associate architects / exterior design: KCF-SHG ARCHITECTS; Associated architects: DEVROUAX + PURNELL ARCHITECTS

Squeezing a major sports facility into a dense urban neighborhood is never an easy task, and it was especially difficult to accommodate a new basketball, hockey, and concert venue entirely within a single block of L'Enfant's plan. In fact, it proved impossible—this arena would fit only if the 600 block of G Street were obliterated. After much controversy, and despite the steadfast opposition of key preservation groups, the developer received permission to close the street. Coincidentally, soon thereafter, the District government decided to reopen several nearby blocks, including the 900 block of G Street, which had been turned into "pedestrian plazas" in the 1970s. Restoring these failed pedestrian malls to vehicular traffic facilitated redevelopment of the city's East End, so the trade-off may have been worth it in the long run, especially since the Verizon Center itself is also widely credited with sparking the area's commercial renaissance.

Because the site was subject to the Chinatown Design Review Guidelines mandated by the D.C. Office of Planning, the architectural team also faced the unusual challenge of incorporating Chinese-inspired motifs into the design of the sports arena—an odd fusion, to say the least. To achieve this, the designers relied primarily on graphic devices and a few larger elements, such as the wavy canopy on the northwestern corner of the building, which vaguely suggest Asian architectural forms. By contrast, the main entry on F Street, with its tall columns and slanted canopy, clearly alludes to the neoclassical porticoes of the Old Patent Office next door. The rest of the façades might be described as cleanly generic. The result is a slightly haphazard building, but one that is now, for better or for worse, a fixture of its neighborhood.

E18 Sidney Harman Hall

610 F Street, NW

2007—Office building: SMITHGROUP; Theater: DIAMOND + SCHMITT ARCHITECTS

Sidney Harman Hall and the Lansburgh Theatre [see E13], which together constitute the Harman Center for the Arts, are the home bases of Washington's vaunted Shakespeare Theatre Company. Harman Hall occupies the lower levels of a commercial office building entered from a "winter garden" to the west side, which aligns with an open arcade running through the adjacent building to the south. The shift of the office entrance to the side allowed the theater's public functions to be expressed on the street front, yielding a marquee-like bay composed of frameless glass panels suspended a few feet over the sidewalk. This projecting bay not only helps protect the box office entrance from the elements, but also establishes a strong connection between the streetscape and the theater's interior while directly advertising the building's cultural function to passersby. A shallower projection, still heavily glazed but with articulated mullions, embraces the marquee and extends another four floors above it, creating a visual transition between the theater and the office building.

At the insistence of the Shakespeare Theatre's artistic director, the interior of the new theater itself bears absolutely no trace of anything "Shakespearean," "Elizabethan," or even "old." It is a state-of-the-art auditorium with an easily altered layout allowing for thrust stage, proscenium, or end stage arrangements, and thus accommodating a variety of performance types from drama to chamber music. Unusual, textured wall panels add visual interest to the space while helping to modulate the acoustics.

E19 Jackson Graham Building

(Washington Metropolitan Area Transit Authority Headquarters)
600 5th Street, NW

1974—KEYES, LETHBRIDGE & CONDON, ARCHITECTS

Extended floor slabs and a parade of widely spaced, cylindrical concrete columns give this office building visual depth, while changing shadows throughout the day animate what might otherwise be a severely plain work of architecture. The building, which is the administrative headquarters of the regional transit authority and is named for its first general manager, was designed so that a Metro car could stop directly beneath it to drop off money collected throughout the system each day.

E20 National Academies Building

500 5th Street, NW

2003—SMITHGROUP; Preservation architects: OEHRLEIN & ASSOCIATES ARCHITECTS

The headquarters of the National Academies, an umbrella organization that includes the National Academy of Sciences, the National Academy of Engineering, the Institute of Medicine, and the National Research Council, was carefully inserted into a block containing some of the few remaining historic row houses in Washington's commercial downtown. Although these buildings were not landmarked at the time that the building was conceived, the architects anticipated strong objections to any proposal that involved tearing them down, and therefore worked with preservation organizations to devise a scheme that would save as many of the historic buildings as possible while making room for significant new construction on the site. Thus the new, tall block is set back substantially from the street line, allowing the preserved buildings to read as discrete structures, rather than just pickled façades as seen in many similar projects from the 1980s and 1990s.

E21 Superior Court of the District of Columbia

(Old City Hall)
451 Indiana Avenue, NW

1820–49—GEORGE HADFIELD
1883—Expansion: EDWARD CLARK
1919—Renovation: ELLIOTT WOODS
2003—Master plan: KARN CHARUHAS CHAPMAN & TWOHEY
2009—Renovation and addition: BEYER BLINDER BELLE ARCHITECTS & PLANNERS; Associated architects: GRUZEN SAMTON; Landscape architects: RHODESIDE & HARWELL

This was the first public building erected by and for the District's municipal government. After the seemingly obligatory funding crises (a "grand National Lottery" was one of several unsuccessful schemes to raise the cash), the mayor laid the cornerstone in August 1820 for "the seat of legislation and of the administration of justice for this metropolis." The central part of the Greek Revival structure is the oldest and simplest, though the well-proportioned Ionic portico that marks the main entry was not finished until 1849. The east and west wings, added in 1826 and 1849, respectively, are a little more adventurous—their southern ends have porches with paired columns *in antis,* meaning that they are bracketed by extensions of the side walls, with arched openings behind and steps leading to ground level. Originally, these wings directly abutted the sidewalk along Indiana Avenue, but the street itself was later re-graded, lowered, and realigned, resulting in a rather nebulous front yard that slightly diminishes the building's visual impact.

Elliott Woods established the basic appearance of the building as it stands today in a major renovation of 1917–19. The work included constructing an entirely new interior, strengthening the walls with steel beams, encasing the original brick-and-stucco exterior in Indiana limestone, and removing the portico on the north side. During the most recent renovation, a new, glass entrance pavilion was added at the spot where the original portico had been removed.

As of this writing, the National Law Enforcement Museum is under construction on the small plot of land between the courthouse and E Street. Most of the museum will be underground, but two transparent pavilions will pop up at street level, joining the newly built entry to the courthouse to form a modern, glass ensemble within the embrace of the older stone buildings.

E22 Henry J. Daly Building

(Municipal Building)
300 Indiana Avenue, NW

1941—NATHAN C. WYETH

One of a number of District government buildings in this vicinity designed by Nathan Wyeth, who served as the city's municipal architect from 1934 to 1946, this is the headquarters of the Metropolitan Police Department. The building is typical of Wyeth's stripped classicism—note the mere hint of classical pilasters inscribed into the stone on either side of each of the major window openings. Be sure to see the ceramic tile friezes that grace the building's two courtyards, illustrating "Democracy in Action" (by Waylande Gregory) in the west courtyard, and "Health and Welfare" (by Hildreth Meière) in the east. Just tell the nice security guards you've come to police headquarters to see the art.

E23 U.S. Tax Court Building

400 2nd Street, NW

1974—VICTOR A. LUNDY; Associated architects: LYLES BISSETT / CARLISLE & WOLFF

The fashion for public buildings in the late 1960s and 1970s tended toward abstraction and extreme monumentality. In the case of the U.S. Tax Court, the result was a forbidding, space-age judicial fortress. The building does have a certain minimalist magnificence, best appreciated from the plaza over the freeway immediately to the east of the site. Along that side, an absurdly wide staircase leads visitors into an inky void obscuring the original main entrance, which has been closed for security reasons for much of the building's history. Suspended above is a huge, windowless, cantilevered slab clad in granite, which holds courtrooms and offices.

TOUR F

Pennsylvania Avenue

Pennsylvania Avenue has long been dubbed "America's Main Street." According to lore, the avenue got its official name as a sop to politicians from the Keystone State, who became disgruntled when Congress decided to build a national capital from scratch instead of bestowing that honor on Philadelphia. If true, the gesture was probably not appreciated—one early 19th-century congressman described Pennsylvania Avenue as "a deep morass covered with elder bushes," and, despite Thomas Jefferson's attempts to beautify the thoroughfare by planting flanking rows of Lombardy poplars, that description remained valid for several decades. While fretting about the street's appearance, Jefferson, perhaps unwittingly, began an honored tradition when he walked down Pennsylvania Avenue for his inauguration in March 1801. Since then, Pennsylvania Avenue has witnessed countless parades and rallies for countless organizations and causes, from the Ku Klux Klan to women's suffrage.

During the Civil War, Pennsylvania Avenue, especially between 7th Street and 14th Street, became the favorite haunt of prostitutes drawn to Washington, in venerable tradition, by the city's hundreds of thousands of soldiers. According to one story, General Joseph Hooker tried to get the prostitutes to confine their activities to a small zone, but the women refused and started taunting him by calling themselves "Hooker's Army," later shortened to "hookers." It's a good tale, but unfortunately, the word *hooker* in that sense seems to have been in use for decades before the general came to town. At any rate, that phase of the avenue's history ended when the District outlawed brothels in 1914. Not long thereafter the southern side of Pennsylvania was transformed by the gargantuan Federal Triangle project.

By the 1960s, the northern side of the ceremonial stretch of Pennsylvania Avenue, despite its historic and symbolic importance, was thoroughly decrepit. President Kennedy, riding down the avenue after his inauguration, expressed shock over what appeared to be a "slum" between the nation's two most prominent public build-

Aerial view of the Federal Triangle, still under construction in the 1930s.

F ST
E ST
12th ST
14th ST
CONSTITUTION AVE
800 ft
11
12
13
14
15
16
17
18
19
20
21
22
23

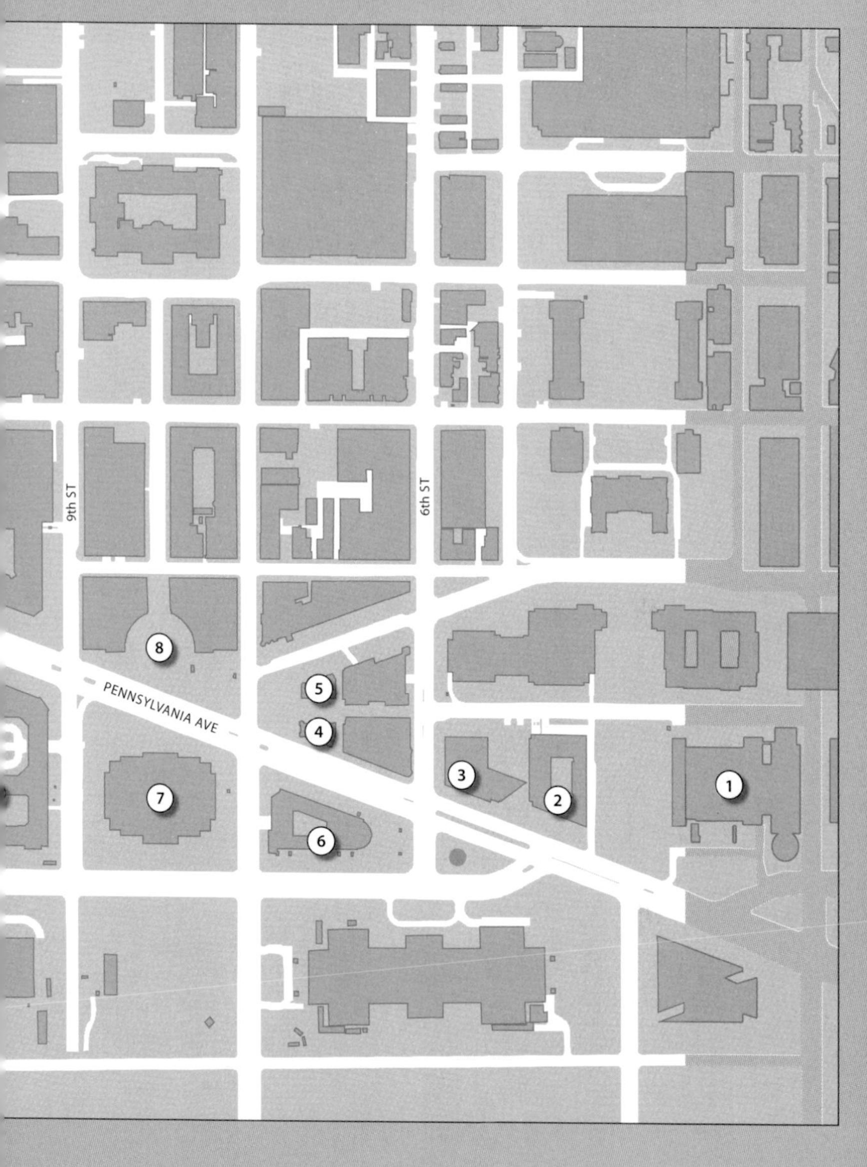
9th ST
6th ST
PENNSYLVANIA AVE
1
2
3
4
5
6
7
8

ings. Kennedy appointed a temporary commission to study possible remedies, and in 1972, Congress established the Pennsylvania Avenue Development Corporation (PADC), an independent federal agency given broad powers to redevelop the area. Over the next 24 years, until its dissolution in 1996, the corporation was extremely successful in acquiring, rehabilitating, selling, and leasing property. PADC used its design oversight authority to guide renovations and new construction, and largely as a result of the agency's work, the once-shabby thoroughfare is now a truly grand, if not especially vibrant, boulevard worthy of the national landmarks that it connects.

F1 E. Barrett Prettyman Courthouse

333 Constitution Avenue, NW

1952—LOUIS JUSTEMENT
2005—Addition and Renovation: MICHAEL GRAVES ASSOCIATES; Preservation architects: OEHRLEIN & ASSOCIATES ARCHITECTS; Associated architects: SMITHGROUP; Courthouse consultants: RICCI ARCHITECTS & PLANNERS

In the realm of stripped classicism, the original Prettyman Courthouse is the Full Monty—as bare as bare can be. Designed and built shortly after World War II, just as modernism was entering its heyday, the courthouse reflects official Washington's continued unwillingness to accept truly modern architecture for major public buildings. The result is a building that looks as if it is trying very hard to be nothing at all.

In contrast, the annex by Michael Graves seems to be trying desperately to be *something,* though what, precisely, is unclear. Oddly reminiscent of the architect's various projects for the Walt Disney Company, the addition, while undeniably monumental, somehow fails to convey the sense of gravitas one would expect in a federal court facility. Instead, it comes off as a teased, fluffy tail wagging a shaved and slightly embarrassed dog.

Immediately west of the original courthouse is John Marshall Park, designed by Carol R. Johnson Associates and completed in 1983. The park's honoree, Chief Justice John Marshall, once lived in a rooming house that, ironically, was one of dozens of structures demolished to make way for this green space.

F2 Canadian Chancery

501 Pennsylvania Avenue, NW

1989—ARTHUR ERICKSON ARCHITECTS

Thanks to Washington's building height limit and other stringent zoning restrictions, many of the city's commercial structures are designed to squeeze in as much square footage as possible, and often look as if they are about to burst beyond the maximum buildable volume allowed by law. In contrast, the Canadian Embassy seems not quite big enough to fill its site, and in fact, that was the case. Guidelines established by the Pennsylvania Avenue Development Corporation dictated the cornice line and basic footprint for any building to go on this prominent plot, and the embassy simply did not need all of the space that the prescribed building envelope would have allowed. As a result, the building is somewhat hollow, with a profusion of architectural elements supporting little substance (though curator and writer Nicholas Olsberg has argued that these seemingly frivolous forms were Erickson's way of poking fun at Washington's stuffy design constraints). On the positive side, the resulting open courtyard is publicly accessible—a rarity in an era of draconian security measures at so many diplomatic facilities.

The most prominent corner of the site, facing the Capitol, is marked by an outdoor rotunda defined by 12 columns, one for each of Canada's provinces and territories at the time the building was completed (such numerological tributes in architecture can quickly become dated—a 13th jurisdiction, Nunavut, was carved out of the Northwest Territories in 1999, and is now represented by a stone cairn in the lobby). Just inside the courtyard is a row of six huge, 80-foot-tall aluminum columns, fluted in a nod to classicism, which incongruously hold up an obviously lightweight glass canopy. The strongest exterior architectural element is the cascading, lushly planted west wall of the courtyard, which recalls similar stepped forms on several of Erickson's governmental and academic projects in Vancouver. The embassy's interior public spaces are serene and elegantly understated.

F3 Newseum

555 Pennsylvania Avenue, NW

2008—POLSHEK PARTNERSHIP ARCHITECTS; Interior architecture and planning for residential component: ESOCOFF & ASSOCIATES | ARCHITECTS; Interior design for residential common areas: MEDITCH MURPHEY ARCHITECTS

Tel: (888) 639-7386
www.newseum.org

Like the news itself these days, the Newseum comes at you as a barrage, with numerous elements vying for your attention. Its design was "inspired by the many ways people get news," and the most obvious gesture in that regard is the vast, rectangular void in the Pennsylvania Avenue façade—a virtual national television set (or computer screen) displaying the people and activities within to passersby. To the left of the giant window is a marble panel bearing the entire text of the First Amendment to the U.S. Constitution, a nod to the Newseum's parent organization, the Freedom Forum, a nonpartisan foundation that seeks to defend the ideals enumerated in the amendment. To the right is the weakest part of the façade—a veritable catalogue of curtain walls, each attractive in its own right, but with no apparent reason for the multiplicity of patterns and glass treatments. Along the sidewalk, however, is the museum's most compelling feature: a line of cases displaying the current front pages of newspapers from all 50 states and the District of Columbia. A direct comparison of the various papers' coverage of similar stories can be very enlightening.

The interior of the museum continues the visual bombardment. The large volume behind the "television screen" fails to provide a clear sense of orientation, and circulation patterns are a bit counterintuitive. The museum offers a wide array of exhibitions and activities, some informative, some entertaining, some vapid. One highlight is the publicly accessible roof terrace, which affords outstanding views of the Capitol and the Federal Triangle.

The project is actually a mixed-use complex including the museum, the headquarters of the Freedom Forum, a large restaurant, and apartments. The foundation's offices and conference facilities are above the museum, nestled among the 250-foot-long trusses that span the main public spaces. The sleekly modern restaurant has its own entrance off of 6th Street. The residential block is behind the museum, aligned with C Street. In contrast to the disjointed front façade of the museum, the residential wing is an extremely orderly composition based on a repeated, asymmetrical window module. A linear balcony at the ninth floor breaks up the block and adds a horizontal accent.

F4 Apex, Gilman, and Brady Buildings

625–633 Pennsylvania Avenue, NW

c. 1840–65—ARCHITECTS UNKNOWN
1888—Apex / Central National Bank Building addition: ALFRED B. MULLETT
Numerous alterations: VARIOUS ARCHITECTS
1984—Addition and restoration design architects: HARTMAN-COX ARCHITECTS; Architects of record: GEIER BROWN RENFROW ARCHITECTS; Preservation architects: JOHN MILNER ASSOCIATES

The westernmost structure of this group was built in the mid-1860s as a hotel in what was then a bustling—sometimes rowdy—part of town. In the 1880s, a bank bought the building for use as offices, and hired Alfred Mullett to give it a stronger presence on the avenue. He added the twin, cylindrical towers, instantly creating a local landmark. From that point, the building's fortunes mirrored those of the broader neighborhood, peaking perhaps in the 1920s before entering a long, slow decline. From 1945 to 1983, it was home to the Apex Liquor Store, which derived its name from the acutely angled site and, in turn, lent its name to the whole building. In the 1960s, the store came to be symbolic of the seedy state of Pennsylvania Avenue that so distressed President Kennedy during his inaugural parade. Many Washingtonians noted the irony of the busy store's location within sight of Henry Cogswell's Temperance Fountain [see following entry].

The two easternmost structures both date from before the Civil War. Mathew Brady, the pioneering photographer, kept his studio and office at 625 Pennsylvania between 1858 and 1881, and expanded into the upper floors of the building at 627 (long the site of Gilman's drugstore on the ground floor) in the 1860s. During a 1967 renovation of the Gilman Building, workers found original glass plates of Brady's photographs amid the debris in the long-vacant upper levels.

In the early 1980s, Sears, Roebuck & Co. bought the row of buildings and converted them into offices for a division that negotiated trade agreements with foreign governments. Hartman-Cox designed a one-story addition atop the Apex Building and a narrow connector—marked by two Doric columns at the base and a pediment at the top—filling in a gap between the historic structures and creating a new entrance. The complex has since been partially subdivided again; the National Council of Negro Women now has its headquarters in the section at 633 Pennsylvania.

F5 Argentine Naval Attache Building

(National Bank of Washington, later Riggs Bank)
630 Indiana Avenue, NW

1889—JAMES G. HILL
1979—Interior renovation: P. T. ASTORE
1982—Renovation: VLASTIMIL KOUBEK

One of the most elegant works of Romanesque Revival architecture in the city, the Argentine Naval Attache's building is made of rough-faced granite with smooth trim. The balance of textures, the rhythm of the windows, and the intricate but modest details all serve to distinguish the building from others using the same vocabulary. A large *trompe-l'oeil* mural, depicting a continuation of these elements, adorns the eastern façade.

In the plaza just west of the Argentine Naval Building stands the Temperance Fountain of 1882. The fountain, which was presented to the city by temperance crusader Henry D. Cogswell, a San Francisco dentist, is now—perhaps more appropriately—dry. Dr. Cogswell picked a good site from which to launch his local anti-vice crusade, since for most of the 19th century this block marked the eastern boundary of the city's large red light district.

F6 Federal Trade Commission

Between 6th and 7th streets and Constitution and Pennsylvania avenues, NW

1937—BENNETT, PARSONS & FROST; Sculptors: MICHAEL LANTZ ET AL.

The most ambitious architectural undertaking in the history of Washington, the Federal Triangle in many ways represents the culmination of the City Beautiful movement. Conceived in the Roaring Twenties and largely executed during the Great Depression, the vast complex—stretching from 6th to 15th streets between Pennsylvania and Constitution avenues—is remarkable for its conceptual and visual cohesion, even as the individual buildings reflect sometimes surprisingly varied attitudes toward ornament and architectural form. The Triangle's buildings were, in fact, designed by many different architects, but they were conceived as a single monumental composition and were guided to completion by a coordinating committee headed by Edward Bennett, architectural advisor to Treasury Secretary Andrew Mellon.

Forming the apex of the Federal Triangle is the Federal Trade Commission, the last of the buildings completed according to the original plan. Not surprisingly, given its construction late in the Depression, this is the plainest structure of the complex. The chastity of the design contrasts with the exaggerated muscularity of Michael Lantz's freestanding equine sculptures depicting, believe it or not, "Man Controlling Trade."

F7 National Archives Building

700 Pennsylvania Avenue, NW (Exhibit Hall Entrance on Constitution Avenue)

1935—JOHN RUSSELL POPE; Sculptors: ADOLPH A. WEINMAN, JAMES EARLE FRASER, AND ROBERT AITKEN
2004—Renovation: HARTMAN-COX ARCHITECTS

Tel: (202) 357-5000
www.archives.gov

Of all the buildings in the Federal Triangle, this one achieves the greatest individual architectural distinction; what success the others enjoy is largely dependent on their cumulative effect. The special treatment accorded this structure is understandable not only because of its exalted purpose, but also because it occupies a site in line with 8th Street, NW, a secondary but still important axis in L'Enfant's plan. Impressive Corinthian porticoes mark the axis on both the north and south elevations of the building.

As with the design for the Scottish Rite Temple on 16th Street [see L26] by the same architect, the National Archives Building seems to have been inspired by a mausoleum—an appropriate reference, really, since it was conceived as a permanent repository for the nation's most important documents. The Declaration of Independence, the Constitution, and other documents are on view in the rotunda, which was recently restored to allow greater accessibility and visibility without compromising the James Bond-like security measures that protect these invaluable items from every imaginable threat. Long-term and rotating exhibitions are on view in other galleries within this building.

F8 Market Square

Pennsylvania Avenue between 7th and 9th streets, NW

1990—HARTMAN-COX ARCHITECTS; Associated architects: MORRIS*ARCHITECTS

The team that planned the rebirth of Pennsylvania Avenue in the 1960s, during the heyday of the heroic period of modernism, could scarcely have imagined that, just a couple of decades later, this prominent site would be occupied by two buildings boasting a phalanx of five-story classical columns. Taking its name from Center Market, which once stood across the street from this site, Market Square is a mixed-use complex with residential units over offices and retail space. The late senator Daniel Patrick Moynihan, a vocal advocate for the avenue's revitalization, put his money where his mouth was and bought one of the apartments boasting spectacular views of the city's monumental core. Nestled within the arc of Market Square is the unmemorable Navy Memorial, by the firm of Conklin & Rossant, with sculptures by Stanley Bleifeld.

F9 J. Edgar Hoover Building

(FBI Headquarters)
Pennsylvania Avenue between 9th and 10th streets, NW

1974—C. F. MURPHY & ASSOCIATES

The swaggering bully of the neighborhood, the FBI headquarters is ungainly, ill-mannered, and seemingly looking for trouble. A cynic could argue that it is all too successful as a piece of architecture to the extent that the building's form so starkly reflects the clandestine work of the agency it houses: the impenetrable base, shadowy courtyard, and looming upper stories bespeak security and surveillance. The prototype for the Pennsylvania Avenue redevelopment plan devised under the direction of Nathaniel Owings, it helped to ensure that the full plan would never be realized.

F10 Robert F. Kennedy Federal Building

(U.S. Department of Justice)
Between 9th and 10th streets and Pennsylvania and Constitution avenues, NW

1934—ZANTZINGER, BORIE & MEDARY
2004—Renovation: BURT HILL KOSAR RITTELMANN ASSOCIATES; Preservation architects: OEHRLEIN & ASSOCIATES ARCHITECTS

The Justice Department building is a curious hybrid—it is fundamentally a neoclassical building, but with Art Deco elements and event hints of ancient Egyptian motifs sprinkled throughout. On the exterior, most of the Art Deco influences are subtle—notice, for instance, the Ionic column capitals, whose scrolls have unorthodox, bulging tops—though the sculpted doors and the exuberant, aluminum light fixtures unabashedly reflect the glamour and audacity associated with the style. Most of the Art Deco elements are inside where, sadly, the average citizen will never get to see them. These include stunning murals, as well as mosaics by local artisan John Joseph Earley. His concrete mosaic ceilings over the driveways are partially visible from the sidewalk.

F11 Internal Revenue Service (IRS) Building

1111 Constitution Avenue, NW

1936—LOUIS A. SIMON
1993—Façade completion: KARN CHARUHAS CHAPMAN & TWOHEY
2005—Renovation: SWANKE HAYDEN CONNELL

The IRS Building is generally less elaborate than most of the other buildings of the Federal Triangle, and that distinction was deliberate—not because it was the IRS per se, but simply because the agency was not a cabinet-level department (and did not share the high profile of the Post Office and the National Archives). The northwestern corner of the site was obviously truncated to accommodate the Old Post Office, which stubbornly lingered to the consternation of the neoclassical crusaders (a raw end at the northwestern corner of the IRS Building was finally finished in 1993, in recognition of the fact that the Post Office simply was not going anywhere). Along 12th Street, only a small portion of the hemicycle that was supposed to complement the one across the street was actually completed.

F12 Nancy Hanks Center / Old Post Office Pavilion

12th Street and Pennsylvania Avenue, NW

1899—WILLOUGHBY J. EDBROOKE
1983—Adaptive reuse: ARTHUR COTTON MOORE / ASSOCIATES; Associated architects: MCGAUGHY, MARSHALL & MCMILLAN
1991—Addition: KARN CHARUHAS CHAPMAN & TWOHEY

Architectural movements do not begin or end at precise moments, of course, but if one had to identify the year in which the fashion for Romanesque Revival buildings faded, 1900 would be a reasonable choice. This building, exemplary of the style and constructed as the headquarters of the U.S. Postal Service, was completed in 1899. In other words, it was finished just in time to be despised. The *New York Times* dismissed it as "a cross between a cathedral and a cotton mill."

Within a couple of years, the Senate Park Commission was hard at work developing its vision for a gleaming, white, politely neoclassical Washington, and structures like the rough-hewn Post Office Building (as it was then known), with its pointy roofs and its attention-grabbing, 315-foot tower, were not welcome at the architectural party. The renderings of the commission's 1902 plan were (literally) a bit fuzzy in their proposals for this specific site, but a quarter century later, Andrew Mellon's Federal Triangle initiative was clearer, and specifically called for the Post Office Building to be torn down in favor of a neoclassical structure that contributed to a coherent plan for the entire precinct.

The vast majority of the Federal Triangle plan was realized—including the *new* headquarters for the Postal Service [see F14]—but somehow the now *Old* Post Office Building hung on, though it faced near-constant threats of demolition. Finally, in the early 1970s, preservationists prevailed and the building was saved in a widely publicized case of adaptive reuse. Upper levels were restored for government offices, and the building's courtyard was turned into a soaring atrium, with food vendors at the base. The tower—the third tallest in the city, after the Washington Monument and the campanile at the Basilica of the National Shrine of the Immaculate Conception—was opened to the public as an observatory. A new shopping pavilion was added next door some years later, but was never a commercial success.

Nowadays, the building looks awfully tired (at least inside), and some of the office employees complain that their workspaces are inadequate and uncomfortable. As of this writing, the government has issued a request for qualifications to identify a private development firm to convert the building to commercial use—a hotel, perhaps, in which the atrium could become a logical amenity rather than merely an unusually copious lightwell. Rumor has it that several major hospitality chains are salivating at the prospect.

F13 Evening Star Building

1101 Pennsylvania Avenue, NW

1899—MARSH AND PETER
1919—Addition: ARCHITECT UNKNOWN
1989—Renovation and addition: SKIDMORE, OWINGS & MERRILL; Preservation architects: OEHRLEIN & ASSOCIATES ARCHITECTS

When this Beaux-Arts building first opened, the *Evening Star*, pleased with

its new digs, ran a full-page story to announce its "architectural triumph." Continuing, the article stated that the paper's publisher had decided to make the District "notable in an artistic sense" and thus chose to erect "such a building as would be harmonious with that future and an inspiration to its speedy attainments." The *Star* pursued many crusades from this building until 1955 (then published from a different location for another generation before its demise).

The original Evening Star Building is notable as a remnant of pre-modern Pennsylvania Avenue, before planners in the 1960s and 1970s decided to broaden the already-wide street by pushing back the building line on the north side (as evident in the adjacent blocks). Fortunately, the building survived long enough for that idea to be reconsidered, and the 1989 addition was built out to the line established by the original structure.

F14 Ariel Rios Building

Pennsylvania Avenue and 12th Street, NW

1935—DELANO & ALDRICH
1998—Façade completion: KARN CHARUHAS CHAPMAN & TWOHEY
2000—Renovation: RTKL ASSOCIATES

Two broad arcs, back to back in plan, lend a Baroque quality to the structure originally known as the Post Office Building (housing the headquarters of the U.S. Postal Service, not to be confused with its predecessor [see F12] or the local post office facilities that once

occupied Postal Square [see A12] and the Hotel Monaco [see E12]). Projecting bays extend all the way to the 12th Street line, providing pedestrian archways over the sidewalk—welcome anomalies in a city where public and commercial buildings rarely engage the streetscape so boldly. The Internal Revenue Service Building across the street was intended to incorporate a complementary arc, creating a full circle, but it was never completed. Meanwhile, the arc on the western side of the Ariel Rios Building was conceived as the apse of a landscaped "Grand Plaza," which was also never realized. That space was instead used as a parking lot for decades until the Ronald Reagan Building filled the site.

F15 Environmental Protection Agency and Andrew W. Mellon Auditorium

Constitution Avenue between 12th and 14th streets, NW

1934—ARTHUR BROWN JR.
2000—Renovation: RTKL ASSOCIATES

Arthur Brown Jr., best known as the architect of San Francisco's elegant City Hall, originally designed this three-unit behemoth to house the Interstate Commerce Commission and the U.S. Department of Labor. Sandwiched between the two office blocks is a spectacularly ornate and impeccably proportioned auditorium now named for Andrew Mellon, who, as secretary of the treasury, was instrumental in the planning of the Federal Triangle. The auditorium is a multipurpose public assembly facility for important lectures, receptions, banquets, and other fancy social affairs, not to mention the occasional treaty signing. Few spaces in Washington can compete with it for sheer grandeur.

The open passageways on either side of the auditorium are the kind of intricate urban spaces that help make many European cities so interesting and pleasant for pedestrians, but are all too rare in the United States.

F16 Ronald Reagan Building and International Trade Center

1300 Pennsylvania Avenue, NW

1998—PEI COBB FREED & PARTNERS; Associated architects: ELLERBE BECKET ARCHITECTS AND ENGINEERS
2001—Center for Association Leadership at the Marriott Learning Complex: VOA ASSOCIATES

Conceived as the very belated completion of the Federal Triangle, the Ronald Reagan Building is a gigantic anachronism. It is ponderously and stodgily neoclassical, stripped of all but minimal ornament—the sort of building one might expect to have been built in the 1930s, like many of its neighbors, but not at the end of the 20th century, when modernism was resurgent. When this design was revealed as the winner of a limited competition in which all of the entries were rather conservative, there were no squeals of glee—just a general sense of resignation that the site was unlikely to inspire a truly contemporary work of architecture. Even so, the building's formalism is astonishing—note the windowless floor near the top, where the clunky cornice took precedence over the need for natural light on the interior.

One might assume that an unabashedly neoclassical building on this site would respect and reinforce the Federal Triangle's Beaux-Arts plan, but strangely, the east side of the Reagan Building arrogantly defies its context. Toward the southern end of the east façade, there is the beginning of a curve in the plan of the new building, suggesting that the architects were thinking about creating a hemicycle to complement the one on the Ariel Rios Building. Then the curve is suddenly interrupted by a long, angled wall extending almost all the way to Pennsylvania Avenue, broken only by a curious bump of a pavilion masquerading as the completion of the hemicycle. Had the architects simply pursued the obvious solution and finished the curve, most anyone—classicist or modernist alike—probably would have acknowledged the resulting oval plaza as a wonderfully grand outdoor space. Instead, visitors are left wondering why, given the enormous expense of cloaking this building in faux-classical garb, its architects worked so hard to avoid the one classical gesture everyone expected.

F17 John A. Wilson Building

(District Building)
1350 Pennsylvania Avenue, NW

1908—COPE & STEWARDSON; Sculptor: ADOLFO DE NESTI
2003—Rehabilitation and addition: SHALOM BARANES ASSOCIATES; Exterior preservation architects: OEHRLEIN & ASSOCIATES ARCHITECTS; Architects of record: KENDALL HEATON ASSOCIATES

Elegant in its way, but also a bit heavy-handed in comparison to many of its Beaux-Arts siblings, the John A. Wilson Building houses the offices of the mayor and council of the District of Columbia. The building was begun in 1904, just a couple of years after the Senate Park Commission issued its recommendations for the city's core. In terms of both style and use, it was essentially consistent with that plan, which envisioned a municipal center in this area. Two decades later, however, the team planning the Federal Triangle had every intention of demolishing this freestanding, marble structure, which did not fit in with their broader plan for a cohesive, limestone enclave, but it managed to survive.

The building was in such bad shape in the early 1990s that city officials actually decamped for leased space in a bland commercial structure on Judiciary Square. The District government then entered into a complicated and rather mysterious deal with the federal govern-

ment and a private developer through which this building was renovated and the U-shaped courtyard was filled in with a glassy addition. (According to the preservation architect, the exterior was so heavily caked in pigeon droppings that it took two years of restoration before the marble approximated its original color.) After lengthy negotiations with the federal government, which had expected to be able to use the building for its own purposes, city officials were eventually able to move back in, restoring the structure's status as Washington's City Hall.

F18 Herbert Clark Hoover Federal Building

(U.S. Department of Commerce)
Between 14th and 15th streets and E Street and Constitution Avenue, NW

1932—LOUIS AYRES / YORK & SAWYER
1989—Law Library restoration: EINHORN YAFFEE PRESCOTT

A rusticated base, a parade of pedimented windows, and deeply etched masonry joints on the third through fifth levels reflect the Italian Renaissance inspirations for this 1,000-foot-long building. When new, it was the largest office building in the city, with more than one million square feet of floor space. The west façade, facing the Ellipse, is punctuated by four tall, shallow porticoes that mitigate its length. The eastern side, by contrast, has an extended central colonnade that seems to emphasize the building's outsize proportions. The monumental façade of this central block was conceived as the terminus of a "Grand Plaza," a huge public space framed on the other end by the western hemicycle of the Ariel Rios Building [see F14]. The plaza was never built, but the shallow arc of the Ronald Reagan Building across the street is a reminder of the intended axial arrangement. A multistage renovation of the Commerce building is ongoing.

F19 Freedom Plaza / Pershing Park

(Western Plaza)
Pennsylvania Avenue between 13th and 15th streets, NW

1980—Freedom Plaza: VENTURI, RAUCH & SCOTT BROWN; Landscape architect: GEORGE E. PATTON
1981—Pershing Park: M. PAUL FRIEDBERG; Associated architect: JEROME LINDSAY

It is ironic that Venturi, Rauch & Scott Brown, a firm known for its populist approach to architecture and urban design, should have created such a desolate and cheerless public space as Freedom Plaza. Laid out on a large, raised terrace, the plaza depicts a portion of L'Enfant's plan for Washington in black granite and white marble, with various quotations about the city—some serious, some less so—inscribed into the stone surfaces. A plaque at the site explains that the city's plan is controlled by two "orders"—the "giant" order of diagonal avenues and the "minor" order of the rectangular street grid—and describes how the plaza itself engages both of these orders. All of this is lost on the typical visitor, who just scurries across the plaza as quickly as possible or avoids it altogether. In fairness, it should be noted that the architects' original design included tall pylons framing views of the Treasury Building and large-scale models of the White House and Capitol, which would have brought some three-dimensional interest to the space, but ultimately would have done little to relieve its wind- and sun-swept barrenness.

Just to the west is the lushly landscaped Pershing Park. With its sense of enclosure and intimacy, this park is a pleasant foil to Freedom Plaza.

F20 Warner Theatre / Office Building

(Earle Theatre and Office Building)
1299 Pennsylvania Avenue, NW

1924—C. HOWARD CRANE AND KENNETH FRANZHEIM
1927—Addition of top floor: ZINK, ATKINS AND CRAYCROFT
1993—Renovation: SHALOM BARANES ASSOCIATES; Addition: PEI COBB FREED & PARTNERS ARCHITECTS

The original Earle Theatre and Office Building was something of a sensation when it opened just after Christmas in 1924. Designed by C. Howard Crane, architect of more than 300 theaters around the world, the project was not only hailed by the *Evening Star* as "Washington's most beautiful commercial building," but also noted as an unusual mixed-use development, incorporating a 2,500-seat Vaudeville theater, a 1,000-person ballroom in the basement, a large restaurant, and substantial commercial office space. The summer after it opened, the Earle hosted outdoor movies and dancing on its roof, but within a couple of years, the roof garden was lost when another floor of office space was added. Office tenants over the years included a variety of nonprofit organizations, among them the Federal Bar Association and the "We Want Beer" association, an anti-Prohibition group. In 1927, the theater was converted into a first-run movie house, though it continued to present live shows until 1945. With the decline of downtown in the 1960s, the theater—by then known as the Warner—was closed for a few years before reopening as a venue for rock concerts and pornographic movies (which must have been astonishing to see on the theater's huge screen). Fortunately, a comprehensive renovation subsequently returned the Warner to its former glory, and it now hosts a wide variety of performances.

The architecture of the building, which is actually at the corner of 13th and E streets despite its Pennsylvania Avenue address, is exemplary of the era, with exuberant terra cotta ornament and an enticing marquee over the theater entrance. The position of the theater within is expressed on the elevations by windowless panels carrying a decorative diamond pattern—the stage being along E Street, with one side of the auditorium along 13th Street. The interiors of the theater and other public spaces are appropriately palatial and decorated in a Renaissance Revival vein.

The large, 1990s addition is articulated along E Street as if it were two buildings—the easternmost part of the façade is a modern recapitulation of the theater façade, while the central part is designed as a slightly different but compatible composition, lending a basic, tripartite symmetry to the entire block.

F21 National Place / J. W. Marriott Hotel

Between E, F, 13th, and 14th streets, NW

1984—Hotel: MITCHELL / GIURGOLA ARCHITECTS; National Place: FRANK SCHLESINGER ASSOCIATES
2005—Renovation of National Place food court: BRIAN G. THORNTON DESIGNS; Exterior canopy at National Place: SOE LIN & ASSOCIATES

The Marriott chain's flagship hotel and the adjoining, mixed-use National Place

complex were among the earliest developments in the renaissance of Washington's former commercial core. The new structures were woven into a block that includes a small remnant of the Capitol Theater (1927—Rapp & Rapp), marked by an apse-like, concave façade on F Street.

F22 Willard InterContinental Hotel

14th Street and Pennsylvania Avenue, NW

1901, 1904 (built in two phases)—HENRY HARDENBERGH
1926—Addition: WALTER G. PETER
1986—Renovation and addition conceptual design: HARDY HOLZMAN PFEIFFER ASSOCIATES; Executive architect: VLASTIMIL KOUBEK; Restoration: STUART GOLDING

Without doubt the most fabled hostelry in town, the present Willard is the last in a succession of hotels that have stood on this site for nearly 200 years. In 1816, John Tayloe, the original owner of the Octagon [see I3], built six houses on this lot and leased them to Joshua Tennison, who established Tennison's Hotel by 1818. Other leaseholders operated hotels under different names on the same site over the next several decades. In 1847, Tayloe's son, Benjamin Ogle Tayloe, leased the property to Henry Willard, a former steamship steward, with an option to buy it at a later date. Willard oversaw an expansion of the hotel and put his own name on it. He eventually bought the property outright, but not until after the U.S. Supreme Court decided in 1869 that his payment in paper currency was valid (at the time the lease had been written, gold and silver were the only widely accepted forms of currency).

During the Civil War, Julia Ward Howe wrote the "Battle Hymn of the Republic" in her room at the Willard and the building played host to so many luminaries that Nathaniel Hawthorne, covering the war for *The Atlantic Monthly,* observed, "This hotel . . . may be more justly called the center of Washington and the Union than either the Capitol, the White House, or the State Department." On a less exalted level, the Willard also supposedly gave rise to the term *lobbyist,* referring to any of the men who prowled the lobby, peering through cigar smoke and potted palms in search of political figures to accost.

The present building was the work of Henry Hardenbergh, who also designed the Plaza Hotel in New York. It exudes a sense of luxury thanks to the robust stone trim and delicate iron railings of some of the lower-level windows; the chunky, projecting keystones above the mid-level windows; and above all (literally and figuratively), the soaring mansard roof, punctuated by huge, two-story dormers. At the sidewalk level, a beefy cast iron railing (which seems to cascade as it follows the slope of 14th Street) protects the areaway that brings light to the basement, while firmly connecting the architecture of the hotel to the streetscape. Inside, the hotel's public rooms—including the main lobby, with thirty-five different types of marble;

Peacock Alley, a block-long promenade of ritzy shops; and the Round Robin Bar, which during Carrie Nation's temperance crusade boasted a sign proclaiming "All Nations Welcome Except Carrie"—rank among the grandest such spaces in the city.

Good times and the Willard remained synonymous until after World War II, when the entire neighborhood suffered an extended, grueling decline. (One of the hotel's few bright postwar moments came in 1963, when Martin Luther King Jr. penned his "I Have a Dream" speech in a room upstairs.) Boarded up and threatened with demolition, the Willard was finally saved through the intervention of the Pennsylvania Avenue Development Corporation and, after a lengthy restoration, reopened its opulent doors in 1986 as the Willard InterContinental Hotel. The large wing added at that time, designed by Hardy Holzman Pfeiffer Associates and executed by Vlastimil Koubek, reflects a concerted effort to replicate the characteristic forms of the existing building while still deferring to it—a challenging task. The architects' solution entailed the use of multiple setbacks, diminishing the apparent scale of the new construction.

F23 W Washington D.C.

(Hotel Washington)
515 15th Street, NW

1918—CARRÈRE & HASTINGS
1985—Renovation: MARIANI AND ASSOCIATES; Materials conservator: IVAN VALTCHEV
2009—Renovation: BBG-BBGM; Interior design: DIANNA WONG ARCHITECTURE & INTERIOR DESIGN

Washington's oldest hotel in continuous use, the former Hotel Washington is widely known for its rooftop restaurant and bar with a terrace that boasts some of the best views in the city. Carrère and Hastings, architects of such masterpieces as the main New York Public Library on Fifth Avenue, sheathed this steel-frame structure in veneers of pale, smooth stone and brown brick. Liver-colored *sgraffito* decorations (in which designs are scratched into layered plaster, revealing colors beneath the surface) adorn the window surrounds and spandrel panels on the upper levels. Starwood Hotels, which manages the property, converted it into a W Hotel in 2009. Despite fears on the part of many local preservationists, key architectural elements of the lobby and other public spaces were retained in the ensuing renovation, though the guest rooms were completely revamped.

TOUR G

Downtown / East End

The early 20th century was the heyday of the American downtown, when shoppers flocked to department stores and streetcars plied their routes amid the throngs of pedestrians. The area east of the White House and above Pennsylvania Avenue was Washington's commercial center during that period, with F Street as its principal retail strip. After World War II, however, the thriving district declined rapidly, as did so many similar areas in cities across the country, leaving dozens of grand works of architecture to decay. New office development in the postwar era shifted toward the west, particularly to thoroughfares like K Street and Connecticut Avenue.

By the 1980s, as developable sites in the West End were growing rarer, commercial interests began to reconsider the old East End. A booming real estate market, interrupted only briefly by a couple of recessions, has subsequently driven a phenomenally rapid rejuvenation of this area. Although only one department store remains in the old center, smaller retailers have moved back in, and residential development is increasingly common. Local political leaders and developers are now hopeful that a truly vibrant downtown is once again on the horizon.

Washington's old downtown was once full of small-to-medium-scale commercial structures, such as this one at 7th and G streets, NW. Most such buildings were demolished in the late 20th century to make way for much larger office buildings.

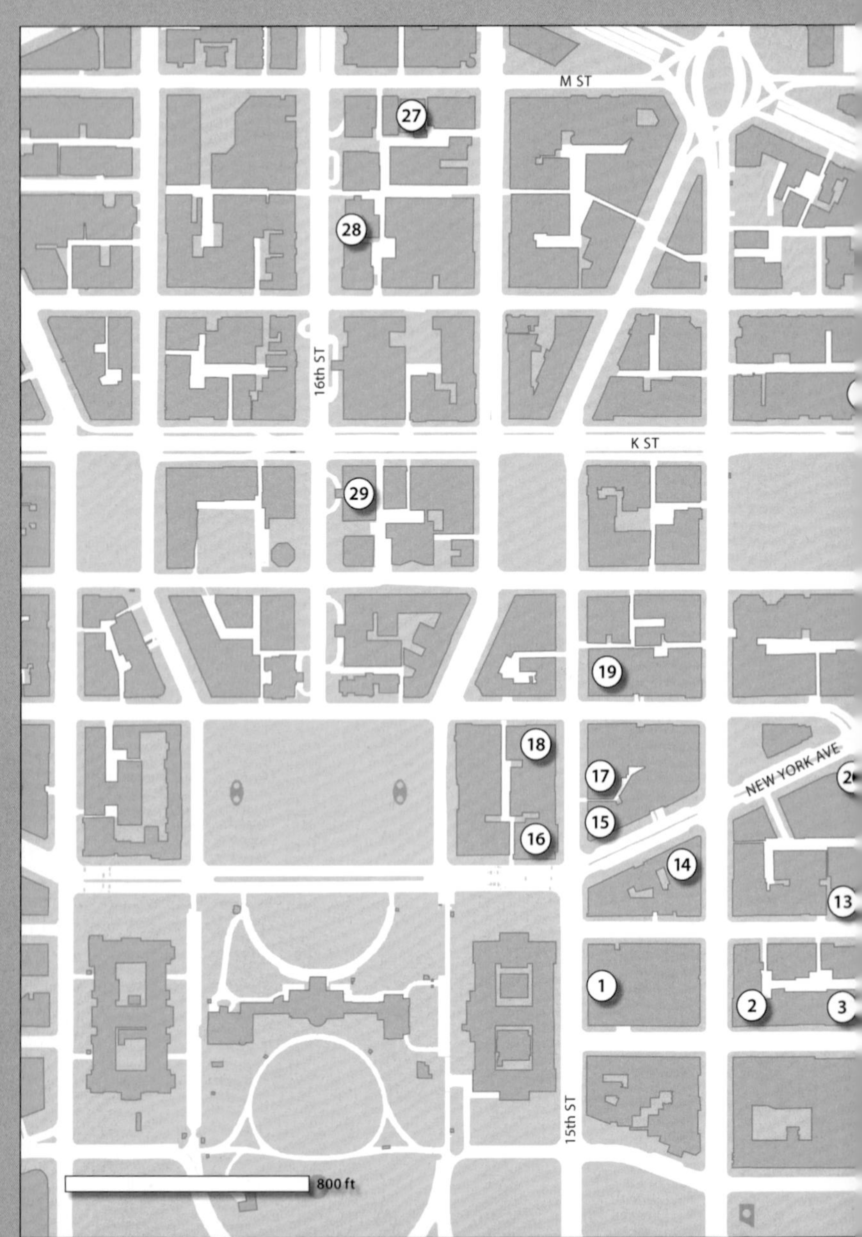

M ST
27
28
16th ST
K ST
29
19
18
17
15
16
NEW YORK AVE
14
13
1
2
3
15th ST
800 ft

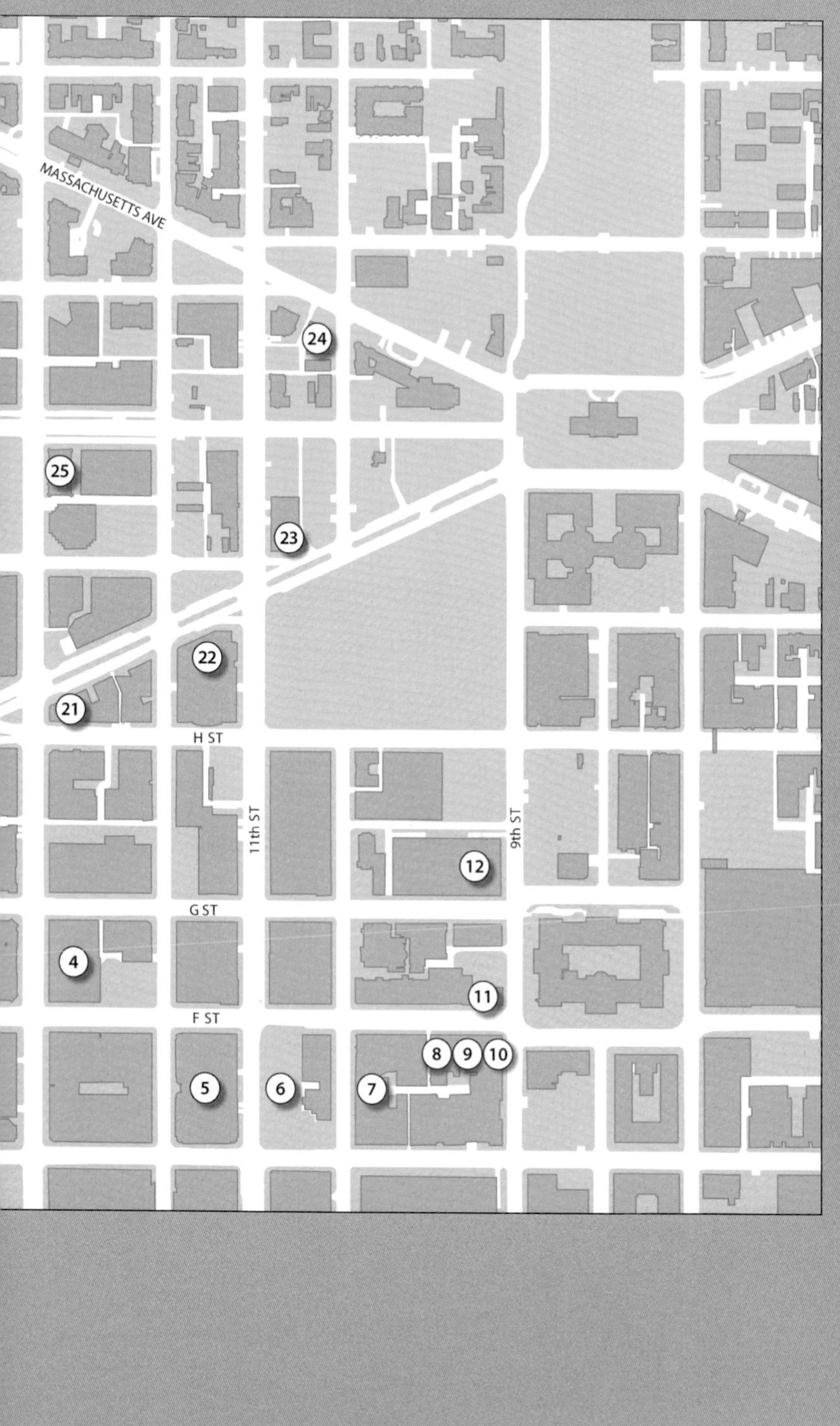

MASSACHUSETTS AVE
H ST
11th ST
9th ST
G ST
F ST
24
25
23
22
21
12
4
11
8
9
10
5
6
7

G1 Metropolitan Square

655 15th Street, NW

1986—VLASTIMIL KOUBEK; Consulting architects: SKIDMORE, OWINGS & MERRILL

For nearly 185 years, the northeast corner of 15th and F streets was occupied by the unassuming but ultra-historic Rhodes Tavern. Opened in 1801, the tavern had served, in effect, as Washington's first town hall, providing a venue for numerous meetings that helped to shape the nascent capital. Shortly thereafter, it housed the rather optimistically named Bank of the Metropolis and, much later, the National Press Club. Having survived the British invasion in 1814 and several construction booms in the late 19th and 20th centuries, the tavern ultimately succumbed in 1984 to make way for the Metropolitan Square project despite fierce opposition from local preservationists. Although the Rhodes was lost, the mixed-use mega-building erected on the site does incorporate façades of several other historic structures, including the National Metropolitan Bank (1907—B. Stanley Simmons; Gordon, Tracy and Swartout) and the Keith-Albee Building (1912—Jules Henri de Sibour), which once contained a 1,838-seat theater, shops, and Turkish baths.

G2 Westory

607 14th Street, NW

1908—HENRY L. A. JECKEL
1990—Renovation and addition: SHALOM BARANES ASSOCIATES; Preservation architects: OEHRLEIN & ASSOCIATES ARCHITECTS
2003—Addition: SHALOM BARANES ASSOCIATES

The new part of this complex facing 14th Street was originally conceived as an addition to the historic National Bank of Washington building at the corner of 14th and G, and was intended to serve as the bank's headquarters, but the company declared bankruptcy before the project got under way. At that point, the project morphed into a speculative commercial development, executed in two phases, which are clearly legible along the F Street façade. At the corner of 14th and F is the original building (with an addition on top); immediately to its east is part of the 1991 addition, designed as an abstraction of the older structure; and following that is the newest addition, which is an abstraction of the abstraction. Note the lions' heads just below the cornice at the seventh floor of the original building.

G3 The Sun Building

1317 F Street, NW

1886—ALFRED B. MULLETT
1983—Restoration: ABEL & WEINSTEIN

Most people would be surprised to hear the word *skyscraper* applied to any structure in Washington, D.C., yet some sources proclaim this building to be the oldest skyscraper in the world. The argument is as follows: it's tall (by 19th-century standards); it contains usable space (as opposed to towers built solely for ornamental or utility purposes); it has a metal structural frame; it is served by an elevator; and all of the earlier buildings that met those criteria (such as the

Home Insurance Building in Chicago, finished in 1885) have been demolished. Ergo, it's the oldest skyscraper still standing.

The problem is that a clear determination of the "first" or "oldest" skyscraper is nearly impossible. Even if everyone could agree on a standard set of criteria for a skyscraper, there was no single building that suddenly met them all perfectly. Regardless, applying the label to this building is a stretch (forgive the pun), since it's really not especially tall, even by the standards of the day (it is about 120 feet high, while the original Home Insurance Building was 180 feet high, and New York already had several taller towers by then). Admittedly, the Sun Building initially sported a pointed spire atop the central dormer, but it was purely ornamental and did not add much to the building's height.

Superlative labels aside, it is an elegantly composed building made of high-quality materials, with limited but effective decoration. Built for *The Baltimore Sun* newspaper, it has a single major façade of rough-hewn granite, with windows, dormers, and projecting bays framed by simple blocks of smooth stone. It was designed by Alfred B. Mullett after he left his position as supervising architect of the Treasury.

G4 Homer Building

601 13th Street, NW

1914—APPLETON P. CLARK JR.
1990—Addition: SHALOM BARANES ASSOCIATES; Preservation architects: OEHRLEIN & ASSOCIATES ARCHITECTS

Appleton Clark anticipated that his original four-story, terra cotta-faced building would eventually be expanded vertically, and so he designed the structure to support the weight of additional stories. As it turned out, however, by the time the addition was finally commissioned many decades later, a Metro line had been constructed beneath the building, posing unanticipated engineering challenges. As a result, an entirely new structural system was required to support the upper floors, and ultimately only the façades of the original building were retained.

G5 555 12th Street, NW

1995 (second phase: 1998)—FLORANCE EICHBAUM ESOCOFF KING ARCHITECTS

In the wake of the postmodern movement, many architects grappled with the question of how to introduce ornament to modern buildings without it looking cheap or simply extraneous. In the case of 555 12th Street, the architects' efforts in that regard were quite successful. Here, all of the decorative elements—including spandrel panels, grilles, canopies, colonnettes resting on the black granite base, and even the door hardware—appear to be holistically conceived, carefully detailed, and well made. As with some roughly contemporaneous buildings by this architecture firm (previously Keyes Condon Florance, and now part of SmithGroup), the effect is reminiscent of the work of the Viennese Secession, which makes sense, as that movement produced buildings that represented a comfortably ornamented modernism.

G6 Lincoln Square

555 11th Street, NW

2001—HARTMAN-COX ARCHITECTS; Preservation architects: OEHRLEIN & ASSOCIATES ARCHITECTS

Hartman-Cox incorporated portions of more than a half-dozen small commercial structures into a new, 12-story building that appears symmetrical from 11th Street but actually has an extra wing on the south end. The newly constructed portions are modest but well proportioned, with fenestration patterns distilled from those commonly found in the existing buildings. The choice of the pale brick for the new skin was clever—it is, of course, compatible with all of the historic buildings' materials, but it not quite the same color as any of them, allowing each of them to read as a distinct structure. The east façade has a surprisingly high-quality finish for the rear of a building facing the middle of a city block.

Across E Street from Lincoln Square is 1001 Pennsylvania Avenue, designed a few years earlier by the same architecture firm, and exhibiting a similar incorporation of smaller, historic buildings. Note the stepped forms that reflect the shift in scale from Pennsylvania Avenue, the only street in the city on which the maximum height is 160 feet (the norm in commercial districts is 130), to the lower-rise surrounding streets.

G7 Ford's Theatre

511 10th Street, NW

1863—JAMES J. GIFFORD
1894—Alterations: ARCHITECT UNKNOWN
1968—MACOMBER & PETER; Restoration: WILLIAM HAUSSMAN
2009—Restoration: ASD

Tel: (202) 426-6924
www.fordstheatre.org

Impresario John T. Ford arrived in town in 1861, flush from a string of successes at Baltimore's Holliday Street Theatre. He began building this theater in 1863 and seemed destined to repeat his Baltimore triumphs until April 14, 1865, when real-life tragedy struck as John Wilkes Booth shot President Lincoln in one of the theater's boxes. After the assassination, the federal government leased the building and then bought it outright, converting it to offices for the War Department. In 1893, the interior collapsed, killing or injuring dozens of government clerks. At that point, the building was relegated to use as a storage facility for government documents, until being transferred to the National Park Service in 1932. It was finally restored to theater use in the 1960s. The government still owns the building, which includes a small museum in the basement as well as the Petersen House, directly across 10th Street at #516, where the wounded president was carried and soon died.

The façade of the theater today looks much as it did in 1865, with a stucco-covered ground floor and a brick wall with simple pilasters above. The block of 10th Street on which the theater stands is noteworthy as one of the most eclectic ensembles in downtown Washington, including, on the east side of the street, a small Second Empire commercial structure and a stolid, early 20th-century office building, and, on the west side, everything from a former 1950s waffle shop, to a sleek Art Moderne building, to a brand-new glass-and-steel tour bus facility by Shalom Baranes Associates. (If the commercial real estate market is booming again by the time this book is published, a few of those buildings may have been demolished or moved to make way for new developments.)

G8 National Union Building

918 F Street, NW

1890—GLENN BROWN
Numerous alterations: ARCHITECTS UNKNOWN
2001—Renovation: ERIC COLBERT & ASSOCIATES

This brawny Romanesque Revival building is an outstanding example of the small commercial structures built in downtown Washington in the late 19th and early 20th centuries. It was designed by Glenn Brown, longtime chief executive of the AIA, whose own architectural practice was housed here until 1905. The main façade of the six-story building is divided into three distinct but complementary two-story sections. The middle section is unusual, with corner piers composed of multiple colonnettes, a curving band at mid-level, and five small Corinthian columns in front of the bay window on each floor. An even more unusual feature of the building is the series of five-story bay windows suspended over the alley, designed to bring extra light and air to the individual offices on the upper levels.

The architects for the 2001 renovation found much of the building's interior intact, including an open-cage elevator that was still being operated by an attendant. Wrapping around the elevator cage was the long, narrow building's only stair. Adding another stair was unfeasible, and the architects were determined to preserve both the old elevator and the existing, open staircase, so they negotiated a solution with the fire marshal that included highly sensitive smoke alarms and automatic door closers at the landings of the staircase. They also oversaw the sensitive conversion of the historic, manual elevator to an automatic version.

A few doors down from 918 F are the remnants of the Atlantic Building at 930 F Street, built around the same time and in a similar style. All but the façade of that building was demolished when the new complex behind it was built. The Atlantic Building was the original home of the legendary 9:30 Club (the name of which was derived from the address), an important venue for hardcore punk and other musical performances in the 1980s and early 1990s, before it moved to V Street, NW.

G9 The Ventana

912 F Street, NW

2006—SHALOM BARANES ASSOCIATES

A slender, Miesian tower reaches out to the street line, quietly announcing the presence of this surprisingly large residential building, most of which is deep within the block. The project incorporates the restored façades of three small, historic buildings, elements of which were salvaged and reinstalled in new structures that replicate the scale and massing of the originals. The tall, narrow wing adjacent to the street contains flats, while the bulkier, mid-block core mostly consists of duplex units, which maximize access to natural light—an important consideration, since many of the apartments face an alley.

G10 Courtyard by Marriott

(Riggs National Bank)
900 F Street, NW

1891—JAMES G. HILL
1912—Interior renovation: ARCHITECT UNKNOWN
1927—Addition: ARTHUR HEATON
1998—Renovation: GORDON & GREENBERG ARCHITECTS

The robust granite façades of this former bank building recall the commercial architecture of late 19th-century Chicago. Notice the alternating courses of narrow and wide stones, a subtle trick that manages to lend the building a surprising degree of delicacy despite its heaviness. Along the F Street face, the vertical line

between the original building and the addition is quite clear thanks to a noticeable change in color. The ornate banking hall and related spaces on the main floor have been respectably restored, though in their adaptation to new uses (as the dining room of a high-volume chain restaurant and common spaces for an ordinary chain hotel), they have certainly lost much of their luster.

G11 Old Masonic Temple

9th and F streets, NW

1870—CLUSS AND KAMMERHUEBER
c. 1921—Alterations: ARCHITECT UNKNOWN
1992—Restoration: OEHRLEIN & ASSOCIATES ARCHITECTS
2000—Renovation and new building: MARTINEZ & JOHNSON; Interiors: VOA ASSOCIATES
2001—Leadership Training Hall in original building: VOA ASSOCIATES

President Andrew Johnson, a loyal Freemason, laid the cornerstone and led the parade that celebrated the start of construction of this Masonic Temple.

The design is essentially Italianate, with a strong cornice and heavy pediments or arches over the windows, but it surely would be labeled Second Empire instead if the mansard roof that the architects originally planned had been executed. In its prime the building accommodated much Gilded-Age revelry: Washingtonians fêted the Prince of Wales here in 1876 at a U.S. centennial banquet, and for decades society matrons fought for the honor of having their daughters' debutante parties here. The Masons moved out in 1908, to be replaced in 1921 by Lansburgh's Furniture Store, which remained until the late 1970s. The elegant building was later abandoned for many years until it was restored in conjunction with the construction of the adjacent structure on 9th Street. The Gallup Organization now occupies both structures, and uses the grand Masonic hall on the second floor of the original building for meetings and ceremonial events.

G12 Martin Luther King Jr. Memorial Library

901 G Street, NW

1972—OFFICE OF LUDWIG MIES VAN DER ROHE
2009—Interior alterations: BELL ARCHITECTS

Tel: (202) 727-0321
www.dclibrary.org/mlk

Washington's central public library is the city's only work by modernist master Ludwig Mies van der Rohe, though it was executed posthumously. The key elements are all classically Miesian, including a structural frame of dark steel, equally dark tinted windows, and large panels of buff brick. For decades, the building suffered from its adjacency to an unpleasant and ill-conceived "pedestrian mall" that occupied the 900 block of G Street. Now that vehicular traffic has been restored to the block, the library seems to have greater potential, though its future is uncertain. Some city officials have advocated the construction of a new, state-of-the-art central library on a different site, which likely would entail the sale of this building to a commercial developer for some undetermined use (unless the District government could figure out something else to do with it). Other civic leaders argue that the current building could be modernized easily—Mies, after all, strove to create easily adaptable "universal space"—yielding an equally state-of-the-art facility. Whatever becomes of the building, one hopes that the desolate outdoor space at its base will be filled with a sidewalk café or some other people-friendly use.

G13 The Church of the Epiphany

1317 G Street, NW

1844—JOHN C. HARKNESS
1857—Addition: AMMI BURNHAM YOUNG
1874—Renovation: HENRY DUDLEY
1892—Addition: EDWARD J. NEVILLE-STENT
1911, 1922—Additions: FREDERICK H. BROOKE
1968—Renovation: ARCHITECT UNKNOWN

Covered in an icing of white stucco, this church is interesting primarily as a reminder of the architectural scale and character that defined the center of antebellum Washington. The interior is a picturesque affair in English Gothic Revival, notable for its hammer-beam ceiling.

G14 Bond Building

14th Street and New York Avenue, NW

1901—GEORGE S. COOPER
1986—Renovation and additions: SHALOM BARANES ASSOCIATES

The renovation of the Bond Building was one of the harbingers of the rebirth of Washington's old downtown. It was among the first commercial projects in the area to include the construction of a new "hat"—that is, the addition of several floors on top in order to fill out the maximum volume allowable under current zoning regulations. The project also incorporated two narrow "bookend" additions whose façades were modeled after a slender building at #19 Lincoln's Inn Fields in London, which is depicted in a book that architect Shalom Baranes keeps in his library.

Other downtown buildings that were expanded vertically during the 1980s and 1990s include the Army-Navy Building at the southeast corner of Farragut Square, also by Baranes, and the Colorado Building at the northeast corner of 14th and G, by KressCox Associates.

G15 SunTrust Bank

(National Savings and Trust Company)
1445 New York Avenue, NW

1888—JAMES T. WINDRIM
1916, 1925, 1985—Additions: VARIOUS ARCHITECTS
2008—Renovation of public spaces: FOX ARCHITECTS

Dark red brick, a copper-clad corner bay, ornamental terra cotta panels, and funny little roof pinnacles make this building a foil to the more staid neoclassical structures on the other three corners of this intersection. A series of additions along New York Avenue spanning many decades remained true to the original building's aesthetic, despite shifts in construction technology and performance expectations. Step inside the corner entrance to get a glimpse of the elegant banking hall.

G16 Bank of America / PNC Bank

15th Street and Pennsylvania Avenue, NW

1902—1503 Pennsylvania: YORK & SAWYER
1905—1501 Pennsylvania: YORK & SAWYER
1924—Addition to 1503 Pennsylvania: APPLETON P. CLARK JR.
1932—Renovation of 1501 Pennsylvania: ARCHITECT UNKNOWN
1986—Restoration of banking hall at 1503 Pennsylvania: JOHN BLATTEAU

These two adjoining bank buildings, though modestly sized, enjoy one of the most prestigious conceivable locations for such institutions—directly across the street from the U.S. Treasury. Built for two different clients in three phases, they were designed in such a harmonious fashion that they are often mistaken as one structure. The first building completed was the pedimented section with two Ionic columns *in antis,* at 1503 Pennsylvania Avenue. It was built for the venerable Riggs National Bank. Riggs originally occupied an older building at the corner, but sold that site to the forerunner of the American Security Bank, which then built the corner building still standing today. In 1924, Riggs added the narrow wing immediately to the west of its original building.

American Security, which occupied the corner building for decades before being absorbed by another bank, used the slogan "When you need a bank for your money, bank with the bank that's *on* the money." The slogan referred to the fact that, on the back of the old $10 bill, the engraving of the Treasury Building included a glimpse of the private bank's flagship facility across the street.

G17 Folger Building and Playhouse Theater

725-727 15th Street, NW

1907—Folger Building: JULES HENRI DE SIBOUR; Playhouse Theater: PAUL PELZ
1985—Addition: MARIANI & ASSOCIATES

Built for a brokerage firm, the Folger Building is small but quite lavish, with gleaming white marble and an exuberant Second Empire crown. Next to it stands the former entrance to the Playhouse Theater, which now serves as the base for a stark, modern addition.

G18 American Bar Association

(Union Trust Building)
740 15th Street, NW

1907—WOOD, DONN & DEMING
1927—Addition: WALTER G. PETER, IN ASSOCIATION WITH A. B. MULLETT & CO.
1983—Renovation and expansion: KEYES CONDON FLORANCE ARCHITECTS

The "UT" crests in the pediments over the ground-floor windows are reminders of this building's original owner, the Union Trust Bank. This is, in fact, a classic early 20th-century bank building, employing a grand, neoclassical vocabulary, fine materials, and impressive massing to convey a sense of stability and rectitude (rental income from office space on the upper floors helped pay for that grandeur). Note the different treatment of the 15th Street and H Street façades on the third through seventh levels: facing 15th the wall is set back behind the massive Corinthian columns and finished in dark cast iron, while on H Street, the wall engages the columns and is finished in matching granite. The odd asymmetry of the ground floor along H Street is the result of the 1927 addition, which doubled the length of that façade, though on the upper levels, the original and the addition are seamlessly matched. A penthouse that was part of the 1980s addition is set back from the building edge and is visible only from a distance.

A small, new office building next door at 1510 H Street (2009—Eric Colbert & Associates) is an interesting example of an attempt to relate simultaneously to dramatically contrasting neighbors on either side. The use of limestone and the balance of horizontal and vertical elements recall the materials and composition of the Union Trust Building, while the tautness and proportions of the curtain wall seem more compatible with the red brick, John Carl Warnecke-designed building to the west [see H4].

G19 Southern Building

805 15th Street, NW

1914—DANIEL BURNHAM AND ASSOCIATES
1986—Restoration and addition: SHALOM BARANES ASSOCIATES; Preservation architects: OEHRLEIN & ASSOCIATES ARCHITECTS

Elaborate terra cotta ornament, including lions' heads poking out from the spandrel panels, contrasts with the plain, buff brick piers of this elegant building by Daniel Burnham. In adding another of his archetypal "hats," Shalom Baranes found justification for the scale and detailing of the addition in several little-known drawings of Burnham's showing designs for mid-rise buildings with two stories above the main cornice line.

G20 Inter-American Development Bank

1300 New York Avenue, NW

1985—SKIDMORE, OWINGS & MERRILL
2004—Addition / conference center: RTKL ASSOCIATES

This project helped to define an emerging Washington "school" of architecture in the mid-1980s, classical in spirit if not in literal detail. The façades are articulated in ways that indirectly evoke common classical motifs, though expressed abstractly and at greatly enlarged scale: recessed bays on the fourth through ninth floors are set behind paired columns that give the impression of a colossal colonnade (compare this, for example, to the façade of the American Bar Association Building [see G18]); the eighth-floor windows are bracketed to suggest huge dentils; and the upper two stories are finished in a darker material and a different fenestration pattern, creating a hint of a giant cornice. An enormous arch announces the main entrance, which leads to a surprisingly large and lush atrium.

G21 National Museum of Women in the Arts

(Masonic Temple)
New York Avenue and 13th Street, NW

1908—WOOD, DONN & DEMING
1987—Renovation: KEYES CONDON FLORANCE ARCHITECTS; Interiors: CAROL LASCARIS
1997—Addition: RTKL ASSOCIATES

Tel: (202) 783-5000
www.nmwa.org

The Masons originally occupied a temple at 9th and F streets [see G11], but when their growing numbers rendered that building inadequate, they hired Waddy Wood's firm to design this much larger structure, which originally included an auditorium on the first floor, with offices, lodge rooms, a library, and a shrine on the upper levels. The identity of the

building's original owner is evident in various decorative motifs, such as stone calipers on the keystones above the fourth-floor windows and other common Masonic symbols. The first-floor auditorium was leased out as a commercial vaudeville and movie theater for most of the period between 1908 and 1983 (during a few of the later years it was a porno house). In 1983, the newly formed National Museum of Women in the Arts bought the building and initiated a complete renovation. The old auditorium was converted into the great hall, a special event space lined with faux marble panels in an attempt to achieve elegance on a limited budget.

G22 1100 New York Avenue

(Old Greyhound Bus Station)

1940—WILLIAM S. ARRASMITH / WISCHMEYER, ARRASMITH & ELSWICK
1991—Restoration: VITETTA GROUP; New building: FLORANCE EICHBAUM ESOCOFF KING ARCHITECTS

The dozens of terminals built by the Greyhound Bus company in the 1930s and 1940s in cities across the country constituted one of the greatest series of Art Moderne buildings in the world. Many of these stations, of which few remain, were designed by Louisville-based architect William Arrasmith. For the Washington terminal, Arrasmith adapted his Art Moderne vocabulary to the capital's conservative architectural culture, avoiding the striking asymmetry and bold colors that often characterized his work, and using such typical Washington materials as limestone and terra cotta for the façade.

The terminal, once known as the "Ellis Island of Washington" since it had welcomed so many African Americans moving from the South, was covered in cheap sheet metal in the mid-1970s, but fortunately, the original structure remained essentially undamaged beneath the crude cloak. It was restored to its sleek glory when the large office building, whose design is inspired by the Art Moderne terminal, was built behind it. The New York Avenue façade of the new building, like that of the terminal itself, initially appears to be symmetrical, but the eastern part of the façade curves away to follow the bend in the street. A close look reveals that the stone skin gradually gets lighter in color as the building rises.

G23 1099 New York Avenue

2008—THOMAS PHIFER AND PARTNERS

From a few blocks away, this appears to be a fairly typical glass box. Upon approach, however, one gradually realizes that the building's skin is no ordinary curtain wall. The glass panes overlap, like shingles or scales on a fish, clearly articulating each floor and adding a subtle three-dimensionality to the façades. The individual panes—with a low-emissivity coating to reduce solar heat gain—are affixed with structural silicone sealant on all four sides, and supported by cast stainless steel brackets that are barely noticeable (the architects worked hard on the bracket design to make sure that would be the case). Clear glass panes continue above the roof-

line, providing a parapet around the roof deck, while at the base, variations on the façade treatment call attention to the building entrances. The lobby is a minimalist space rendered vibrant by a backlit installation by artist Matthew Ritchie.

G24 Cato Institute

1000 Massachusetts Avenue, NW

1993—HELLMUTH, OBATA + KASSABAUM
2012—Renovation and addition: GENSLER

One of the most purely geometrical responses to the irregular intersections characteristic of L'Enfant's plan, the Cato Institute building, which houses a libertarian think tank, looks a bit like a three-dimensional puzzle. The atrium breaks away from the main body of the building to align with Massachusetts Avenue, while the masonry block containing offices is oriented to the rectilinear street grid. Subtle architectural details add interest—note the asymmetrical motifs at the intersections of the metal grid enclosing the atrium and the overlapping geometries in the window patterns of the main block. The new addition is clad in white metal panels that contrast with the ruddy masonry but relate to the metal frame of the atrium.

G25 Franklin School

13th and K streets, NW

1869—ADOLF CLUSS
1992—Exterior restoration: OEHRLEIN & ASSOCIATES ARCHITECTS

The notion of the District of Columbia Public Schools being touted as a paradigm for the world seems farfetched today, yet that was precisely the case in 1873, when the school system received a "Medal for Progress" at the Vienna Exposition. The primary reason for the award was the design of the Franklin School, which was represented in the exposition by a high-quality scale model. It caused a sensation, inspiring educators from all over Europe to make detailed notes and sketches in the hope of emulating the school's progressive features. Interest in the project extended to as far away as Brazil, Argentina, and Japan.

Designed by German American architect Adolf Cluss, the building expanded upon and perfected innovations he had introduced in an earlier school (now demolished). In plan, the Franklin School consisted of three principal bays running the width of the structure and separated by circulation zones. On the first and second floors, each bay was divided into two classrooms back to back. To ensure sound isolation and cleanliness, each classroom was separated from the corridor by a cloakroom. Immediately behind the cloakroom wall was a raised platform for the teacher's desk, sitting in front of a curved niche that helped to focus sound. Boys and girls entered through separate doors and were sequestered throughout the day—each classroom in the middle bay could be assigned either to girls or to boys as necessary. The third floor included a thousand-seat auditorium along with separate spaces for "the two grammar schools." Large windows brought abundant natural light into all of the learning spaces.

The exterior of the school is typical of the German *Rundbogenstil,* or "round arch style," perhaps showing some Second Empire influence in the mansard roof and even a hint of Indian architecture in the cupolas crowning the octagonal towers that originally served as ventilation shafts (the bell towers, the large dormer window, and the caps on the slender chimneys all had been removed but were replicated as part of the restoration in the early 1990s). The building's careful composition, high-quality materials, and fine details, both inside and out, reflected a very deliberate effort to demonstrate to students the value of beauty. It is a lesson that, sadly, has been forgotten all too often in schools and other works of public architecture.

The Franklin School housed the school system's administrative headquarters for many years and more recently served as a homeless shelter. As of this writing, the building sits empty, and its future is unclear.

G26 One Franklin Square

1301 K Street, NW

1990—Design architects: HARTMAN-COX ARCHITECTS; Architects of record: DEWBERRY & DAVIS / HABIB; Preservation of Almas Temple: OEHRLEIN & ASSOCIATES ARCHITECTS

Washington's famous building height limit has always allowed certain exceptions, such as ornamental "spires, towers, domes, minarets, [or] pinnacles." One Franklin Square was among the first late 20th-century commercial buildings to take advantage of that loophole. Known colloquially as the "Twin Peaks" building, it recalls the stepped massing of 1920s New York skyscrapers. To make room for the new building, the historic Almas Temple (1930—Allen Hussell Potts) was dismantled and reconstructed slightly to the west, in a project supervised by Oehrlein & Associates. Only one piece out of more than 7,000 was lost in this move.

During the period of the old downtown's decrepitude, the area around Franklin Square was the city's pornography and prostitution headquarters (one longtime porn shop in the area bore a sign that proudly identified the propri-

etors as "Purveyors of Fine Smut"). In the 1990s, however, commercial developers succeeded where the Metropolitan Police had consistently failed, and soon the sex workers were supplanted by lawyers and lobbyists.

G27 Metropolitan A.M.E. Church

1518 M Street, NW

1886—SAMUEL MORSELL (WITH GEORGE DEARING)
1924—Renovation: JOHN A. LANKFORD
1994, 1998—Renovations and expansion: BAKER COOPER & ASSOCIATES

This church, known as the National Cathedral of African Methodism, is a noteworthy example of red brick, Gothic Revival architecture. Its numerous stained glass windows depict milestones in the growth of the A.M.E. church during the 19th century. Tracing its roots to the founding of the Union Bethel A.M.E. Church in 1838, Metropolitan played a significant role in the abolition of slavery and in the 20th-century civil rights movement. It was also the site of Frederick Douglass's funeral in 1895.

G28 Russian Embassy

(Pullman House)
1119–1125 16th Street, NW

1910—NATHAN C. WYETH
c. 1915—Addition: ARCHITECT UNKNOWN
1934—Remodeling: EUGENE SCHOEN AND SONS
1977—Addition: ARCHITECT UNKNOWN

Harriet Sanger Pullman, whose husband invented the railroad sleeping car, commissioned this mansion for her daughter and son-in-law, Illinois Congressman Frank Lowden. The design of the house is ostensibly based on French Baroque models, with its simple, horizontally striated ground floor and, of course, its mansard roof, but the composition is idiosyncratic and does not correspond to any specific historical period or style. Seen today, the house is distinguished, curiously enough, by the two narrow bands of patinated copper at the top and bottom of the mansard—these thin, horizontal accents provide a subtle but significant counterpoint to the steepness of the roof.

Health problems kept Lowden from running for re-election in 1910, so in 1913 Mrs. Pullman sold the house to the wife of a wealthy mining engineer, who sold it to the Russian government a few months later for a tidy profit. The Russians soon added the two-story wing to the south of the main house. Following the 1917 revolution, caretakers occupied the building until the United States officially recognized the Soviet Union in 1933, at which point a modest remodeling of the building ensued. The Soviets moved most diplomatic operations to a huge new chancery complex on Wisconsin Avenue in the 1980s, retaining this as the ambassador's residence. Both properties passed to the new Russian government following the dissolution of the Soviet Union in 1991.

G29 St. Regis Hotel

(Carlton Hotel)
923 16th Street, NW

1926—MIHRAN MESROBIAN
1976—Renovation: ARCHITECT UNKNOWN
1988—Renovation: SMITH, SEGRETI, TEPPER, MCMAHON & HARNED
2008—Interior renovation: SILLS HUNIFORD; Restaurant and bar interiors: ROCKWELL GROUP

This elegant hotel was designed in the manner of a late Italian Renaissance *palazzo,* with simple massing, a rusticated base, and strongly articulated quoins at the corners. It is almost a perfectly freestanding block, save for a small commercial structure that adjoins it on the K Street side (a garden separates the hotel from the neighboring building to the south). The relative austerity of the façades is relieved by a parade of arches along the ground floor and elaborate window surrounds on the third and seventh stories. A heavy cornice line above the sixth story gives the impression that the building is shorter and more horizontal than it actually is.

Between 1934 and about 1958, the hotel's interior boasted a dazzling, Art Moderne bar designed by Nat Eastman. Highlights of the bar's design included several enamel-and-metal murals and a neon "fireplace." The star feature, however, was surely the "servidor"—a revolving bar that allowed the bartender to make and serve drinks without being seen by patrons.

Previously known as the Carlton, the hotel was designed by Mihran Mesrobian, a Turkish-born Armenian, who immigrated to the United States in 1921 and became the primary in-house architect for legendary Washington developer Harry Wardman. After Wardman declared bankruptcy in 1930, Mesrobian established his own practice, which produced a variety of residential and commercial work over the ensuing quarter century.

TOUR H

White House / Lafayette Square

Henry Adams, who occupied a grand house overlooking Lafayette Square from 1885 until his death in 1918, wrote that in this neighborhood's early days, "[b]eyond the Square the country began." Adams also wrote that when he moved to the capital city, "No literary or scientific man, no artist, no gentleman without office or employment, had ever lived there. It was rural and its society was primitive. . . . The happy village was innocent of a club. . . . The value of real estate had not increased since 1800, and the pavements were more impassable than the mud."

Indeed, when L'Enfant selected the site for the President's House and the "President's Park" immediately to its north, the area was filled with a flourishing orchard. Construction of what came to be called the Executive Mansion began in 1792, and President and Mrs. John Adams (Henry's great-grandparents) moved into the semi-habitable dwelling in November 1800. Thomas Jefferson, who succeeded Adams in March of the following year, wrote, "we find this a very agreeable country residence . . . free from the noise, the heat, . . . and the bustle of a close-built town," which makes clear how undeveloped Washington was in 1801.

L'Enfant intended that the President's Park serve as an extension of the Executive Mansion grounds, but Jefferson and others with strongly democratic proclivities found such a large lawn uncomfortably imperial. Before long, a new stretch of Pennsylvania Avenue was laid down in front of the mansion, dividing the green space in two and creating the separate square, which was named (informally at first, and later officially) for the Marquis de Lafayette during his triumphant return to Washington in

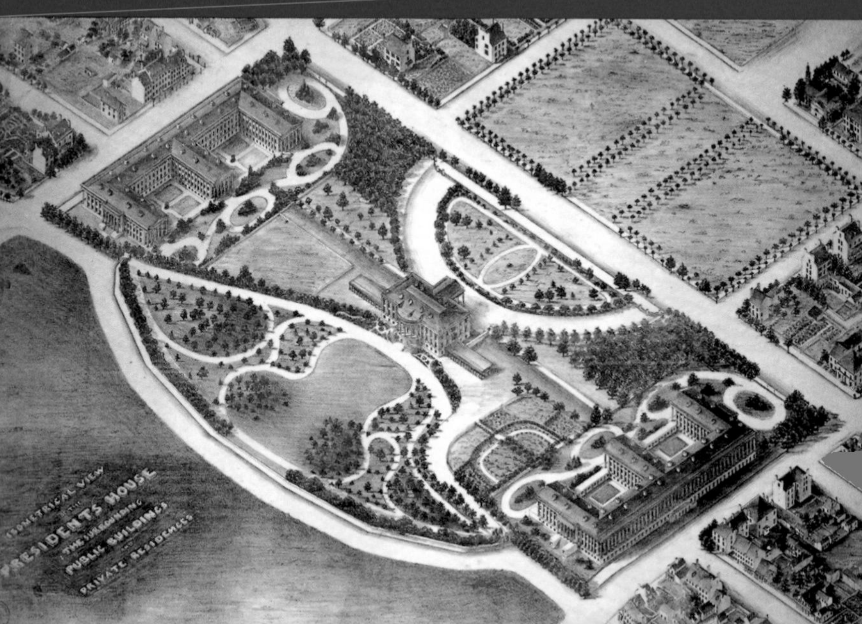

This isometric drawing shows the White House and Lafayette Square sometime before 1851, when the park was landscaped in accordance with plans by Andrew Jackson Downing. The drawing also shows idealized, symmetrical, E-shaped buildings for the War and Navy departments (left) and the Treasury (right).

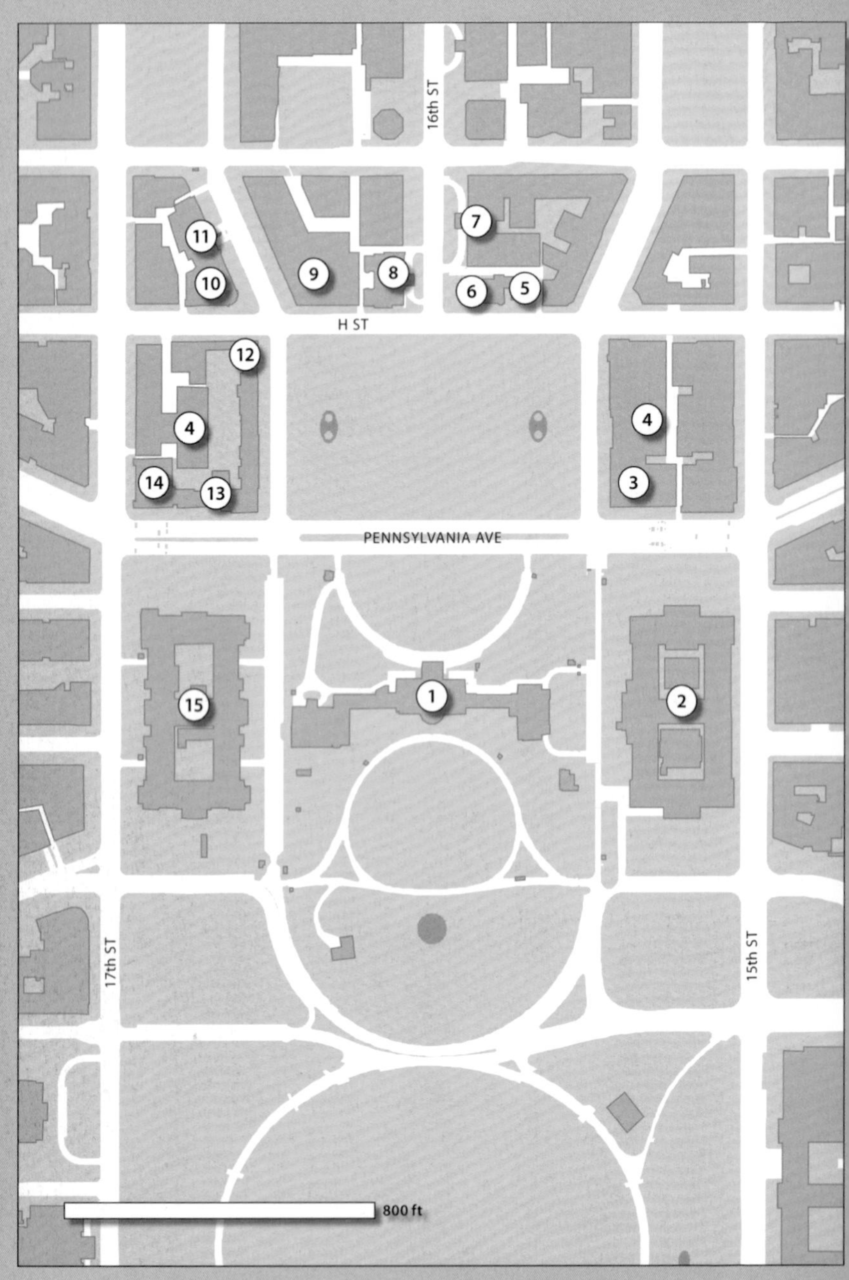
16th ST
H ST
PENNSYLVANIA AVE
17th ST
15th ST
800 ft
1
2
3
4
4
5
6
7
8
9
10
11
12
13
14
15

1824. In 1829, after Andrew Jackson had defeated Henry Adams's grandfather for the presidency, he held boisterous, whiskey-fueled inauguration festivities in the square. During the Civil War, soldiers bivouacked in the park. In the 1870s, Ulysses S. Grant started a small zoo here. By the 1920s, improbably enough, the park—virtually in the shadow of the White House—was firmly established as a safe meeting place for closeted gay men. In the late 20th century, for obvious reasons of visibility, the park had become a popular site for political protests of various kinds.

The Senate Park Commission Plan of 1901–2 envisioned a wholesale reconstruction of Lafayette Square and its adjacent blocks to create a unified enclave of enormous, neoclassical government office buildings, but only two buildings were eventually built in accordance with this plan. In the early 1960s, the character of the square was threatened again, and it was only through the personal and active intervention of Jacqueline Kennedy that the remaining town houses facing the square were saved. Sadly, security concerns following the bombing of the Oklahoma City federal building in 1995 led to the closure of Pennsylvania Avenue in front of the White House to vehicular traffic, and the once-busy thoroughfare suddenly became a rather desolate stretch disfigured by makeshift barriers. A serviceable if bland redesign of the block was finally completed in 2004, and while vehicular traffic is still banned, the appearance of the avenue now at least suggests the hope that it could once again become a vital urban street in some happier, more secure future.

H1 The White House

1600 Pennsylvania Avenue, NW

1792–1803—JAMES HOBAN
1803–14—Renovations and terrace additions: BENJAMIN HENRY LATROBE
1814–17—Reconstruction after fire: JAMES HOBAN
1823, 1830—Portico additions: JAMES HOBAN, BASED ON DESIGNS BY LATROBE
1902—Addition of West Wing and renovation of interior and East Terrace: MCKIM, MEAD & WHITE
1909—Expansion of West Wing: NATHAN C. WYETH
1927—Addition of third floor: WILLIAM ADAMS DELANO
1934—Expansion of West Wing: ERIC GUGLER
1942—Addition of East Wing: LORENZO S. WINSLOW
1948—South Portico balcony: LORENZO S. WINSLOW AND WILLIAM ADAMS DELANO
1949–52—Reconstruction of interior: LORENZO S. WINSLOW
1970—Renovation of West Wing and North Portico: ARCHITECT UNKNOWN

Tel: (202) 456-7041
www.whitehouse.gov

Few buildings are as laden with symbolism as the White House. Its name is invoked to represent the president, as well as his (and, someday, her) administration, and indeed the entire executive branch of the federal government. It is alternately an emblem of national pride and an object of political scorn, which sometimes makes it difficult to appreciate the building itself as a work of architecture.

The White House today seems immutable, yet it reflects more than two centuries of nearly constant alterations and additions. As with the Capitol, the basic design was selected through a competition (and there is evidence that Thomas Jefferson entered and lost the competition under a gentlemanly pseudonym). The winning proposal was submitted by James Hoban, an Irish architect practicing in Charleston, South Carolina, whose somewhat conservative design was inspired by Leinster House in Dublin, Ireland, a mid-18th-century palace that is now home to the Irish Parliament. It is probably not an accident that Hoban chose the less-formal Ionic order instead of the Corinthian used on Leinster House, however, since his design reflected an effort to strike a careful balance between dignity and modesty.

Construction began in the fall of 1792, but the building was still unfinished when the government moved from Philadelphia in November 1800. The first residents, President and Mrs. John Adams, were not impressed by their new accommodations. Abigail wrote to her daughter, complaining, "There is not a single apartment finished. . . . We had not the least fence, yard, or other convenience, without, and the great unfinished audience-room [the East Room] I make a drying room of, to hang up the clothes in." Jefferson displaced the grumbling Adamses in 1801, but he wasn't enamored of the mansion, either, supposedly grousing that it was "big enough for two emperors, one Pope, and the grand lama in the bargain" (some sources attribute the quote to an unnamed satirist instead). A diligent amateur architect, Jefferson designed low pavilions for either side of the main building, moderating the structure's grandeur. He worked in association with the omnipresent Benjamin Henry Latrobe, who humored the president even while quietly dismissing Jefferson's proposals as "a litter of pigs worthy of the great sow it surrounds." Latrobe's own designs for the pavilions were actually built, and several of his other proposals inspired subsequent additions to the mansion.

Set ablaze by the British in August 1814, the Executive Mansion was saved

James Hoban's competition-winning design for the President's House, 1792.

from total destruction by a violent thunderstorm. After the fire, James and Dolley Madison rented the Octagon [see I3], and brought in Hoban to oversee the mansion's restoration. The building received a thick coat of white paint to cover charring from the fire (though it had been whitewashed even before it was finished). It is not known who first called it the "White House," but when Theodore Roosevelt made the name official in 1902 he was merely giving formal sanction to longstanding common usage.

In 1824, Hoban, following Latrobe's plans, added the semicircular South Portico, thereby creating the house's signature façade, which is actually the rear of the building. He added the North Portico a few years later. The interior underwent frequent alterations, but in 1902, Theodore Roosevelt ordered an especially extensive renovation. He brought in McKim, Mead and White to remodel the original building, remove a run of Victorian conservatories, and add the West Wing. The famous Oval Office actually did not appear until the 1909 renovation by Nathan Wyeth, and even then it was not in its current location (it was moved in 1934).

Investigations during Harry Truman's administration revealed that the aging mansion was on the verge of catastrophic structural failure. Although the exterior walls, which were, in one inspector's memorable phrase, standing "purely from habit," were salvaged, little else was—the building was gutted. Steel replaced the crumbling stone and wood structure, and while the original paneling and trim were removed, repaired, and reinstalled, many historic elements were, shockingly, simply discarded. The rooms of the main house are thus largely replicas rather than true originals, but this does not diminish the awe that these historic and venerable spaces inspire in general visitors, foreign dignitaries, and even the families afforded the temporary privilege of calling the White House home.

H2 Treasury Building

1500 Pennsylvania Avenue, NW

1836–42—East and central wings: ROBERT MILLS
1855–64—South and west wings: AMMI B. YOUNG AND ISAIAH ROGERS, BASED ON INITIAL DESIGN BY THOMAS U. WALTER
1866–69—North wing: ALFRED B. MULLETT
1910—Renovation and addition: YORK & SAWYER
1986—East Executive Avenue redesign: ARTHUR COTTON MOORE/ASSOCIATES
1996–2005—Exterior restoration: QUINN EVANS ARCHITECTS; Interior restoration: SHALOM BARANES ASSOCIATES; Historic materials consultants: JOHN MILNER ASSOCIATES; Project management and space planning: MCKISSACK & MCKISSACK

The oldest cabinet-level departmental headquarters, the Treasury Building also represents one of the earliest serious infringements upon L'Enfant's plan. According to legend, it was President Andrew Jackson who, tired of delays in determining the exact site for the building, stood at a spot on the diagonal axis of Pennsylvania Avenue, pounded his cane into the ground, and barked, "Put it here!" Actually, even if the story is true, his choice of location would not have blocked the reciprocal vista between the President's House and the Capitol, since the first wing of the new building did not extend that far south. But indeed, once the inevitable addition was built at that end, one of the most important symbolic features of L'Enfant's design of the city was forever compromised.

The Treasury took more than three decades to build, and reflects the work of several of the country's most important 19th-century architects. Robert Mills was responsible for the original design, which called for an E-shaped plan with the open ends facing the White House. Like the Patent Office [see E10], it was a Greek Revival design, but whereas the former relied on a simple, brawny Doric portico for visual power, the Treasury Building was defined by an audacious, uninterrupted Ionic colonnade running the entire length of the east façade, a distance of 466 feet. The Ionic order is typically more delicate than the Doric in its proportions and details, but when repeated at such scale, the result was a level of grandeur exceeding that of the Patent Office. The main entrance to the building was in the middle of that façade, behind the colonnade, and was reached by a staircase from 15th Street. The interior of Mills's original structure incorporated his signature, brick-vaulted structural system, considered the best defense against the ravages of fire.

Mills oversaw construction of the long spine and the central wing between 1836 and 1842. In 1855, Thomas U. Walter, who was busy at work on the extension of the Capitol, was hired to "complete" Mills's plan. He proposed filling in the open ends of the E-shaped plan to create a large rectangle with a bar across the middle. He also altered Mills's design by adding shallow porticos bracketing the Ionic colonnade along 15th Street, and proposing deep porticos in the centers of the north and south wings, as well as the new west wing facing the White House. As with the Old Patent Office, Walter abandoned Mills's masonry vault system in favor of a cast iron structure. The south and west wings were built, largely according to Walter's design, under Ammi Young in his capacity as supervising architect of the Treasury, and his successor, Isaiah Rogers.

Construction of the north wing was delayed until after the Civil War. In completing it, architect Alfred Mullett respected the precedents set by Mills and Walter on the exterior, but designed the interiors in a much more elaborate, Renaissance Revival vein. The most notable of Mullett's spaces is the capacious Cash Room, which originally served as something like a commercial banking hall. It is lined with seven different types of marble, lit by enormous gilded chandeliers, and surrounded by a balcony with intricate iron railings.

Between 1908 and 1910, the building underwent a renovation that included removal of the entry staircase on 15th Street and replacement of the long row of Ionic columns, which had been built of fragile Aquia sandstone, with more durable granite replicas. In 1996, repairmen accidentally set fire to the roof, and while the building's structure held up well, there was significant water and smoke damage. The incident provided the impetus for a long-overdue renovation that restored the key public spaces and corridors, many of which had been cluttered with haphazard lighting, wiring, and ducts, and created open-plan offices that make the most of the building's unusual structural bays.

H3 Treasury Annex

Madison Place and Pennsylvania Avenue, NW

1919—CASS GILBERT

The Senate Park Commission Plan of 1901–2 called for an enclave of public buildings that would have obliterated all of the row houses surrounding Lafayette Square, and in 1917, Cass Gilbert de-

veloped specific designs for the palatial marble structures the commission envisioned. Only this building and the Chamber of Commerce [see H9] were executed, however. Intended to alleviate the severe overcrowding that was plaguing the main Treasury Building at the time, the annex exudes the sturdy rectitude one would expect given its purpose. While the long, Ionic colonnades on the two exposed elevations are impressive, the lack of a portico on either side is a sign of the building's subordinate status.

H4 Lafayette Square Federal Buildings

Blocks adjacent to Jackson Place and Madison Place, NW

1969—JOHN CARL WARNECKE & ASSOCIATES

Lafayette Square, the pride of 19th-century Washington, lost several of its greatest treasures to 20th-century wrecking balls, yet things could have turned out much worse. A scheme to raze nearly all of the remaining row houses on the square was under consideration again in 1961, when First Lady Jacqueline Kennedy intervened and asked John Carl Warnecke to devise a plan that would save what remained of the historic fabric. Warnecke's solution somehow seemed both radical and sensible at the time—the houses would be preserved while taller, "background" buildings would be built in the houses' back yards. The new buildings (the U.S. Court of Claims to the east and the New Executive Office Building to the west) were intended to relate to the historic houses by virtue of their similar materials, bay windows, and mansard roofs. Unfortunately, as constructed, the buildings are still intrusive, with large, unrelieved, red brick walls, stingy windows, and awkwardly proportioned projecting bays. Still, the essential character of the square, as perceived from street level, was largely preserved—an act of deference, rare at the time, to existing architecture.

H5 St. John's Parish Building

1525 H Street, NW

1837—ARCHITECT UNKNOWN
1854—Renovation: THOMAS U. WALTER
1877—Addition and renovation: ARCHITECT UNKNOWN
1955—Renovation: HORACE PEASLEE

Matthew St. Clair Clarke, once and future clerk of the House of Representatives, began building this house in 1836, but he soon ran into financial trouble and was forced to sign over the property to his bankers. It was subsequently leased to a number of distinguished people, including British diplomats such as Lord

Ashburton and Sir Henry Bulwer (brother of Edward Bulwer-Lytton, the novelist responsible for the infamous opening line, "It was a dark and stormy night . . ."). Originally finished in brick, the house was given a coat of stucco in 1854, along with new, bulky window trim and a heavy cornice. The oversized mansard roof was added in 1877. The American Federation of Labor eventually bought the building and later sold it to St. John's for use as a parish hall.

H6 St. John's Church

16th and H streets, NW

1816—BENJAMIN HENRY LATROBE
1820—Addition: GEORGE BOMFORD
1822—Steeple: ARCHITECT UNKNOWN
1842—Renovation: ARCHITECT UNKNOWN, THOUGH POSSIBLY ROBERT MILLS
1880s—Alterations and addition: JAMES RENWICK JR.
1919—Renovation: MCKIM, MEAD & WHITE
2009—Renovation: BOWIE GRIDLEY ARCHITECTS

Benjamin Henry Latrobe once claimed that this church "made many Washingtonians religious who had not been religious before." It's hard to know whether he was joking or just being arrogant, but regardless, his initial design—a simple, dignified, well-proportioned structure with a plan in the shape of a Greek cross—was surely an impressive sight in 1816 despite its small size. His chaste little chapel did not last long, however, before it began to be altered by a succession of architects, who extended the nave toward 16th Street (creating a more typical, Latin cross plan), added both a portico and a tall steeple, and later replaced clear windows with stained glass, among many other changes. One can, however, sense the original plan while sitting in a pew under the central dome. Known as the "Church of the Presidents," it has hosted every chief executive since Madison. By tradition, pew 54 is reserved for the current president and First Family.

H7 AFL-CIO National Headquarters

815 16th Street, NW

1956—VOORHEES, WALKER, SMITH AND SMITH
1971—Addition: MILLS PETTICORD & MILLS
2002—Renovation: GROUP GOETZ ARCHITECTS (GGA) WITH EHRENKRANTZ ECKSTUT & KUHN ARCHITECTS

An organization hoping to influence federal policy could hardly find a more auspicious site for its headquarters, practically within shouting distance of the White House. The main body of the building is fairly typical of Washington's post-

Rendering of St. John's Church in 1816, the year it was built, with the President's House in the background, still scarred from damage inflicted by the British in the War of 1812.

World War II commercial architecture—essentially a slightly modernized version of the stripped classicism that was so common before the war—but the top is unusual, with barrel-vaulted mechanical penthouses punctuated by perforated stone panels. With the top and bottom floors recessed behind simple colonnades, the effect is somewhat reminiscent of Mussolini-era government buildings in Rome. A skillful 2002 renovation moved the main entrance off center, providing space for conference facilities and a welcoming lobby featuring a stunning restored mosaic that is now visible to passersby. Site improvements yielded a pleasant front yard, with benches and other elements that both enhance building security and provide places for people to take a break or have lunch in nice weather.

H8 Hay-Adams Hotel

800 16th Street, NW

1928—MIHRAN MESROBIAN
1983—Renovation: LEO A DALY
2002—Interior renovation: BBG-BBGM; Interior design: THOMAS PHEASANT
2009—Exterior restoration: HARTMAN-COX ARCHITECTS
2011—Rooftop addition: HARTMAN-COX ARCHITECTS; Interior design: THOMAS PHEASANT

The Hay-Adams Hotel derives its name from two spectacular buildings that, unfortunately, were demolished to make way for it—adjoining houses for John Hay and Henry Adams designed by H. H. Richardson and built in 1885. Mesrobian's hotel is a somewhat stolid but dignified structure, anchored by a slightly rusticated base and heavy

quoins at the corners and along the sides of the projecting central bays (the *porte-cochère* is not original—it was added in 1983). The exterior is loosely derived from Italian Renaissance models, while the interior is more directly inspired by the style of the English Renaissance.

H9 U.S. Chamber of Commerce Building

1615 H Street, NW

1924—CASS GILBERT
1956—Addition: CHATELAIN, GAUGER AND NOLAN
1980—Addition and renovation: JOHN S. SAMPERTON
2010–11—Interior renovations: MORGAN, GICK, MCBEATH AND ASSOCIATES

This and the Treasury Annex [see H3] are the only completed portions of Cass Gilbert's plan to unify the architecture of Lafayette Square in a neoclassical fashion. This particular building replaced a brace of houses owned by several prominent historical figures: Daniel Webster lived at the corner of H Street and Connecticut Avenue, and the adjacent house was home to John Slidell, antebellum congressman from Louisiana, Confederate minister to France, and one half of the "Mason and Slidell Affair," which nearly brought the British into the Civil War on the side of the South.

H10 800 Connecticut Avenue, NW

1993—FLORANCE EICHBAUM ESOCOFF KING ARCHITECTS

This commercial office building strongly evokes the architecture of the Viennese Secession in its basic forms, fenestration, and ornamental details. Given its location amid the centers of political power, the building was conceived with high-powered lobbyists in mind as potential tenants, and the architects therefore sought to provide as many "power perches" as possible, hence the profusion of corner offices and terraces. The upper levels are popular vantage points for television news cameras because of their clear views of the White House.

H11 816 Connecticut Avenue, NW

1987—SHALOM BARANES ASSOCIATES

This elegant, 28-foot-wide sliver borrows a trick from the bay-fronted row houses that characterize many of Washington's residential neighborhoods. The architect obtained permission from the District government for the projection over the sidewalk by arguing that the narrowness of the site created a unique aesthetic opportunity to accentuate the building's verticality. The advantage for the city is a slick exclamation mark that terminates the vista from up 17th Street. Vertical slits lined with glass block and lit from behind emphasize the building's proportions.

H12 Stephen Decatur House Museum

748 Jackson Place, NW (visitor entrance at 1610 H Street, NW)

1819—BENJAMIN HENRY LATROBE
1876—Renovations: ARCHITECTS UNKNOWN
1944—Restoration: THOMAS T. WATERMAN
2004—Restoration of original kitchen: DAVIS BUCKLEY ARCHITECTS AND PLANNERS
2008—Restoration of entry and stair hall: DAVIS BUCKLEY ARCHITECTS AND PLANNERS

Tel: (202) 842-0920
www.decaturhouse.org

The Decatur House was both the first and the last building on Lafayette Square to be occupied as a private residence. Built for Commodore Stephen Decatur, scourge of the Barbary Pirates, and his wife, Susan, the original house was a textbook example of Federal-style archi-

tecture, with restrained details, a flat façade, and carefully considered proportions. A little over a year after the Decaturs moved in, however, Latrobe was dead of yellow fever in New Orleans and the commodore was killed in a duel. Susan Decatur decamped for a smaller house in Georgetown, and rented the Lafayette Square property to a number of prominent residents, including several British, French, and Russian diplomats. The house was the unofficial residence of secretaries of state from 1827 to 1833, as Henry Clay, Martin Van Buren, and Edward Livingston all rented the place during their tenures in that office.

John Gadsby, owner of the Washington Hotel and Gadsby's Tavern in Virginia, bought the house in 1836, and then Western explorer Edward Fitzgerald Beale and his wife, Mary, bought it from Gadsby's heirs in 1872. (It was Beale, then based near San Francisco, who in 1848 galloped east to announce that gold had been discovered at Sutter's Mill.) The Beales embarked on a thorough Victorianization of the chaste old Federal house, and proceeded to throw lavish parties that made it a nexus of social life in the Gilded Age. They left the house to their son, Truxtun, whose widow lived there until she bequeathed it to the National Trust for Historic Preservation in 1956.

In 2010, Decatur House became the site of the National Center for White House History, established by the National Trust and the White House Historical Association. The center promotes research and conducts educational programming related to the history of the White House and Lafayette Square. Restoration of the house is ongoing.

H13 Blair-Lee House

1651–1653 Pennsylvania Avenue, NW

1824—Blair House: ARCHITECT UNKNOWN
1850s—Addition of third and fourth stories and east wing: ARCHITECTS UNKNOWN
1859—Lee House: ARCHITECT UNKNOWN
1931—Blair House restoration: WALDRON FAULKNER
1988—Restoration and addition: MENDEL MESICK COHEN WAITE HALL ARCHITECTS; ALLAN GREENBERG, ARCHITECT

When the U.S. Department of the Interior placed a historical marker at Blair House in 1939, the building became, in effect, the first federally designated historic landmark in the country. In arguing for the marker, the National Park Service noted the building's construction of hand-hewn lumber with handmade nails and hardware. It's a safe bet, however, that Franklin Delano Roosevelt's desire to protect a historic house across the street from the Executive Mansion didn't hurt the nomination.

The original Blair House was built by Surgeon General Dr. Joseph Lovell; its current name came from Francis Preston Blair, who bought it in 1837. Blair was a newspaper editor from Kentucky who helped shape American politics through his influential publications, *The Globe* and *The Congressional Globe.* The house was later occupied by his son, Montgomery Blair, an attorney who represented Dred Scott in the infamous Supreme Court case and served as postmaster general under Lincoln. The adjacent house was built by the senior Blair for his daughter and her husband, Samuel P. Lee, a cousin of Robert E. Lee.

In 1942, as World War II was raging, the federal government bought Blair House to serve as guest quarters for visiting heads of state, and then purchased Lee House next door for the same purpose the following year. According to a story told by Franklin D. Roosevelt Jr., his mother, Eleanor, enthusiastically supported the idea of an official guest house after a late-night encounter with British Prime Minister Winston Churchill, whom she found wandering the halls of the White House in his nightshirt, carrying a cigar, and looking for the president in order to resume a discussion from earlier in the evening. There is also evidence, however, that one reason for buying the property was to avoid potential embarrassment when foreign leaders "of non-Caucasian extraction" came to town, since such visitors might not have been accepted at racially segregated hotels.

From 1948 to 1952, President Harry Truman and his family lived here while the White House underwent major structural renovations. During this time, the Marshall Plan for the reconstruction of postwar Europe was hatched in the Lee House dining room, which served as Truman's cabinet room. In 1950, two Puerto Rican nationalists stormed Blair House in an attempt to assassinate the president. One of the would-be assassins and White House Police Officer Leslie Coffelt were killed in the gunfight on the front sidewalk.

H14 Renwick Gallery of the Smithsonian American Art Museum

(formerly Corcoran Gallery and U.S. Court of Claims)
Pennsylvania Avenue at 17th Street, NW

1861—JAMES RENWICK JR.
1874—Renovation: ARCHITECT UNKNOWN
1972—Exterior restoration: JOHN CARL WARNECKE & ASSOCIATES; Interior restoration and remodeling: HUGH NEWELL JACOBSEN
2000—Renovation of Grand Salon: EHRENKRANTZ ECKSTUT & KUHN ARCHITECTS

Tel: (202) 633-1000
www.americanart.si.edu

William Wilson Corcoran, cofounder of Washington's storied Riggs Bank, commissioned this building as a pub-

lic gallery for his substantial art collection. Construction began in 1859, but when the Civil War broke out, the federal government appropriated the nearly completed building from Corcoran, a southern sympathizer, and used it as a military warehouse and later as the headquarters of Quartermaster General Montgomery C. Meigs. The building was returned to Corcoran in 1869, and he finally opened his museum in 1874 following extensive renovations. The institution moved to a new facility in 1897 [see I5], and in 1899, the U.S. Court of Claims moved in and stayed for 65 years. Fortunately, the Smithsonian then took possession of the building and returned it to museum use, as a branch of the Smithsonian American Art Museum focusing on crafts. It opened to the public in 1972.

The Renwick—probably the only museum named for its architect, rather than its benefactor—imitated the elaborate French Second Empire style, most notably in the characteristic mansard roof. The use of red brick as the primary finish material seems to be a distinctly American touch, however, as are the column capitals bearing ornamental motifs based on tobacco and corn (surely inspired by Latrobe's similar designs at the Capitol). Heavy, vermiculated quoins (with irregular, wormlike patterns etched into the stone) and swags bearing Corcoran's initials add to the liveliness of the façades. The interior is relatively intimate for a museum, though it does boast a quite grand staircase, leading to an equally grand salon with walls intended to be, in the words of E. J. Applewhite, "the color of crushed mulberries."

H15 Dwight D. Eisenhower Executive Office Building

(Old Executive Office Building / State, War, and Navy Building)
Pennsylvania Avenue and 17th Street, NW

1871–88—ALFRED B. MULLETT, WITH WILLIAM POTTER, ORVILLE BABCOCK, AND THOMAS LINCOLN CASEY; Interior engineering and design: RICHARD VON EZDORF
1997–2001—Various interior restoration projects: KEMNITZER, REID & HAFFLER ARCHITECTS; QUINN EVANS ARCHITECTS; EINHORN YAFFEE PRESCOTT; SMITHGROUP
2004–11—Modernization design architects: SMITHGROUP; Architects of record: AECOM

> The transitory taste for French neoclassicism, fostered by the École des Beaux-Arts in Paris, has few more striking expressions.
> —*The WPA Guide to Washington, D.C.*, 1942

Washington's largest Second Empire-style building took 17 years to build, and

when finally finished, it was widely reviled as a symbol of Gilded-Age excess. Its ornate style had fallen out of fashion, and the building's great cost—more than $10 million—was considered scandalous. Henry Adams infamously dubbed it an "architectural infant asylum." Alfred Mullett, who designed the building while serving as supervising architect of the Treasury, resigned his position in 1874, and later committed suicide after unsuccessfully suing the federal government for additional compensation.

The building was repeatedly threatened with radical revisions that seemed almost punitive in spirit. In 1917, the U.S. Commission of Fine Arts asked John Russell Pope to cloak the hulking structure in more orthodox classical garb, and in 1929, after President Herbert Hoover groaned about the "architectural orgy" that loomed over the White House, Waddy Wood was given a similar assignment. Neither Pope's nor Wood's drastic proposal came to pass thanks to a lack of money, but the building's fate was still far from secure. In 1957, a presidential commission recommended total demolition, and it was not until the 1960s that general opinions of the building began to soften.

Built of dense, dark granite from Virginia and Maine, the structure is lined with some 900 columns, accented with dramatically projecting bays, and topped with a steep mansard roof and tall chimneys. Immense and undeniably eccentric, the building managed to survive decades of ignominy and is now, at long last, widely beloved as a welcome exception to the sedate architecture more typical of the nation's capital.

TOUR I

Foggy Bottom

There are various stories about the origins of this neighborhood's moniker, which suggests a dismal fen to be avoided at all costs. Some say the name commemorates the noxious fumes emanating from several now-defunct industries—the Heurich brewery, the city gas plant, and a glass factory—while others believe that it was simply an apt description of a low-lying, marshy area that was often shrouded in fog rolling off the Potomac. Then again, the name may have been a euphemistic reference to the fetid Tiber Canal, which emptied into the river near the neighborhood's southeast corner. By the time the Civil War broke out, the canal had degenerated into an open sewer, swarming with flies and mosquitoes.

Before the establishment of the District of Columbia, part of what is now Foggy Bottom was an inchoate town called Hamburgh, also known as Funkstown, conceived as a kind of suburb to the bustling port of Georgetown. Hamburgh never developed on its own, and its modest street grid was wiped out when L'Enfant's plan was imposed upon the landscape. Currently, Foggy Bottom is known primarily as the seat of the U.S. Department of State and of George Washington University, a growing institution whose facility-related requirements often lead to conflicts with neighbors fearful that what remains of the area's residential character is endangered.

Aerial view of Foggy Bottom, on the far side of the Potomac River, with Roosevelt Island and the Rosslyn area of Arlington, Virginia, in the foreground.

H ST
VIRGINIA AVE
23rd ST
800 ft
18
17
16
15
14
13
12

PENNSYLVANIA AVE
19
1
2
F ST
21st ST
19th ST
4
3
NEW YORK AVE
5
6
17th ST
9
7
C ST
10
8
CONSTITUTION AVE

I1 Office of Thrift Supervision/ Liberty Plaza

1700 G Street, NW

1977—MAX O. URBAHN ASSOCIATES;
Courtyard: SASAKI ASSOCIATES

The present-day architecture buff, weary of the terrorism-inspired paranoia that has rendered many "public" buildings nearly inaccessible, may long for the comparatively halcyon days of 1976. In that year, Congress passed the Public Buildings Cooperative Use Act, which directed the head of the General Services Administration to "encourage the location of commercial, cultural, educational, and recreational facilities and activities within public buildings." This call for the integration of mixed uses into governmental structures was part of a broader initiative intended to break down barriers between federal agencies and the citizens they serve, and to encourage true urban vitality around such facilities.

The building that now houses the Office of Thrift Supervision, which regulates savings banks, was among the first federal projects to reflect this new spirit of openness, accommodating shops and restaurants beneath bureaucratic office space while also meeting increasingly strict energy conservation standards. Architecturally, it is remarkable in its use of a very standard 1970s vocabulary—cylindrical concrete columns, thin concrete slabs, and dark-tinted glass—to create façades of unusual depth and character. This spare vocabulary also alludes, in a highly abstract way, to the multi-columned façades of the Eisenhower Executive Office Building across the street. Perhaps reflecting a lesson learned from the nearby AIA headquarters and its relationship to the Octagon [see I3], the new building wraps around, and is highly deferential to, the historic Winder Building. The courtyard that connects the two, while not exactly festive, is reasonably inviting and successfully draws pedestrians to the commercial establishments within.

I2 Winder Building

600 17th Street, NW

1848—RICHARD A. GILPIN
1930–48—Various renovations: ARCHITECTS UNKNOWN
1975—Restoration: MAX O. URBAHN ASSOCIATES
1990—Exterior restoration: ARCHITRAVE, P.C., ARCHITECTS

It may not look like it now, but when new, the Winder Building was one of the most innovative structures in the city—the first to employ a central heating system and cast iron beams throughout, it was also the tallest (75 feet) and largest (130 rooms) office building in the capital. The building was among the earliest examples of a now-ubiquitous Washington type—speculative office space developed in order to be sold or leased to the federal government. Indeed, the builder, William H. Winder, sold it to the government in 1854, and for much of its history it was used by the Navy, War, and Treasury departments. It now houses the headquarters of the U.S. Trade Representative.

I3 The Octagon

1799 New York Avenue, NW

1802—WILLIAM THORNTON
1817—Alterations: GEORGE HADFIELD
1898—Interior restoration: GLENN BROWN
1911–70—Numerous restoration projects: VARIOUS ARCHITECTS
1989–95—Restoration: MESICK COHEN WAITE ARCHITECTS

The Octagon isn't. In plan, it is actually more like a "pregnant hexagon," in the words of Sherry Birk, former director of the Octagon Museum and Collections. The origins of the misnomer are unclear, but regardless, the building's unusual geometry was an inventive response to the acutely angled site, yielding one of the most distinctive houses of the Federal period in Washington. The plan also allowed for a number of atypical spaces inside the house, including a copious, circular entry hall and an oval stair hall that affords surprisingly vertiginous views between floors. Several doorways in the house are shaped to fit seamlessly within curved walls.

The house was designed by Dr. William Thornton for Colonel John Tayloe III, a scion of one of Virginia's most prominent families. Legend maintains that, on the whole, Tayloe would rather have been in Philadelphia, a much larger and more sophisticated city at the time, but he settled in the new capital at the urging of his friend George Washington. During the British invasion of 1814, Tayloe's wife, who had been at the Octagon alone as the city began to burn, convinced the diplomatic minister of France to occupy the house and fly his country's flag from its roof, most likely saving the structure from the torch. From 1814 to early 1815, James and Dolley Madison lived here while workmen repaired the charred Executive Mansion. In 1815, in the Octagon's second-floor parlor, President Madison signed the Treaty of Ghent, formally ending hostilities with Great Britain, following its ratification by the Senate.

In the mid- to late 19th century, the building had a succession of occupants, including a girls' technical school, and gradually fell into disrepair. The American Institute of Architects (AIA) leased the house as its headquarters beginning in 1898, and soon purchased it outright. The AIA eventually moved into a larger structure next door (which was torn down when the present headquarters was built), and in 1968, the AIA Foundation—later known as the American Architectural Foundation—assumed control of the Octagon and converted it into a historic house museum. In 2010, the property was transferred once again, this time to a new, affiliated organization called AIA Legacy.

14 American Institute of Architects Headquarters

1735 New York Avenue, NW

1973—THE ARCHITECTS COLLABORATIVE
1989—Interior renovation:
MALESARDI + STEINER / ARCHITECTS
1993—Library expansion:
THE ARCHITECTS COLLABORATIVE;
MALESARDI + STEINER / ARCHITECTS

Tel: (202) 626-7300
www.aia.org

In the 1960s, the AIA sponsored a competition for the design of a new headquarters building to be set behind the Octagon. First place went to the entry by Mitchell / Giurgola Architects, which featured an expansive, concave, glass curtain wall stretching almost all the way across its primary façade. A revised version of this design, bolder and more complex, was rejected by the U.S. Commission of Fine Arts, which feared that it would overwhelm the historic house at the corner. Ultimately, Mitchell / Giurgola withdrew from the project, and the institute hired The Architects Collaborative (TAC) to devise a simpler solution, which ultimately won approval from the commission.

TAC's design, with its largely unrelieved ribbons of concrete and dark glass, might be overlooked among the many other 1970s-era structures based on a similar architectural language. The AIA building, however, offers greater visual interest than most of its contemporaries, thanks to the boomerang shape of its plan and the bold, projecting volume in the New York Avenue wing, which houses the boardroom. Originally, the area beneath this projection was a dark, disused corner of the otherwise pleasant courtyard between the new structure and the Octagon, but during the 1993 renovation, this space was enclosed as part of the expansion of the library (it is now used for offices). This change was a great improvement, alleviating the ominousness of the broad overhang and helping to direct visitors to the main entrance just to the left of the new space.

I5 The Corcoran

(Corcoran Gallery of Art / Corcoran College of Art + Design)
500 17th Street, NW

1897—ERNEST FLAGG
1915—Renovation: WADDY B. WOOD
1928—Addition: CHARLES ADAMS PLATT

Tel: (202) 639-1700
www.corcoran.org

Officially established in 1869, the Corcoran Gallery of Art was the first art museum in Washington and one of the first in the nation. It initially occupied the building that is now the Renwick Gallery [see H14], but moved to this location after outgrowing the original facility.

The current Corcoran makes a powerful impression thanks to its closeness to the street, its rusticated base, and its strong horizontal banding, not to mention the pair of lounging lions imperturbably guarding its entrance. The simplicity of the inscription above the doorway—"Dedicated to Art"—only enhances the building's aura of nobility. But the most commanding aspect of the exterior is the broad, blank stone panel between the main floor and the row of attic-level windows (which are actually vents) along the 17th Street façade. The masterful proportions of this panel in relation to the rest of the façade, coupled with the sheer audacity of incorporating such a vast, unadorned surface into an otherwise richly ornamented composition, make the Corcoran one of the most elegant and self-assured buildings in the city.

A skylit atrium, surrounded by a parade of simple, fluted Doric columns on the main floor and Ionic columns on the balcony, is the gallery's primary interior space. Glass panels in the floor, originally intended to bring natural light to art studios in the lower level, add a surprisingly modern touch, especially when lit from below at night, making the entire space feel a bit like a trendy dance club. A grand staircase, flanked by stepped pedestals for the display of sculpture, carries visitors to upper-level galleries.

The northeast corner of the building was originally a two-story, curved room known as the hemicycle, which served as a sort of knuckle connecting the museum to the New York Avenue wing housing the art school. This space was split into two separate levels in 1915, with the lower floor becoming an amphitheater for lectures and the upper floor becoming additional gallery space. A new wing was added along E Street in the 1920s to accommodate a substantial bequest from Montana Senator William A. Clark that included paintings, sculptures, tapestries, and an entire room known as the Salon Doré. Originally part of an 18th-century private residence in Paris, this heavily gilded chamber previously had been dismantled and reinstalled in Clark's mansion in New York.

In 1999, the Corcoran conducted a limited competition for the design of an addition to be built adjacent to the school wing. The winning design, by Frank Gehry, featured the architect's signature billowy, metal-clad forms, in striking contrast to the formality of the existing building. Whether one thinks this would have been a great enhancement or a tragic defacement does not matter, since the project was ultimately cancelled. In 2010, a real estate development firm agreed to a long-term lease of the site, on which it will build an office building designed by SmithGroup and intended to generate income for the museum and school.

16 American National Red Cross

17th Street between D and E streets, NW

1917—A. BRECK TROWBRIDGE AND GOODHUE LIVINGSTON
1930, 1932—North and west buildings: TROWBRIDGE AND LIVINGSTON
2005—Renovation: SHALOM BARANES ASSOCIATES; Preservation consultants: JOHN MILNER ASSOCIATES

President Wilson laid the cornerstone in 1915 for the main building in this complex, which was conceived as a memorial "to the heroic women of the Civil War, both North and South." It is a straightforward but stately neoclassical building, with a Corinthian portico and a recessed third story, partially obscured by a balustrade. The highlight of the interior is the Board of Governors Hall, featuring a trio of Tiffany windows depicting evocative figures such as St. Filomena, the patron saint of the sick, and, appropriately enough, the Redcrosse Knight from Edmund Spenser's *The Faerie Queene.* Two other buildings, designed by the same architects in a complementary fashion, were completed in 1930 and 1932.

17 National Society Daughters of the American Revolution (DAR) Headquarters

1776 D Street, NW

1910—Memorial Continental Hall: EDWARD PEARCE CASEY
1923—Administration Building: MARSH AND PETER
1929—Constitution Hall: JOHN RUSSELL POPE
1950—Addition to Administration Building: EGGERS AND HIGGINS
1994–97—Renovations of Constitution Hall: BLACKBURN AND ASSOCIATES; KRESSCOX ASSOCIATES

Tel: (202) 628-1776
www.dar.org

Reputed to be the largest complex of buildings in the world owned exclusively by women, this is the headquarters of the Daughters of the American Revolution, one of the nation's most prominent patriotic organizations. Facing 17th Street is Memorial Continental Hall, an imposing structure boasting heavy quoins, a dense balustrade at the roof level, and an abundance of gleaming marble. The main entrance is marked by an unusual *porte-cochère,* with columns set on tall pedestals and steps rising between them. On the south façade is a semicircular porch with 13 columns representing the original colonies.

At the center of this building is a magnificent, skylit space that originally served as the DAR's main auditorium. This was the venue for the annual "Continental Congress," drawing thousands of members from across the country. It is now the library and is worth a visit even if you have no interest in conducting research there. Surrounding the library are more than 30 distinct rooms, each of which was sponsored by a DAR state chapter. Some of these rooms served as offices until the administrative wing was added to the west of the main building, at which point they were restored as period salons. Visitors may tour all of these spaces, as well as the museum in the central wing.

The Continental Congress soon outgrew the original building, necessitating the addition of a large auditorium dubbed Constitution Hall. John Russell Pope's preliminary designs for the addition were extremely grand, but budgetary constraints forced him to tame his ambitions. The completed structure is staid in comparison to the main building, with large expanses of blank wall relieved only by subtle recesses and belt courses. Two long, copper canopies—one on C Street and the other on D—add welcome, jaunty touches.

Constitution Hall became one of the most prominent performance venues in 20th-century Washington, and was the primary home of the National Symphony for more than four decades. But this site is most famous for the concert that did *not* take place here in 1939, when African American singer Marian Anderson was denied the opportunity to perform because of her race, prompting First Lady Eleanor Roosevelt to resign her DAR membership and arrange an outdoor concert by Anderson at the Lincoln Memorial. Anderson subsequently performed here on several occasions, and fortunately, everyone is now welcome at the DAR.

18 Organization of American States (OAS)

(Pan-American Union)
17th Street and Constitution Avenue, NW

1910—ALBERT KELSEY AND PAUL P. CRET
1912—Annex: KELSEY AND CRET
2005—Renovation: JOHN MILNER ASSOCIATES

Tel: (202) 458-3000
www.oas.org

Funded in part by a $750,000 gift from Andrew Carnegie, the "House of the Americas" was built as the headquarters of the Pan-American Union (now the Organization of American States [OAS]), and intended to symbolize the peaceful relations among the countries of North, South, and Central America. It occupies the former site of the Van Ness mansion, designed by Benjamin Henry Latrobe, which was built around 1816 and thought to be the most expensive residence in the United States in its day. A former stable of that estate, also by Latrobe, still stands at 18th and C streets, though its stucco finish is not original.

The OAS building was the first major commission for the French-born Paul Philippe Cret, who had collaborated with Philadelphia-based architect Albert Kelsey on the winning entry in the design competition conducted in 1907. The exterior of Kelsey and Cret's building is in keeping with Beaux-Arts traditions, but is inflected with elements alluding to the Spanish Colonial architecture of Latin America, such as the red tile roof and bronze gates. The sculptures flanking the entrance represent North America (to the right, by Gutzon Borglum, best known for his work on Mount Rushmore) and

South America (to the left, by Isidore Konti). The bas-relief panels above the large sculptures depict the "great liberators" of the Americas: George Washington in the northern panel, and Simón Bolívar and José de San Martín in the southern panel.

Inside, classical formality yields to tropical exoticism, as the building is organized around a lushly planted patio that was originally covered with a sliding glass roof, though modern air-conditioning now precludes the use of this feature. The centerpiece of the garden is Gertrude Vanderbilt Whitney's fountain incorporating references to Mayan, Aztec, and Zapotecan art. The building also contains elegant event and conference rooms, most notably the 100-foot-long, barrel-vaulted Hall of the Americas at the rear of the second floor.

Behind the main building is the Annex, also by Kelsey and Cret, which now houses the Art Museum of the Americas. The highlight of this structure is the interior loggia, which is a riot of colorful, glazed tile. Between the two buildings lies the Blue Aztec Garden, featuring a small reflecting pool. Presiding over the garden is a statue of Xochipilli, the Aztec god of flowers, which seems pleasant enough, though he was also associated with hallucinogenic drugs and human sacrifice.

I9 Stewart Lee Udall Department of the Interior Building

1849 C Street, NW

1936—WADDY B. WOOD

Tel: (202) 208-4743
www.doi.gov

The first project undertaken by the Depression-era Public Works Administration, the U.S. Department of the Interior's headquarters is enormous and severe. Behind those forbidding façades, however, there are some entertaining surprises. Most noteworthy are the dozens of spectacular New Deal murals and sculptures, some of them addressing Native American themes, others representing "The Negro's Contribution in the Social and Cultural Development of America." There is also a small museum on the first floor, as well as an Indian Craft Shop (sadly, the Federal Duck Stamp Office, a longtime Interior Department oddity, has migrated to Arlington). The building's floor plan is unusual for its era: instead of the more typical courtyards to bring light to office spaces within a huge block, architect Waddy Wood organized the plan around a central, north-south spine, with six pairs of narrow wings projecting east and west. An ongoing renovation of the building by Shalom Baranes Associates is currently under way.

I10 Federal Reserve Building

(Marriner S. Eccles Building)
Constitution Avenue between 20th and 21st streets, NW

1937—PAUL PHILIPPE CRET

Tel: (202) 452-3149
www.federalreserve.gov/generalinfo/virtualtour

E. J. Applewhite called the Federal Reserve the "Valhalla of the dollar," and Paul Cret won an invited design competition to create an appropriately monumental temple for America's gods of economic policy. The exterior design may be the apotheosis of starved classicism in Washington, and with the eagle sculpture over its main doorway starkly lit at night, the building is perhaps uncomfortably reminiscent of the contemporary work of Albert Speer (suggesting that stylistic trends often trump ideology in architecture). The eagle motif is carried throughout the building, even appearing as an outline in the glass ceiling of the atrium, an elegant space lined with buttery travertine and intricate railings by notable Philadelphia ironworker Samuel Yellin. The public may visit the Federal Reserve Building, which also hosts limited art exhibitions, but reservations are required.

I11 National Academy of Sciences

2101 Constitution Avenue, NW
(2100 C Street, NW)

1924—BERTRAM GROSVENOR GOODHUE;
Sculptor: LEE LAWRIE
1962, 1965, 1970—Additions:
HARRISON & ABRAMOWITZ
1979—Landscape design for Einstein statue: OEHME, VAN SWEDEN & ASSOCIATES;
Sculptor: ROBERT BERKS

Tel: (202) 334-2436
www4.nationalacademies.org/nas/nashome.nsf

Bertram Goodhue tried to convince the National Academy of Sciences—chartered by Congress in 1863 to advise the government on science and technology policy—to hire another architect for its headquarters because he felt uncomfortable designing a building so near the Lincoln Memorial and other major neoclassical landmarks. He finally relented and went on to create a subdued structure—a boiled-down Beaux-Arts palace with hints of the Spanish Colonial style that Goodhue favored. The exterior walls appear at first glance to be perfectly flat planes of stone, but in fact each course is set back slightly from the one below, creating subtly battered—or inwardly sloping—façades. Goodhue himself dubbed the style of the building "Alexandrian," allegedly referring to a late period in ancient Greek culture when Alexandria, Egypt, was a center of learning and style. However one might describe it, the building represents a magnificent integration of art and architecture. Famed sculptor Lee Lawrie did all of the three-dimensional artistic works, including the enormous bronze entry doors and spandrel panels depicting major figures and events in scientific history, while Hildreth Meière created the exuberant mosaics in the Great Hall, the original building's principal space, which initially served as an auditorium.

In the 1960s, Wallace K. Harrison, who had worked in Goodhue's office in his younger days, designed a trio of additions, the last of which houses a new, futuristic auditorium encased in a wildly faceted shell. In 1979, the endearingly frumpy Albert Einstein Memorial, by Robert Berks, was dedicated in the academy's front yard. The map at the base of the monument has more than 2,700 metal studs representing planets, stars, and other heavenly bodies in their relative positions as of the dedication date.

As of this writing, Quinn Evans Architects is overseeing a thorough renovation of the building.

I12 American Pharmacists Association

(American Pharmaceutical Association)
2215 Constitution Avenue, NW

1933—JOHN RUSSELL POPE
1958—Addition: EGGERS & HIGGINS
2009—Renovation and addition:
HARTMAN-COX ARCHITECTS

The tourist coming upon this complex for the first time would be excused for guessing that the small, marble-faced structure in front is a shrine of some kind—a war memorial perhaps, or a dignified little museum dedicated to some archaic, vaguely remembered civic cause. In fact, it is the headquarters of a professional association, and for nearly seven decades, it was the only private building on Constitution Avenue, NW (the new private office building at 101 Constitution [see A20] now anchors the other end of this important thoroughfare). The building was financed entirely by the organization's members, but because of its sensitive location, federal design review authorities dictated its siting, the treatment of the surrounding landscape, and the choice of white marble as the finish material.

The shrine-like character of John Russell Pope's design may derive from its basis in an earlier project. He originally developed it in 1908 for the Lincoln Birthplace Museum in Kentucky, where it would have served as a shell for Lincoln's natal log cabin, but the design proved too expensive—not to mention oddly urbane for its rustic setting—so Pope prepared a revised scheme for that site that was simpler and more robust (and which was executed). Some 20 years later, he conjured up the initial Lincoln Birthplace design and, with a few modifications, turned it into the pharmaceutical building.

The architects of the recent addition to the rear, which contains more than 20 times the floor space of the Pope building, deliberately chose a contrasting stone and set the new wing back as far as possible to allow the original structure to continue to read as a freestanding form.

I13 U.S. Institute of Peace

Constitution Avenue at 23rd Street, NW

2011—SAFDIE ARCHITECTS

The location and scale of the U.S. Institute of Peace make it one of Washington's most prominent new buildings in decades (the site, ironically enough, used to be part of the military complex immediately to the north). The building consists of three rather stolid blocks, sheathed in acid-etched, precast concrete with punched windows, separated by two atria that fan out from the entrance at the northeast corner. The atria are covered by milky-white, translucent panels that appear opaque from the outside by day but glow from within when artificially lit at night. The latter quality caused some consternation among federal design review authorities, who insisted on thorough study of the lighting scheme to ensure that it would not visually overwhelm the nearby Lincoln Memorial.

Knowing the building's purpose, one cannot help but interpret the billowing, white roofs of the atria as abstractions of a dove's wings, yet curiously, the architects contend that these forms were in-

tended only to suggest the idea of peace in some more general way. Regardless, they are graceful additions to Washington's skyline, even if the contrast between the curving, translucent forms and the uninspired, rectilinear blocks is too stark.

I14 Pan American Health Organization

525 23rd Street, NW

1965—Design architect: ROMÁN FRESNEDO SIRI; Architects of record: JUSTEMENT, ELAM, CALLMER & KIDD
2001—Renovation: AI

Like many Latin American architects of the mid-20th century, Román Fresnedo Siri, of Uruguay, was enthralled by Corbusian modernism. His competition-winning design for this complex reflects Le Corbusier's influence in the visual interplay between the cylindrical structure (housing a council chamber and related spaces) and the gently curved "secretariat" tower; the *brise-soleil* that shades the cylinder's glass curtain wall from the sun; and the *pilotis* that lift the main office block off the ground.

As of this writing, the firm of KCCT has been engaged to design the conversion of the ground-floor library in the cylindrical wing into a "Knowledge / Emergency Operations Center."

I15 John F. Kennedy Center for the Performing Arts

2700 F Street, NW

1971—EDWARD DURELL STONE ASSOCIATES; Landscape architect: EDWARD DURELL STONE JR.
1979—Terrace Theater: PHILIP C. JOHNSON
1997—Concert Hall renovation: QUINN EVANS ARCHITECTS; Design architects: HARTMAN-COX ARCHITECTS
2003—Opera House renovation: QUINN EVANS ARCHITECTS; Renovation of public spaces: TOBEY DAVIS WITH POLSHEK PARTNERSHIP
2005—Family Theater: RICHTER CORNBROOKS GRIBBLE

Tel: (202) 467-4600
www.kennedy-center.org

If a Las Vegas developer were to open a casino under the theme of "Palace of the Soviets"—and unlikelier things happen hourly in Vegas—the result might look something like the Kennedy Center. Cut off from the adjacent neighborhood by a tangle of freeways, and from the Potomac riverfront by an enormous cantilevered balcony, the building was designed as a gaudy concoction of vast marble planes, spindly bronze columns, overwrought chandeliers, and acres of bordello-red carpet. It brings to mind the work of Morris Lapidus, but without the sensuous curves (though Stone produced an earlier scheme with a curvilinear plan) and with, instead, a hefty dose of Stalinist bombast. Critic Ada Louise Huxtable decried the center as "a cross between a concrete candy box and a marble sarcophagus in which the art of architecture lies buried."

Some government officials had been calling for a major performing arts facility in central Washington since the 1930s, but the effort did not get under way in earnest until the Eisenhower administration. After Kennedy's assassination, the project was rechristened in his name as a "living memorial." It opened in 1971 with a requiem mass in honor of the slain president. Since then, various renovations of the theaters and other spaces have mitigated the architectural shortcomings of the complex, which has become a successful hub for music and theater. As of this writing, plans for a set of steps connecting the terrace to the riverfront below are pending.

I16 The Watergate

2500–2700 Virginia Avenue, NW, and 600–700 New Hampshire Avenue, NW

1963–71—LUIGI MORETTI WITH MARIO DI VALMARANA; Associated architects: CORNING, MOORE, ELMORE & FISCHER
1994—Renovation of office building public spaces: BASS ARCHITECTS; NORA FISCHER DESIGNS
2000—Renovation of hotel: RJSHIRLEY & ASSOCIATES ARCHITECTS; Interior designers: HUGHES DESIGN ASSOCIATES

Even without its tawdry fame as the site of a bungled, politically motivated burglary, the Watergate complex—which includes residences, offices, and a hotel—would still have a rich history because so many people of power and influence have lived, worked, or stayed here. Monica Lewinsky and Bob and Liddy Dole were, for a brief period, improbable next-door neighbors, as were the personal secretaries to Richard Nixon and Lyndon Johnson.

The Watergate's lead designer, Luigi Moretti, rose to fame as one of Benito Mussolini's favorite architects, and he never fully recanted his fascist sympathies. He was hired to design this complex by the Italian investment firm that developed it. Moretti consciously produced a design that departed from what he saw as the rigid formality of official Washington architecture. While much of the detailing is awkward—the chunky balcony railings, for example, look as if they might have been borrowed from Fred Flintstone's house—overall the complex succeeds in bringing a welcome fluidity to a generally linear and angular city. From certain vantage points, in fact, the buildings almost suggest ocean liners, with gentle curves and prow-like balconies.

The complex's curious name derives from the nearby Watergate Steps, an arc of stairs providing access to the Potomac riverfront. Completed in 1932, the steps were originally intended as a ceremonial entrance to the city for dignitaries arriving by water and as a docking point for recreational boats. As it turned out, not a lot of 20th-century dignitaries actually arrived by water, but from 1935 until the 1970s, the steps served as an amphitheater for musical performances, the stage for which was a barge anchored at their base.

The Watergate Hotel closed in 2007, when it was sold and later resold after the initial buyer defaulted on a loan. As of this writing, it remains "closed for renovations," though no work appears to be under way.

I17 St. Mary's Episcopal-Anglican Church

730 23rd Street, NW

1881—Parish hall: ARCHITECT UNKNOWN
1887—Church: RENWICK, ASPINWALL AND RUSSELL
1909—Parish house: ARCHITECT UNKNOWN
1913—Rectory: ARCHITECT UNKNOWN
2005—Restoration: FETTERMAN ASSOCIATES

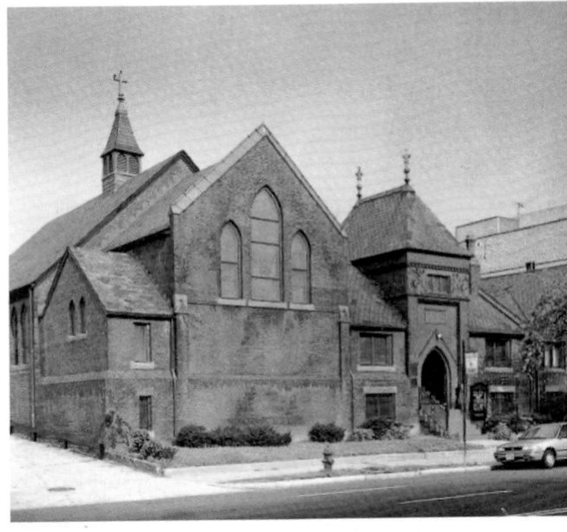

St. Mary's is the oldest African American Episcopal congregation in Washington. It held its first service on this site in 1867 in a reconstructed wooden chapel

(later demolished) formerly attached to the Kalorama Hospital. The congregation prospered and grew, necessitating the new church by James Renwick Jr., built a couple of decades later. Above the altar are painted glass windows, made in France, depicting saints of African descent, including St. Cyprian, a Carthaginian who became a Christian bishop and martyr.

I18 George Washington University

Primarily between F Street and Pennsylvania Avenue, from 20th to 24th streets, NW

The most urban of Washington's major collegiate institutions, George Washington University does not enjoy a cohesive campus, and partially as a result, lacks a clear architectural identity. Nonetheless, the school includes a number of notable individual buildings. The Law School (1926—Albert Harris and Arthur Heaton; 1967–70—Mills, Petticord & Mills; 1984—Keyes Condon Florance Architects), at 20th and H streets, NW, is interesting as a mélange of quite different structures that seem to have grown together over time. The Lisner Auditorium (1940—Faulkner & Kingsbury) at 730 21st Street, NW, is a stripped classical block with a swoopy, Art Moderne interior that was one of the primary performance venues in Washington before the opening of the Kennedy Center. The formerly undistinguished Marvin Center, at 800 21st Street, NW, now boasts an inviting entrance (2002—SmithGroup) and provides a sense of place amid the otherwise generic campus.

I19 World Bank

1818 H Street, NW

1997—KOHN PEDERSEN FOX ASSOCIATES; Associate architects: NÄGELE HOFMANN TIEDEMANN UND PARTNER, KRESSCOX ASSOCIATES

Kohn Pedersen Fox became famous in the 1980s for designing corporate office buildings that had one foot in the modern movement and the other in the turbid waters of postmodernism. The World Bank Headquarters was one of a series of buildings the firm designed in the 1990s that reflected a kind of retro-modernist approach. The complex takes up an entire city block, and actually incorporates two pre-existing buildings along G Street. The cheerless gray concrete wall that ties the old and new structures together at ground level is the most unfortunate aspect of the design. Above that level, however, things get much livelier, especially along the north façade, facing Pennsylvania Avenue, which is dynamically canted outward and emphatically articulated by horizontal muntins. At several points, distinct volumes break from the main building envelope, providing visual relief from the insistent geometry and marking important interior spaces, such as the board room high up on the northeast corner of the building, which is capped by a swooping, upturned roof.

TOUR J

Downtown / West End

Strategically located between the White House and the elegant neighborhoods of Georgetown and Dupont Circle, the West End was the primary focus of Washington's commercial development during the major post–World War II economic booms. Although development in the old, eastern part of downtown took off again beginning in the 1980s, the area west of 16th Street and north of Pennsylvania Avenue continues to be a prestigious precinct of nonprofit organizations and corporate offices. The area also contains the most consequential stretch of K Street, a thoroughfare synonymous with high-powered law firms and lobbyists. The streetscapes in this neighborhood tend to be rather bland, but they do contain a number of architecturally noteworthy individual buildings.

The Demonet Building, built in the 1880s at the corner of M Street and Connecticut Avenue, with a 1980s addition by Skidmore, Owings & Merrill behind it. The west end of downtown was the first area in central Washington to benefit from the boom in commercial real estate in the late 20th century.

19
M ST
16
NEW HAMPSHIRE AVE
17
18
15
25th ST
23th ST
1200 ft

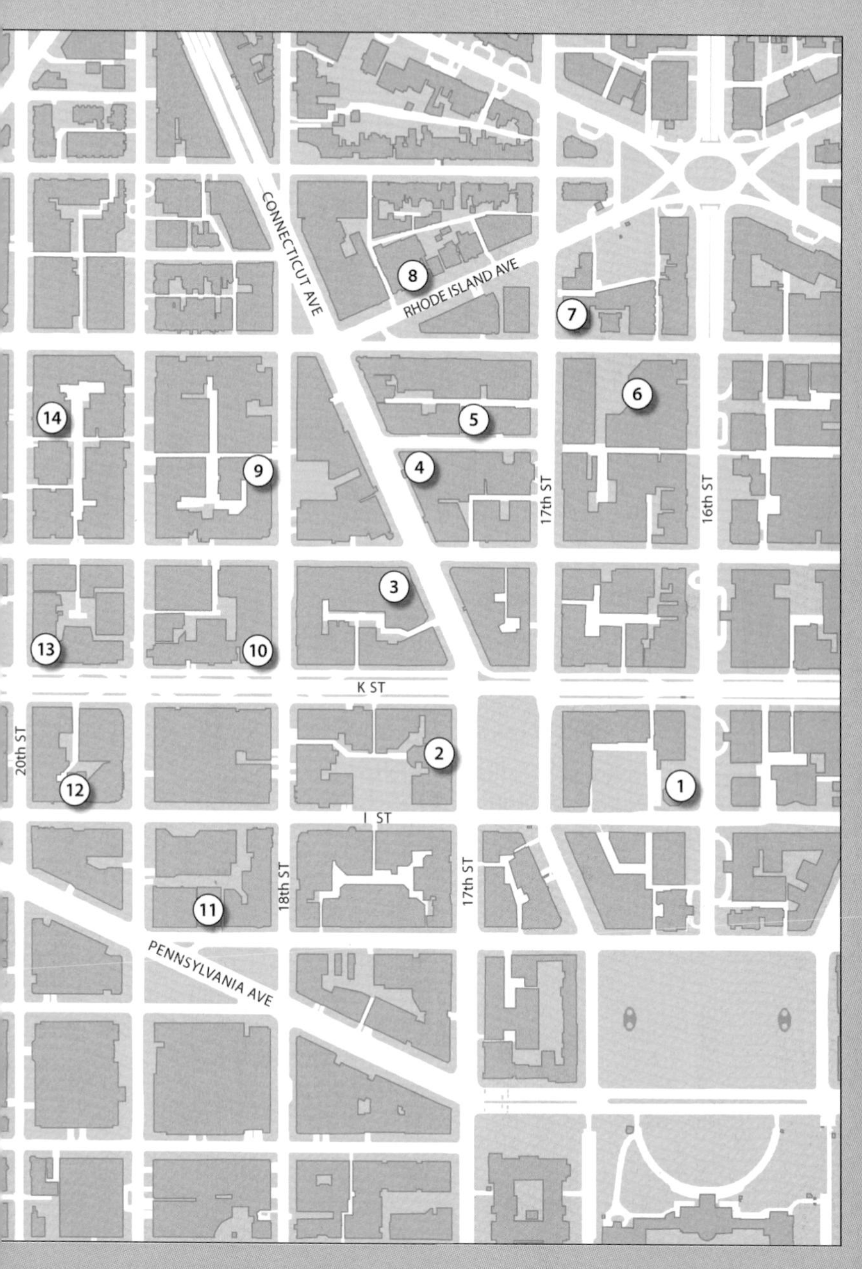
CONNECTICUT AVE
RHODE ISLAND AVE
17th ST
16th ST
K ST
20th ST
I ST
18th ST
17th ST
PENNSYLVANIA AVE
1
2
3
4
5
6
7
8
9
10
11
12
13
14

J1 Third Church of Christ, Scientist / Christian Science Monitor Building

900–910 16th Street, NW

1971—I. M. PEI & PARTNERS (PRINCIPAL DESIGNER: ARALDO A. COSSUTA)

The Christian Science Church has a long track record as a patron of progressive architecture, including important, early 20th-century works in California by Bernard Maybeck and Irving Gill. The church's world headquarters in Boston is a fascinating enclave incorporating several modern buildings by the firm of I. M. Pei & Partners, which also designed this much more modest church and office complex.

The octagonal sanctuary, whose shape was inspired by the Romanesque Baptistery in Florence, Italy, is clad in concrete panels, and is mostly windowless—light enters the interior primarily through a skylight tracing the perimeter of the roof. A carillon, cantilevered over the public sidewalk along 16th Street, is the most engaging element of the design; the low point is the decidedly inelegant emergency exit doorway on I Street, which passersby are presumably expected to ignore. The main entrance to the church faces a forlorn plaza, across which stands a small office building housing the Christian Science Reading Room. This slender building, with its rectilinear plan and long ribbons of glass, is a geometrical and textural foil to the main structure.

In recent years, this humble little complex became the center of a vigorous preservation debate. The congregation, claiming that the church not only failed to meet its needs but also created a strongly unpleasant environment, sought permission to demolish it. Various preservation groups and other organizations protested, arguing that this was an important example of Brutalist architecture and that it played a critical role in modulating the scale and character of this mostly commercial district. In the end, the D.C. government sided with the church and issued a demolition permit. As of this writing, the buildings still stand, but by the time you read this, they may be gone.

J2 Barr Building

910 17th Street, NW

1926—B. STANLEY SIMMONS

Rich ornament in the English Gothic Revival style lends an ecclesiastical character to this office building—indeed, the vacant niches on its façade look as if they were destined to accommodate saintly statuary. E. J. Applewhite declared the Barr Building to be "a rebuke to the boring borax banality of the computer-designed structures which adjoin it at either side." Although the adjacent structure to the north is new since Applewhite's time, his remark remains apt.

J3 Washington Square

1050 Connecticut Avenue, NW

1982—CHLOETHIEL WOODARD SMITH & ASSOCIATES

The intersection of Connecticut Avenue and L Street is sometimes called "Chloethiel's Corner" because the architect designed three of its four buildings (all but the one on the northeast corner). Of these, Washington Square is by far the most stylish, thanks to its serrated façades composed of shallow bay windows, its mezzanine-level outdoor terrace, and its pair of glassy, towering atria, all of which make it look more like a glitzy convention hotel than a typical downtown office building.

J4 Mayflower Hotel

1127 Connecticut Avenue, NW

1925—WARREN & WETMORE; Associated architect: ROBERT S. BERESFORD
1941—Partial interior renovation: DOROTHY DRAPER INC.
1958—Apartment wing converted to hotel rooms: ARCHITECT UNKNOWN
1984—Renovation and addition: VLASTIMIL KOUBEK; Interiors: LOUIS CATAFFO

Best known as the architects of New York's Grand Central Terminal, Warren & Wetmore also designed dozens of luxurious hotels, mansions, and office buildings that epitomized gentility and urbanity in early 20th-century America. The Mayflower Hotel is emblematic of the era in its subdued elegance. The main body of the building is actually quite plain, with simple windows set into unadorned brick walls, but the hotel achieves quiet dignity thanks to its tastefully ornamented limestone base, the bold terra cotta quoins climbing the corners of each wing, the subtle curves of the two wings facing Connecticut Avenue, and the parade of loosely spaced urns running along the edge of the roof.

The interior of the hotel is pretty much what one would expect, but it did contain some surprises in the past. In 1941, famed interior designer Dorothy Draper redid all of the guest rooms on the fifth floor. Draper was known for an over-the-top, florid decorative style, but curiously, this project in conservative Washington was one of her simplest and most modern. All of the hotel's rooms have since been redone a number of times.

The Mayflower has been closely associated with numerous famous people and events. Local resident J. Edgar Hoover ate lunch in the hotel's restaurant with his colleague and companion, Clyde Tolson, virtually every day for two decades. More recently, the hotel garnered loads of tabloid coverage as the site of the infamous tryst between "Client-9"—a.k.a. Eliot Spitzer, then-governor of New York—and a very expensive prostitute.

J5 ABC News Washington Bureau

1717 DeSales Street, NW

1981—KOHN PEDERSEN FOX ASSOCIATES

Now a global mega-firm, Kohn Pedersen Fox started out in 1976 as an office comprising only the three partners. ABC was the client that gave the young architects their big break, and the firm went on to design a number of facilities for the network, including the Washington News Bureau, one of their earliest completed projects. The taut, convex curve of the façade distinguishes the mid-block building from its neighbors without unduly disrupting the streetscape.

J6 National Geographic Society Headquarters

M Street between 16th and 17th streets, NW

1903—Hubbard Memorial Library: HORNBLOWER & MARSHALL
1904—Interior of Hubbard Memorial Library: ALLEN & COLLINS
1913/1932—Administration building (facing 16th Street): ARTHUR B. HEATON
1964—17th Street building: EDWARD DURELL STONE
1984—M Street building and renovation of Hubbard Memorial Library: SKIDMORE, OWINGS & MERRILL

Tel: (202) 857-7588
www.nationalgeographic.com

The National Geographic Society complex is a small, tightly packed campus composed of several quite disparate buildings. At the corner of 16th and M

streets stands the original building, now known as the Hubbard Memorial Library, named after Gardiner Greene Hubbard, the society's first president. It was Hubbard's son-in-law, inventor Alexander Graham Bell, who succeeded him and laid the groundwork for the organization's transformation into the famously popular enterprise that it is today. Bell's wife, Mabel, had a strong interest in architecture and was the de facto client for the Hubbard building. Local architects Hornblower & Marshall won a limited competition for the project, but Mrs. Bell was never fully pleased with their work, which she considered "showy." Well ahead of her time, she constantly pushed for a simpler, more "functional" design. The architects tried to accommodate her wishes—and frankly, to modern eyes the building they created seems quite dignified and understated—but Mrs. Bell remained dissatisfied and ultimately fired them, bringing in another firm to complete the interior.

Adjacent to the library on 16th Street is an administrative building executed in a complementary Renaissance Revival style in two phases ending in 1913 and 1932. The initial phase included the five northernmost bays visible today plus the "hyphen" connecting it to the Hubbard building. Arthur Heaton's preliminary designs for the second phase included a tall homage to an Italian campanile, but this was eliminated in favor of a wing matching the earlier expansion and linked to it by a pedimented portico.

At the 17th Street corner is Edward Durell Stone's 1960s tower, which is strangely reminiscent of an unbuilt Frank Lloyd Wright project from 1913 for the *San Francisco Call* newspaper, with slender, tightly spaced columns and a boldly cantilevered, perforated "cornice." Unlike Stone's widely reviled Kennedy Center [see I15], which languishes by the Potomac like a beached whale, this building is welcoming and comfortable in its urban setting. It also houses the society's Explorers Hall, a small museum with rotating exhibitions.

At the center of the block lies the newest element of the complex, a modern rendition of a ziggurat, with an L-shaped plan creating a courtyard as a focal point for the motley campus. The new building's insistent horizontality contrasts with the equally emphatic verticality of Stone's structure, while mediating between the modern tower and the older, neoclassical buildings to the east.

J7 Sumner School and Sumner Square

17th and M streets, NW

1872—Sumner School: ADOLF CLUSS
1887—Magruder School: ARCHITECT UNKNOWN
1985—Restoration and additions to existing buildings: EHRENKRANTZ GROUP; New structures: HARTMAN-COX ARCHITECTS; Associated architects: NAVY, MARSHALL, GORDON, WITH RTKL ASSOCIATES; Preservation architects: OEHRLEIN & ASSOCIATES ARCHITECTS

Named for abolitionist Charles Sumner, this was a well regarded school for African Americans during the era of segregation. Ironically, with integration came neglect, and the Sumner School sat, largely ignored and rapidly decaying, until the District's Board of Education finally decided to restore it and the Magruder School next door.

The two historic schools became the centerpieces of a new commercial development, though the Sumner School was retained by the Board of Education for its own use. The underground component of the project required that the Magruder building be dismantled and reconstructed on a new foundation. The bulk of the new structure, by Hartman-Cox, is unobtrusively rendered in a gray curtain wall, making it a true background building that avoids visual competition with the schools. One wing of the new building comes out to the street line, however, and for that part, the architects broke from the pure background approach. Instead, they covered it in a buff brick, which deftly relates the new wing to the existing buildings on either side—its primary material, brick, is the same as that of the Magruder School, while its beige color ties it to the Jefferson Hotel (1923—Jules Henri de Sibour) at the corner of M and 16th streets.

J8 St. Matthew's Cathedral

1725 Rhode Island Avenue, NW

1893-1913—C. GRANT LA FARGE (HEINS AND LA FARGE)
2003—Restoration: OEHRLEIN & ASSOCIATES ARCHITECTS

The 190-foot-tall copper dome of St. Matthew's, the seat of Washington's Catholic Archdiocese, was a prominent landmark for a half century before it was gradually surrounded by mid-rise office buildings. The cathedral's spartan façade recalls the sober architecture of early Christian churches (the one bit of relative exuberance, the mosaic over the main door, was added in 1970). The severe exterior, however, belies the opulence of the interior, which teems with rich marble and colorful mosaics bearing a debt to Byzantine architecture. Heins and La Farge, both of whom apprenticed in the office of H. H. Richardson, were also the original architects of the gigantic and perpetually unfinished Cathedral of St. John the Divine in New York.

J9 1150 18th Street, NW

1991—DON M. HISAKA & ASSOCIATES
2010—Renovation: GROUP GOETZ ARCHITECTS (GGA)

In designing this small office building, Don Hisaka was eager to avoid not only the "granite or marble cliché" of traditional Washington architecture but also the banal glass curtain walls so common in the city's more recent commercial buildings. Nonetheless, the architect felt that his project must still fit comfortably into the cityscape. His solution was to create an elaborate, sunscreen-like façade of white-painted steel. In its color, depth, and interplay of light and shadow, the façade alludes abstractly to the city's classical landmarks, while its extruded steel components and industrial detailing firmly establish its modernity. By organizing the interior around a bright atrium and cantilevering the upper floors over an adjacent alley, Hisaka was able to maximize both square footage and access to natural light on a very constricted site.

J10 1801 K Street, NW

1972—HENRY HOLLE ASSOCIATES
2009—Renovation: SKIDMORE, OWINGS & MERRILL

Sometimes profit is the mother of invention. The owner of this building, which was formerly clad in drab, brown panels with narrow, widely spaced windows, wanted to upgrade the property inside and out without having to break the leases of existing tenants. He hired Skidmore, Owings & Merrill to devise an appropriate renovation strategy. After laboratory analysis revealed that the existing mullions were capable of supporting a new curtain wall with only minor reinforcement at the floor slabs, the architects came up with an innovative plan in which new glass panels were affixed to the mullions and sealed, and then the old metal-and-glass units were removed *from the inside*. Because the overall building envelope remained airtight throughout this process, the recladding could take place on a piecemeal basis as specific tenants' leases expired or were renegotiated. As a result, 75 percent of the tenants were able to remain in place during the work.

At the same time, the lobbies on K and L streets, which are on different floors, were also renovated and unified through the use of similar materials, including richly figured Calacatta marble from Italy and a vibrant light installation by Leo Villareal.

J11 1875 Pennsylvania Avenue, NW

2006—SHALOM BARANES ASSOCIATES

The address is a cheat, of course—the building is actually on H Street, but laid claim to Pennsylvania Avenue since it faces one of the remnant green spaces, or "reservations," that occur where L'Enfant's diagonal avenues intersect the grid. But that may be the least complicated aspect of this project, which began when a huge law firm wanted to take the entire southern half of the block bounded by 18th, 19th, H, and I streets to build its new Washington headquarters. The firm's initial plan called for razing the existing—and fairly new—buildings at the two corners. From an environmental standpoint, this would have been an unconscionable waste, so it is fortunate that the firm changed its plans (for economic and logistical reasons), and instead asked Shalom Baranes Associates to design a new building in the middle of the block and tie the three structures together to create a single complex.

In addition to entailing obvious structural and planning difficulties, this scheme posed aesthetic challenges. The two existing buildings were quite different, but both were relatively staid and formal, with towers extending above the roofline. Since the new structure was to incorporate the main entrance, some architects might have been tempted to outdo the flanking buildings, relying on grander forms or a taller tower to assert dominance. Baranes, however, decided to avoid one-upmanship, eschewing symmetry and strong vertical accents to create a surprisingly dynamic composition. The gambit was successful—the new structure draws the eye first, avoids visual competition with its siblings, and enlivens the entire block.

J12 1915 I Street, NW

1917—FRANK RUSSELL WHITE
1982—Addition: KERNS GROUP ARCHITECTS

While the addition to this structure echoes the form of the original building's Dutch gable, its animated, multiple setbacks change what was previously an inconspicuous structure into a minor landmark. The stepped façades unabashedly reveal their false historicism at their edges, where they are offset from the side walls by glazed notches.

J13 1999 K Street, NW

2009—MURPHY/JAHN

Among the many brand-new, glass-box buildings in downtown Washington, this one stands out for three reasons. First, of course, is the Big Gesture—the angled, glass screen wall on the K Street side that is anchored at the sidewalk, soars above the roofline, and then extends around to the eastern end of the upper floors. Vertically cantilevered from the outermost curtain wall, this huge fin serves no functional purpose, but it lends a sense of depth to the façade while helping to solve the compositional challenge posed by the setback of the top few floors from the building next

door (which makes room for a three-story outdoor terrace, barely visible behind the curtain wall at the upper right). The screen wall also draws the eyes of passersby upward, encouraging them to notice the building's second distinguishing feature: the array of smaller glass fins set into the curtain wall, which are as subtle as the big fin is bold, but add a surprising amount of visual interest, especially as light conditions change throughout the day and night. Finally, there is the building's luminous lobby, whose backlit panels dematerialize the space and constitute a room-size piece of minimalist art that also can be appreciated from the street.

J14 Brewood Office Building

1147 20th Street, NW

1974—WILKES & FAULKNER

A small surprise among the generic behemoths so common in this part of town, the Brewood Building is unusual in its use of board-formed concrete that reveals the pattern of the wood used as formwork. The façade details go a step further to suggest the patterns, scale, and connection methods of wood construction. As a result, the small building has an almost hand-crafted quality that is rare in modern commercial architecture.

J15 International Finance Corporation Headquarters

2121 Pennsylvania Avenue, NW

1997—MICHAEL GRAVES & ASSOCIATES; Associated architect: VLASTIMIL KOUBEK (KOUBEK ARCHITECTS)
2005—Store: MICHAEL GRAVES & ASSOCIATES

A division of the World Bank Group—which, if it were any bigger, would require its own world—the International Finance Corporation (IFC) occupies this mammoth building comprising more than one million square feet of office space. An example of the Aldo Rossi-esque style that Michael Graves has come to favor for commercial and civic structures, the IFC Building is daunting with its no-nonsense massing, its ominously tall, four-story "base," and its dizzying array of perfectly cylindrical columns (especially on the K Street façade).

J16 22 West Condominium

1177 22nd Street, NW

2008—SHALOM BARANES ASSOCIATES

Occupying a narrow, triangular block conveniently located between downtown and Georgetown, this site seemed ideal

for a high-end residential development, except for one snag—a gas station ensconced at the northwest corner with an unbreakable, long-term lease. The architects' solution was to close the gas station temporarily, modernize its facilities, and then cover as much of it as possible with a green roof. The result is effective from the condominium's perspective—the elevator lobby on each floor, for example, has a view over the station and from that vantage point, the roof comes off as a simple garden, and one is hardly aware of the facility beneath it.

The condominium building itself has two distinct façade treatments. The New Hampshire Avenue façade is layered, incorporating broad expanses of glass and substantial balconies, taking advantage of an eight-foot projection into public space. It is an ordered but varied composition, slightly softened by the array of plants that residents have placed on their balconies. The west façade, which is more subject to problematic heat gain on warm, sunny afternoons, is covered in an irregular pattern of tall, narrow windows and zinc panels. Although apparently random, the placement of the windows is actually quite pragmatic, reflecting the varied arrangements of the apartments within—living areas have more glass, for instance, while bedrooms have less. The contrasting façade patterns meet along the short north and south ends of the building, creating interesting juxtapositions and emphasizing the narrowness of the structure's plan.

J17 2401 Pennsylvania Avenue, NW

1991—KEYES CONDON FLORANCE

This mixed-use building employs a whimsical assortment of materials and decorative motifs. Many of the details are subtly amusing, such as the donkey- and elephant-head brackets holding the cables that support the ground-floor canopies, while others are downright kitschy, such as the cast stone flags on either side of the curved bay at the southeast corner. The sweeping curve of the Pennsylvania Avenue façade prefigures the sculptural forms in more recent projects by Phil Esocoff [see E4 and M1], who was the lead architect for this building before establishing his own firm.

J18 Barclay House

2501 K Street, NW

1980—MARTIN AND JONES

In Washington, the term *postmodern architecture* is popularly associated with rather straightforward historicism. Actually, the city has relatively few *truly* postmodern buildings—those that expressly and provocatively challenged modernist orthodoxies. The Barclay House is an example of this more mischievous brand of postmodernism. Dozens of conventions are broken here—expected hierarchies are subverted, grids and planes dissolve and reappear seemingly at random, and projecting bays seem to hang illogically from columns.

J19 1250 24th Street, NW

(B and W Garage)

1925—Designer-builder: PETER REINSEN
1988—New building incorporating existing façade: HISAKA & ASSOCIATES ARCHITECTS

This office building, like the garage that originally occupied the site, is simultaneously industrial and classical in spirit. The front façade of the two-story garage was preserved (though the deteriorating brick had to be painted), and now serves primarily as a screen defining small courts in front of the new building, which features a curving curtain wall bracketed by two painted brick towers that replicate the architectural vocabulary of the old garage. The bowed façade gives the building a formal presence, but does not overwhelm the low wall of the original structure.

TOUR K

Georgetown

Founded in 1751, Georgetown was originally a small Maryland river town known simply as George—named not for America's first president, as many people suppose, but most likely for King George II of England (or possibly for George Gordon and George Beall, the two men who owned most of the land on which the town was established). The initial community covered about 60 acres between the Potomac and a line south of N Street (then known as Gay Street), bounded on the east by what is now 30th (then Washington) Street, and on the west by the land now occupied by Georgetown University. Even after it was absorbed into the newly established District of Columbia in 1791, Georgetown remained legally a separate jurisdiction until formal annexation by "Washington City" 80 years later.

While Georgetown is now virtually synonymous with gentility, much of its history is actually rather gritty. In its early days, Georgetown was a bustling port, thanks to its strategic location near the falls of the Potomac and its proximity to vast tobacco plantations that provided the primary commodity to be shipped. Like most ports of that era, it was a scrappy town, home to workaday wharves and rowdy taverns, populated by notoriously crude sailors and probably more than a few merchants with fungible business ethics. Abigail Adams dismissed the place as "a dirty little hole," and many other contemporary accounts were equally unfavorable.

Busy ports may be seedy, but they also generate substantial wealth for those positioned to reap the profits of commerce. Georgetown quickly grew a substantial class of prosperous entrepreneurs, many of whom were quite cultured, and who built houses that still reign as some of the most elegant in the District. In fact, George-

This View of Georgetown D.C., *published by E. Sachse & Co. in 1853, reveals that parts of the area retained a pastoral quality well into the 19th century.*

RESERVOIR RD
35th ST
33rd ST
PROSPECT ST
42
3
4
2
1B
1A
1
1C
8
7
6
5
9
12
10
11
13
14
17
18
15
16
1600 ft

R ST
31st ST
Q ST
O ST
N ST
M ST
K ST
29th ST
27th ST
3
41
44
40
38
37
39
36
35
34
30
31
32
33
29
28
27
9
23
24
20
21
22
25
26

town's elite regarded the nascent—and, at the time, absolutely distinct—capital city to the east with some skepticism, suspicious as they were of the questionable enterprises (i.e., politics and government) practiced there. As late as 1826, one observer noticed that "the people of Georgetown . . . form a striking contrast to their neighbors in Washington, their minds being generally more cultivated. It is hardly possible to conceive how towns so near . . . should differ so widely."

As the 19th century progressed, however, Georgetown did not fare well. The river soon silted up, and the C&O Canal, dug to lure the rich Midwest trade to the Potomac, proved no match for the B&O Railroad, so trade bypassed Georgetown's once-flourishing port in favor of Baltimore. The Civil War brought significant social rifts, since Georgetown, though situated in the capital of the Union, still housed a number of prominent Confederate sympathizers (Georgetown University's official colors, blue and gray, reflect the school's divided loyalties). Following the war, the town absorbed an influx of freed slaves, most of whom were of course quite poor, and whose presence displeased some affluent Georgetowners, who moved elsewhere. The community grew increasingly shabby, and eventually even officially lost its name when, upon annexation in 1871, it became legally known as "West Washington."

Georgetown then entered a period of quiescence that lasted until the New Deal, when the growth of the federal government—and the consequent rise in Washington's population—brought about the rediscovery of "West Washington" as a choice place to live, with convenient access to the office buildings of Foggy Bottom and downtown. The pace of this rediscovery quickened after World War II until it began to look as if Georgetown might be spoiled by its success. To ensure the preservation of the architectural character of their town, residents pushed the Old Georgetown Act through Congress in 1950. The act officially made Georgetown a historic district, and gave the U.S. Commission of Fine Arts the authority to appoint an advisory panel—the Old Georgetown Board—which to this day reviews proposals for additions and alterations to both public and private structures throughout the neighborhood.

Tourists are often surprised to learn that a substantial percentage of the "historic" houses in present-day Georgetown were actually built in the aftermath of the 1950 legislation. Many of these "Eisenhowerian" structures fit quite stealthily into the historic fabric, thanks to their modesty and reliance on red brick as the primary finish material. Even so, they are generally readily distinguishable by their less-grand proportions, smaller windows, shallower façades, and, in many cases, brick patterns that were uncommon in the 19th century.

Today, Georgetown may be appreciated as a microcosm of American urbanism, miraculously encapsulated within a small precinct of a large metropolis. Starting at the waterfront and walking northward, one passes the remnants of the town's industrial origins, moves through a thriving commercial and entertainment zone, and then traverses dense residential blocks. Continuing, one discovers streets lined with larger, detached houses, followed by an area of palatial "country" estates, and finally, the edge of Rock Creek Park—a swath of wilderness (well, almost) in the heart of the city.

K1 Georgetown University

The nation's oldest Catholic institution of higher learning, initially known as Georgetown Academy, was formally established in 1789 by Father John Carroll, the first American Catholic bishop. Carroll considered placing the new school on what is now Capitol Hill, but dismissed the site as being "too far in the country." Instead, he opted for a high spot just upriver from the bustling port, enjoying a commanding view. The present campus is organized around two primary centers, with most of the historic academic buildings and residential clusters toward the southern end, and a sprawling medical school and hospital complex at the northern edge along Reservoir Road.

K1a Healy Hall

1877–1909—SMITHMEYER & PELZ
1970—Renovation: LEO A DALY
1982—Restoration of Riggs Library: ENVIRONMENTAL PLANNING & RESEARCH
1995—Renovation: EINHORN YAFFEE PRESCOTT

The architectural centerpiece of the campus is named for Father Patrick Healy, the university's dynamic president from 1874 to 1881. The son of an Irish American father and a mixed-race mother who was a slave, Healy was the first person of acknowledged African American descent to earn a PhD and the first to head a predominantly white university. Designed by the stylistically ambidextrous architects of the original Library of Congress building, Healy Hall has exterior walls of dark gray Potomac gneiss and is capped by a 200-foot clock tower, making it one of low-rise Washington's most widely visible landmarks. Glimpsed from the Potomac River or various spots along the Virginia banks, the imposing structure could almost be mistaken for a baronial fortress overlooking the Rhine. The building's most notable interior space is the Riggs Library, distinguished by four levels of delicate cast iron stacks.

K1b Old North Hall

1795—ARCHITECT UNKNOWN
1926—Renovation: MARSH AND PETER
1983—Restoration: MARIANI & ASSOCIATES

The oldest extant academic building at Georgetown, Old North is typical of the simple but dignified Georgian and Federal structures found on a number of the country's most venerable campuses, though the two octagonal towers at the rear are unusual. It now houses the university's Public Policy Institute.

K1c Joseph Mark Lauinger Memorial Library

1970—JOHN CARL WARNECKE & ASSOCIATES
1990, 1993—Renovations: EINHORN YAFFEE PRESCOTT

The exposed-aggregate concrete surfaces and angular forms of the Lauinger Library are not widely favored today, but when it opened, the structure was praised—if rather faintly—for being deferential to its historic neighbors. *Washington Post* critic Wolf Von Eckardt declared that the architects of the library "managed to blend it into the cityscape, if not unobtrusively, successfully." Indeed, the new building's low physical

profile preserves views to and from the older structures, while its incorporation of dark gray aggregate in the concrete and its abstract, asymmetrical towers are clear allusions to Healy Hall.

K2 Georgetown Visitation Preparatory School / Convent of the Visitation

1524 35th Street, NW

1821—Chapel: JOSEPH PICOT DE CLORIVIÈRE
1832—Monastery: ARCHITECT UNKNOWN
1857—Additions/alterations to monastery and chapel: RICHARD PETTIT
1874—Founders' Hall (Academy Building): NORRIS G. STARKWEATHER
1995—Restoration of Founders' Hall: KRESSCOX ASSOCIATES
1996—Renovation of chapel: KRESSCOX ASSOCIATES
1998—Athletic and Performing Arts centers: KRESSCOX ASSOCIATES

Founded in 1799 by three "Pious Ladies"—French nuns who had fled the revolution—under the auspices of Georgetown University's president, this is one of the oldest Catholic girls' schools in America. The campus is a catalogue of period architecture, from the austere, Federal-style "monastery" building (at the corner of 35th and P), to the neo-Gothic, stuccoed chapel, to the ornate Victorian Founders' Hall, with its mansard roof and elaborate brickwork. The last of these was the victim of a spectacular fire in 1993, after which the nuns not only oversaw a meticulous restoration of the damaged structure, but also embarked on a broader building and renovation campaign, adding new ancillary facilities designed in a low-key historicist mode. From around the corner, in the 3500 block of P Street, one can catch glimpses of the long wooden porches that line the rear of the monastery.

K3 Volta Bureau

1537 35th Street, NW
(3417 Volta Place, NW)

1894—PEABODY AND STEARNS
1949—RUSSELL O. KLUGE
2000—Renovation architects of record: HORSEY & THORPE; Interior: RTKL ASSOCIATES

After the French government awarded Alexander Graham Bell the Volta Prize of 50,000 francs (about $10,000) in recognition of his invention of the telephone, Bell invested the money in further research that led to the graphophone, an improved version of the phonograph. The profits from this device helped him to establish the Volta Bureau, dedicated to the diffusion of knowledge about deafness, a subject near to Bell's heart because both his mother and his wife, Mabel Hubbard Bell, were deaf. The temple-like bureau seems to be mined from the same architectural vein as the small but impeccably detailed classical bank buildings that once stood on Main Streets in countless American towns. The entrance is marked by a pair of intricately decorated columns *in antis,* meaning that they are bracketed by the extensions of the side walls of the building. Note the contrasting east façade, which is composed of a series of slit windows reminiscent of the rear of the former Central Library on Mount Vernon Square.

K4 Pomander Walk

Volta Place, between 33rd and 34th streets, NW

1885—ARCHITECTS UNKNOWN
C. 1950—Renovations: ARCHITECTS UNKNOWN

Formerly called Bell's Court, this row of ten tiny houses was once an alley inhabited by former slaves living in desperate poverty. In 1950, the houses were condemned and the remaining residents forcibly evicted. Following renovation, the street was renamed after a small, private enclave in Manhattan's Upper West Side, which in turn had been modeled on the set of an early 20th-century comedic stage play of the same name.

K5 St. John's Episcopal Church, Georgetown Parish

3240 O Street, NW

1806—WILLIAM THORNTON
1843–1951—Numerous alterations and additions: VARIOUS ARCHITECTS
1878—Rectory: NORRIS G. STARKWEATHER
1995—Renovation and addition: EGBERT & HOUSTON

William Thornton, the original architect of the Capitol, as well as of Tudor Place and the Octagon, provided drawings for this church, but most likely did not supervise its construction. Early members of the congregation, which was founded in 1796, included Benjamin Stoddert and Francis Scott Key. President Thomas Jefferson contributed $50 to the building fund. Despite auspicious beginnings, the church was bankrupt by 1829. A few years later, the building was sold to William Corcoran in order to pay back taxes, but Corcoran, who had attended the church as a child, soon donated the building back to the congregation. The structure has been modified greatly over the years, but the foundations and most of the walls seem original. A modern atrium connecting the church and the parish hall is crowned by a row of skylights between timber trusses. As of this writing, the church has hired Hartman-Cox Architects to oversee a renovation of the sanctuary.

K6 Smith Row

3255–3263 N Street, NW

C. 1815—WALTER AND CLEMENT SMITH, OWNER-BUILDERS
Numerous alterations: VARIOUS ARCHITECTS

Along with Cox's Row one block down N Street [see following entry], these five houses are classic examples of domestic architecture of the Federal period, with flat fronts, arched doorways, and generally restrained ornament. The houses in this series are more refined than the neighboring row in several subtle ways, most notably their raised parlor floors, elegant entrance steps, slightly more elaborate door treatments (note #3259 in particular), and intimate relationship with the street.

K7 Cox's Row

3327–3339 N Street, NW

C. 1818—JOHN COX, OWNER-BUILDER
Numerous alterations: VARIOUS ARCHITECTS

Built by Colonel John Cox, this row of Federal houses shows traces of Victorian remodeling and recent restoration projects, but enough remains of them to give a sense of how they must have looked when new. Cox engineered the gerrymandering of city boundaries so he could run for mayor of Georgetown; he won, entering office in 1823 and holding the post for a record 22 years. When the Marquis de Lafayette returned to town in 1824, he accepted Cox's offer to reside at 3337 N Street for his entire

visit. In Lafayette's honor, it is said, local school girls sketched welcoming decorative flowers on the floor of the house with colored chalk. Cox and his wife lived next door at 3339.

K8 Holy Trinity Catholic Church

3513 N Street, NW

1794—Original church (now Chapel of St. Ignatius Loyola): ARCHITECT UNKNOWN
1851—Present church: ARCHITECT UNKNOWN
1869—Rectory: FRANCIS STAUNTON
1979—Renovation of main church: GIULIANI ASSOCIATES ARCHITECTS
2000—Renovation of chapel and parish facilities: KERNS GROUP ARCHITECTS

The three primary structures in this complex reflect three quite different eras in religious history. The original brick church on N Street was the first building in the District of Columbia erected for public Catholic services, and its small scale and modest character testify to the still-tenuous state of Catholicism in late 18th-century America. By the mid-19th century, that tiny church had become inadequate for the growing congregation, and it was superseded by the dignified, Greco-Roman revival structure on 36th Street, whose larger size and more refined architectural expression suggest American Catholicism's improved condition. Finally, the more elaborate, mansard-roofed rectory, around the corner on O Street, attests to the financial stability that came with the arrival of millions of industrial-era immigrants from Ireland, Italy, and elsewhere, swelling the ranks of the Roman Catholic Church in the United States. Less notable school and office structures complete the complex.

K9 Prospect House

3508 Prospect Street, NW

C. 1788–93—JAMES MACCUBBIN LINGAN, OWNER-BUILDER
1861–1951—Numerous alterations: VARIOUS ARCHITECTS

A great view down the Potomac provided the name for this quintessential freestanding Federal-era town house. It is believed that James Lingan designed the residence himself, perhaps using one of the architectural pattern books then popular among America's educated builders. One of 19 landowners who agreed to sell their holdings to establish the District of Columbia, Lingan decided that the future lay in the new, distinct capital city to the east, so he moved there and sold Prospect House in 1793. An outspoken opponent of the War of 1812, Lingan met his end in Baltimore when a hawkish mob stoned him to death.

A later resident was James Forrestal, the first person to hold the title of secretary of defense and namesake of the U.S. Department of Energy's building at L'Enfant Plaza [see C1]. After Forrestal's death, apparently by suicide, in 1949, the federal government leased the residence as a guest house for foreign dignitaries (while the Trumans were living at Blair House during the renovation of the White House). In 1950, the *Washington Times-Herald* published an exposé about the "scores of Congressmen" who sullied the grand dwelling with "stag entertainments . . . featuring liquor and feminine companionship."

K10 Capitol Traction Company Union Station

(Georgetown Car Barn)
3600 M Street, NW and 3520 Prospect Street, NW

1897—WADDY B. WOOD
1911—Expansion and alterations: ARCHITECT UNKNOWN
1960—Renovation: ARCHITECT UNKNOWN
1986—Renovation: ARTHUR COTTON MOORE / ASSOCIATES
1999—Renovation: RTKL ASSOCIATES

Engaging the precipitous bluff at the western end of the Georgetown waterfront, this former streetcar storage facility towers over M Street but appears from Prospect Street to be merely a series of modestly scaled pavilions and sunny terraces. In its original form, this was a highly complex building incorporating multiple levels of streetcar tracks, passenger stations, and offices. It is now used by Georgetown University for classrooms and office space. The steep staircase immediately to the west of the Car Barn is the one made famous in the movie *The Exorcist*—happily, it is now more commonly populated by ambitious joggers than by plunging priests.

K11 Washington Canoe Club

K Street, NW, above Key Bridge

1904—GEORGES P. HALES

A classic example of early 20th-century recreational architecture, this shingle-style boathouse conjures up images of the days of full-body bathing suits and Teddy Roosevelt's vigorous, outdoorsy antics. Supposedly built by the club's members using wood salvaged from derelict barns, the structure contains a large ballroom with a massive brick fireplace, and a grill room on the first floor decorated by a cartoon frieze, executed by *Evening Star* cartoonist Felix Mahony, showing early members of the Washington Canoe Club. Floods and ice have wreaked havoc with the building numerous times, but amazingly, it has never been damaged beyond repair. The organization was instrumental in the establishment of flatwater canoe racing as an Olympic sport.

K12 Halcyon House

(Benjamin Stoddert House)
3400 Prospect Street, NW

C. 1787—BENJAMIN STODDERT, OWNER-BUILDER
1900–1938—Numerous alterations and additions: ALBERT ADSIT CLEMONS
1994—Renovations and additions: STAVROPOULOS ASSOCIATES; Landscape architect: JAMES URBAN

The bizarre history of this large urban estate, one of Washington's quirkiest buildings, could warrant a book in its own right. The short version begins with Benjamin Stoddert, merchant, landowner, and America's first secretary of the navy, who built Halcyon House "after the manner of some of the elegant houses I have seen in Philadelphia," which then reigned as the American model of urban sophistication. The south façade, which actually resembles those of several other local houses as much as it does anything in Philly, remains largely intact, but the north is another matter.

Albert Adsit Clemons acquired the mansion around 1900, and soon began to alter it. Supposedly convinced that he would die if he stopped working on the house, Clemons spent nearly four decades obscuring Stoddert's chaste structure in a labyrinth of rooms, hallways, and stairs, most of which no one ever used. The peculiar results of his obsession are still visible on the north façade—note, just for starters, the mix of irregularly shaped stone and brick, the Mannerist, broken bases under the engaged columns, the vertical recesses in the brickwork between windows on the second and third floors, and the chamfered windows in the pediment. According to the *Washington Times-Herald,*

Clemons subsisted on money "provided by his wife on condition that he stay away from her." That condition apparently didn't bother Clemons, who, legend has it, was particularly fond of one of his carpenters, with whom he lived in the basement while they both worked feverishly on the upper levels.

Georgetown University bought the property in 1961 and used it as a dormitory for a few years before selling it. In 1978, sculptor John Dreyfuss moved into the mansion, and during the 1980s, he and his then-wife removed many of Clemons's greater excesses. They also commissioned a cavernous new studio space, under a revamped rear garden, which is illuminated by large skylights made of translucent, composite panels.

K13 Embassy of Ukraine

(Forrest-Marbury House)
3350 M Street, NW

C. 1790—URIAH FORREST, OWNER-BUILDER
Numerous alterations: ARCHITECTS UNKNOWN
1988—Addition: GEIER BROWN RENFROW ARCHITECTS; Restoration: MMP INTERNATIONAL

In this house, in March 1791, Georgetown mayor Uriah Forrest hosted a consequential dinner party—one that proved critical to the creation of the District of Columbia. At the urging of George Washington, Forrest gathered the area's leading landowners and convinced them, according the Washington's diary entry the following day, "to surrender for public purposes, one half of the land they severally possessed within bounds which were designated as necessary for the city." The agreement stipulated, among other points, that the landowners would receive £25 per acre for land to be used for public purposes and the rights to wood from the trees on their property. It was a win-win proposition—the young federal government would acquire the land necessary to build its new capital, and the landowners would benefit from the increased value of their remaining holdings.

A few years after hosting these successful negotiations, Forrest sold the stolid brick house in Georgetown and moved to Rosedale [see O16], his farm in what is now Cleveland Park. The next owner was Baltimore attorney William Marbury, who gained fame in 1803 as the plaintiff in the landmark Supreme Court case of *Marbury v. Madison,* which established the principle of judicial review. The large Marbury family, which owned the house for more than a half century, added a two-story wing to the east around 1840 and a third story above the main block about a decade later. After an extended period of neglect, the house was adapted in the late 20th century to new use as part of the Embassy of Ukraine.

K14 Cady's Alley

Between 33rd and 34th streets, NW, and between M Street and the C&O Canal

2004—Master plan and bridge: SHALOM BARANES ASSOCIATES; Individual buildings and stores: SORG AND ASSOCIATES, FRANK SCHLESINGER ASSOCIATES, MCINTURFF ARCHITECTS, MARTINEZ & JOHNSON ARCHITECTURE, AND SHALOM BARANES ASSOCIATES WITH LEOPOLD BOECKL; Landscape architects: THE FITCH STUDIO

Cady's Alley runs between 33rd and 34th streets just north of the C&O Canal, but the name is also used loosely to refer to a broader area containing a burgeoning collection of stores selling high-style furniture and housewares. This publicly accessible design center was the brainchild of developer Anthony Lanier, who saw the long-neglected western end of M Street as ripe for rejuvenation as a retail destination. The complex is all the more interesting because a number of different architects had a hand in the various buildings, some of which are relatively edgy for Georgetown. Note in particular the corrugated metal façade of 3335 Cady's Alley and the addition on top of 1028 33rd Street at the eastern end of the alley.

K15 3303 Water Street

2004—FRANK SCHLESINGER ARCHITECTS IN ASSOCIATION WITH GARY EDWARD HANDEL + ASSOCIATES

Inspired by the 19th-century industrial architecture of the Georgetown waterfront, this condominium building—containing some of the most expensive apartments in the city—achieves elegance through the interplay of plain brick surfaces and a curtain wall divided into relatively small units with dark metal frames. The curtain wall appears in several different forms. On the north and south façades, the main block of the building is divided into regular bays in which the outermost plane of the curtain wall is flush with the brick piers, but then is notched back at both corners, creating spaces for small balconies. On the east and west ends of the building, the curtain wall begins to break out from the brick armature, creating several fully glazed corners. On the south façade of the wing extending toward the river, a three-story section of curtain wall is cantilevered out from the brick structure to become the dominant compositional element. The butterfly-wing panel immediately adjacent to the freeway was conceived as being convertible to a glass curtain wall should the elevated road ever be torn down.

K16 The Flour Mill

1000 Potomac Street, NW

1845—GEORGE BOMFORD, OWNER-BUILDER
1883, 1932—Alterations: ARCHITECTS UNKNOWN
1980—PETER VERCELLI

Mills for cotton and flour were once fairly common near the Georgetown waterfront, yet of the many such buildings erected hereabouts, this is the sole survivor. Colonel George Bomford started a cotton mill on this site in the 1840s; later owners converted that structure into a flourmill in 1866; still later owners built additions in 1883 and some more in 1932.

Peter Vercelli used the extant structure as the base for a large condominium complex. The serrated balconies of the new buildings contrast dramatically with the planar façades of the original structure. This was one of a number of late 20th-century projects in Georgetown reflecting an almost fetishistic reliance on red brick as a medium for creating clearly modern buildings that still seemed sympathetic to their historic contexts. While the results can be a little overwhelming, the technique was usually successful. The vaguely threatening bollards at the corner of the plaza to the northeast of the site are inexplicable, however.

K17 Dean & Deluca

(Georgetown Market)
3276 M Street, NW

1865—ARCHITECT UNKNOWN
1992—Renovation: JACK CEGLIC, DESIGNER; Associated architects: CORE GROUP

Public markets have been located on this site since 1795, and in 1802, the ground was formally deeded to the town "for the use of the market aforesaid forever, and for no other use, interest or purpose whatsoever." The current structure, reminiscent of a small Victorian train station, dates to the Civil War. Generations of hucksters enjoyed a brisk business in the market until chain stores rendered the independent vendors obsolete. After a period of neglect, the old building, with its round-arched windows, bracketed cornices, and central parapet, has been carefully restored and now houses a highly fashionable food store. Excellent lighting and well-maintained displays conspire to make the fresh fruit, vegetables, and other foodstuffs on view almost irresistible.

K18 Chesapeake & Ohio Canal Warehouses

(Canal House / Georgetown Park Apartments)
Along the C&O Canal

c. 1828 and after—ARCHITECTS UNKNOWN
1977–82—CHLOETHIEL WOODARD SMITH / LOCKMAN ASSOCIATES ET AL.

The C& O Canal, which runs roughly 185 miles from Cumberland, Maryland, to Washington, D.C., never enjoyed the commercial success its backers had anticipated. The canal, obsolete even when new, could not compete with its archrival, the Baltimore & Ohio Railroad, which easily garnered most of the lucrative Ohio Valley trade. Closed to commerce since 1923, the canal is now simply a tourist attraction and a popular venue for evening constitutionals. A passenger barge operated by the National Park Service provides a sedate amusement ride for those so inclined.

Back in the early to mid-19th century, the canal carried enough traffic to warrant several large warehouses, which, more than a century later, caught the eye of developers eager to address the growing interest in loft spaces for both residential and commercial purposes. These dour, muscular buildings—rare in a city nearly bereft of industrial heritage—proved readily adaptable for modern living, retail, and office use. Old and new elements, while distinguishable by virtue of their differing materials and details, are nonetheless seamlessly integrated into a coherent and vibrant whole.

K19 City Tavern

3206 M Street, NW

1796—ARCHITECT UNKNOWN
1962—Reconstruction: MACOMBER & PETER

During the 18th century, Georgetown, which was located on a much-traveled post road, boasted several inns and taverns. Some voyagers used these more or less reputable establishments as places to refresh themselves with a glass of ale

or a spot of dinner; others sought rest in the (literally) lousy upstairs sleeping quarters. While most of the inns went out of business and were demolished as the importance of the post road declined in the 19th century, this one managed to endure. Rather, parts of it have endured: the upper-floor rooms are original, but the lower floor and brick façade are new and date to the building's painstaking reconstruction. The tavern now functions as a private social club.

K20 Grace Church

1041 Wisconsin Avenue, NW

1867—ARCHITECT UNKNOWN
1895—Rectory: ARCHITECT UNKNOWN
1898—Parish hall: ARCHITECT UNKNOWN
1922—Renovation: ARCHITECT UNKNOWN

Set back on a raised and tree-shaded courtyard, this humble, granite, Gothic Revival church, built as a mission for boatmen on the nearby Chesapeake & Ohio Canal, seems oblivious to the passage of time and the substantial development that has occurred around it. Viewed from certain angles, the property evokes images of classic New England churchyards.

K21 Waterfront Center

(Dodge Center)
1010 Wisconsin Avenue, NW

1813–24—Original warehouses: ARCHITECTS UNKNOWN
1975—HARTMAN-COX ARCHITECTS

Its angled profile mimicking the natural bluff that rises steeply from K Street (formerly known as Water Street), this office building is one of several projects offering a modern take on the industrial character of the old Georgetown waterfront. The finish brick replicates the texture of that used in surrounding historic structures, including the onetime warehouse of Francis Dodge, at the corner of Wisconsin and K, which was incorporated into the new complex. The building's open-air atrium has a Piranesian quality—its overall shape not fully intelligible, its concrete frame soaring into the mysterious upper reaches of the space. This atrium recalls the raw visual power of the area's old mills and warehouses, while affording intriguing views between the various offices and circulation spaces throughout the building.

K22 Ritz-Carlton Georgetown

3100 South Street, NW

1932—Incinerator: ARCHITECT UNKNOWN
2002—Renovation and additions: GARY EDWARD HANDEL + ASSOCIATES AND SHALOM BARANES ASSOCIATES; Hotel interiors / architects of record: GARY EDWARD HANDEL + ASSOCIATES; Theater

interiors: ROCKWELL GROUP; Preservation architects: BRAWER & HAUPTMAN, ARCHITECTS

Talk about adaptive reuse. This swanky hotel and condominium complex occupies the site—and remnants—of a Depression-era garbage incinerator. The project posed substantial regulatory and technical challenges, not the least of which was the need to blast out an enormous volume of rock in order to make room for the complex's parking garage, theaters, and other lower-level components. Meanwhile, a clump of little, historic houses, standing just to the west of the hotel entrance on South Street, had to be carefully picked up, moved to a temporary site, and later moved back to their original locations to ensure that they didn't go sliding down the hill during all that blasting. And, of course, the 130-foot smokestack and the incinerator building, an attractive work of industrial Art Deco, were contributing structures in the Georgetown Historic District and had to be preserved.

To avoid overwhelming the small-scale structures on the site and adjacent blocks, the architects broke up the massing of the complex into relatively small blocks, and organized them so as to preserve views to and from the various components, thus maintaining as much as possible of the "village-like" atmosphere that Georgetowners cherish. Not surprisingly, the architects chose red brick as the principal material for the new structures, matching the incinerator building and smokestack, as well as most of the larger buildings in the area. They also picked up on the dark window frames of the incinerator, using a matte black metal both in the frames for individual punched windows and as cladding for larger sections of the new structures, lending some variety to the façades. Battered, stone walls at the base of the building along K Street define a separate zone, creating a distinct identity for the entrance to the movie theaters while alluding to the tons of rock that had to be removed in order for the theaters to exist.

The incinerator building itself has been incorporated into the hotel, accommodating the lobby, lounge, and restaurant spaces. The highlight of the complex, however, is surely the chimney stack room—a space accommodating a single dining table at the base of the old smokestack, which is now protected by a glass roof and highlighted with appropriately dramatic lighting. Patrons inclined toward vertigo are advised to go easy on the martinis before gazing upward.

K23 Canal Square

1054 31st Street, NW

C. 1850—ARCHITECT UNKNOWN
1970—ARTHUR COTTON MOORE / ASSOCIATES

This seminal project was among the earliest successful examples of the adaptation of antique industrial facilities to contemporary commercial purposes. The new complex incorporates an existing warehouse that was the site of a historically significant event: here, in the 1880s, the computer age arguably began when Herman Hollerith perfected his pioneering punch-card tabulating machines. In 1890, the Census Bureau used Hollerith's new gadget to tabulate that year's survey data, accomplishing the job in a fraction of the time it had taken clerks to process the information from the previous census. Hollerith secured other important commissions, and in 1911 his Tabulating Machine Company merged with several other firms to create an entity that came to be known primarily by its initials: IBM.

K24 The Foundry

1055 Thomas Jefferson Street, NW

1856—ARCHITECT UNKNOWN
1977—Renovation and new construction: ARTHUR COTTON MOORE / ASSOCIATES; Architect of record: VLASTIMIL KOUBEK; Landscape architects: SASAKI ASSOCIATES

William Duvall's 1856 machine shop at 1050 30th Street, which was once used as a veterinary hospital for the mules that worked the C&O Canal, inspired the design and name of this complex. The modern building may not look like much from the side streets, but from the canal side, it can be appreciated for its simple lines, expansive windows, and sensitive massing. This development has struggled to retain retail and entertainment-oriented tenants—its movie theaters closed years ago, for instance—perhaps because it is somewhat removed from the bustle of Georgetown's primary commercial corridors.

K25 Washington Harbour

3000–3020 K Street, NW

1986—ARTHUR COTTON MOORE / ASSOCIATES

Dubbed "Xanadu on the Potomac" by the late J. Carter Brown, longtime chairman of the Commission of Fine Arts, Washington Harbour is a curious concoction of architectural motifs, which, according to the architect, refer to such diverse antecedents as the "exuberant three-dimensional vocabulary of Victorian Georgetown," the "classic, rhythmic, columnar quality" of Washington's monumental architecture, and even what he calls "Jeffersonian domes." Add to this the cartoonish metallic ornamentation that exemplifies Moore's "industrial baroque" style, and the result is visually staggering.

The mixed-use complex is, however, unquestionably successful in creating a *place,* predictably aswarm with diners, drinkers, boaters, and strollers on any remotely pleasant day. The slightly skewed, cross-shaped plan incorporates an implied continuation of Virginia Avenue (which actually dead-ends on the other side of Rock Creek), intersected by a pedestrianized extension of Thomas Jefferson Street, culminating in an oval plaza with a fountain and an extremely idiosyncratic tower. The relative narrowness of the complex's "streets" provides a respite from the famous—and, sometimes, seemingly relentless—broad avenues of Washington. The freestanding columns that dot the perimeter of the development provide support for floodwalls that can be raised from below ground when the Potomac has one of its destructive mood swings.

K26 House of Sweden

2900 K Street, NW

2006—GERT WINGÅRDH AND TOMAS HANSEN; Architects of record: VOA ASSOCIATES

Leave it to the Swedes to rethink the very concept of an embassy. This building houses not only the Swedish chancery, but also separate exhibition and event spaces, as well as corporate apartments and, in a gesture of international cooperation, the Embassy of Iceland. These days, "diplomatic" facilities are often fortresses set back far from surrounding streets, but the House of Sweden is transparent, open, and easily accessible by the general public.

Glass—the primary exterior material—is used in several different ways. On the lowest level, large windows allow passersby to get clear views into the building. On the next level, glass panels are suspended in front of the exterior wall, lending a slightly mysterious sense of depth to that part of the façades. One level above that, the building is girdled with ribbons of laminated glass containing a layer of film imprinted with wood grain patterns. The architects originally intended to use actual, thinly sliced sheets of wood to achieve this effect, but determined that Washington's infamous humidity would wreak wrinkly havoc on them. The alternative was risky—a reliance on fake, computer-generated wood grain might seem like a recipe for kitsch—but thanks to the exaggerated scale of the grain, coupled with the semi-regularity of the pattern embedded in each pane of glass, the effect is intriguingly abstract.

The interior is an essay in blond wood, stone, and more glass. Ceilings in key spaces are sheathed in maple panels with arrays of small holes drilled in them, allowing pinpoints of light to shine through. On the lower level, which contains most of the conference facilities, a reflecting pool with a sleek black basin provides a visual foil to all of the light-colored wood, while also making an architectural reference to Rock Creek, which flows right by the building before emptying into the Potomac. Throughout the building, circulation patterns are straightforward, making orientation easy.

With its simple but rich material palette, its organizational clarity, and even the slight frivolity of its translucent, faux wood-grain glass panels, the House of Sweden perfectly captures the aesthetic spirit of its home country. In the words of one staff member, "This building speaks Swedish."

K27 3001–3003 M Street, NW

C. 1794—THOMAS SIM LEE, OWNER-BUILDER
C. 1955—Restoration: HOWE, FOSTER AND SNYDER
Numerous alterations and additions: VARIOUS ARCHITECTS

Thomas Sim Lee served as a delegate to the Continental Congress and put in two terms as governor of Maryland. Like many prominent area politicians of the day, he dabbled in Washington real estate. One of his ventures involved building 3001–3003 M Street, originally a single, six-bay town house. Around 1805, however, Lee divided the building in two, selling one part and keeping the other. The structure is typical of Federal-era residential architecture in Georgetown, but one subtle aspect of the façade is worth noting: a water table (a projecting, horizontal course of bricks normally used to deflect water away from a building's foundation) appears between the first and second floors, instead of just above the ground as one might expect. That is because M Street was later substantially re-graded, entailing a dramatic drop in elevation that required these houses and most other older buildings on the street to add a floor *below* what used to be the ground level.

By the 1950s, the Lee houses had been neglected for decades and faced demolition. A group of private citizens led by Dorothea de Schweinitz and the nascent Historic Georgetown, Inc., stepped in, bought the properties, and restored them. The successful project spurred others to similar actions and may have been the single most important factor in bringing Georgetown's commercial district back to life.

K28 Old Stone House

3051 M Street, NW

1765—CHRISTOPHER AND RACHAEL LEYHMAN (OR LAYMAN), OWNERS-BUILDERS
1767, 1775, 1790—Additions: ARCHITECTS UNKNOWN
1959—Restoration: NATIONAL PARK SERVICE

Tel: (202) 426-6851
www.nps.gov/olst

The aptly if unimaginatively named Old Stone House is generally recognized as the oldest extant structure *built in* the District (but arguably not the oldest structure *in* the District [see P15]). Supported by thick walls of blue granite and fieldstone, the house probably survived only because generations of locals were told either that George Washington was headquartered here while surveying the area or that L'Enfant used it while drawing up plans for the new capital city. These and other traditional stories have been debunked, and it now seems that this was just a simple house and shop begun by a Pennsylvania-born cabinetmaker and completed by his widow. Purchased by the National Park Service and restored in the 1950s, the house is open to the public, as is the narrow garden to the rear of the property.

K29 Washington Post Office, Georgetown Branch

(Customhouse)
1215 31st Street, NW

1858—AMMI B. YOUNG
Numerous alterations: ARCHITECTS UNKNOWN
1997—Restoration: SORG AND ASSOCIATES

This former customhouse serves as a reminder that Georgetown remained a prominent port well into the 19th century. The architect, a native of New Hampshire, had already designed the Greek Revival Vermont State House (1833–38) and the Boston Custom House (1837–47) when the federal government called him to Washington in 1852 and made him supervising architect of the treasury. In that capacity Young designed a number of customhouses across the country, including this impressively solid building with granite façades and trim. During this period, the U.S. Treasury Department sometimes reused specific building designs—an exact duplicate of the Georgetown building, but made of limestone instead of granite, was erected at the same time in Galena, Illinois.

K30 Wheatley Houses

3041–3043 N Street, NW

1859—FRANCIS WHEATLEY, BUILDER
Numerous alterations: ARCHITECTS UNKNOWN

This almost mirror-image pair combines the flat façades more typical of Federal-era row houses with details that reveal their true Victorian character: tall, narrow parlor windows, pronounced cast iron window hoods (sporting huge medallions on the lower floors), and strongly rhythmic decoration on the cornices. By placing the first floor well above street level, Wheatley could drop the windows on that level to the floor and still preserve privacy for the rooms inside. Note the service entrance, suitable for hobbits, between the two houses.

K31 Laird-Dunlop House

3014 N Street, NW

c. 1798—Original (central) section: ATTRIBUTED TO WILLIAM LOVERING
Various alterations and additions: ARCHITECTS UNKNOWN

In the 1990s, German automaker BMW used a block of N Street in Georgetown as the backdrop for a series of ads for one of its most expensive models, elevating the street to iconic status as a province of the wealthy. Exuding class and unimpeachable taste, this stretch of the street is lined with quietly elegant row houses, including the storied Laird-Dunlop residence.

The inset, arched windows on the main floor of this house were unusual

during the Federal period, though William Lovering, a self-trained, amateur architect, used a similar motif on the Law House in Southwest Washington [see C9]. Thanks to slight setbacks and changes in height, the additions mimic the scale and rhythm of separate row houses, and thus disguise the true bulk of this mansion. John Laird, a wealthy tobacco merchant, built the original house. It later passed to his daughter, Barbara, and son-in-law, James Dunlop, a judge whose Confederate sympathies led to his ouster by President Lincoln. Coincidentally, a subsequent owner was none other than Robert Todd Lincoln, Honest Abe's only surviving son. The most recent famous occupants are former *Washington Post* editor Ben Bradlee and author Sally Quinn.

K32 Foxall House

2908 N Street, NW

c. 1820—HENRY FOXALL, OWNER-BUILDER
Various alterations and additions: ARCHITECTS UNKNOWN

Dwarfed by its three-story neighbors, this small, three-bay residence with a rare, wall-enclosed entry court has been much expanded. Foxall, who owned a thriving munitions foundry on the western outskirts of Georgetown and briefly served as the city's mayor, has gained immortality (and an "h") thanks to the 20th-century suburban neighborhood that sprawls over the family farm just west of Georgetown University [see Tour Q: Foxhall].

K33 Susan Decatur House

2812 N Street, NW

C. 1779—ARCHITECT UNKNOWN
Various alterations: ARCHITECTS UNKNOWN

The date of this house's original construction is unclear—various sources indicate that it was anywhere from 1779 to 1813. At any rate, it is a quintessential Georgetown Federal-period house, with a well-articulated doorway, planar façade, and simple staircase that seems to leap toward the entry. Stephen Decatur's widow, Susan, moved here after he was killed on the dueling field in 1820.

K34 Trentman House

1350 27th Street, NW

1968—HUGH NEWELL JACOBSEN

Hugh Newell Jacobsen is best known for his abstract, freestanding houses—assemblages of white pavilions whose simple, iconic shapes remind some people of Monopoly houses. In historic settings, however, Jacobsen tended to pursue a more contextualist path. Ac-

knowledging, but not quite replicating, the scale, color, and certain compositional elements of classic Federal row houses, the Trentman House is clearly modern, with sleek bay windows popping out from frames of highly unusual curved bricks.

K35 Mount Zion United Methodist Church

1334 29th Street, NW

1884—ARCHITECT UNKNOWN
1904—Alterations and addition: ARCHITECT UNKNOWN

The area of Georgetown east of 29th Street and below P was once a predominantly African American neighborhood known as Herring Hill. Mount Zion, believed to have been the first organized African American congregation in the District of Columbia, was a major fixture of the community. The original church, built around 1816, stood on 27th Street, and served as a station on the

Underground Railroad. This larger brick structure, built after the old church was destroyed by fire, bears a sober brick façade, though the sanctuary contains a rather elaborate stamped iron ceiling.

K36 Christ Church

31st and O streets, NW

1887—CASSELL & LAWS / HENRY LAWS
1923—Addition: ARCHITECT UNKNOWN
1968—Chapel of St. Jude: PHILIP IVES
2003—Interior restoration: STUDIOS ARCHITECTURE

With its acutely angled gables and almost skeletal tower, this church suggests a Gothic cathedral rendered in miniature and in dark red, pressed brick rather than stone. Note the sharp right triangle implied by the overall composition of forms along the O Street side. Inside, the ceiling is supported by exposed scissor trusses.

K37 The National Society of the Colonial Dames of America

(Dumbarton House)
2715 Q Street, NW

C. 1800—SAMUEL JACKSON, OWNER-BUILDER
1805—Alterations: ATTRIBUTED TO BENJAMIN HENRY LATROBE
1915—Moved to present site
1931—Restoration: HORACE W. PEASLEE AND FISKE KIMBALL
1991—Renovation: MARTIN ROSENBLUM

Tel.: (202) 337-2288
www.nscda.org

One of the oldest of Georgetown's large houses, Dumbarton was originally known as Cedar Hill, and later as Belle Vue, because of its spectacular site just beyond where Q Street once dead-ended on the east side of Rock Creek. The developer, Samuel Jackson, went bankrupt, and the house was unoccupied until Joseph Nourse, the first person to hold the position of register of the treasury, bought it in 1804. It is believed that Benjamin Henry Latrobe had a hand in adding the front portico and the two semicircular bays at the rear of the house not long after Nourse moved in.

The origin of the Dumbarton name is convoluted. In 1703, Ninian Beall, a Scot who had been taken prisoner by Oliver Cromwell in the Battle of Dunbar in 1650, obtained a "patent" for a large tract of land in what is now Georgetown. He named the estate "Rock of Dunbarton" (sometimes rendered as "Dunbar-ton"), a wry reference to his defeat many years earlier, but also a bit of a pun, referring to the famous Dumbarton (with an "m") Rock, a castle in Scotland.

Demolition of Dumbarton House seemed imminent in 1915, when the District government unveiled plans to extend Q Street into Georgetown across the new Buffalo Bridge. Preservationists managed to save the building and move it about 100 feet to its present location. The National Society of the Colonial Dames of America, an organization dedicated to historic preservation and education, bought the house in 1928 to serve as its headquarters. The society soon undertook a restoration to remove pseudo-Georgian appliqués, such as stone quoins at the corners of the house, which had been added in the early 20th century. A more recent renovation added modern services and various facilities to meet the organization's needs.

K38 R. E. Lee House

2813 Q Street, NW

C. 1890—ARCHITECT UNKNOWN
1961—Addition: HUGH NEWELL JACOBSEN
2005—Renovation: ROBERT PAHNKE

This property began as a typical, 19th-century Georgetown row house. At some point, however, the owners bought the vacant lot next door and moved the house's entrance around to that side. Much later, the mid-20th-century owners decided they needed more living space, and hired Hugh Newell Jacobsen to design an expansion. He created a mirror image of the existing house's projecting bay and connected the two with a "hyphen" containing a new entrance. The rear wall and ceiling of this architectural isthmus are of glass, bringing natural light into the house and affording direct views from the foyer to the rear garden. Jacobsen also lowered the sills of the windows on the existing façade and inserted more contemporary mullions (which he matched on the new wing), sending Georgetown's aesthetic rear guard into a tizzy, but the subdued modern solution seems to have won many converts after the fact.

K39 Francis Dodge House

1517 30th Street, NW

1853—ANDREW JACKSON DOWNING AND CALVERT VAUX
Numerous alterations: VARIOUS ARCHITECTS

One of a pair of houses built for the Dodge brothers, Francis and Robert, who made their fortunes in shipping, this grand residence is quite literally a textbook example of Victorian Italianate design. Calvert Vaux described both dwellings at length in his book *Villas and Cottages* (1857), though he lumped them together as "Design No. 17—Suburban Villa." He noted accurately that "although these two houses have their principal features in common, neither is a servile imitation of the other." As designed, each house was an asymmetrical but balanced composition, intended to accommodate the informality of daily domestic life while yielding a pleasing, "painter-like effect." The architects did not supervise the construction of either house directly. When Vaux wrote to Francis Dodge seeking a report on the progress of the work, Dodge replied, "We find the cost of our houses to be much beyond what Mr. Downing led us to expect—say about $15,000 each; yet we have fine houses, and very comfortable and satisfactory in every respect."

Robert Dodge's house still stands at 1534 28th Street, at the corner of Q Street, but was substantially altered during the 20th century.

K40 Cooke's Row

3007–3029 Q Street, NW

1868—STARKWEATHER AND PLOWMAN
2009—Renovation of 3007 Q Street: CHRISTIAN ZAPATKA ARCHITECT
Numerous other alterations: ARCHITECTS UNKNOWN

This parade of picturesque duplexes hints at the stylistic promiscuity of the Victorian era, while dramatically refuting

the perception of Georgetown as solely an enclave of Federal-style architecture. The row's two end units are quintessentially Second Empire, while the middle two are equally classically Italianate. All four pairs sport some of the more effusive roof brackets in the city, but the ones supporting the porches at 3007 and 3009 deserve particular note.

K41 Tudor Place

1644 31st Street, NW

1795—East and west wings: ARCHITECT UNKNOWN
1805–16—Central section and connecting structures: WILLIAM THORNTON
1876—Kitchen addition: ARCHITECT UNKNOWN
1914—Renovation: WALTER GIBSON PETER

Tel: (202) 965-0400
www.tudorplace.org

Tudor Place—William Thornton's masterpiece—marks a significant break with the Georgian architecture of the preceding generation as represented by the Bowie-Sevier House, directly across Q Street. Like the Capitol, for which Thornton was the original architect, Tudor Place began ingloriously as a pair of wings with no connecting body. Then, in 1805, these stubs and the eight-and-a-half-acre property on which they stood were bought by Thomas Peter and Martha Custis Peter, granddaughter of Martha Washington, using $8,000 left to Mrs. Peter by her step-grandfather, George. The Peters hired Thornton to remodel the wings and design the central connecting piece. The house is linear in plan, with the public rooms marching along the south side of the ground floor, and circulation and service spaces lining the north side. The engaged porch, which is a full circle in plan, leads to the "saloon," a curious room given the convex arc of the porch that projects into the space. Huge windows in the arc can be lifted up into a hidden pocket above, creating a doorway through which guests once entered.

Incredibly, Tudor Place was continuously occupied by six generations of the Peter family over the course of more than 180 years. It is now a museum boasting extensive collections of art objects and household items, as well as meticulously maintained gardens. Martha Peter planted some of the Old Blush roses and the boxwood parterre, and her direct descendants added specimen trees and other features. Both the house and the gardens provide unparalleled insights into the evolution of domestic life in Washington in its first two centuries.

K42 Scott-Grant House

3240 R Street, NW

1857—A. V. SCOTT, OWNER-BUILDER
1907, 1930—Alterations: ARCHITECTS UNKNOWN

Representative of the gracious, freestanding estates that give the northern end of Georgetown its genteel suburban character, this highly formal house is loosened up by relatively florid decorative elements. Alabaman A. V. Scott, who built the place, had no use for it during the Civil War for obvious reasons and leased it to a variety of tenants. General Ulysses S. Grant himself rented it during at least one summer, hence the second half of the house's name, but the most

memorable lessee may have been General Henry Walker Halleck. He earned the enmity of his neighbors by quartering enlisted men in the house, turning R Street into a drill field, and having the company bugler sound reveille and taps at dawn and dusk each day.

K43 Dumbarton Oaks

Museum entrance: 1703 32nd Street, NW
Garden entrance: R Street at 31st Street, NW

c. 1801—WILLIAM HAMMOND DORSEY, OWNER-BUILDER
c. 1805-15—Orangery: ARCHITECT UNKNOWN
c. 1865—Alterations: EDWARD LINTHICUM, OWNER
1922-59—Landscape architect: BEATRIX FARRAND
1923—Alterations: FREDERICK H. BROOKE
1926—Service Court buildings: LAWRENCE WHITE / MCKIM, MEAD & WHITE
1929—Music room: LAWRENCE WHITE / MCKIM, MEAD & WHITE
1938-46—Byzantine wing and other additions: THOMAS T. WATERMAN
1963—Garden library: FREDERIC RHINELANDER KING / WYETH AND KING
1989—Museum addition: HARTMAN-COX ARCHITECTS
1995—Pool renovation: RICHARD WILLIAMS ARCHITECT
2000-07—Library, Gardeners' Court, and rehabilitation of existing structures: VENTURI, SCOTT BROWN AND ASSOCIATES; Preservation architects: OEHRLEIN & ASSOCIATES ARCHITECTS

Tel: (202) 339-6450
www.doaks.org

The house at Dumbarton Oaks has been renovated and extended so many times that little of the original architecture is intact. The main structure is characteristic of the Federal period, with planar brick walls, evenly spaced windows, and a modest cornice. Some slight scroll work above the main entry and a series of subtle, inset panels between the first- and second-floor windows are among the few decorative flourishes—if that's

even the right word—on the primary façade of this grand but understated building.

Robert and Mildred Bliss (stepbrother and -sister, who were unrelated by blood, raised together, and later married) acquired the house and 53 acres in 1920 and proceeded to change the already much-altered dwelling to accommodate their exceptional collections of Byzantine and pre-Columbian art. They also set to work on the gardens. Beatrix Farrand's evolving design for the property, with its numerous terraces and "garden rooms," is a masterpiece of American landscape architecture and the summation of her distinguished career. Her Dumbarton work captures her spirit of romance: she once wrote to the Blisses about a patch of woods near the music room, urging them "to keep it as poetic as possible . . . the sort of place in which thrushes sing and . . . dreams are dreamt."

The Blisses, whose wealth derived from their family's ownership of the patent for Fletcher's Castoria, a children's medicine, moved to California in 1940. After donating 27 acres north of the house to the city as a public park and selling ten acres to the government of Denmark for its embassy on Whitehaven Street, they gave the rest of the estate to Harvard University for use as a study center and museum. Before heading west, Mrs. Bliss asked Farrand to draw up some maintenance guidelines for the grounds. Farrand complied and urged the university always to respect the dual nature of the property—on the one hand it offers "a pleasant sense of withdrawal from the nearby streets," while on the other it allows "an intimate connection with all that a great city can offer."

Between August and October 1944, the estate was the site of a series of meetings collectively known as the Dumbarton Oaks Conference, in which senior representatives of the United States, Great Britain, Russia, and China laid the organizational groundwork for the United Nations.

K43a Pre-Columbian Collection Pavilion

1963—PHILIP JOHNSON
2007—Restoration: VENTURI, SCOTT BROWN AND ASSOCIATES; Preservation architects: OEHRLEIN & ASSOCIATES ARCHITECTS

In a long but erratic career, which on the one hand produced the sublime Glass House in New Canaan, Connecticut, but also yielded a series of fatuous postmodern skyscrapers, Philip Johnson produced a few masterpieces. The Pre-Columbian Museum is among them.

It was the 1960s, and the idea of appending an abstract molecule of little pavilions made of marble, teak, bronze, and glass to a historic, brick Georgetown mansion was less surprising than it would be now. For the visitor who can set aside any preconceptions about such a juxtaposition, this gem of a museum is a wondrous building to experience. It consists of eight circular, domed exhibition pods surrounding a central, open court with a fountain. Each pod is itself defined by a constellation of robust, round columns, subtly recapitulating the larger organization of the structure. Curved glass walls blur the boundary between inside and out. Despite its heavy classical and Byzantine undertones, this was the only Washington building to be included in the Museum of Modern Art's landmark 1977 survey exhibition of modern architecture.

K44 Oak Hill Cemetery

30th and R streets, NW

1833—Van Ness mausoleum: GEORGE HADFIELD
1850—Chapel: JAMES RENWICK JR.
1853—Gatehouse: ATTRIBUTED TO GEORGE DE LA ROCHE
1867—Additions to gatehouse: ARCHITECT UNKNOWN
1872—Van Ness mausoleum moved from original site on H Street, NW

Oak Hill Cemetery was laid out in a fashionably romantic manner over naturally terraced land donated by banker and philanthropist William Corcoran in 1849. Local luminaries interred here include architect Adolf Cluss, politico James G. Blaine, and Corcoran himself.

The Italianate gatehouse is believed to have been designed by George de la Roche, who was also responsible for the overall cemetery plan (though there is some evidence that Andrew Jackson Downing played a role in the landscape design). Inside the grounds, but visible from the street, is James Renwick's impeccable little Gothic Revival chapel—a giant paperweight made of gray Potomac gneiss and sharply contrasting red sandstone. The large rose window over the entrance beckons visitors from across the adjacent lawn. At the eastern end of the cemetery is the Van Ness family mausoleum, the design of which was based on the ancient Temple of Vesta in Rome. Although it seems perfectly at home here, the structure was actually built for the family's private burial grounds in what is now downtown Washington, and was later moved to this site.

TOUR L

Dupont Circle

During much of its first century, Washington was generally a scruffy and inconsistently developed town with a few monumental buildings that stood out like ermine-clad royalty among the mud-soaked peasants. That began to change in the 1870s with Boss Shepherd's highly successful (but fiscally disastrous) public works campaign. The city soon began to show more signs of architectural maturity and sophistication, and by the 1890s, to the astonishment of the upper classes everywhere, Washington was becoming a fashionable place for the wealthy—especially the newly wealthy—to hobnob, throw fabulous parties, and build immense mansions.

Around the turn of the 20th century, more than 100 grand residences sprang up along Massachusetts and Connecticut avenues and on Dupont Circle itself, making this once-quiet section of the city suddenly the rival of New York's Fifth Avenue as *the* place in the nation to live. Perhaps Henry Adams was thinking of this trend when he wrote in 1904: "The American wasted money more recklessly than any one did before; he spent more to less purpose than any extravagant court aristocracy; he had no sense of relative values, and knew not what to do with his money when he got it, except to use it to make more, or throw it away." Later, the Dupont Circle phenomenon prompted Phillip Wylie to use his 1942 book, *Generation of Vipers,* to attack "every

Dupont Circle in the mid-1920s, after the original statue of Admiral Samuel Francis du Pont had been replaced with the more impressive fountain by sculptor Daniel Chester French and architect Henry Bacon (the same team responsible for the Lincoln Memorial). The Patterson House (now the Washington Club) is visible at the middle left. The large house at right was the mansion of dry-goods magnate Levi Leiter. It was demolished in 1947 to make way for what is now the Dupont Circle Hotel.

19th ST
CONNECTICUT AVE
MASSACHUSETTS AVE
21st ST
800 ft
1
2
3
4
5
6
7
8
9
10
11
12

T ST
S ST
R ST
Q ST
P ST
18th ST
16th ST
NEW HAMPSHIRE AVE
27
28
29
30
26
25
24
23
22
21
20
19
17
18
16
15
14

sullen, rococo, snarling, sick, noxious and absurd form of vainglorious house . . . [built here] to assuage the cheap pretensions of the middle class and the Middle West."

The evolution of the park in the circle itself reflects the broader trends in the neighborhood during that period. In 1882, Congress decided to commemorate Admiral Samuel Francis du Pont, a Civil War naval hero, by naming this new circle for him (the area had been known as "The Slashes") and by placing a small bronze statue of him in the center. That wasn't enough for the admiral's family, who, in good Gilded-Age style, decided to circumvent the federal government by directly hiring the team that gave the city the Lincoln Memorial—architect Henry Bacon and sculptor Daniel Chester French—to create the present, far grander, monument. At some point, the spelling of the admiral's last name was modified to yield the one-word version applied to the circle today.

The Great Depression obliterated much of the wealth that had made all of this possible, and when World War II came, many of the grand mansions were lent, sold, or donated to governmental and other agencies to aid the war effort. By the 1950s, a number of the buildings here had been converted to boarding houses. The riots of the late 1960s along the nearby 14th Street corridor triggered a further decline in property values. Not coincidentally, at the same time, the circle itself and some nearby buildings were becoming popular with hippies, artists, and other alternative types that the decade produced in abundance. Soon the area was recognized as a historic district, and, repeating a pattern common to analogous areas in so many American cities, gay men and lesbians began to move here in large numbers, leading a wave of renovation. Over the past generation, the Dupont Circle neighborhood has blossomed once again, becoming one of the most vibrant residential areas in the country, attracting new residents and boasting housing prices that suggest the arrival of a new Gilded Age.

L1 Dupont Circle Building

1350 Connecticut Avenue, NW

1931—MIHRAN MESROBIAN
1942—Conversion from apartments to offices: ARCHITECT UNKNOWN
1987—Renovation: OLDHAM AND SELTZ

The genius of this wedge-shaped structure lies in its masterful bas-relief ornament, which lends visual depth and rhythm to the main façades, but keeps the profile of the building taut and planar so as not to distract from its apparent geometrical purity when viewed on end. In this regard, it outdoes New York's famous Flatiron Building, which has a heavily sculpted skin that competes with the acutely angled form for attention. Another notable element of the Dupont Circle Building is its stepped mechanical penthouse—a technical necessity that Mesrobian turned into an architectural asset.

L2 1818 N Street, NW

1984—DAVID M. SCHWARZ / ARCHITECTURAL SERVICES; Associated architect: VLASTIMIL KOUBEK

Since John Carl Warnecke's project for Lafayette Square set a Washington precedent for preserving low-rise structures and adding taller buildings behind them, local architects have experimented with numerous variations on that theme. This complex on a narrow block of N Street represents a hybrid approach—in its materials, gabled forms, and stepped massing, the newly constructed portion clearly draws on elements of the existing

row houses but stops short of replicating their decorative motifs or other historical details.

L3 Sunderland Building

1320 19th Street, NW

1969—KEYES, LETHBRIDGE & CONDON, ARCHITECTS
2005—Renovation and lobby addition: ENVISION DESIGN

This relatively small office building is an intriguing geometrical exercise. The façades of the rectilinear structure are animated by several asymmetrical design gestures: first, the exterior columns (some of which house ventilation ducts, rather than structural supports) are flared on just one side of each vertical slit window; second, the regular grid of these slit windows on the second through seventh floors is interrupted by a large blank panel to the right; and third, on the top floor, the pattern of solid and void is switched, with a large expanse of glass to the right and a smaller blank panel to the left. Taken together, the four virtually identical façades thus create a dynamic composition suggesting rotational movement.

L4 The Brewmaster's Castle

(Christian Heurich House Museum)
1307 New Hampshire Avenue, NW

1894—JOHN GRANVILLE MYERS; Interiors: CHARLES H. AND HUGO F. HUBER
1914—Addition: APPLETON P. CLARK

Tel: (202) 429-1894
www.brewmasterscastle.org

Knotty and lugubrious, the Heurich House is an example of what historian Richard Howland dubbed "beer-barrel baronial" grandeur. Its New Hampshire Avenue façade, made of dark, rough sandstone, is punctuated by a chunky *porte-cochère* bristling with gargoyles. Around the corner on Sunderland Place, a somewhat less intimidating brick, terra cotta, and sandstone façade ends with a copper-and-glass conservatory, the delicacy and bright green patina of which contrast sharply with the main body of the house. Supporting all of the robust masonry is a structure that was innovative in its day—the first significant use of reinforced concrete in a residential building in the United States.

The shadowy interiors, intact and original, attest to the extravagant taste of the house's builder, Christian Heurich, a German immigrant who became a highly successful brewer and, at one time, the second largest landowner in the nation's capital after the federal government. Heurich, whose company's slogan was "Beer recommended for family use by Physicians in General," made no bones about acknowledging the source of his wealth. The breakfast room in the basement is a case in point. Its walls are covered with murals depicting the virtues of beer-drinking interspersed with aphorisms such as "Raum ist in der kleinsten Kammer für den grossten Katzenjammer" ("There is room in the smallest chamber for the biggest hangover"). Clearly, Heurich, who actively managed the business until his death at the age of 102, was a man who loved his work.

Heurich's widow donated the house to the organization now known as the Historical Society of Washington, D.C. When the society moved to its new headquarters at Mount Vernon Square in 2003, two of Heurich's grandchildren bought the house back, and formed a foundation to preserve it as a museum, to which they have now applied the regrettable, Disneyesque moniker "The Brewmaster's Castle."

L5 21 Dupont Circle, NW

(Euram Building)

1971—HARTMAN-COX ARCHITECTS

All too often, a project that begins as an elegantly simple architectural diagram, when finally realized in three dimensions, lacks the purity and clarity of the initial concept. This modestly scaled building is a brilliant exception. Structurally, 21 Dupont Circle is composed of a series of post-tensioned concrete bridges, spanning between unadorned, brick-clad piers at the corners of the site, and surrounding an open courtyard. The resulting office spaces are narrow and column-free, affording all tenants access to views outside and plenty of natural light. The principal façades neatly express the essential structural scheme, thanks in large part to the bands of floor-to-ceiling, mullionless windows, which allow the bridge-like concrete beams to be read clearly.

L6 Blaine Mansion

2000 Massachusetts Avenue, NW

1882—JOHN FRASER
1921—Renovation and additions: GEORGE N. RAY
1949—Conversion to office use: MAURICE S. MAY
2009—Renovation and addition: VAN DUSEN ARCHITECTS

This brooding pile of bricks is the last of several stern Victorian-era mansions that once loomed near Dupont Circle. The house was built for James G. Blaine, a man known to his friends as "the Plumed Knight of American Politics" and to his enemies as "Slippery Jim." One of the founders of the Republican Party, Blaine held a number of important posts, including Speaker of the House and secretary of state, and thrice ran unsuccessfully for the presidency. Soon after this house was finished, Blaine decided that it was too expensive to maintain and leased it to some of his more cash-laden contemporaries, such as Levi Leiter, an early partner of Marshall Field, and George Westinghouse, whose surname speaks for itself. Westinghouse bought the place outright in 1901 and lived here until his death in 1914.

John Fraser, a former partner of the great Philadelphia architect Frank Furness, originally designed the house for a different site, which helps explain its rather incidental relationship to the surrounding streets. There are subtle but significant variations in the treatment of the façades—note, for instance, how some of the chimneys are flush with the walls below the cornice line, while others bulge from the wall plane at the second floor. The one-story retail strip along P Street was added in 1921 and was updated during the most recent renovation, which also involved the addition of a major new wing to the west. The contrasting materials, colors, and forms of this addition allow the original structure to continue to be perceived as a free-standing block. In fact, on the Massachusetts Avenue side, the new wing angles away from the mansion so dramatically that it almost looks as if it were an addition to the building next door. The complex now contains a mix of establishments, including restaurants along P Street, office space, and apartments on the upper levels.

L7 Embassy of the Republic of Indonesia

(Walsh-McLean House)
2020 Massachusetts Avenue, NW

1903—HENRY ANDERSEN
1952—Renovation: ARCHITECT UNKNOWN
1982—Addition: THE ARCHITECTS COLLABORATIVE

In 1869, an Irish teenager named Thomas Walsh came to the United States to seek his fortune, and he soon found it during the Black Hills Gold Rush. He then struck it richer, as it were, when he bought the Camp Bird Mine, which was marked by one of the thickest veins of gold in the world (he later sold the mine for the then-remarkable sum of $3 million plus a percentage of future yields). Obscenely rich, he moved his family to Washington in 1897 with the goal of joining "society."

Walsh quickly realized that one of the most important instruments of social status was an impressive mansion, so he commissioned this 60-room extravaganza, and proudly embedded a slab of gold ore into the front porch to proclaim the source of his wealth. The house is organized around a three-story, galleried Art Nouveau stairwell that was supposedly copied from one of Walsh's favorite White Star ocean liners. The exterior, with its undulating walls, rounded corners, and even curving chimneys, defies stylistic nomenclature, but could be described generically and with some understatement as "neo-Baroque." "Baroque" also describes Walsh's lifestyle: "At one New Year's Eve party," reported the *New York Times*, "325 guests consumed 480 quarts of champagne, 288 fifths of scotch, 48 quarts of cocktails, 40 gallons of beer and 35 bottles of miscellaneous liquors."

Walsh later grew reclusive, and in 1910 he died in virtual isolation. His daughter, Evalyn, inherited the house but refused to move into it, stating that "it was cold, but its deepest chill lodged in my breast." She married publishing heir Edward Beale McLean (his family owned the *Post*), and the pair lived lavishly at their estate on Wisconsin Avenue. According to James Goode's *Capital Losses*, the pair "managed to dissipate almost all of the vast McLean and Walsh fortunes, amounting to 100 million dollars." (She "dissipated" a portion of the money when she bought the Hope Diamond.) The Indonesian government purchased the Massachusetts Avenue mansion in 1951 for $335,000—less than half of its original cost—and later added a new wing with a curving façade echoing the fluid form, but not the quirky character, of the exuberant main house.

L8 The Society of the Cincinnati Headquarters Library and Museum

(Anderson House)
2118 Massachusetts Avenue, NW

1905—LITTLE AND BROWNE
1968—Restoration and renovation: CLAS, RIGGS, OWENS & RAMOS
1998—Exterior restoration and interior alterations: ARCHETYPE

Tel: (202) 785-2040
www.societyofthecincinnati.org

Career diplomat Larz Anderson III and his heiress wife, Isabel Weld Perkins, commissioned this neo-English Baroque mansion as their winter residence to take advantage of Washington's "social season." And social they were, hosting foreign dignitaries, industrialists, members of Congress, and at least a couple of U.S. presidents. They also gladly made the house available to visiting heads of state—the royal couples of Belgium and Siam were among those who surely found the 50-room house appropriately palatial.

After Mr. Anderson's death, his widow, following her husband's wishes, donated the mansion to the Society of the Cincinnati, a hereditary organization of which Mr. Anderson was a member. The society was founded by a group of Revolutionary War officers and took its name from Lucius Quinctius Cincinnatus, a Roman "civilian general" who humbly returned to his farm after each of two victorious military campaigns. He was therefore seen as a parallel to America's own nonprofessional military hero, George Washington. Washington somewhat reluctantly agreed to become the organization's first "president general" despite the objections of contemporary politicians who feared that it represented the beginnings of an American aristocracy.

The house's arched gateways and stately forecourt are highly unusual in Washington, and suggest the presumption that all visitors would arrive by carriage rather than on foot. Huge lanterns, suspended from curved iron armatures, hang just inside the archways. The mansion's cavernous interior, which is open to the public as a museum, is eclectically decorated, to say the least. Notable items on display include a set of Brussels tapestries originally woven as a gift of Louis XIII to Cardinal Barberini, papal representative at the French court. The premier space is the ballroom on the first floor, which boasts an astonishing cantilevered staircase leading to a musicians' balcony supported by spiral, red Verona marble columns. The building also houses a library notable for its 18th-century military history collections.

L9 Phillips Collection

1600 21st Street, NW

1897—HORNBLOWER & MARSHALL
1907—Music room: HORNBLOWER & MARSHALL
1920—Second-floor addition: MCKIM, MEAD & WHITE
1923—Fourth floor: FREDERICK H. BROOKE
1960—Original annex: WYETH & KING
1989—Renovations and addition: ARTHUR COTTON MOORE / ASSOCIATES
2006—Addition and renovation: COX GRAAE + SPACK ARCHITECTS

Tel: (202) 387-2151
www.phillipscollection.org

The first museum of modern art in the United States, the Phillips Collection was born in 1921, when Duncan Phillips and his mother opened two rooms of their own residence as a public gallery in memory of Duncan's recently deceased father and brother. Today, despite a succession of additions and renovations, the institution largely retains the intimate, domestic character of its original incarnation. Even when the museum is crowded with art lovers, a visitor almost expects a member of the Phillips family to pop in and invite everyone to sit down for tea.

The Phillips Collection, which is best known for its Impressionist and Post-Impressionist paintings, was actually conceived as a museum of "modern art and its sources," reflecting Duncan's interest in both contemporary art and past works that he considered to be important antecedents. An heir to the Jones and Laughlin steel fortune, Duncan developed his avocation early on—while still an undergraduate he wrote an article titled "The Need of Art at Yale," and he called his first book, published when he was 28, *The Enchantment of Art*. His wife, Marjorie, was a well-regarded painter in her own right.

The original mansion is a subdued, mildly eclectic affair, combining Georgian and Federal elements, and even a hint of Art Nouveau in the decoration on the columns and frieze of the entrance bay. The house was modestly expanded several times in the early 20th century, and the mansarded fourth floor was added to provide more living space after the initial rooms were opened to the public. By 1930, the collection had grown so large that the family had to move out entirely.

The original annex, as completed in 1960, was a necessary but uninspired addition, lending a more institutional tone to the complex. In 1989, the annex was thoroughly revamped to make it more compatible with the older structures and a more commodious setting for art in its own right. Yet another renovation of the complex, including the incorporation of an existing apartment building to the north, was completed in 2006. A small fire in 2010 damaged office areas in the mansion, but all of the art came through unscathed.

L10 Cosmos Club

(Townsend House)
2121 Massachusetts Avenue, NW

1901, 1904—CARRÈRE & HASTINGS; Landscape architects: OLMSTED BROTHERS
1909—2164 Florida Avenue: SPEIDEN & SPEIDEN ARCHITECTS
1952—Alterations and addition: HORACE W. PEASLEE
1962—Alterations and addition: FRANK W. COLE
1997—Renovation of 2164 Florida Avenue (Hillyer House): O'NEIL & MANION ARCHITECTS

Railroad money lay behind this entry to the unspoken contest to build the grandest house in turn-of-the-20th-century Washington. Richard Townsend's fortune came mostly from the Erie and Pittsburgh line and Mary Scott Townsend's from the Pennsylvania, among other sources. The couple had the new house built around an older one, because a gypsy had once predicted that Mrs. Townsend was destined to die "under a new roof."

The Townsends told Carrère and Hastings that they wanted a Washington château based on the Petit Trianon at Versailles, an apt choice given the New York architects' predilection for things French. The tall, central portion of the house has a strong vertical thrust, thanks to its two-story-tall pilasters and the trio of arched dormer windows set into the mansard roof. The grandest interior spaces, however, are actually in the horizontal, flanking wings. The ballroom and the library are on the second floor of the north and south wings, respectively, and each is marked with a single window framed by two blank panels. Lest the effect of all this be insufficiently regal, the architects added a quartet of ring-chomping lions' heads to the frieze above the first floor of the central pavilion.

The Townsends' daughter, Mathilde, inherited the house in 1935; she had married Sumner Welles, a diplomat who played several crucial roles in FDR's administration. The prestigious and exclusive Cosmos Club acquired the property in 1950. In adapting the place for its new use, Horace Peaslee had to take away much of the original landscaping by the Olmsted Brothers—parking lots do take up room—but he was able to maintain surprisingly large sweeps of Carrère's interiors. Thus, the original structure, largely intact, forms a veritable museum of railroad-financed, Gilded-Age grandeur.

L11 1718 Connecticut Avenue, NW

1982—DAVID M. SCHWARZ / ARCHITECTURAL SERVICES

An architectural Jekyll and Hyde—which side is which depends on the viewer's own stylistic proclivities—this retail and office building is fancifully neo-Romanesque in front and no-nonsense International Style in back. A bold diagonal line, best observed from a vantage point a few blocks up Connecticut

Avenue, strikingly cleaves the two halves of the building. Although obviously more deliberate in this case, the dichotomy evokes that of many historic Washington row houses and commercial structures, which were often built with relatively ornate fronts and quite plain rear façades.

L12 Woman's National Democratic Club

(Whittemore House)
1526 New Hampshire Avenue, NW

1894—HARVEY L. PAGE
1967—Addition: NICHOLAS SATTERLEE

Tel: (202) 232-7363
www.democraticwoman.org

A great cape of a roof—punctuated by an occasional raised-eyelid window—drapes languidly over this spectacular mansion. Sarah Adams Whittemore, an opera singer and cousin of Henry Adams, commissioned the house, whose modest entrance is partially sheltered by an overhanging, copper-and-leaded-glass bay window. A parade of rather simple and serviceable brackets remarkably turns the roof gutter into a substantive architectural element. Now the headquarters of the Woman's National Democratic Club, the building contains a small museum mostly devoted to political memorabilia, including items pertaining to Eleanor Roosevelt, a club member who, when she became First Lady, used the organization as a vehicle to advance her social agenda. A starkly contrasting, rough concrete addition houses event spaces and peripheral functions.

L13 The Washington Club

(Patterson House)
15 Dupont Circle, NW

1903—MCKIM, MEAD AND WHITE (STANFORD WHITE)
1951–56—Alterations and addition: ARCHITECTS UNKNOWN
1985—Restoration: OEHRLEIN & ASSOCIATES ARCHITECTS

Designed by Stanford White for Robert Wilson Patterson, publisher of the *Chicago Tribune,* this palazzo appears extremely grand from Dupont Circle, but assumes a surprising intimacy up close, thanks to its tiny forecourt defined by the two wings and angled entry connecting them. Lavishly iced with swags, fruit, and other sundries, the façades of glazed terra cotta and marble are further decorated with flat panels of variegated marble, abstractly suggesting framed paintings. This same variegated marble appears on the columns of the central porch, which became famous in 1927, when Charles Lindbergh, freshly returned from his daring flight across the Atlantic, was photographed there waving to crowds below. (Lindbergh was visiting President and Mrs. Calvin Coolidge, who were living at the Patterson mansion temporarily while the White House was undergoing renovation.)

The most famous Patterson to live in the house was not Robert, but his redoubtable and scandal-prone daughter, "Cissy," who worked her way up through the family publishing business and ultimately purchased two newspapers that she combined to create *The Washington Times-Herald.* Briefly a countess by marriage, Cissy was a vociferous opponent of Franklin Roosevelt, and she used the medium at her disposal to disseminate a blizzard of highly sensational "news" that made her the *bête noire* of official Washington. "The trouble with me," she once said, "is that I am a vindictive old shanty-Irish bitch." Cissy's death in 1948 marked the end of a feverish era in the capital's social life. She left the building to the Red Cross, which sold it to the Washington Club in 1951.

L14 Chancery of Iraq

(Boardman House)
1801 P Street, NW

1893—HORNBLOWER & MARSHALL
Numerous alterations: ARCHITECTS UNKNOWN

Tricks with bricks—such as the splayed jack arches over the windows and the eccentric, zigzag frieze between the first and second floors—help to animate this otherwise staid, quasi-Romanesque block. Also noteworthy are the balustrades along the top of the bay window and on the small balcony above, comprising rows of tiny Ionic columns. Curiously, the house's most elaborate decorative element, a beautiful mosaic, is tucked under the entry arch, where, on a sunny day, it is sometimes almost invisible in the shadows. Mabel Boardman, the house's most notable occupant, was well known for her work with the Red Cross. Boardman also cofounded the Sulgrave Club, whose members met here until 1932, when they were able to buy and remodel their present building across the street [see following entry]. Now, after more than a decade of disuse between the two Persian Gulf wars, this house serves once again as the Iraqi Chancery.

L15 Sulgrave Club

(Wadsworth House)
1801 Massachusetts Avenue, NW

1901—GEORGE CARY
1932—Remodeling: FREDERICK H. BROOKE
1952—Alterations: ARCHITECT UNKNOWN

When built, this was a drive-through house, incorporating an unusual carriageway running from what is currently the main entrance on Massachusetts Avenue all the way to P Street. The residence was commissioned by Herbert Wadsworth, an engineer who also owned vast farms in the Finger Lakes region of New York State, and his wife, Martha. During World War I, the Wadsworths turned the entire house over to the Red Cross. In 1932, it was sold to a small group of women who formed a private club named for George Washington's ancestral home in England, Sulgrave Manor. Architect Frederick Brooke, hired to convert the house to club use, also worked as the local consulting architect for Lutyens's British Embassy on Massachusetts Avenue [see P23].

L16 National Trust for Historic Preservation

(McCormick Apartments)
1785 Massachusetts Avenue, NW

1917—JULES HENRI DE SIBOUR
1941–50—Interior alterations: ARCHITECT UNKNOWN
1979—Restoration/renovation: YERKES, PAPPAS AND PARKER

The most assured and sophisticated of the numerous Beaux-Arts buildings in

Dupont Circle, the current headquarters of the National Trust for Historic Preservation would be perfectly at home in, say, the 8th *arrondissement* of Paris. Incredibly, the elegant structure was commissioned as a rental apartment building, albeit one with only six units. Full-floor apartments, each measuring a total of 11,000 square feet spread over 25 rooms, occupied the second through fifth floors.

The building was designed by the mellifluously named Jules Henri de Sibour. A descendant of French royalty, de Sibour arrived in Washington around 1900 following study at the famed École des Beaux-Arts. His client for this building was ostensibly Stanley McCormick, son of Cyrus and heir to the International Harvester fortune. Stanley had wanted to build "the most luxurious apartment house in Washington" but soon became incapacitated by mental illness, leaving his wife, Katharine Dexter McCormick, to oversee the completion of the project. (Katharine became famous herself as a supporter of Margaret Sanger and single-handedly funded the vast majority of research that led to the development of the birth control pill.)

The McCormick Apartments quickly became some of the most sought-after residences in the city, attracting such tenants as Pearl Mesta (later known as the "Hostess with the Mostest"), Lord Joseph Duveen, and Andrew Mellon. Duveen, an international art dealer, never actually lived in his apartment—he rented it as a private gallery for the express purpose of selling a large collection of paintings and sculptures to Mr. Mellon. The strategy worked. After padding downstairs—often in his robe and slippers—almost daily for three months, Mellon finally bought the entire lot in one fell swoop for a record-shattering $21 million. He later donated these and other artworks to the nation as the basis for the National Gallery of Art.

The armies of servants who looked after these nabobs lived in tiny rooms crowded onto eight mezzanine levels facing a narrow light well—you can catch a glimpse of this disparity from the alley at the northeast corner of the building, seen from P Street, where the larger number of shorter floors is apparent. Fortunately, the building offered several amenities to make work easier for the housekeeping staff, including a central vacuum system, centrally refrigerated tap water, and laundry chutes to individual washing machines in the basement.

L17 Peter G. Peterson Institute for International Economics

1750 Massachusetts Avenue, NW

2001—KOHN PEDERSEN FOX ASSOCIATES

A modern jewel set among the grand old buildings of Massachusetts Avenue, the Peterson Institute for International Economics demonstrates that sensitive historic contexts can readily accommodate contrasting architecture when it is thoughtfully designed and appropriately scaled. The new building's roofline suggests a gable that has been split and reassembled in an unexpected way, creating a dynamic composition without relying on fussy details or decoration. The specialty glass wall to the left of the entrance filters light and lends an ethereal quality to a conference area within. At night, when the interior lights are on, the curtain wall on the upper levels almost disappears, and the tidy individual offices read as rooms in a dollhouse. The only unfortunate note is the long, blank party wall along the east side of the property, next to the Embassy of Uzbekistan—if only it could have been executed in metal or stone rather than cheap artificial stucco.

L18 Embassy of the Republic of Uzbekistan

(Old Canadian Embassy)
1746 Massachusetts Avenue, NW

1909—JULES HENRI DE SIBOUR WITH BRUCE PRICE
1917—Addition: JULES HENRI DE SIBOUR
Various alterations: ARCHITECTS UNKNOWN

Clarence Moore, a West Virginia tycoon, commissioned this Louis XV-style *palais*, but was able to enjoy it for only a few years before he had the misfortune to book passage on the maiden voyage of the *Titanic* in 1912. (Moore, a noted horseman and master of the hounds at the Chevy Chase Club, had been in England to buy dogs or ponies, depending upon which story you believe.) With its light-colored Roman brick, elaborate stone and iron ornament, and mansard roof, this house contrasts with the much more subdued Wilkins House (now the Peruvian Chancery), down the street at 1700 Massachusetts, which de Sibour designed a few years later. The Canadian government acquired the Moore property in 1927 and maintained it as a chancery until 1988, when embassy staff moved to their new quarters on Pennsylvania Avenue. It now serves as the Embassy of Uzbekistan.

L19 Benjamin T. Rome Building of the Johns Hopkins University

(Forest Industries Building)
1619 Massachusetts Avenue, NW

1961—KEYES, LETHBRIDGE & CONDON, ARCHITECTS
2000–2010—Renovations: BOWIE GRIDLEY ARCHITECTS

Carefully considered proportions and deeply set windows distinguish this office building from more run-of-the-mill contemporaries. As a nod to the forestry-related association that commissioned the building, the window frames were originally made of wood—very unusual for a commercial struc-

ture—but were later replaced with metal versions.

L20 Carnegie Institution of Washington

1530 P Street, NW

1909—CARRÈRE & HASTINGS
1938—DELANO & ALDRICH; Auditorium murals: J. MONROE HEWLETT
1998—Rehabilitation: FLORANCE EICHBAUM ESOCOFF KING; Preservation architects: OEHRLEIN & ASSOCIATES ARCHITECTS

In 1902, Andrew Carnegie gave funds to establish an institution to "encourage investigation, research, and discovery [and] show the application of knowledge to the improvement of mankind." This headquarters building by Carrère and Hastings soon followed. The architecture itself, though impressive, is a little odd in several respects. The huge portico, for instance, with its paired Ionic columns and heavy balustrade, appears as though it aspired to introduce a much larger structure—in fact, the architects diminished the building's scale several times during the design process in response to Carnegie's directive to avoid excessive grandeur. The scale of the portico seems particularly excessive now that it no longer serves as the primary entrance. The main door is actually around the corner on the P Street side, under a relatively modest canopy, at the point where the original building meets the addition by Delano & Aldrich. The exterior of the addition is a slightly watered-down version of the original, while the interior boasts a sleek, Art Moderne auditorium lined with spectacular murals.

L21 Church Place Condominium

1520 16th Street, NW

1964—ARCHITECT UNKNOWN
2000—Renovation: ERIC COLBERT & ASSOCIATES

The original, exceedingly banal apartment building had degenerated into a crowded tenement when an electrical fire and flood led to its condemnation. Colbert's colorful metal appliqués, suggestive of a de Stijl painting, give life to the once-drab façades. The architect worked to maximize window area in the new apartments to compensate for their low ceiling heights.

Next door is the Hightowers, a classic, late Art Deco apartment building by Alvin E. Aubinoe Sr. and Harry L. Edwards, completed in 1938.

L22 The Cairo

1615 Q Street, NW

1894—THOMAS FRANKLIN SCHNEIDER
1904—Additions: THOMAS FRANKLIN SCHNEIDER
1976—Renovation: ARTHUR COTTON MOORE / ASSOCIATES
2000—Lobby renovation: JAMES CUMMINGS AIA: A COLLABORATIVE DESIGN GROUP

The Cairo is a very large curio. Some might equate the building with one of those rare objects occasionally encountered that appear so ugly or ungainly as to attract rather than repel.
—*Sixteenth Street Architecture, Volume 2,* The Commission of Fine Arts, 1988

Contrary to popular belief, the structure that engendered the District of Columbia's first building height limitation was neither the Capitol nor the Washington Monument, but rather this bizarre, "Moorish" pile of bricks and limestone. At a height of more than 160 feet, the 12-story tower—the upper floors of which were beyond the reach of fire ladders available at the time—so alarmed its neighbors that they successfully lobbied the District's Board of Commissioners to enact restrictive zoning regulations in July 1894, before the building was even finished (the first federal *legislative* height restriction was enacted by Congress in 1899; the current law was passed in 1910). In truth, the Cairo's opponents probably represented a strange alliance of architectural sophisticates appalled by its ungainly design and Luddites who feared that it was only a matter of time before such a "skyscraper" would topple from sheer weight and hubris.

The architect was the enterprising T. F. Schneider, who had visited the 1893 Columbian Exhibition in Chicago, marveled at the fair's literally spectacular architecture, and, apparently, learned little. The Cairo is ill-proportioned and capped by a ridiculously boxy cornice, and its fancy front façade stops abruptly after turning the corners, leaving bare brick walls on the sides and back. Nonetheless, the building certainly has its charms—note, for instance, the attenuated elephant heads that bracket the sills of the two outermost windows on the first floor, and of course the great entry arch, with its wispy lettering.

One of the first residential towers in America to employ steel-frame construction, the Cairo was built in less than ten months. An effusive promotional brochure touted it as "the most thoroughly equipped establishment of this nature south of New York," and even promised pleasant summer living thanks to "cooling zephyrs" from Rock Creek Park, despite the fact that the park is at least a half mile away. The flyer also acclaimed the establishment's bakery, two billiard rooms, and rooftop garden complete with tropical plants and electrically powered fountains "bubbling here and bursting forth there." The building originally had a dining room on the top floor, marked by a change in window pattern that is still visible on the east façade.

The Cairo was converted into a hotel in the 1920s, beginning a slow but dramatic decline. By the 1960s, it was visited more frequently by police than by tourists, and rats outnumbered both. Finally, in 1976, a HUD-sponsored renovation, accomplished on the cheap, returned the building to apartment use. It became a condominium in 1979, and now, for all its quirks, the awkward tower reigns as one of Washington's guilty architectural pleasures.

L23 The Tapies Apartments

1612 16th Street, NW

2005—BONSTRA ARCHITECTS

Squeezed onto a 21-foot-wide site previously occupied by a much-abused little wood-frame house, this svelte apartment building was conceived as a stretched, abstracted version of a typical row house with an asymmetrical bay. It accommodates just five apartments, four of them duplexes with living rooms almost as tall as the building is wide. A ladder-like trellis on the front façade, intended to serve as an armature for greenery, provides a series of small, horizontal counterpoints to the building's overall verticality. The landscaping of the front yard creates a surprisingly dense grove shading the sidewalk that zigzags toward the entrance.

L24 Church of the Holy City (Swedenborgian)

1611 16th Street, NW

1896—HERBERT LANGFORD WARREN; Associated architects: PELZ AND CARLISLE
1912—Parish house: WARREN & SMITH; Associated architect: PAUL PELZ

This rugged neo-Gothic structure was designed by Herbert Langford Warren, a Swedenborgian who later served as the first dean of Harvard University's Faculty

of Architecture. Construction was overseen by Paul Pelz, architect of the main Library of Congress building. The south wing, added in 1912, contains a glorious, cantilevered spiral staircase that begins just inside the arched doorway.

L25 Toutorsky Mansion

1720 16th Street, NW

1894—WILLIAM HENRY MILLER

This 12,000-square-foot mansion was built for Supreme Court Justice Henry Brown, and later housed the Persian Legation and the American Zionist Organization (no, not at the same time). In the minds of longtime neighborhood residents, however, the house is indelibly associated with the Russian music teacher Basil Toutorsky and his Mexican wife, María, who ran the Toutorsky Academy of Music here for four decades beginning in 1947. Upon retiring in 1988, the Toutorskys donated the house to the Peabody Conservatory of Music in Baltimore, which soon sold it to a private buyer who turned it back into a residence. It was recently purchased by the Republic of the Congo for use as its embassy.

With its stepped and scroll-edged gables, insistent rows of windows, dark red brick, and strong horizontal stone courses, the Toutorsky Mansion is a rare iteration of Flemish Renaissance architecture in a city whose architectural ancestry is overwhelmingly Roman, English, and French. The façades are intriguing assemblages of symmetrical and asymmetrical components, making the building appear simultaneously balanced and dynamic. The interior is replete with dark wood and over-the-top, ornate fireplaces.

L26 Scottish Rite Temple

(House of the Temple)
1733 16th Street, NW

1915—JOHN RUSSELL POPE; Consulting architect: ELLIOTT WOODS

Tel: (202) 232-3579
www.srmason-sj.org/web/index.htm

"Supreme Council," answers the receptionist at the headquarters of the Ancient and Accepted Scottish Rite of Freemasonry, Southern Jurisdiction, USA. It goes without saying that subtlety is not a hallmark of the Masons, who are known for their pomp and elaborate rituals. Inspired by all that showmanship, John Russell Pope had a field day in designing the organization's seat. Basing his building on the Mausoleum at Halicarnassus, one of the Seven Wonders of the Ancient World, Pope erected an awe-inspiring temple in the midst of a relatively quiet enclave of houses and apartment buildings.

As one would expect, the temple is replete with symbolism—some of it obvious, some requiring a good deal of esoteric knowledge on the part of the viewer. The colonnade surrounding the building, for instance, consists of 33 columns, an allusion to the 33rd Degree (sometimes abbreviated as 33°), an honorary designation bestowed upon Masons for outstanding service to the fraternity. The front steps rise in flights of 3, 5, 7, and 9, alluding to Pythagoras's fascination with odd numbers (note also the organization's telephone number listed above). The steps are bracketed by a pair of monumental sphinxes—representing *Power* on the left and *Wisdom* on the right—which guard the entry. Inside the great bronze doors is the "Atrium," resplendent in Greek and Egyptian decorative motifs and rich in Masonic associations. The chairs, for example, are modeled after the throne at the Temple of Dionysus, and a pair of statues in ancient Egyptian style—three-dimensional representations of the hieroglyph that precedes the name of a god or of a sacred place—flanks the grand staircase.

Upstairs awaits the temple chamber, soaring roughly 88 feet (the original height of Jenkins Hill, where the Capitol now stands—why does this seem significant?) to the inside of the stepped pyramidal roof. Visit the space on a bright day, if possible, to witness the spectacle of sunlight streaming in through the giant windows. The room is dripping with sumptuous materials, including marble, granite, bronze, and . . . and . . . are those *acoustical tiles lining the walls?* It seems that even the Masons occasionally must succumb to mundane practical considerations (though these tiles will be removed as part of a comprehensive renovation by Hartman-Cox now under way). Back downstairs are other intriguing spaces and displays, including a handsome library with stacks radiating along a gentle curve, and a room dedicated to none other than J. Edgar Hoover, 33°.

L27 Lauriol Plaza Restaurant

1835 18th Street, NW

1999—SINGLETARY RUEDA ARCHITECTS

This outrageously popular Tex-Mex restaurant benefits from its inviting sidewalk café, large expanses of glass, and trellis-covered roof deck. Resisting the many clichés that such an establishment might have invited—from cartoonish "Mexican" decorations based on the restaurant's theme to pseudo-historical motifs intended to make it "fit" in Washington—the architects designed a resolutely modern structure in brick, sheet metal, and wood. Although the exterior has a slightly industrial character, it sits comfortably in the residential neighborhood, thanks to its modest scale and carefully thought-out details. Inside, the soaring main space, with a mezzanine under a half-barrel vault, is one of the brightest and airiest dining rooms in the city. The viewer should try to ignore the various temporary "additions"—such as plastic sheeting to enclose the roof deck—that currently diminish the appearance of the building from the street.

L28 American Institute for Cancer Research

(Thomas Nelson Page House)
1759 R Street, NW

1896—MCKIM, MEAD & WHITE (STANFORD WHITE)
1903—Alterations: STANFORD WHITE

Stanford White designed this house for Thomas Nelson Page, the famous southern author, and his wife in a Federal

Revival style, making a clean break from the faux châteaux then so popular with Washington's architects and their clients. The two main façades are quite different from each other—the R Street face, which presaged McKim, Mead & White's later design for the Percy Rivington Pyne House on New York's Park Avenue, is extremely reserved and perhaps a bit institutional, while the façade along New Hampshire Avenue is glassier and more clearly domestic.

L29 International Headquarters, Order of the Eastern Star

(Perry Belmont House)
1618 New Hampshire Avenue, NW

1909—PAUL-ERNEST EUGÈNE SANSON; HORACE TRUMBAUER

The Belmont House is symbolic of the era when many of the nation's wealthiest families routinely "wintered" in Washington to take advantage of the capital's then-fashionable social scene. In effect, this enormous slice of limestone pie with all the trimmings was built as a party house.

Diplomat Perry Belmont, a grandson of Commodore Matthew Perry, imported Paul-Ernest Sanson, a popular French architect, to design the house. Horace Trumbauer, who had a substantial portfolio of estates for American plutocrats, served as associate architect. The $1.5 million mansion was laid out in the preferred French manner of the time, with bedrooms on the first floor and the primary public rooms elevated to a *piano nobile.* Its highly ornate interior is decorated with Italian marble, German woodwork, and metalwork from France.

Belmont sold the house during the Great Depression to the General Grand Chapter of the Order of the Eastern Star, an organization accepting both women and men as members, but widely known as the distaff counterpart to the Masons. The price tag of just $100,000 came with the stipulation that the order's Right Worthy Grand Secretary must live in the house. Thus, despite the building's institutional use, it is now actually a year-round residence—an awful lot of house for one family, no matter how right, worthy, or grand.

L30 Schneider Row Houses

1700 block of Q Street, NW

1889–92—THOMAS FRANKLIN SCHNEIDER
Numerous alterations: VARIOUS ARCHITECTS

Built by Thomas Schneider of Cairo Hotel fame, these three-story brown- and greenstone row houses form a parade of turrets, projecting bays, tiled mansard roofs, and Richardsonian Romanesque decorative detailing. Called a "young Napoleon" by one of his contemporaries, Schneider paid $175,000 for the long row of lots on the north side of Q Street and audaciously developed the whole tract in one fell swoop.

TOUR M

Logan Circle / Shaw

No area in Washington experienced greater change in the 1990s and early 2000s than the interconnected neighborhoods of Logan Circle and Shaw, centered on the commercial spines of 14th Street and U Street, respectively. These long-decrepit business corridors—vexing symbols of urban decay—have rebounded dramatically and are now home to dozens of trendy shops, restaurants, and nightclubs. The surrounding residential blocks, many of which were nearly abandoned just a couple of decades ago, now contain some of the city's priciest real estate.

The 14th Street corridor had its heyday in the 1920s, when it was Washington's "automobile row." Elegant but architecturally restrained car dealerships, typically sporting huge windows to show off their merchandise to good effect, lined the street. Peripheral businesses, such as auto repair shops, were also common along 14th and on the adjacent blocks of several cross streets.

During the same period, U Street was a vibrant entertainment center for African Americans, rivaling and often exceeding the glamour of even the most exclusive "white" establishments in segregated Washington. Arguably the cultural capital of black America before the Harlem Renaissance, U Street was synonymous with jazz, attracting many of the world's great African American musicians to its theaters and dance halls. Ironically, it was desegregation that ended all of this, as African Ameri-

The duplex at 1–2 Logan Circle, built c. 1877 on what was then called Iowa Circle, exemplifies the elegant housing built for affluent Washingtonians in this neighborhood during the last quarter of the 19th century.

W ST
U ST
10th ST
14th ST
13th ST
Q ST
P ST
11th ST
RHODE ISLAND AVE
N ST
1
2
3
4
5
6
7
8
9
10
11
12
13
14
15
16
17

cans quickly took advantage of their new freedom to visit previously segregated clubs and theaters, leaving U Street businesses with fewer and fewer patrons.

In 1968, a series of riots in the wake of the assassination of Martin Luther King Jr. dealt a devastating blow to the Logan/Shaw area. Angry mobs set fire to businesses that refused to close in mourning of the slain civil rights leader, laying waste to much of 14th Street and U Street. The physical and psychological scars of that tragic period are still evident in many corners of these neighborhoods. The District government tried to spur redevelopment by building the Reeves Center (1986—VVKR, Devrouax + Purnell Architects, Robert Coles) at the corner of 14th and U to house various city services. It was the real estate boom of the 1990s, however, coinciding with resurging interest in urban living, which finally engendered a true resurrection of the area. In a city with little industrial heritage, the old car dealerships have proved to be popular for conversion to loft apartments and galleries, and U Street is once again one of the city's great spots for dining out and nightlife. Gentrification remains a delicate issue, as longtime residents are displaced by buyers of luxury condominiums, but for now at least, the 14th and U Street corridors form the core of a diverse and vital community.

M1 Post Massachusetts Apartments

1499 Massachusetts Avenue, NW

2002—ESOCOFF & ASSOCIATES | ARCHITECTS

The exterior design of this large apartment building is clever in several respects. Its scalloped façades and vibrant blue projecting bays establish a strong rhythm of vertical elements that diminish the building's apparent bulk, while also yielding a sculptural quality that is rare in the bottom-line world of developer-driven construction. This design strategy was no mere caprice, however. It emerged logically from two factors: first, the prevalence of flat-plate concrete construction in Washington—commonly used because it often allows architects to squeeze an extra floor in commercial buildings governed by the city's height restrictions—and second, the District's public space regulations, which allow parts of residential buildings to project beyond the property line within certain guidelines. In flat-plate construction, it is relatively easy to create unusual shapes at the edges of the concrete floor slabs, so the scalloped façade design took advantage of local building traditions to make curved forms efficiently and economically. Meanwhile, under District law, the projections into public space—in this case, over the sidewalks—do not count against the maximum floor area permitted by zoning regulations, so the developer can build a larger building, gaining extra rentable space on a given piece of land.

The architect cites the work of Antoni Gaudí as one source of inspiration, and indeed, this building would fit well in Barcelona or many other European cities. It is one of a series of structures by Esocoff employing similar façade design strategies, including 400 Massachusetts Avenue, NW [see E4] and Quincy Park at 1001 L Street, NW.

M2 National City Christian Church

14th Street and Massachusetts Avenue, NW (Thomas Circle)

1930—JOHN RUSSELL POPE
1954—Addition: LEON CHATELAIN JR.
1962—Wilfley Memorial Prayer Chapel: CLAIR S. BUCHART
1980–86—Renovation and addition: CARL T. COOPER JR.

This huge structure—its immense size becomes apparent only as the viewer approaches—was inspired by the early 18th-century church of St. Martin-in-the-Fields, on Trafalgar Square in London, designed by James Gibbs. National City is thus in good company, as Gibbs's iconic composition of pedimented front and stepped tower has served as the inspiration for countless Protestant churches throughout the United States. John Russell Pope took some liberties, however, most notably by placing the structure atop a substantial mound, thereby necessitating the intimidating staircase leading to the portico, and by terminating the tower in a small dome rather than a pointy, conical spire. Inside, the sanctuary is a bright rendition of the English Baroque, with a stunning coffered ceiling and a semicircular apse covered by a hemispherical dome.

The curious little hexagonal structure

outside the church, surrounded by an open-air arcade, is a replica of the study used by Alexander Campbell, considered the founder of the Disciples of Christ, the denomination that built this complex.

M3 Luther Place Memorial Church

1226 Vermont Avenue, NW
(at Thomas Circle)

1874—JOHN C. HARKNESS AND HENRY S. DAVIS, BASED ON ORIGINAL DESIGN BY JUDSON YORK
c. 1884—Towers: ARCHITECT UNKNOWN
1905—Restoration: FRANK H. JACKSON
1951—Parish house: L. M. LEISENRING
1969—Renovations: NEER AND GRAEF
1990—Parish house addition and renovation: WEIHE PARTNERSHIP
2006—Renovation of sanctuary: KERNS GROUP ARCHITECTS

Built as a gesture of thanksgiving for the end of the Civil War, this red sandstone, Gothic Revival church contrasts sharply with the neoclassical National City Christian Church across the street. The structure's splayed plan derives from the acute angle of its site. The sanctuary is somewhat spartan, but gains visual interest from the unusual wooden trusses that support the roof. A recent renovation involved restoration of the stained glass, refinishing of wood surfaces, and installation of new entry doors. A curving corridor separates the sanctuary from a rectilinear office wing, which is angled in plan to align with N Street.

M4 Washington Plaza Hotel

(International Inn)
10 Thomas Circle, NW

1962—MORRIS LAPIDUS

One could easily walk or drive by the Washington Plaza Hotel and barely notice it, but it becomes much more interesting when one discovers that it was designed by Morris Lapidus, the architect of glitzy Miami Beach hotels such as the Fontainebleau and the Eden Roc, whose motto was "Too much is never enough." Admittedly, this hotel would have been easier to recognize as a Lapidus work in its early years, when the principal façade was still clad in its original alternating black and white panels, and the swimming pool just off Thomas Circle was covered by a retractable glass dome that was probably described as "groovy" back in the day. The dome was dismantled in 1981, and the horizontal concrete bands on the façade have long been painted a uniform white, but one can still appreciate the Lapidus touch in the building's curving plan and some remaining elements of the lobby.

Lapidus designed several buildings in Washington, including the Capitol Skyline Hotel on South Capitol Street, currently the scene of popular, summertime pool parties attracting crowds for whom the words *buff* and *tan* are not colors of brick.

M5 Logan Circle

1875 to present—VARIOUS ARCHITECTS

Proof that preservation is often the handmaiden of neglect, the houses surrounding Logan Circle, along with those lining adjacent streets (note, for example, the beautiful rows along the 1300 block of Rhode Island Avenue), form Washington's finest enclave of intact and carefully restored Victorian town houses. Most were built during a 25-year period from about 1875 to 1900 to house the District's powerful and wealthy, such as John A. Logan, prominent Civil War general and, later, senator from Illinois, who lived at 812 12th Street. Logan originated the idea of Memorial Day. The government named the former Iowa Circle for him in 1930 notwithstanding his efforts to have the national capital moved to St. Louis. (Perhaps as vengeance, city officials allowed his house to be destroyed to make way for a parking lot.) In the early 20th century, Washington's fickle society folk abandoned the neighborhood for Dupont Circle, and Logan Circle entered a deep sleep. Having miraculously survived an excruciating period as one of the city's most prominent drug and prostitution centers, the neighborhood is now regarded once again as a highly desirable place to live.

M6 The Studio Theatre

14th and P streets, NW

1919—1501 14th Street: MURPHY & OLMSTED
1920—1507 14th Street: ARCHITECT UNKNOWN
1922—1509 14th Street: JOHN MAHON DONN
1987—Renovation: DEVROUAX + PURNELL ARCHITECTS; Theater designer: RUSSELL METHENY
1997—Renovation: RUSSELL METHENY; O'MARAH & BENULIS
2004—Renovation and addition: BONSTRA ARCHITECTS; Theater designer: RUSSELL METHENY

One of the harbingers of the urban revitalization to come, the Studio Theatre, founded in 1978, moved to a former automobile showroom at 14th and P streets in 1987. The original renovation preserved the essential character of the existing building, while adding striking graphic elements—a giant sign, rendered in dressing room-style lights, cleverly set within the windows along P Street, and large, high-contrast black-and-white photographic images of faces, filling in the window areas to create the enclosure necessary for the theater spaces.

The well-regarded and successful theater company embarked on a major expansion in 2002, buying the two buildings along 14th Street immediately to the north of the original facility. The separate structures were combined and visually unified by a glassy atrium atop the middle building, where the entrance to the complex is now located. Inserting a new theater in the northernmost building, long occupied by the Ace Electric Company, required the removal of the second-floor slab, and the transfer of structural forces to a series of three-foot-deep steel beams spanning the width of the building. The latest renovation also updated the large photographic faces, adding backlighting to create a glowing band of images.

M7 Whole Foods Market

1440 P Street, NW

2000—MUSHINSKY VOELZKE ASSOCIATES / MV+A
2010—Renovation: MUSHINSKY VOELZKE ASSOCIATES / MV+A

When the parent company of what was then called Fresh Fields announced an interest in opening one of its markets on an urban site in Washington, a group of Logan Circle residents launched a concerted effort to bring the natural food store to their neighborhood. The campaign was successful, and all parties are apparently thrilled with the results. Not only is the store, now officially a Whole Foods Market, an excellent performer for the chain, it also served as a major catalyst for additional commercial and residential development in the area. Built on the site of a former service garage, the new building includes both underground and rooftop parking. Conceptually, the main façade is a stretched and folded storefront inspired loosely by the industrial architecture of the neighborhood, though it also bears hints of Art Deco, Amsterdam School modernism, and 1950s commercial architecture. Note the subtle green and blue colors in the small panes of glass at the top of the serrated windows.

M8 Rainbow Lofts

1445 Church Street, NW

1929—ARCHITECT UNKNOWN
2004—Renovation and addition: ERIC COLBERT & ASSOCIATES

A façade-wide sign of individual letters declares the original purpose of this former auto body repair garage, and explains the derivation of the condominium project's otherwise corny-sounding name. The apartments in the existing, three-story, brick-faced structure have an intentionally raw character, with exposed masonry walls and industrial, pivoting steel-frame windows. The addition, running up the west wide and across the top, is a dramatic contrast, sheathed in white Alucobond panels (each composed of a polyethylene core sandwiched between two aluminum sheets) and large expanses of glass.

Sunscreens partially shield the windows of the addition, while minimalist glass railings line the edges of the roof deck and upper-level terraces.

M9 Lincoln Theatre

1215 U Street, NW

1922—REGINALD GEARE
1994—Restoration architects of record: LEO A DALY; Preservation architects: OEHRLEIN & ASSOCIATES ARCHITECTS; SORG AND ASSOCIATES

At the height of the jazz era, U Street reigned, in the words of native Washingtonian Pearl Bailey, as the "Black Broadway." Its grand theaters and lively nightclubs, which regularly featured the most inventive and talented musicians in the world, provided elegant entertainment venues for African Americans living in segregated Washington. The Lincoln Theatre was instantly popular as a first-run movie and Vaudeville house, which the *Washington Afro-American* declared to be "perhaps the largest and finest for colored people exclusively anywhere in the United States." Immediately behind the theater once stood the Lincoln Colonnade, a dance hall that was a prestigious site for proms and other celebratory events, and which was among the establishments frequented by jazz greats like Duke Ellington, who grew up in the neighborhood. The Colonnade was demolished in the 1960s, and the Lincoln Theatre itself closed its doors in 1979.

As the U Street corridor began its slow resurgence in the early 1990s, the District of Columbia government assumed ownership of the theater and sponsored its restoration. Behind the unprepossessing façade is a somewhat more ornate interior, with a lobby that instantly evokes the era of silent films, and an auditorium surrounded by curved balconies and an elaborate proscenium stage bracketed by large Palladian arches. The restored theater hosts live performances, film festivals, and a variety of special events.

M10 True Reformer Building

1200 U Street, NW

1903—JOHN A. LANKFORD
2001—Renovation: SORG & ASSOCIATES

Commissioned by the Grand Fountain of the United Order of True Reformers, an African American benevolent society that provided insurance and financial services to its members, the True Reformer Building was the first major commercial structure in the nation designed, financed, and built solely by African Americans. John Lankford, believed to have been the first African American registered architect in the District of Columbia, produced a building of restrained elegance, with tall floors, subtle pilasters that match the wall surface behind them, and a contrasting frieze of swags just below the cornice. The building housed shops, offices, meeting rooms, and an auditorium, in which Duke Ellington—who grew up nearby—gave his first paid performance (the cover charge was five cents). A mural on the west-facing party wall commemorates that musical milestone and contributes to the building's status as a U Street landmark. Today, the building is owned by the Public Welfare Foundation.

M11 W Street Residence

1024 W Street, NW

2007—DIVISION1 ARCHITECTS

As of 2011, there were 46 officially designated Historic Districts in Washington, covering a substantial percentage of the territory originally laid out by L'Enfant. This is particularly true of the inner residential areas in the Northwest quadrant. Just north of U Street, NW, however, there is a little pocket of L'Enfant's plan, bounded roughly by 12th Street, V Street, and Florida Avenue, that remains outside of any Historic District. This compact neighborhood has become known as one in which relatively adventurous architecture is possible, since projects are not subject to the approval of design review authorities. Several of the most interesting recent buildings were designed by the same architecture firm: Division1.

The W Street Residence was not the firm's first foray into this neighborhood [see next entry], but it is the most striking. The composition is completely abstract—the architects acknowledge that they made no effort whatsoever to allude to specific forms or motifs common among nearby row houses—and yet in its scale, its proportions, and especially the layering of its façades, the house seems to fit comfortably within the neighborhood (which, admittedly, was already something of an architectural hodgepodge).

Surprisingly for a single-family house, the W Street Residence has a structure of steel rather than wood. The architects, who developed this speculative project themselves, worked so hard to come up with a composition they liked, they wanted to discourage future owners from modifying it willy-nilly. A steel structure, they reasoned, would make casual changes difficult, and was therefore worth the added cost.

M12 Logan Heights Row Houses

2114–2122 10th Street, NW

2002—DIVISION1 ARCHITECTS

This was Division1's first project in the neighborhood. As with the W Street Residence [see previous entry], the architects developed it themselves—and served as general contractors to boot. The freely composed façades contrast with neighboring houses in their lack of traditional hierarchy and their divergent colors and materials, but they remain sympathetic to the essential scale and rhythm of the streetscape. The interior spaces are surprisingly open and light-filled for row houses, and more classically modern than the slightly offbeat exteriors.

M13 The Floridian

919–929 Florida Avenue, NW

2008—ERIC COLBERT & ASSOCIATES

The Floridian condominium consists of a pair of fraternal twin towers designed by the same firm at the same time, though that was not the original intention. The architects were initially hired to design what is now the south building, and were well into the construction document phase when the project's developer purchased the lot immediately to the north and decided to build on that parcel

simultaneously. Having studied the prospects for reworking the existing design to create a larger building, the architects determined that maintaining two separate cores would actually yield more sellable square feet. So they proceeded with plans for the first tower while developing a complementary design for the second one.

The façade treatments of the two sections are both lively, but in very different ways. The north tower is primarily an exercise in patterns and colors, while the south tower relies on layers and textures in various shades of gray. On the southernmost wing, set back from the street, notice the perforated metal panels, which filter sunlight entering the rooms within. Both towers are crowned by simple, metal canopies that are lit from below at night and serve as open-air pavilions where residents can gather on the shared roof deck. The notched plan of the buildings helps to maximize views, especially from apartments in the western wings, many of which have clear lines of sight to the Washington Monument.

M14 Speck House

990 Florida Avenue, NW

2008—Designer: JEFF SPECK; Architect of record: BRIE HUSTED

In designing this house for his own family, urban planner Jeff Speck had to figure out how to fit a square peg in a triangular hole—or at least, on an acute, triangular site. Speck had long been fascinated by the many small, "flatiron"-shaped plots within L'Enfant's plan and was eager to demonstrate that such a site, despite its apparent constraints, could accommodate a comfortable house by means of a few clever geometric tricks. After a lengthy search, he discovered this 500-square-foot property but had to hire a private detective to track down the owners and pay back taxes before he could take possession of it. Having finally obtained the perfect canvas for his experiment, he developed a design taking advantage of projections over public space (not unlike the bay windows in many 19th- and 20th-century Washington row houses) in order to maximize the structure's habitable area. He then had to convince local regulatory authorities, who ultimately granted him three distinct zoning variances in order to build a surprisingly roomy house totaling some 2,200 square feet.

Rounded bricks at the apex of the acute triangle lend the house a vaguely nautical character. On the east side, a few feet behind the apex, is the projecting bay that makes it all work, accommodating the main living area on the second floor and the master bedroom on the top floor—both of them perfectly rectangular. On the opposite side, balconies project from the brick façade at an angle similar to that of the enclosed bay, providing slivers of private, outdoor space and ensuring that the house appears balanced when viewed from the acute corner.

M15 The Lacey

2250 11th Street, NW

2008—DIVISION1 ARCHITECTS

It's a safe bet that when Lacey Wilson Sr. and his wife, Bertha, opened a soul food restaurant in an almost exclusively African American neighborhood in 1944, they could never have imagined that someday, apartments in the building next door would be selling for nearly $1 million. But when their son, Lacey Jr., sold the venerable Florida Avenue Grill and the adjacent parking lot to a New York lawyer in 2004, it was a sign of imminent change. While the new owner had no intention of messing with the success of the grill, he had an ambitious vision for the adjacent site.

He hired Division1 to design a condominium building, giving the young architects a chance to develop ideas they had explored in nearby town house projects at a larger scale. Several key elements distinguish the building. The curtain wall on the street façade is an intricate, three-dimensional composition, with an irregular pattern of clear and etched glass in various shades of blue and fully glazed balconies set behind the primary plane. At ground level are four units with direct entrances from the street, establishing a rhythm that mimics that of the row houses common to the neighborhood. On the south façade, a relatively solid wall clad in cement-bonded particle board is interrupted by an open, partially screened staircase that appears poised to leap from the body of the building. That stair aligns with a spacious atrium running longitudinally through the building, intended to facilitate chance meetings of residents and foster a sense of community.

M16 Meridian Public Charter School

(Manhattan Laundry Building)
1328 Florida Avenue, NW

1937—BEDFORD BROWN IV
1986—Renovation: KRESSCOX ASSOCIATES

This surprisingly festive, Depression-era building once housed the offices of a commercial laundry operation. The façade cleverly uses flat materials—mostly porcelain-enamel panels and glass block—to create a cartoon of the three-dimensional ornament typically found on fancier, historic buildings. On the first floor, for instance, the narrow green bands alternate with wider white bands to suggest rusticated stone. A colorful Greek key design, framed in turn by an egg-and-dart pattern, surrounds the entrance. At the top of the façade is a "cornice" made of alternating bands of green and white metal tiles, punctuated by red diamonds.

The architects of the renovation in the 1980s initially wondered where they might find a manufacturer capable of producing porcelain-enamel panels to match the originals. They ultimately found a company that, as it turned out, had been making the panels for some time for a steady client: the White Castle hamburger chain.

M17 Union Row

2125 14th Street, NW

2007—SK&I ARCHITECTURAL DESIGN GROUP

This condominium and retail development consists of two separate components. The "Flats" occupy the new, nine-story structure running along 14th Street, which is divided into three distinct segments articulated in a way that lends a vertical emphasis to the long façade. Midway along the block is a one-story, open-air passage that leads to the second component—the "Warehouses," which is where things get interesting. A linear courtyard, running perpendicular to the main building, is flanked by two historic structures that have been renovated and expanded vertically, creating a sort of industrial mews. Black metal canopies modulate the scale of the complex while calling attention to the individual unit entries. Simple light fixtures suspended from cables spanning the courtyard add visual rhythm and evoke the streetlight systems found in many European cities.

TOUR N

Meridian Hill / Adams Morgan

In the late 1880s, former Missouri Senator John Brooks Henderson, who had drafted the constitutional amendment abolishing slavery, built a gruff stone "castle" at the corner of 16th Street and what is now Florida Avenue, just beyond the boundary of L'Enfant's plan. His wife, Mary Foote Henderson, seemingly alarmed to find herself suddenly living in quasi-rural suburbia, soon began an audacious—and ultimately quite successful—campaign to turn the pastures around her house into a fashionable residential enclave. Mrs. Henderson thus became, in effect, one of the country's earliest female real estate developers, and however selfish her motivations, and despite numerous setbacks, her efforts yielded an extraordinary park and a collection of grand buildings that brought new glamour to the capital.

One of Mrs. Henderson's earliest ideas for improving her neighborhood was to try to convince Congress to declare the area Washington's official Embassy Row. She failed, but a few brave—or possibly intimidated—governments did establish outposts here. She later sought to have 16th Street rechristened the "Avenue of the Presidents"—she succeeded briefly, before Congress changed its collective mind and restored the numerical name. Other ambitious schemes included commissioning Paul Pelz to design an imperially scaled new Executive Mansion for "her" hill, and lobbying Congress to place the proposed new Lincoln Memorial there. Even though all of these initiatives came to naught, Mrs. Henderson nonetheless was highly successful in her broader goal of acquiring socially desirable neighbors. Meridian House, perhaps the most elegant private house in town, bears witness to her labors.

As for "Henderson Castle" itself, the main structure was demolished in 1949, leaving only the dark red stone retaining walls running along 16th Street and Florida Avenue. The actual site of the house is now occupied by the regrettably mundane Beekman Place condominiums.

The "castle" of Senator and Mrs. John Henderson once loomed over 16th Street at the base of Meridian Hill, just beyond the boundary of L'Enfant's original plan. All that remains of the estate today are the craggy walls along the public sidewalk.

CALVERT ST
12
COLUMBIA RD
CHAMPLAIN ST
18th ST
11
800 ft

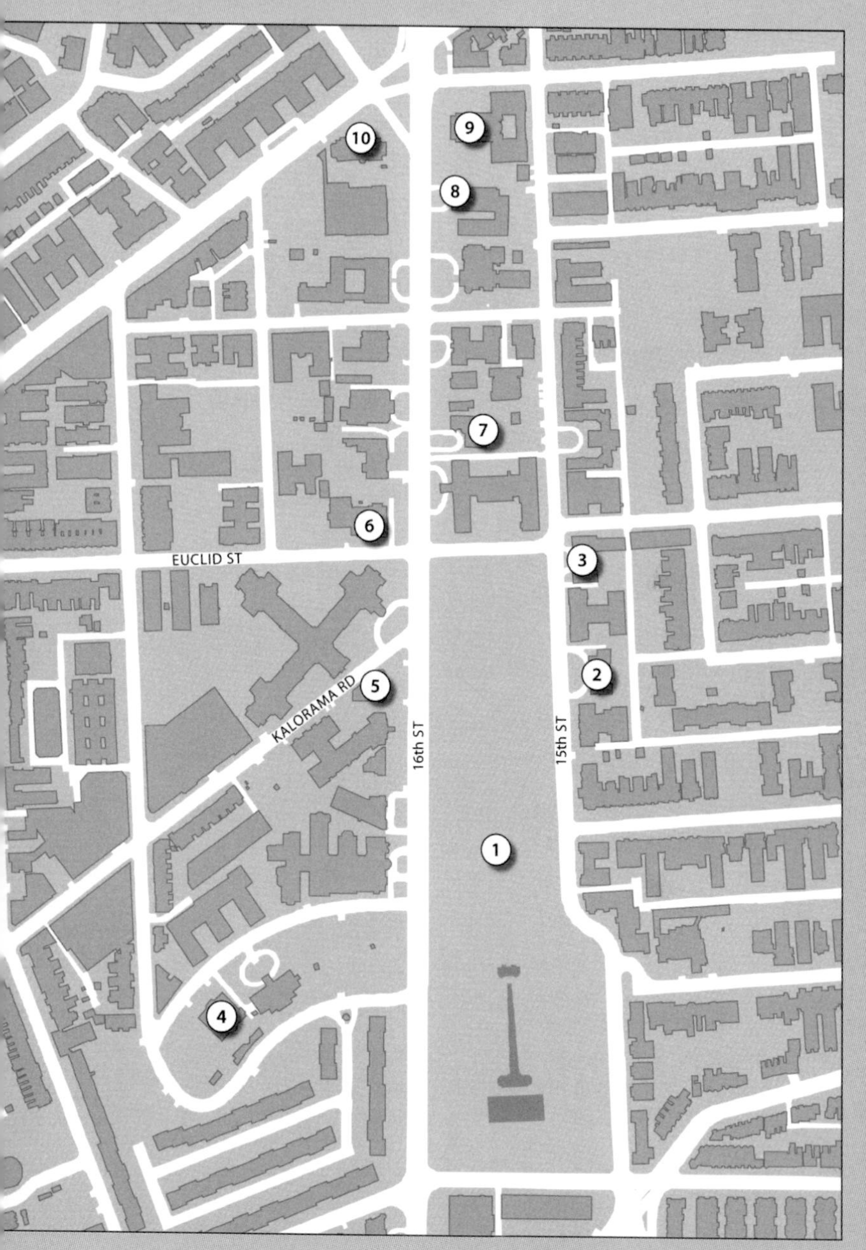

EUCLID ST
KALORAMA RD
16th ST
15th ST
1
2
3
4
5
6
7
8
9
10

N1 Meridian Hill Park

16th Street between Florida Avenue and Euclid Street

1912–36—HORACE W. PEASLEE; Concrete designer: JOHN JOSEPH EARLEY; Landscape architects: VITALE, BRINCKERHOFF & GEIFFERT; BASED ON DESIGN BY GEORGE BURNAP
2006—Restoration: ARCHITRAVE, P.C., ARCHITECTS

Meridian Hill gets its name from the official meridian of the United States, which runs through the center of the White House. The "hill" is actually the edge of the fall line, a steep bluff that served as a natural boundary to L'Enfant's original plan for the city. The top of this bluff affords outstanding views of the capital's monumental core. Placing a park here was, not surprisingly, the brainchild of Mary Foote Henderson, who proposed the idea in 1906, and secured the approval of the Commission of Fine Arts in 1914. Construction of the park spanned two decades. Horace Peaslee wrote that he based the park's lower level, with its axial plan, 13 graduated pools, and cascading falls, on "the Pincian Hill in Rome," but at other times he said he relied on the Villa d'Este for inspiration. At any rate, the upper terrace is clearly of French origin—flat for some 900 feet from the edge of the hill, it is centered on a broad grass mall with promenades and hemlock hedges all culminating in a bronze statue of Joan of Arc.

Peaslee's luxuriant plantings contrast with the rough, exposed-aggregate concrete, a surprising choice of material used throughout the park in the massive retaining walls, walks, and basins. As the city's chief engineer observed in 1926, "Meridian Hill Park is neither wholly architecture nor yet is it landscape design. There is nothing like it in this country." Miraculously, the park has survived more or less as Mrs. Henderson and Peaslee envisioned it, despite a period in the 1970s and 1980s when it was a notorious haven for drug dealers. Unofficially but commonly called Malcolm X Park, the site was, to many, a symbol of racial and economic strife. The real estate boom of the 1990s, abetted by a nationwide drop in drug-related crime, led to rapid gentrification of the surrounding neighborhood and, in turn, to the park's rejuvenation.

N2 Josephine Butler Parks Center

2437 15th Street, NW

1927—GEORGE OAKLEY TOTTEN JR.

Architect George Oakley Totten Jr., working on Mary Foote Henderson's dime, designed nearly a dozen residences in the Meridian Hill area as part of his sponsor's grand plan to make the neighborhood a center of international society. Formerly the Embassy of Hungary and of Brazil, this building now serves as the headquarters of Washington Parks & People, along with a number of other small cultural and service organizations. It is named in honor of Josephine Butler, a longtime community activist who was a founder of the District of Columbia statehood movement and an influential advocate of urban park revitalization, including Meridian Hill Park. The *porte-cochère*, yellow stucco, generous windows, and metal balcony railings lend the building a decidedly Mediterranean air.

N3 Ecuadorian Embassy

2535 15th Street, NW

1927—GEORGE OAKLEY TOTTEN JR.

Another of the speculative mansions developed by Mary Foote Henderson, the Embassy of Ecuador suggests that Totten was looking toward the 17th-century French architect François Mansart for inspiration here, at least for the elements above the cornice line (most notably the tall, mansard roof—a term derived from Mansart, after all). The rest of the façade is more modest, though Totten managed to create a good deal of interest in the main body of the building using only simple pilasters, a few vertical reveals, and barely articulated panels beneath the third-floor windows.

N4 Meridian House

(Meridian International Center)
1630 Crescent Place, NW

1922—JOHN RUSSELL POPE
1960—Alterations: FAULKNER, KINGSBURY & STENHOUSE
1994—Renovation: ARCHETYPE

John Russell Pope designed Meridian House for Irwin Boyle Laughlin, heir to one of the country's greatest steel fortunes. Laughlin, a career diplomat, purchased the hilltop site in 1912, but postings abroad kept him from building anything until 1920. A recognized scholar of 18th-century French art, Laughlin worked closely with Pope on the project. A 1929 article on the building in *Architectural Record* commented, "Because of [Laughlin's] detailed knowledge of the art and architecture of that period and because of his indefatigable interest in every detail, Meridian was immediately recognized as one of the finest examples of architecture in the French style in America." Laughlin continued the French themes out into the terraced garden, whose pollarded linden trees and raked gravel strongly evoke the quietly elegant landscapes of Parisian palaces.

Laughlin maintained his interest in art and architecture throughout his life. He helped his friend, Andrew Mellon, organize and plan the new National Gallery of Art and, according to David Finley, the gallery's first director, the steel heir influenced everything about the original building—also designed by Pope—including the choice of fountains for the garden courtyards and paint colors for the galleries. Laughlin died in 1941, just missing the National Gallery's opening.

Next door to the Meridian House is the White-Meyer House (1912), yet another Pope design. It was for many years the home of Eugene Meyer, owner of *The Washington Post,* and his wife, Agnes (their daughter, Katherine Graham, later became the newspaper's publisher). Both the Meridian House and the White-Meyer House are now parts of the Meridian International Center, an organization that promotes international understanding through cultural exchange and other programs.

N5 Council for Professional Recognition

(Old French Embassy)
2460 16th Street, NW

1908—GEORGE OAKLEY TOTTEN JR.
1962—Renovation: MILTON SCHEIMGARTEN

"Let me build an embassy for you." This was Mary Foote Henderson's simple offer

to French ambassador Jean Jules Jusserand, who had been complaining about his country's current diplomatic quarters sometime around 1907. Monsieur Jusserand accepted, and Mrs. Henderson—thrilled to have landed such a prestigious tenant for her budding embassy row—called on Totten to design an appropriately French château for her future neighbors.

Totten responded with an opulent, if not especially large, Beaux-Arts mansion in limestone with terra cotta trim. The design exploits the shape of the site—essentially a right triangle, with the hypotenuse facing the side street—to create a distinctive, vertically accentuated composition. A domed, cylindrical tower anchors the right angle at the southeast corner, rather than the acutely angled northeast corner as one might expect. The short sides of the triangle (facing south and east) contain the principal rooms, while the hypotenuse is lined with circulation and service spaces. This arrangement seems odd now, but when the building was finished, there were no structures on the lots immediately to the south, so the rooms on that side had excellent, open views toward the city. Still, the long façade facing the side street and the two short, gabled ends facing north and west appear almost unfinished in contrast to the building's principal elevations.

Around 1930, the French government announced plans to build a new embassy on Euclid Street across from Meridian Hill Park, and hired Paul Philippe Cret to design it, but the project never materialized. In 1936, the embassy moved to what is now the French ambassador's residence in Kalorama. Incredibly, within a few months, the Totten building, which had served for nearly three decades as a prominent diplomatic mission, was converted into a run-of-the-mill rooming house. It was later bought by the government of Ghana for use as its embassy, and is now the headquarters of a nonprofit organization.

N6 Inter-American Defense Board

(Pink Palace)
2600 16th Street, NW

1906—GEORGE OAKLEY TOTTEN JR.
1912, 1920—Addition and alterations: GEORGE OAKLEY TOTTEN JR.
1923–86—Numerous alterations: VARIOUS ARCHITECTS

This neo-Venetian Gothic mansion, known as the Pink Palace because of the original color of its stucco walls, was the first building completed as part of Mary Foote Henderson's efforts to make Meridian Hill the center of Washington's social life. Notable residents included Secretary of the Treasury Franklin MacVeagh (before he moved down the street to 2829 16th), and Delia Spencer Caton Field, the extremely wealthy widow of

Marshall Field. The building has been altered significantly, including the removal of several balconies on the south and east façades and the enclosure of the formerly open-air galleries along the south face. It is now occupied by an international organization dealing with defense-related issues throughout the Americas.

N7 Warder-Totten Mansion

2633 16th Street, NW

1888—H. H. RICHARDSON
1925—Reconstruction: GEORGE OAKLEY TOTTEN JR.
2002—Renovation/restoration: SADLER & WHITEHEAD ARCHITECTS / COMMONWEALTH ARCHITECTS

Benjamin Warder commissioned Henry Hobson Richardson's firm to design this house, but Richardson himself seems to have had a rather limited role in the project, which began construction just two months before his death. It is likely that George Shepley, Charles Rutan, and Charles Coolidge, who were the senior designers under Richardson, shared responsibility for the faux château. The house originally stood on K Street, between 15th and 16th streets, NW. When George Oakley Totten Jr., himself a pupil of Richardson's, learned that the house was being demolished, he bought most of the original structure's elements from the wrecker, hauled them across town, and reassembled them in a slightly different configuration on this site. After years of neglect and abandonment, the building was renovated in 2002 and converted into a 38-unit corporate apartment complex, though as of this writing it looks as though the building still could use some TLC.

N8 Mexican Cultural Institute

(Mexican Embassy)
2829 16th Street, NW

1911—NATHAN C. WYETH
1922—Additions: CLARENCE L. HARDING
1942—Addition: MARCUS HALLETT

Tel: (202) 728-1628
www.portal.sre.gob.mx/imw

Commissioned by Emily MacVeagh as a surprise gift for her husband, Franklin, who was secretary of the treasury under William Howard Taft, this mansion is marked by a high ratio of wall to window area, and rather oddly stretched proportions. After his wife died, MacVeagh made the building available to the federal government as a guesthouse for visiting dignitaries. In 1921, the Mexican government purchased it for use as its embassy, and shortly thereafter added the boxy Italianate portico and a new office wing.

Mexico produced a number of great muralists, and the three-story stairwell of this building features a colorful and richly layered mural by Roberto Cueva del Rio, depicting the history of the country. The building now houses the embassy's cultural arm, which sponsors a variety of programs and events.

N9 All Souls Church, Unitarian

16th and Harvard streets, NW

1924—COOLIDGE & SHATTUCK / COOLIDGE, SHEPLEY, BULFINCH AND ABBOTT
1936—Expansion: ERNEST D. STEVENS
1968—Alterations: GRIGG, WOOD, AND BROWNE

The design of this Unitarian church, the result of a limited architectural compe-

tition, is very directly derived from the Baroque church of St. Martin-in-the-Fields on London's Trafalgar Square. The tall spires of All Souls, the Unification Church [see following entry] across the street, and the National Baptist Memorial Church a block to the north make this stretch of 16th Street one of the most architecturally dramatic nongovernmental enclaves in the city. All Souls has a long history of social activism, particularly in its early advocacy of abolition of slavery and, in the 20th century, support for civil rights. The church's bell, which was moved from an earlier structure, was cast by Paul Revere's son, Joseph, in 1822.

N10 Unification Church

(Church of Jesus Christ of Latter-day Saints)
2810 16th Street, NW

1933—DON CARLOS YOUNG JR. AND RAMM HANSEN

Severe and insistently vertical, this former Mormon church is reminiscent of the multi-spired Mormon Temple (not the Tabernacle) in Salt Lake City, but also reflects the influence of Art Deco and the stripped classicism so prevalent in the 1930s. One of the architects, Don Young, was a grandson of Brigham Young, the influential successor to Mormon Church founder Joseph Smith. The bird's-eye marble that covers the church was quarried in Utah. Rather surprisingly, the underlying structure is steel frame. The building is now owned by the controversial Unification Church of Sun Myung Moon.

N11 The Lofts at Adams Morgan

2328 Champlain Street, NW

2001—Project designers for base building: DEVROUAX + PURNELL ARCHITECTS; Interior architects and architects of record: ERIC COLBERT & ASSOCIATES
2003—Addition on 18th Street: ERIC COLBERT & ASSOCIATES

Decades ago in New York and other industrial cities, loft apartments developed logically as architects and property owners sought new uses for deserted warehouses and similar structures that no longer served their original purposes. The result was a new type of urban dwelling with unusually generous interior space and a chicly gritty character that many buyers and tenants found refreshing. In white-collar Washington, however, there were few industrial buildings available for conversion, so when local developers sensed a market for loft-style living, they decided to create facsimiles from scratch.

Thus derives the faux-warehouse aesthetic of the Lofts at Adams Morgan, one of the earliest loft apartment projects in Washington built from the ground up as such. It is composed of two main wings on either side of a pedestrian passage, which also accommodates cars entering a large parking garage beneath the apartments. Contrary to appearances, this passage is not a public right of way—it is actually on private land, and was incorporated as a civic amenity in response to community concerns raised during an arduous and lengthy public review process. Spanning the passage is a glassy, two-level bridge that contains lobby-like lounge spaces for residents. A third wing, completed a couple of years later, reaches out to 18th Street and contains apartments above retail space.

N12 Fitch/O'Rourke Residence

1918 Calvert Street, NW

1999—ROBERT M. GURNEY

The front of this row house offers few hints that it is anything out of the ordinary, but the rear elevation is an architectural gem that warrants a walk down the alley. A skillful, balanced composition of horizontal and vertical lines and

planes, the façade combines transparent, translucent, and solid surfaces to suggest a beautifully intricate three-dimensional puzzle. Inside, curved walls and other elements generate geometrically complex spaces. Perhaps most remarkable is the architect's success in controlling a diverse mix of materials—including Kalwall, sandblasted glass, various metals, concrete, and wood—which could have easily devolved into visual cacophony but instead yields a congenial array of colors and textures.

TOUR O

Cleveland Park / Woodley Park

In the 19th century, many people believed that low-lying urban areas harbored "miasmic vapors"—mysterious gases that somehow caused illness, especially during hot, humid weather. An easy solution for Washingtonians who had the wherewithal was to seek weekend or summer refuge in the nearby sylvan highlands. Though now considered quite close to downtown, Cleveland Park and Woodley Park were, in those days, unquestionably "in the country," and were popular sites for second houses of wealthy city dwellers. Named after a prominent summer visitor (Grover Cleveland, who stayed at Red Top, now demolished) and a specific estate (Woodley, built by Philip Barton Key), these areas gradually developed into bucolic, close-in suburbs replete with commodious, detached houses. Today they are among the most storied neighborhoods in the city, popularly—and not inaccurately—associated with well-to-do professionals with a penchant for driving Volvos and listening to National Public Radio. Meanwhile, the Woodley Park and Cleveland Park commercial strips along Connecticut Avenue attract patrons from throughout the city, while the National Zoo and Rock Creek Park, which rambles nearby, are major recreational attractions for the entire region.

In 1905, Easter Monday was a popular day for a stroll at the National Zoo.

RENO RD
VAN NESS ST
WISCONSIN AVE
CONNECTICUT AVE
LINNEAN AVE
TILDEN ST
PORTER ST
ORDWAY ST
NEWARK ST
MACOMB ST
CATHEDRAL AVE
34th ST
CALVERT ST
3200 ft
1
2
3
4
5
6
7
8
9
10
11
12A
12B
12C
12D
12E
12F
13
13A
14
15
16
17

01 Duke Ellington Bridge

(Calvert Street Bridge)
Calvert Street over Rock Creek, NW

1935—PAUL PHILIPPE CRET

One of several notable bridges in the area, this handsome structure, with wide sidewalks and graceful stone-covered concrete arches, carries motorists and pedestrians over Rock Creek, which gurgles along more than 100 feet below. The triangular pylons that buttress the bridge are embellished with stylized sculptures symbolizing travel by air, rail, water, and highway. Unfortunately, the bridge, which was named in Duke Ellington's honor following his death in 1974, became a popular platform for suicidal jumpers, leading to the addition of spiky metal railings, which, though reasonably well integrated, greatly diminish the pleasure of crossing.

02 Omni Shoreham Hotel

2500 Calvert Street, NW

1930—WADDY B. WOOD
1935—Addition: JOSEPH ABEL / DILLON AND ABEL
1946-64—Numerous alterations and additions: VARIOUS ARCHITECTS
1997-2000—Renovation: BBG-BBGM; Interiors: HUGHES DESIGN ASSOCIATES

The exterior of the Shoreham is a somewhat timid rendition of jazz-age architecture, bearing hints of Art Deco, Renaissance Revival, and even the work of Frank Lloyd Wright. In its heyday, this was one of those places that attracted countless famous performers and guests, from Rudy Vallee to the

Beatles. The best aspect of the complex lies at the rear, where elegant dining and recreational terraces overlook the lush greenery of Rock Creek Park. Partially embraced by the building's sprawling wings, the pool deck in particular is remarkably secluded from the bustle of the city that surrounds it.

03 Wardman Tower

(Wardman Park Marriott Hotel)
2600 Woodley Road, NW

1928—MIHRAN MESROBIAN
Numerous alterations: VARIOUS ARCHITECTS

The Wardman Tower was built as an apartment annex to the adjacent Wardman Park Hotel, completed about ten years earlier. Developer Harry Wardman tore down his own house to make way for the tower, which initially enjoyed a pastoral but still convenient setting that quickly made it one of the most prestigious addresses in Washington. The roster of famous residents remains unmatched by any other single structure in the capital save the White House, and includes former president Herbert Hoover, future president Lyndon Johnson, a bevy of cabinet officials, and more senators than you could shake a gavel at. Beginning in 1973, the apartments were gradually converted to hotel use, relegating the tower to secondary status as part of the larger complex. A few years later, the original Wardman Park Hotel next door was demolished and replaced by the current red brick behemoth.

Mesrobian's design skillfully diminishes the apparent bulk of the cross-shaped building while establishing a tone of posh domesticity. Subtle brick quoins modulate the scale of the tower at the corners, while stacks of balconies lend vertical emphases to counter the building's great breadth. His cleverest design move, though, was the incorporation of diagonal bays at the intersection of the two cross axes, thereby reducing the apparent length of each wing while providing prime spots for what were originally grand parlors with spectacular views from the upper floors.

04 Embassy of Switzerland Chancery

2900 Cathedral Avenue, NW

1959—WILLIAM LESCAZE
2004—Renovation: LEO BOECKL AND HERBERT FURRER

Characteristically Swiss in its no-nonsense modesty, this chancery could almost be confused with a relatively refined suburban elementary school. Designed late in William Lescaze's career, the structure suggests the influence of Mies van der Rohe, with a simple office block of buff-colored brick and steel-and-glass pavilions housing more ceremonial spaces. Lescaze, who was born in Switzerland and immigrated to America in 1920, is best known for the Philadelphia Saving Fund Society (PSFS) Building (1932), which was designed in partnership with George Howe and widely acknowledged as the first International Style skyscraper in the United States.

04a Swiss Ambassador's Residence

Adjacent to Swiss Chancery

2006—STEVEN HOLL ARCHITECTS AND RÜSSLI ARCHITEKTEN

The ambassador's residence, designed by a Swiss-American team led by Justin Rüssli and Steven Holl, may be just as reticent as the chancery, yet it is far more striking. In plan, the house is a slightly skewed and distorted Swiss cross set on a rectangular podium. Such literal symbolism is surprising in Holl's work, but given the building's quasi-public function and the Swiss penchant for spending time outdoors, the shape has a certain logic to it. The building comfortably accommodates groups of different sizes, whether just a few people gathering in one wing or a large group spread throughout the public spaces on the first floor. The plan also allows each public room to be adjacent to at least one outdoor terrace, while ensuring that all rooms have access to plenty of natural light.

The building's predominant materials—gray, integrally colored concrete and sandblasted, structural glass planks—abstractly evoke the wintry landscape of alpine Switzerland. Up close, one can see that the concrete, which appears smooth from a distance, is actually horizontally striated, creating a sharp contrast to the verticality of the glass planks. Clear windows penetrate the sandblasted glass at irregular intervals; in some areas, the sandblasted glass continues across an opening in the wall, admitting filtered light to the interior.

05 Woodley

(Maret School Main Building)
3000 Cathedral Avenue, NW

C. 1801—PHILIP BARTON KEY, OWNER-BUILDER
1867, 1900, 1929—Additions: ARCHITECTS UNKNOWN
1952—Renovation: ARCHITECT UNKNOWN

Philip Barton Key, an uncle of Francis Scott Key, was a loyalist who joined the British army soon after the colonies declared independence. He was captured and imprisoned by Revolutionary forces, and then fled to England upon being paroled. Key later returned to the United States, renounced his allegiance to the crown, and eventually managed to redeem himself sufficiently in the eyes of his countrymen to get elected to Congress representing Maryland. He reportedly modeled this mansion on Woodley Lodge, an 18th-century manor house that he had visited in Reading, England (and which was demolished in 1962). Key's estate went on to serve as the summer White House for several presidents, including Martin Van Buren and Grover Cleveland, and housed a number of prominent cabinet members. In 1946, then-owner Henry Stimson, former secretary of war, gave Woodley to the Phillips Academy Andover. The Maret School acquired the property in 1950.

06 Smithsonian National Zoological Park

3001 Connecticut Avenue, NW

1890—INITIAL LAYOUT BASED ON PLAN BY FREDERICK LAW OLMSTED AND FREDERICK LAW OLMSTED JR.
1907 to present—WILLIAM RALPH EMERSON, HORNBLOWER & MARSHALL, GLENN BROWN, AND MANY OTHERS

Tel: (202) 633-4800
www.nationalzoo.si.edu

Established in 1889 and incorporated into the Smithsonian Institution the following year, the National Zoo was born of an initiative to create a "city of refuge" for bison and other endangered American species. The zoo's basic plan reflects the vision of landscape architect Frederick Law Olmsted, who worked with Smithsonian Secretary Samuel P. Langley and animal curator William T. Hornaday on the project. Hornaday resigned in 1890 over disagreements with the secretary about the design, but Langley continued to develop the plan in collaboration with Olmsted and later with his son, Frederick Jr.

Several of the earliest structures at the zoo were designed by Boston architect William Ralph Emerson. The prominent firm of Hornblower and Marshall was commissioned to renovate an existing building into an aquarium, possibly on the basis of their experience incorporating fish tanks into the Children's Room at the Smithsonian Castle (though the tanks were actually designed by the institution's secretary himself). The firm's Small Mammal House, the oldest extant building at the zoo, was completed in 1906. It later served as the Monkey House, and now houses the Think Tank, an exhibition exploring cognitive thinking in primates.

07 Kennedy-Warren Apartments

3133 Connecticut Avenue, NW

1931—JOSEPH YOUNGER
1935—Addition: ALEXANDER SONNEMANN, BASED ON PLANS BY YOUNGER
2004—Restoration and addition: HARTMAN-COX ARCHITECTS; Interior design: JOHNSON-BERMAN, HARTMAN DESIGN GROUP
2012—Renovation of original building: HARTMAN-COX ARCHITECTS

The Kennedy-Warren represents the zenith of Art Deco architecture in the nation's capital. Named after its developers, who, like so many of their cohort, went bankrupt during the Great Depression, the building is richly ornamented without seeming as frenetic as many other works of the same era and style. The welcoming forecourt, jazzy aluminum marquee, exuberant lobby, and ornate ballroom give the apartment house a decidedly theatrical air.

The building is even larger than it first appears. Taking advantage of the dramatic slope of the land at the northern and eastern sides of the site, there are six floors below the entrance level, including two floors of apartments, the ballroom, and several levels of parking and service spaces. In the days before air-conditioning was common, the building featured an innovative ventilation system that used giant fans at the rear of the building to suck in cool air from the park floor and distribute it through the corridors.

More than 70 years after the building's opening, the owner obtained necessary approvals to build the unrealized south wing that had been part of the initial plan. The addition is remarkable in its impeccable replication of the original's buff brick, aluminum spandrel panels, and other details, though the apartments differ from the earlier ones in size and character.

08 Klingle Mansion

(Linnean Hill)
3545 Williamsburg Lane, NW

1823—JOSHUA PEIRCE, OWNER-BUILDER
1840s–1850s—Additions: ARCHITECTS UNKNOWN
1936—Renovation: NATIONAL PARK SERVICE STAFF ARCHITECTS
1994—Rehabilitation: NATIONAL PARK SERVICE STAFF ARCHITECTS

Established by a son of mill owner Isaac Peirce (whose relatives sometimes spelled the name as "Pierce" or even "Pearce"), this estate contains many elements that reflect the family's Pennsylvania origins, including a beehive oven and a bank barn. Young Peirce, a noted horticulturist, created extensive gardens around the granite-walled, center-hall dwelling; a few of his plantings have survived, as has his two-story utility house with its built-in potting shed. The National Park Service restored the house and grounds in the 1930s, and now uses it as the park's administrative headquarters.

09 Peirce Mill

2311 Tilden Street (at Beach Drive), NW

C. 1820—ISAAC AND ABNER PEIRCE, BUILDERS
1936—Restoration: THOMAS T. WATERMAN; Landscape architect: MALCOLM KIRKPATRICK
2011—Rehabilitation: QUINN EVANS ARCHITECTS

Rock Creek's formerly strong current once powered eight separate mills, grinding corn, rye, oats, and wheat grown by local farmers. The 1932 *Washington Sketch Book,* in fact, observed that the creek "was originally a racing stream, deep enough where it flowed into the Potomac to anchor seagoing ships," but "gradually the little harbor filled up." Simultaneously, changes in land use spelled extinction for major local agricultural enterprises. Of those original eight mills, only this one remains.

Peirce Mill and surrounding acreage were absorbed into the park in 1892 and the Works Progress Administration restored the mill to working order in 1936. Flour produced here helped to stock government cafeterias of the 1930s and 1940s, but the mill stopped working again in 1993. Other survivors of the once-flourishing Peirce family compound include a distillery (c. 1811), which is now private property, a stone springhouse (c. 1801), and the adjacent Linnean Hill / Klingle Mansion [see previous entry].

010 Hillwood Estate, Museum, and Gardens

4155 Linnean Avenue, NW

1926—JOHN DEIBERT; Landscape architect: WILLARD GEBHART
1957—Renovation: ALEXANDER MCILVAINE
1955–65—Landscape architect: PERRY WHEELER
1985—Indian artifacts collection: O'NEIL & MANION ARCHITECTS
1986—Café: O'NEIL & MANION ARCHITECTS
1988—Conversion of chauffer's house to library: FISHER GORDON ARCHITECTS
1998—Visitors' center and renovation of greenhouse: BOWIE GRIDLEY ARCHITECTS; Visitor Center schematic design: QUINN EVANS ARCHITECTS
1999—French garden renovation: RICHARD WILLIAMS ARCHITECT
2000—Restoration of main house: BOWIE GRIDLEY ARCHITECTS; Preservation architects: OEHRLEIN & ASSOCIATES

Tel: (202) 686-5807
www.hillwoodmuseum.org

This multifaceted museum complex is the legacy of cereal heiress Marjorie Merriweather Post, who in 1955 bought what was then known as Arbremont, a red brick, neo-Georgian mansion standing amid 25 acres of gardens and woods, and promptly changed the estate's name to Hillwood. She then embarked on what might be called, in contemporary parlance, an "extreme makeover" to create a showcase for her unparalleled collections of French and Russian art.

Post had begun collecting French decorative arts while she was in her thirties and still married to her second husband, financier E. F. Hutton, who took over her family's company and turned it into General Foods Corporation. She divorced Hutton in 1935, and soon married Joseph E. Davies, who became the American ambassador to the Soviet Union. While living in Moscow, she developed a profound love of Russian imperial art, examples of which she was able to amass easily in exchange for the hard currency the Soviets then desperately needed. After divorcing Davies, Post (who eventually returned to using her maiden name after her fourth and final marriage, to Herbert May) bought the glorious estate that was to become her favorite project.

Mrs. Post, as she is still reverentially called by many Hillwood staff members decades after her death, terrorized workmen for years, micromanaging the remodeling of the mansion to ensure that it would provide the perfect architectural complement to her collections. On the interior, the result is sort of a Beverly Hills take on the 18th-century French mode—the materials are impeccable, and most of the details quite credible, but one gets the (accurate) sense that the lavish rooms were fundamentally incompatible with the character and proportions of the Georgian-style house into which they were inserted. At any rate, meanwhile, Post was commanding various landscape designers and architects to add a French parterre, a Japanese garden, a rose garden, and so on, to the rolling grounds. Once Hillwood finally met her standards, she began to fill it with her treasures, including an array of Russian Orthodox icons and a very impressive clutch of Fabergé eggs.

Upon her death in 1973, Post bequeathed Hillwood to the Smithsonian Institution along with a substantial endowment, but the Smithsonian deemed the funds insufficient to support the conversion of the estate to a museum, and in 1976 returned the property to the Post Foundation, which, fortunately, made a go of it. Additions to the estate since then include a building modeled after Post's camp in the Adirondacks, where she kept a significant collection of Native American artifacts, and a Russian dacha.

011 Intelsat Headquarters

3400 International Drive, NW

1988—JOHN ANDREWS INTERNATIONAL; Associated architects: NOTTER FINEGOLD + ALEXANDER

A rare example of high-tech architecture in Washington, this assemblage of steel-and-glass pods and cylindrical, glass-block stair towers serves as the headquarters of a telecommunications satellite consortium. The building incorporates a number of environment-conscious features, including a network

of atria that bring natural light to interior spaces, roof gardens that enhance insulation and minimize unnecessary water run-off, and shimmering sunscreens that reduce thermal gain. Without being overly literal about it, the precisely honed structure suggests a flotilla of spacecraft.

012 International Chancery Center

Both sides of Van Ness Street Between Connecticut Avenue and Reno Road, NW

1970 to present—Initial plan: EDWARD D. STONE JR. AND ASSOCIATES; Landscape architects: OEHME, VAN SWEDEN & ASSOCIATES

In the 1960s, as foreign governments were clamoring for more space for their Washington outposts and real estate pressures were making inner-city neighborhoods less viable for such facilities, the State Department began seeking a large tract of land to accommodate a number of completely new embassy buildings. The chosen site, formerly occupied by the National Bureau of Standards, was divided into 23, one-acre plots plus one larger parcel that was set aside for Intelsat. The State Department decreed that each embassy must be of essentially domestic scale and somehow reflect the architectural character of the home country. The result is the International Chancery Center, though a better name for this suburban assemblage of disparate, detached buildings might be "Embassy Acres." Although a few buildings in the complex stand out, most are dreadful pastiches of pseudo-vernacular forms.

012a Embassy of Singapore Chancery

3501 International Place, NW

1993—RTKL ASSOCIATES

With its cruciform plan, low-pitched roof, broad eaves, and horizontally striated façades, this chancery inevitably suggests a debt to Frank Lloyd Wright's Prairie Style houses, but the resemblance is accidental. Such forms are also characteristic of the vernacular buildings of Singapore (of course, Wright's work was strongly influenced by Asian architecture, so the correlation is understandable). The result, however, is a chancery that reflects certain building traditions of both the home and the host countries without resorting to hokey, superficial imitation.

012b Embassy of the People's Republic of China, Chancery Building

3505 International Place, NW

2008—PEI PARTNERSHIP ARCHITECTS WITH I. M. PEI ARCHITECT; Associate architects: CHINA IPPR ENGINEERING INTERNATIONAL

Famed Chinese American architect I. M. Pei collaborated with his sons' firm to design the new chancery of China. It is by far the largest building in the International Chancery Center, with more than 115,000 square feet of space. Clad in French limestone with relatively few windows and virtually no ornament, the building appears substantial but nondescript from most viewpoints. Along the Van Ness Street façade, the only sign that this structure is anything out of the ordinary is a huge, open-air, diamond-shaped frame that emerges from the wall plane. This serves as a clue not only to the building's signature planning motifs, but also to its authorship, since 45-degree angles and rotated squares have figured prominently in other recent works by the senior Pei, such as the Museum of Islamic Art in Qatar, and by his sons, such as the Suzhou Museum in China.

The main entrance is off of International Place, a short, L-shaped street entirely within the international compound. A circular, transparent dome—the only hint of glitz in the entire project—is suspended over the driveway to create a partial *porte-cochère.* Immediately inside the door is the entrance hall, one of three circulation nodes with 45-degree-chamfered corners and topped by square, skylit towers that are also offset at 45 degrees. Public rooms, including a banquet hall and a 200-seat auditorium, occupy the central section of the building, with offices in the east and west wings. Several key rooms also have chamfered corners and light fixtures that recapitulate the rotated-square motif.

The chancery was built entirely by Chinese workers who were brought to the United States solely for this project. For years, they could be seen in unmarked vans being shuttled between the construction site and an anonymous motel where they were all housed for the duration.

012c Embassy of Kuwait Chancery

3500 International Drive, NW

1982—SKIDMORE, OWINGS & MERRILL

One of the first buildings in the new International Center enclave was the sleekly geometrical Kuwaiti Chancery. As with the new Chinese Chancery, this building employs 45-degree angles as a compositional motif in both plan and elevation. Although relatively small, the structure has great presence thanks to the cantilever shielding its glassy corner entrance and the bold, diagonal struts on the second floor. In certain light, an elaborate, filigree screen in the lobby can be seen from the outside.

012d Embassy of Bangladesh Chancery

3510 International Drive, NW

2000—SMITHGROUP

Water is an ever-present feature in swampy Bangladesh, and the architects of the country's new chancery incorporated a number of design elements alluding to this essential aspect of the nation's culture. The inverted gable hovering over the building, for example, is intended to suggest a water lily, while on the interior, various colors and textures of slate flooring are used to suggest a riverbed running through the main space. Kasota limestone on the front and rear façades adds warmth, and hints at the sandstone common in Bangladesh; for budgetary reasons, groundface concrete block was used instead on the side elevations.

012e Embassy of Nigeria Chancery

3519 International Court, NW

2001—SHALOM BARANES ASSOCIATES

In approaching the Nigerian Chancery, the visitor first passes alongside a sweeping, limestone-clad wall that closely adheres to the curve of the street. Although this is the rear façade of the chancery, and it reflects the setback requirements common to all of the embassies in the International Center, its detailing, its fenestration pattern, and

especially its respect for the street line make this one of the more urbane buildings in the complex. Around front, the primary façade, which is rectilinear and unpretentious, culminates in a modest, angular tower that houses a ceremonial "grand hall." In the middle of the building is a glass atrium that unites the curving wing and the rectilinear wing. The basic plan abstractly refers to a common West African building typology, in which separate structures surround a courtyard covered with a communal roof.

012f Embassy of Brunei Darussalam

3520 International Court, NW

1999—RTKL ASSOCIATES

Brunei Darussalam is a tiny sultanate on the island of Borneo in the South China Sea, and both the country and its monarch virtually ooze wealth thanks to huge deposits of oil and gas. The design of this chancery draws not only on building strategies that are common in Southeast Asia, such as post-and-beam construction and steeply pitched roofs, but also on forms that are more particularly associated with Brunei. The chancery's most direct antecedent is the "Kampung Ayer," or "Water Village," in Brunei's capital city, which is filled with simple, gable-roofed houses on stilts.

013 Sidwell Friends School Administration Building

(The Highlands)
3825 Wisconsin Avenue, NW

C. 1827—CHARLES JOSEPH NOURSE, OWNER-BUILDER
Numerous alterations: VARIOUS ARCHITECTS
2004—Interior renovation: OUTERBRIDGE HORSEY ASSOCIATES

One of the few remaining 19th-century houses in this part of the city, the Highlands once presided over hundreds of acres of farmland. Joseph Nourse, who as register of the treasury from 1781 to 1829 played a vital role in managing the federal government's financial affairs, gave the land to his son Charles, chief clerk at the War Department, and daughter-in-law, Rebecca. The couple then built this house using stone quarried on the property. As Anne Hollingsworth Wharton observed in *Social Life in the Early Republic* (1904), "[N]o house in the vicinity of Washington is more replete with associations of the past than The Highlands, where the Madisons, Thomas Jefferson, . . . and other distinguished people of the day were wont to congregate." The second floor and the square pillars on the west front were later additions. The building now houses administrative offices of the prestigious Sidwell Friends School, which has attracted the children of several sitting U.S. presidents, including Barack Obama.

013a Sidwell Middle School

Sidwell Friends School Campus

2006—KIERAN TIMBERLAKE

The Sidwell Middle School was the first building in the District of Columbia, and the first K–12 educational facility in the United States, to be awarded LEED Platinum certification. The project began with an existing, two-story brick structure that was renovated—as minimally as possible, to avoid wasting energy and materials—and incorporated into the three-story addition. The addition is largely sheathed in reclaimed wood, including vertical slats on the main west-facing wall to reduce heat gain from the afternoon sun. Where the old and new structures meet, some of these wood slats extend down over the windows of the existing building, literally embracing it. On the south-facing wall of the new wing, horizontal louvers shield the interior from the sun's heat while allowing filtered light to enter the adjacent spaces. The building has a green roof, of course, as well as solar chimneys, which vent hot air from classrooms on multiple levels. Nestled between the old and new wings is a terraced courtyard that the architects describe as a "constructed wetland," which filters gray water for reuse in the building.

The school's leaders did not begin the project with the goal of achieving LEED certification—in fact, some board members were skeptical about the extra costs of "going green." Then several faculty members made the case that a state-of-the-art, sustainable building could be a valuable teaching tool. The results have exceeded the teachers' expectations. Students actively monitor the building's performance and incorporate their findings into science classes and other subject areas, while teachers routinely use aspects of the building, the green roof, and the courtyard as instructive case studies. The middle school's groundbreaking credentials even inspired a group of parents to start a buying club for hybrid cars.

014 Slayton House

3411 Ordway Street, NW

1960—I. M. PEI & ASSOCIATES; Associated architect: THOMAS W. D. WRIGHT
2003—Renovation: HUGH NEWELL JACOBSEN; Landscape architect: JAY GRAHAM
2010—Renovation: MAURICE WALTERS ARCHITECT; Interior design: FORMA DESIGN

A trio of barrel vaults peeks out impishly from behind a plain brick wall, inviting observant passersby to stop and investigate the unexpected form on an otherwise typical Cleveland Park street. Standing amid a well-landscaped garden is a modern pavilion rendered in concrete, brick, and glass. The house was one of a very small number of private residences designed by the firm of I. M. Pei, architect of the National Gallery of Art's East Building. The client, William Slayton, managed this coup because

he was a former associate of Pei's who came to Washington to serve as commissioner of the U.S. Urban Renewal Administration and later became executive vice president of the AIA. He was locally renowned as the centerpiece of the "Slayton Irregulars," an amorphous group of architects and related professionals who often got together for conversation and lengthy meals.

The house is a zigzag in section—a sort of tri-level plus basement—with the main living space in front facing the street, two bedrooms on the upper level toward the rear, and a dining room, kitchen, and guest room below. As renovated by Hugh Newell Jacobsen, the house was remarkably improved while remaining true to Pei's fundamental intent. The top level of the central bay, for instance, which was originally enclosed, is now an open library and sitting area, allowing views from the front yard all the way through the house. Since then, a new owner has made additional changes while retaining the open layout.

015 Winthrop Faulkner Houses at Rosedale

Ordway and 36th streets, NW

1964–78—WINTHROP FAULKNER

Son of architect Waldron Faulkner and grandson of famed architectural patron Avery Coonley, Winthrop Faulkner designed this group of houses—including 3530 Ordway, 3540 Ordway, 3407 36th Street, and 3411 36th Street—as neighbors for his own residence at 3403 36th Street. Simultaneously modest and striking in their simplicity, the cleanly modern houses fit comfortably among more traditional neighbors.

016 Rosedale

3501 Newark Street, NW

C. 1793—URIAH FORREST, OWNER-BUILDER
2003—Addition and renovation: MUSE ARCHITECTS

Rosedale was the summer retreat of General Uriah Forrest, whose house in Georgetown [see K13] was the site of the crucial dinner party at which George Washington convinced prominent area landowners to sell property to the government for the new District of Columbia. Within a few years Forrest decided to abandon his M Street residence and live in the farmhouse at Rosedale year-round. The small cottage that constitutes the oldest part of the house is believed by some historians to date to 1740, which would make it the oldest extant structure in the District, but this has not been proved, and at any rate, the cottage has been changed a great deal.

In 2002, Youth for Understanding, a nonprofit group that owned the property, which then included the farmhouse, several mid-20th-century dormitories, and six-and-a-half acres of land, put it up for sale. Neighbors were alarmed by the possibility that the green space they had all freely used for recreational purposes might be rendered inaccessible—or, worse, fully developed—by a new owner, so a group of them got together and raised $12 million to buy the site. One of the families bought the farmhouse and renovated it, the dormitories were demolished, and most of the green space was placed in trust to be preserved in perpetuity. A portion of the property along Ordway Street was subdivided, and a row of houses by several different architects was built there.

Other notable houses in the immediate vicinity of Rosedale include 3530 Newark Street, NW, by Travis Price Architects, an elegant composition in copper, glass, wood, and stone.

017 Highland Place

Between 34th and Newark streets, NW

Late 19th to early 20th centuries—
VARIOUS ARCHITECTS

Romantic architecture, copious porches, and yards full of majestic, gnarled oaks make Highland Place one of the most picturesque streets in the city. Sequestered in the middle of a city block and easily overlooked, it is unknown even to many longtime Washingtonians. Several of the houses are interesting on their own, but the street warranted a collective entry in this book because of the houses' overall quality and intriguing variations on a similar architectural vocabulary.

TOUR P

Massachusetts Avenue / Kalorama

Kalorama is an artificial word derived from the Greek for "good view." It is the fitting name that poet, liberal activist, and diplomat Joel Barlow gave to the estate he bought in 1807 near the present-day intersection of 23rd and S streets, overlooking the nascent federal city and Georgetown. Barlow, one of Thomas Jefferson's most trusted friends, embraced whatever was new and advanced in any field—politics, literature, science—as long as he thought it would improve the condition of humankind. For him, that included improving the condition of the new United States: "My object is altogether of a moral and political nature," he wrote. "I wish to encourage and strengthen in the rising generation, the sense of the importance of republican institutions."

Barlow's house burned during the Civil War, was rebuilt, and then was demolished in the 1880s. Soon thereafter, Kalorama Woods, as realtors originally called the neighborhood, began to attract rich, famous, and powerful families who raced in to build their mansions and gardens. The area's architectural purity and unimpeachably tasteful landscaping prompted Russell Baker to quip, "Kalorama has the quiet, slightly sinister atmosphere of the aristocratic quarter of a Ruritanian capital."

Baker might have extended his criticism to cover most of Massachusetts Avenue, the city's longest and grandest boulevard, a stretch of which skirts the western edge of Kalorama. "Mass Ave," as it is colloquially known, was perhaps the most sought-after address for the many robber barons and aristocrats who moved to Washington in droves during the late 19th and early 20th centuries. Life along the avenue changed perforce, however, during the Great Depression, as suddenly impoverished dowagers and debutantes slipped out the back door and diplomats from around the world strode in the front, and "Embassy Row" was born.

Cyril Farey's preconstruction (c. 1925) impression of the British ambassador's residence. Architect Edwin Lutyens signed the watercolor, apparently to signify his approval.

26
27
25
MASSACHUSETTS AVE
34th ST
WISCONSIN AVE
24
23
22
20
21
2000 ft

CONNECTICUT AVE
KALORAMA RD
24th ST
S ST
19th ST
Q ST

P1 Buffalo Bridge

(Dumbarton Bridge)
23rd and Q streets, NW

1914—GLENN AND BEDFORD BROWN;
Sculptors: A. PHIMISTER PROCTOR (BUFFALO) AND JOHN JOSEPH EARLEY (HEADS)

Brown *père* and *fils* designed this amazing bridge to join Georgetown with the then-developing Dupont/Kalorama area. Curving in plan, supported on large semicircular arches, and crowned by a cantilevered row of smaller, bracketed arches supporting the walkways, it is a visually powerful structure evoking Roman aqueducts and medieval fortifications. In contrast to such ancient European imagery, the decorative scheme is pure Americana, from the giant buffalo that give the bridge its unofficial but widely used name, to the series of heads sculpted from a life mask of the Sioux chief Kicking Bear.

The lower part of Rock Creek is traversed by a number of other noteworthy bridges, including the majestic William Howard Taft Bridge of 1906, which carries Connecticut Avenue over the creek (George Morison, architect; Roland Hinton Perry, sculptor), Paul Cret's 1931 bridge over Klingle Valley (Connecticut Avenue just north of the Kennedy-Warren Apartments), and the Duke Ellington Bridge at Calvert Street [see O1].

P2 Turkish Ambassador's Residence

(Everett House)
1606 23rd Street, NW

1915—GEORGE OAKLEY TOTTEN JR.
2006—Renovation and restoration: ARCHETYPE

The prolific George Oakley Totten Jr., like many architects of his day, was stylistically promiscuous—compare his Venetian Gothic "Pink Palace" on Meridian Hill [see N6] or his Beaux-Arts Moran House [see P6] to this restless Renaissance Revival mansion. The gently bowed front portico brings to mind the south façade of the White House before the addition of the Truman Balcony, but the two buildings differ greatly in almost every other respect (this mansion is primarily of French derivation, whereas the White House was inspired by Anglo-Irish precedents). A wing to the south, containing a conservatory and a trellised, rooftop terrace, breaks the symmetry of the façade. The tripartite windows on the third floor of the main block add an unexpected and rather awkward horizontal component. In fact, the best-resolved elevation may well be the short one facing Sheridan Circle, which exhibits a better balance between the primary architectural forms and the delicate ornamentation of the frieze and window surrounds.

Edward Hamlin Everett, who commissioned the mansion and moved here from his native Cleveland, was one of scores of industrialists who flocked to Washington in the Gilded Age. Everett derived some of his evident wealth from the usual sources, such as mining, oil, and gas, but he was also a pioneer in the automated manufacture of beer and soda bottles, and for a time was a major shareholder in Anheuser-Busch.

Although built for Everett, the house may have been destined to serve as the Turkish Embassy. Totten had visited Turkey in 1908, and designed the American Chancery there, as well as a residence for the prime minister. Sultan Abdul-Hamid was so impressed with these buildings that he offered Totten the position of "personal and private architect to the sultan." The architect accepted, but the sultan was deposed the following year and Totten returned to the United States to resume his career.

P3 Embassy of Latvia

(Alice Pike Barney Studio House)
2306 Massachusetts Avenue, NW
(on Sheridan Circle)

1902—WADDY B. WOOD
2005—Renovation: BALODEMAS ARCHITECTS

In the early 1900s, this eccentric house was a nexus of cultural life in Washington, under the auspices of artist, patron, and social activist Alice Pike Barney. Designed by Waddy Wood with substantial input from Barney herself, it was the site of concerts, theatrical performances, exhibitions, and parties where artists and socialites mixed liberally. Barney once complained, "What is capital life after all? Small talk and lots to eat, an infinite series of teas and dinners. Art? There is none." Doing her part to change this situation, she painted and wrote plays, one of which was attended by Sarah Bernhardt, who arrived in a litter carried by four liveried footmen. Also a well-regarded musician, Barney received a commission from no less than Anna Pavlova to score a ballet for the great Russian dancer to use on her triumphant 1914–15 tour of America.

Barney died in 1931, and several decades later her daughters donated the house to the Smithsonian Institution, which never quite figured out what to do with it. The Smithsonian finally unloaded the charming but fallow building in 1999, and it now serves as the Latvian Embassy.

The Barney Studio House faces Sheridan Circle, named after General Philip H. Sheridan, who built his reputation on the scorched-earth Valley Campaign in Virginia during the Civil War and subsequently on the slaughter of countless Native Americans out west. The equestrian statue of the general is the work of Gutzon Borglum, who later showed what he could do at a larger scale when he created Mount Rushmore.

P4 Egyptian Ambassador's Residence

(Joseph Beale House)
2301 Massachusetts Avenue, NW

1909—GLENN BROWN
2002—Renovation and restoration: ARCHETYPE

Commissioned by Joseph Beale and now the Egyptian ambassador's residence, this neo-Renaissance *palazzo* is an exceptionally skillful composition. The central Palladian arch, marking a recessed loggia, creates a void that plays off against the subtle, convex curvature of the façade. Note how the bulging belt course low on the façade meets the projecting benches.

P5 Embassy of Haiti

(Fahnestock House)
2311 Massachusetts Avenue, NW

1910—NATHAN C. WYETH

Haiti is one of several underdeveloped countries whose Washington embassies occupy incongruously opulent mansions. This soaring Beaux-Arts town house, commissioned by financier Gibson Fahnestock, harmoniously blends with the rows of similar structures that line the blocks around Sheridan Circle. In contrast with the Moran House next door, however, this is a rather restrained and tightly controlled composition. Because of the tautness of the façade and shallowness of the pilasters, the Corinthian capitals seem to explode like fireworks from the wall plane.

P6 Moran House

2315 Massachusetts Avenue, NW

1909—GEORGE OAKLEY TOTTEN JR.

This building and its counterpart next door were commissioned by different plutocrats and designed by different architects, but appear as harmonious neighbors, sharing similar materials, thin pilasters, aligned cornices, and mansard roofs. Even so, the effects are not the same—the Moran House is much more idiosyncratic, with unusual figural sculptural motifs and surprisingly large windowless panels on what would seem to be the primary floor. The bold tower is an architectural exclamation point terminating one of the city's most elegant blocks. Long serving as the Pakistani Chancery, the house became vacant when a new facility was built in the International Chancery Center. The Embassy of Pakistan expects to renovate the Moran House but has announced no specific plans for its future use.

P7 Embassy of the Republic of Cameroon

(Hauge House)
2349 Massachusetts Avenue, NW

1907—GEORGE OAKLEY TOTTEN JR.
1934—Addition: SMITH BOWMAN JR.

This romantic limestone mansion marks the western end of Massachusetts Avenue's grand turn-of-the-century Beaux-Arts residences, a procession that begins with Jules Henri de Sibour's Wilkins House at 17th Street. As with many of the buildings along this stretch of the avenue, the design of the Hague House was derived from French sources, but in this case, the inspiration lay in the early Renaissance period, closely associated with the great châteaux of the Loire Valley. Christian Hauge, a Norwegian diplomat, commissioned the mansion shortly after he was appointed his nation's first minister to the United States in 1905 (the year Norway gained its independence from Sweden). Hauge died in 1907, while snowshoeing back home, but his Kentucky-born and quite rich widow stayed on in the house, holding sway as one of the city's more influential hostesses until her own death in 1927.

P8 Woodrow Wilson House

2340 S Street, NW

1916—WADDY B. WOOD
1921—Remodeling: WADDY B. WOOD
2005—Exterior restoration: ARCHETYPE

Tel: (202) 387-4062
www.woodrowwilsonhouse.org

President and Mrs. Wilson occupied this Georgian revival house, which was inspired by the work of the 18th-century Scottish architect Robert Adam, from the end of his latter term as president, in 1921, until his death in 1924. Mrs. Wilson called it "an unpretentious, comfortable, dignified house, fitted to the needs of a gentleman," and she continued to live here until she died in 1961. Although the Wilsons did not commission the house—they purchased it from its builder, businessman Henry Parker Fairbanks—it is the only one the couple ever owned.

Waddy Butler Wood, from a prominent family of Virginia, enjoyed a successful career as one of upper-class Washington's favored architects and designed more than 30 mansions in the Kalorama area alone. He was a particular favorite of the Wilsons, perhaps because they shared his deep Old Dominion roots, and he was chosen to design the inaugural stands for both of Wilson's inaugurations. Wood's professional views were quite conservative—in an unpublished essay, he decried originality for its own sake, which he termed "Architectural Bolshevism."

P9 Thai Ambassador's Residence

(Codman-Davis House)
2145 Decatur Place, NW

1907—OGDEN CODMAN JR.

The entry courtyard of this mansion would be at home in Paris, but the house itself, designed by Ogden Codman Jr. for his cousin, Martha, is more in the English Georgian style. The building's prim aspect is hardly surprising, since Mr. Codman was Edith Wharton's collaborator on that classic book of architectural dos and don'ts, *The Decoration of Houses* (1897), in which the authors purse their lips and take a firm stand against such modern horrors as electric lighting, with its "harsh white glare, which no expedients have as yet overcome" (they encouraged their readers to rely on wax candles instead). The building now serves as the residence of the Thai ambassador, who probably uses electric lights without a trace of shame.

The stairway just west of the house, connecting 22nd Street to S Street and nicknamed "the Spanish Steps," is one of Washington's hidden treats.

P10 Friends Meeting House

2111 Florida Avenue, NW

1930—WALTER F. PRICE; Landscape architect: ROSE GREELY
1950—Addition: LEON CHATELAIN II

Made possible by a gift from a Rhode Island Quaker, and built in part for President and Mrs. Herbert Hoover, who were also Quakers, this simple stone meeting house recalls similar structures that dot rural Pennsylvania, the religious sect's historic center (in fact, the structure is faced with fieldstone from a Pennsylvania quarry). One of the ground-floor rooms includes ceiling beams that had been installed in the White House when it was repaired after the War of 1812, but were later removed during another renovation. Rose Greely designed and planted the informal, tranquil grounds to resemble a small private park.

P11 Russian Trade Representation

(Lothrop Mansion)
2001 Connecticut Avenue, NW

1909—HORNBLOWER & MARSHALL

Alvin M. Lothrop and Samuel W. Woodward founded the business that eventually became the prominent local department store chain, Woodward and Lothrop, which sadly was subsumed into a national retail company in the 1990s. Lothrop commissioned this 40-room house for one of the most spectacular residential sites in the city, commanding the view down Connecticut Avenue. The main façade is actually the rear of the house, designed purely for the public impression; the entrance is on the opposite side, facing a small courtyard. For years the building has housed the offices of the Russian (previously Soviet) Trade Representation [sic], a branch of that country's embassy.

P12 2029 Connecticut Avenue

1916—HUNTER AND BELL

What Gilded-Age mansions are to Massachusetts Avenue, elegant apartment houses are to Connecticut Avenue. Some of the earliest luxury apartment buildings in the city are found on this stretch of the street, and none can surpass 2029 Connecticut for opulence. With just three huge apartments on each of the main floors, it has long been a favorite of Washington's elite, from former president William Howard Taft to entertainer Lena Horne. The velvet-voiced Horne occupied one of the units facing the avenue, running the entire width of the building and featuring a 43-foot-long foyer, a 33-foot-long living room, and five bedrooms. The base and top of the building are sheathed in glazed terra cotta, as are the two projecting porticoes, whose decorative sculptures include salamanders and fleurs-de-lis, favorite symbols of French king Francis I.

P13 The Dresden

2126 Connecticut Avenue, NW

1910—ALBERT H. BEERS
1974—Renovation: PETER VOGHI
1996—Restoration: OEHRLEIN & ASSOCIATES ARCHITECTS

While serving as the chief architect for developer Harry Wardman (a position later held by Mihran Mesrobian), Albert Beers designed a large number of apartment buildings all over Washington. The Dresden is distinct because of its curving, neo-Georgian façade, holding the street line of the avenue. One of the side effects of the curve is that the apartments running along that façade contain rooms that are slightly tapered in plan.

P14 Woodward Condominium

2311 Connecticut Avenue, NW

1910—HARDING AND UPMAN
1970—Renovation: ARCHITECT UNKNOWN

Not long after Mr. Lothrop built his mansion at the corner of Connecticut and Columbia [see P11], his partner, Mr. Woodward, developed this apartment house. The design is a rather tame Spanish Colonial affair, but with one big splash of ornament: the polychrome terra cotta frame surrounding the main entrance, which adds a touch of Baroque exuberance. Crowning the narrow tower at the oblique corner of the building is a little open-air pavilion for residents' use. The Woodward, which was converted into

a condominium in 1973, was notable as one of the earliest apartment buildings in Washington to contain duplex units, though there are just a few of them facing Connecticut Avenue.

P15 The Lindens

2401 Kalorama Road, NW

1754—ROBERT "KING" HOOPER, OWNER-BUILDER
1934—Moved to Washington
1935—Restoration: WALTER MACOMBER
1985—Renovation: SHARON WASHBURN ARCHITECT, WALTER MACOMBER

This wood-frame Georgian house defensibly claims the title of oldest building in Washington, even though it was not built here. Its complex history begins with Robert Hooper, a prosperous Yankee merchant, who erected the house in Danvers, Massachusetts. More than a century and three quarters later, Mr. and Mrs. George Maurice Morris bought the building, dismantled it, moved it in sections, and reconstructed it on a sloping Kalorama lot, where it immediately seemed at home among its eclectic neighbors.

The house's entrance bay, carried up three stories to the pedimented attic and partially defined by the flanking Corinthian columns, adds a strong vertical thrust to the otherwise foursquare dwelling. The rusticated wooden façades were covered in sand-infused paint to resemble more expensive stone.

P16 Ambassador's Residence, Embassy of the Sultanate of Oman

(Devore Chase House)
2000 24th Street, NW

1931—WILLIAM LAWRENCE BOTTOMLEY
1965—Addition: DOUGLAS STENHOUSE

William Bottomley, a specialist in creating "new-old" houses, is perhaps best known for the James River, neo-Georgian brick villas he built in and around Richmond in the 1920s and 1930s. The Devore Chase House, covered in textured limestone, suggests more of a French influence, though traces of the Georgian are still evident in its overall demeanor of extreme restraint.

P17 Turkish Chancery

2525 Massachusetts Avenue, NW

1999—SHALOM BARANES ASSOCIATES

The Turks must like the neighborhood, since they built this new chancery just down the street from their ambassador's residence on Sheridan Circle. The building cuts into a steeply sloping site, resulting in massive retaining walls visible

at the sides. Eschewing the usual hierarchical grandeur associated with such buildings, the chancery seems unusually domestic in scale, with two distinct wings linked by a low-rise connector. (One result of this modest design approach is that a house located up the hill behind the chancery actually figures very prominently in the view from the avenue.) References to vernacular Turkish architecture are subtle, and largely consist of abstract geometrical patterns that suggest the intricacies of traditional Mediterranean and Islamic decorative motifs.

P18 Japanese Embassy (Old Ambassador's Residence)

2516 Massachusetts Avenue, NW

1931—DELANO & ALDRICH
1960—Teahouse: NAHIKO EMORI

The main building of this complex, which was, unlike most of its contemporaries, designed expressly as an embassy, has a simple, pedimented Georgian Revival façade that makes the structure seem modest by comparison with the architectural stage sets that dominate this stretch of Massachusetts Avenue. Note the "swept eaves," which curve up slightly as if lifted by a breeze, and the unusual radial arch above the main door. The rear gardens contain an authentic teahouse that was built in Japan, taken apart, shipped to America, and reassembled on this site; the little structure marks the 100th anniversary of diplomatic relations between the two nations.

P19 Islamic Center

2551 Massachusetts Avenue, NW

1957—EGYPTIAN MINISTRY OF WORKS WITH MARIO ROSSI; IRWIN PORTER AND SONS, ASSOCIATED ARCHITECTS

Officially serving as the religious center for all American Muslims, this steel-framed mosque was built through a joint initiative of the ambassadors of the leading Islamic countries. While the main façade of the building follows the line of Massachusetts Avenue, the mosque proper, in the center, is canted so that the *mihrab,* or altar-like niche, is oriented toward Mecca. Persian carpets cover the floors, the ebony pulpit is inlaid in ivory, stained glass sparkles in the clerestory, and verses from the Koran are rendered in mosaics around the entrance, throughout the front courtyard, and atop the 160-foot minaret. The designers did make a few concessions to the building's physical context, particularly in deciding to face the mosque in limestone, the favorite material of Massachusetts Avenue's château builders. Visitors of any or no faith are welcome except during prayer times, provided that they observe customs of dress, which guides can explain to those not in the know.

P20 Embassy of Italy Chancery

3000 Whitehaven Street, NW

2000—SARTOGO ARCHITETTI ASSOCIATI; Associated architects: LEO A DALY

This is an example of a chancery expressly designed to relate to its physical context while evoking the architectural culture of the country it represents. The building is essentially a diamond in plan, split down the middle to create two right triangles separated by an atrium, and oriented so that one side is parallel to Massachusetts Avenue (meaning that the points of the diamond align with the cardinal points on a map). In other words, the chancery's plan is an abstraction of the original map of the District of Columbia—before Arlington and Alexandria were retroceded to Virginia—which was a perfect diamond with the Potomac River slicing lengthwise through it. Most visitors are unlikely to make this connection on their own, but it does help to explain what would otherwise seem to be an illogical design move resulting in multiple acute corners within the building.

Having devised this rationale for the plan, the architects turned their attention to issues of massing and façade composition, creating an abstract rendition of a Tuscan *palazzo,* with pinkish stone walls, relatively small windows, and a projecting, patinated copper roof. A couple of larger openings along the Massachusetts Avenue façade, one of which features panels of copper to match the roof, help to break up the vast, solid plane of stone. The result is rather forbidding, though it has become less so over time as the surrounding trees have visually enveloped the building.

P21 Danish Embassy

3200 Whitehaven Street, NW

1960—VILHELM LAURITZEN; Associated architects: THE ARCHITECTS COLLABORATIVE
2006—Renovation design architects: VILHELM LAURITZEN; Architects of record: VOA ASSOCIATES

An excellent example of coolly rational Scandinavian modernism, the Danish Embassy combines chancery functions and the ambassador's residence in a single building. While visiting the newly finished embassy, the architect, who is perhaps best known for his design of two generations of terminals at Copenhagen's airport, wrote in a letter home that "[Benjamin] Thompson from [The Architects Collaborative] was here yesterday and said that it was the only building in Washington worth looking at." Lauritzen went on to write, "I would like to show the servants' wing to the Americans. They say that we are socialists and perhaps we are; here they can see how it works." Unfortunately, the parking lot at the entrance compromises the initial impression of the aesthetically pure building.

P22 Brazilian Ambassador's Residence and Chancery

(McCormick House)
3000 Massachusetts Avenue, NW

c. 1910—Ambassador's residence: JOHN RUSSELL POPE
1973—Chancery: OLAVO REDIG DE CAMPOS

Built as the Washington lair of retired diplomat Robert S. McCormick, whose uncle invented the reaper, the Brazilian ambassador's residence presents

another variation on John Russell Pope's *palazzo* formula. Here the architect created a recessed entrance, derived from that of the famed Palazzo Massimo alle Colonne in Rome, and placed the house perpendicular to Massachusetts Avenue so that all of the main rooms face the quiet side street (and enjoy more-or-less southern exposure).

To the north of the residence is the chancery, a classic example of space-age, glass modernism seemingly hovering just off the ground. Note the swooping spiral reception desk visible inside the lobby.

P23 British Embassy

3100 Massachusetts Avenue, NW

1928—SIR EDWIN LUTYENS; Associated architect: FREDERICK H. BROOKE

With its broad entry court and tall, narrow wings reaching out to the avenue, the British Embassy is simultaneously imposing and welcoming. The plan is actually quite unusual, and reflects the building's dual purpose as chancery and residence (the much larger, modern chancery next door, of course, came later). The two functions are separated on the ground floor by a *porte-cochère* deep within the complex, behind the U-shaped office building, but on the upper level, the ambassador's study, which spans the driveway, serves as both a literal and a figurative bridge between the public offices and the private residence. The central axis of the chancery flows into the residence where, in the main foyer, it is reoriented 90 degrees to face the elegant gardens.

As earnest revivalists were sweating to create classical references to an idealized (and largely fanciful) American past, Lutyens, who called architecture "the great game," mischievously employed colonial American associations for the new embassy. The Massachusetts Avenue façade is a pastiche of Williamsburg—then very much in the news—and the work of Sir Christopher Wren, while the garden façade of the residence, dominated by a giant Ionic portico, suggests vintage movies about the Old South.

P24 Finnish Embassy

3301 Massachusetts Avenue, NW

1994—HEIKKINEN-KOMONEN ARCHITECTS; Associate architects: ANGELOS DEMETRIOU & ASSOCIATES

The Finnish Embassy is simultaneously sensational and subtle, confident and modest, coolly rational and arrestingly picturesque. Its opening in 1994 caused quite a stir in both architectural and diplomatic circles. Here was a chancery that not only eschewed the typical grandeur of official Washington but also subverted common assumptions about the visibility, accessibility, and security of foreign missions. Plus, it had a sauna.

The building is organized as a series of linear zones running parallel to the main façade. First comes the porch-like layer defined by an ivy-covered copper trellis. Just inside is a zone of security and reception spaces, followed by the main circulation spine. A graceful but dramatic curving staircase breaks the rectilinear geometry, connecting the lobby to the main public event space one level below. A glazed rear porch, which can be opened up to the main space or closed off depending on the weather and other factors, runs the length of the rear facade. The back-yard surprise is a pier-like walkway, partially sheltered by tensile fabric awnings, that juts into the woods, affording visitors a view back to the building, which is particularly beautiful when lit at night.

In its simplicity, its sleek materials, and its deference to the natural setting, the embassy seems quintessentially Finnish, and yet it also incorporates a number of allusions to the landscape and culture of its host country. The narrow, linear atrium, for example, was inspired by the Grand Canyon, which the architects considered to be America's most glorious natural feature. And that curving staircase was partially inspired by the glamorous sets in classic Hollywood musicals.

A former press counselor for the em-

bassy once remarked, "I had no idea a building could be such an important diplomatic tool." The Finns take full advantage of that tool, graciously hosting exhibitions, receptions, lectures, and other events for Washingtonians who enjoy spending time in such a serenely elegant building.

P25 St. Albans School, Marriott Hall

Massachusetts Avenue at Garfield Street, NW

2009—SKIDMORE, OWINGS & MERRILL

Like the National Cathedral School for girls [see following entry], the St. Albans School for boys is administered by the Protestant Episcopal Cathedral Foundation though its earliest building predates the cathedral itself. The school gradually grew and added various buildings without benefit of a master plan, and by the dawn of the 21st century, the campus was picturesque but disjointed. The new Marriott Hall does a remarkably good job of tying the campus together without upstaging the historic structures that it connects. Through a system of terraces, staircases, and passageways, the addition deftly negotiates its dramatically sloping site while creating a sensible circulation pattern linking four existing buildings. Although the new building is much glassier and sleeker than its Gothic Revival neighbors, it blends in by virtue of its copious use of bluestone (which closely matches the Potomac gneiss common in the older buildings), its landscaped terraces, and its green roof.

P26 National Cathedral School, Hearst Hall

3101 Wisconsin Avenue, NW (at Woodley Road)

1900—ROBERT GIBSON; Superintendent of construction: ADOLF CLUSS

The main building of what is now the National Cathedral School was completed years before the church itself was even begun. Today it stands out as a regal, Renaissance Revival work amid the predominantly Gothic Revival cathedral compound. The hall was named after Phoebe Hearst, the mother of William Randolph Hearst, who donated $200,000 to build a girls' school under the auspices of the National Cathedral Foundation. The bas-relief sculptures between the arches on the Wisconsin Avenue façade, by Louis Amateis, depict "Qualities of Womanhood," to wit: Purity, Faith, Art/Music, Motherhood, and Nursing. Seen from the rear, the steeply pitched roof appears almost as tall as the building's base walls.

P27 Washington National Cathedral

(Cathedral Church of St. Peter and St. Paul)
Massachusetts and Wisconsin avenues, NW

1907—GEORGE FREDERICK BODLEY AND HENRY VAUGHAN
1907–17—HENRY VAUGHAN; Superintending architect: ARTHUR B. HEATON
1921–44—FROHMAN, ROBB & LITTLE; Consulting architects (1921–29): RALPH ADAMS CRAM AND FRANK FERGUSON
1944–72—PHILIP HUBERT FROHMAN
1971–73—Superintending architects: GODWIN & BECKETT

1973-81—Superintending architect: HOWARD BUCKNER TREVILLIAN JR.
1981-90—Superintending architects: SMITH SEGRETI TEPPER ARCHITECTS AND PLANNERS
1989—Landscape architects, West Front: EDAW INC.
2007—Visitor Gateway project: SMITHGROUP; Landscape architects: MICHAEL VERGUSON

Tel: (202) 537-6200
www.cathedral.org

The notion was preposterous, really: to build from scratch a "true" Gothic cathedral, icon of feudal Europe, in the capital of the world's first modern democracy and the epicenter of the classically inclined City Beautiful movement. Having overcome this improbable genesis and the infamously protracted construction process that ensued, the Washington National Cathedral today stands majestically atop Mount St. Albans, one of the highest points in the District of Columbia.

The idea for a nondenominational cathedral in Washington dates back to L'Enfant, who envisioned a "great church for national purpose . . . equally open to all" on the present-day site of the Old Patent Office [see E10]. There was no sustained effort to create such a church, however, until 1893, when Congress chartered the Protestant Episcopal Cathedral Foundation as a private, nonprofit organization. To get the cathedral going, the Episcopal hierarchy first had to create a new diocese, since Washington was then part of the Diocese of Maryland. Then came a years-long search for the right site, followed by design competitions, or rather, a series of what the longtime clerk of the works, Richard Feller, called "wranglings." Church officials initially approved a design by Ernest Flagg for a domed, Renaissance-style cathedral, but Bishop Henry Yates Satterlee, a devoted Gothicist, traveled to England to persuade the aged George Frederick Bodley to develop a Gothic alternative, which was ultimately adopted. Then came the inevitable fundraising, a process helped initially by Charles Carroll Glover, president of Riggs Bank. Finally, in 1907, Theodore Roosevelt tapped the cornerstone into place and cried, "God speed the work!" But the work was anything but speedy—construction continued in spurts for 83 years until the building was finally officially finished in 1990.

Bodley's design, not surprisingly, was primarily derived from English Gothic precedents, with a Latin cross plan, a tall, square tower at the intersection of the two axes, and twin towers flanking the west façade. Construction began at the eastern end and proceeded gradually westward. The walls were built using traditional masonry techniques similar to those used in actual Gothic churches, though reinforcing steel rods were added for greater stability and the roof is partially supported by steel trusses. As successive architects took charge of the project, they adjusted the design of subsequent sections, while generally remaining true to Bodley's intentions. Many aspects of the cathedral's lengthy construction period are legible in the architecture. One subtle surprise, for instance, is the slight kink in the plan of the nave, best witnessed from the choir area behind the altar—curiously, this minor discrepancy goes a long way toward making the cathedral seem genuinely Gothic.

Like its architectural forebears, the National Cathedral is replete with fascinating details, artworks, and historical connections. The strangely erotic sculptures by Frederick Hart in the tympanums (the areas within the arches over the main doors) are among the numerous artistic elements that seem strikingly modern in comparison to the structure they adorn. On the north side of the building is a colonnade in which the column capitals are decorated with highly unusual motifs reflecting aspects of American culture and geography, from animals to igloos. Inside the sanctuary, of course, there is the famous stained glass window with an embedded Moon rock.

Despite its congressional charter and continuing management by the Episcopal Diocese of Washington, the National Cathedral receives no federal funding and is officially nondenominational, thus preserving at least some semblance of separation between church and state.

TOUR Q

Foxhall

The thoroughly suburban—at some points almost pastoral—character of the Foxhall area belies its proximity to Georgetown and central Washington. Indeed, it was not all that long ago that much of the property along Foxhall Road was open farm country. As recently as the 1920s and 1930s, cows from the nearby Palisades Dairy Farm grazed the land now occupied by the Mount Vernon Campus of The George Washington University.

The neighborhood takes its name from Henry Foxall (without the "h"), whose family farm, Spring Hill, was near where Foxhall Road and P Street now intersect. Foxall was a close friend of Thomas Jefferson—the two occasionally met for violin duets—and a major cannon manufacturer. His foundry, located in what is now Glover Archbold Park, was an obvious target during the War of 1812; when a timely thunderstorm prevented British troops from attacking the facility, Foxall credited divine providence, and in gratitude, established the Foundry Methodist Church, which initially stood at 14th and G streets and later moved to its current location on 16th Street, NW.

Agricultural enterprises became increasingly impractical within the District of Columbia during the late 19th century, and the Foxall farm was sold in 1910. By 1927, construction was under way on the neo-Tudor Foxhall Village (with the "h"—according to legend, a careless sign-maker bears responsibility for the misspelling) just below Reservoir Road, and station wagons, cocktail parties, and bridge games soon supplanted plows, cattle, and chicken coops.

Much of the Foxhall area was quite rural in character well into the 20th century, as evidenced by this house on Reservoir Road, made partially of logs and dating to the early 1800s.

48th ST
FOXHALL RD
W ST
WHITEHAVEN PARKWAY
RESERVOIR RD
1200 ft
1
2
3
4
5
6

Q1 Embassy of Germany Chancery

4645 Reservoir Road, NW

1964—EGON EIERMANN

The two major buildings in the German Embassy complex, the chancery and the ambassador's residence, both reflect the Teutonic penchant for precision and orderliness, but with strikingly different results. The sleek and finely detailed chancery, one of the most underappreciated buildings in Washington, demonstrates that rationalist, hard-edged modernism can also be visually rich and inviting. Architect Egon Eiermann skillfully obscured the bulk of the building by nestling it into the sloping terrain and stepping down its mass at both ends. The intricate façade, composed of layered grids in wood, metal, and glass, further dematerializes the structure. An influential architect in post–World War II Germany, Eiermann was perhaps best known for his hauntingly beautiful additions to the ruins of the Kaiser Wilhelm Memorial Church in Berlin.

As of this writing, the chancery is undergoing a major renovation by Geier Brown Renfrow Architects.

Q2 German Ambassador's Residence

1800 Foxhall Road, NW

1994—O. M. UNGERS

In contrast to the delicate chancery, the German ambassador's residence is monumental and forbidding. Despite its almost sepulchral severity, however, the building does have its charms. Many of the forms and patterns visible in the residence, such as the repeated grids of open squares, recall the starkly elegant motifs of Josef Hoffman and the Viennese Secession. Architect O. M. Ungers, who studied under Egon Eiermann, is notoriously obsessive—his contract for this project empowered him to dictate the exact and unalterable placement of all furniture in the building's public spaces.

Q3 Florence Hollis Hand Chapel

George Washington University,
Mount Vernon Campus
2100 Foxhall Road, NW

1970—HARTMAN-COX ARCHITECTS

Conceived as the last element of a master plan for an independent college (now a satellite of The George Washington University), the Hand Chapel was actually the first new structure to be built, following a gift from a generous benefactor. From the main entrance, one descends through a sequence of spaces that offer glimpses of the main sanctuary, which is used for both religious and secular purposes. Inspired by the restrained interiors of American colonial churches and by the work of Alvar Aalto, the unpretentious main hall is, by day, awash in remarkably even light that enters through a series of stepped clerestories.

Q4 Belgian Ambassador's Residence

(Anna Thomson Dodge House)
2300 Foxhall Road, NW

1931—HORACE TRUMBAUER
2006—Modernization: QUINN EVANS ARCHITECTS

Mansions are almost commonplace in Northwest Washington, but few can compete with this one for sheer, Gatsbyesque opulence. It was commissioned by the widow of Horace E. Dodge, the car

manufacturer, as a wedding gift for her daughter. The house's stately façade was inspired by that of the early 18th-century Hôtel de Rothelin-Charolais in Paris. The architect, Horace Trumbauer, whose prolific Philadelphia-based firm designed palatial houses for many of America's wealthiest families, was also involved in the design of the imposing Philadelphia Museum of Art and the campus plan for Duke University. Like many projects by Trumbauer's firm, however, this one is now believed to have been the work of his chief designer, Julian Abele, one of the most prolific African American architects of the early 20th century.

Q5 Spanish Ambassador's Residence

2350 Foxhall Road, NW

2003—JOSÉ RAFAEL MONEO;
MONEO BROCK STUDIO

Pritzker Prize winner José Rafael Moneo tends to rely on the inherent beauty of high-quality materials to lend character to his buildings, and such is the case with the unadorned walls of narrow Roman brick that define this very large but unassuming residence. Several interior spaces stand out, including the barrel-vaulted reception hall whose bold, simple dormers are visible from the street, and the skylit orangerie adjacent to the baronial formal dining room. Without resorting to literal historical quotation, Moneo imbued the residence with a distinctly Spanish feel through such devices as the use of Moorish-inspired tiles, reflecting the influence of seven centuries of Muslim presence on the Iberian Peninsula during the Middle Ages.

Q6 Kreeger Museum

2401 Foxhall Road, NW

1967—PHILIP JOHNSON AND RICHARD FOSTER

Tel: (202) 338-3552
www.kreegermuseum.org

When insurance executive David Lloyd Kreeger and his wife, Carmen, commissioned Philip Johnson to design a house that could accommodate their burgeoning art collection, they were already planning for its eventual conversion into a museum. Johnson's design strongly evokes ancient Mediterranean villas, with travertine walls, outdoor sculpture terraces, and groin-vaulted interior spaces reminiscent of the great Roman baths. Inside, the unusual choice of cotton carpet as a wall covering serves two practical purposes: it enhances the acoustics for musical performances and facilitates the quick rearrangement of paintings.

TOUR R

Arlington National Cemetery

Though outside the current boundaries of the District of Columbia, Arlington National Cemetery is so integral to the identity and character of the capital's monumental core that it warrants inclusion in this book. The green hills of the cemetery provide a placid backdrop for views from the Capitol and other spots along the Mall, and its principal architectural elements are important satellites of the city's network of landmarks.

Arlington House is barely visible as a light-colored speck in the center background of this annotated 1927 photograph, which shows the construction of the Arlington Memorial Bridge.

ARLINGTON BLVD
MEMORIAL DR
EISENHOWER DR
JEFFERSON DAVIS HIGHWAY
McPHERSON DR
I-395
1
2
2A
2B
2C
2D
3
4
3200 ft

R1 Arlington Memorial Bridge

1932—MCKIM, MEAD & WHITE; Sculptors: LEO FRIEDLANDER, JAMES EARLE FRASER, AND C. PAUL JENNEWEIN

Proposals for a bridge at this site date back at least to the time of President Andrew Jackson, who suggested a structure that would symbolically and physically link North and South. In the late 19th century, military engineers developed various schemes for a bridge beginning near the foot of New York Avenue, but in 1902, the Senate Park Commission, citing the planned placement of the new Lincoln Memorial, issued a statement supporting the alignment of the bridge as built. It was not until the 1920s, however, that the firm of McKim, Mead & White was finally chosen from a short list of architectural candidates and construction began.

The elegant result completely transformed the adjacent areas on both sides of the river into the coherent visual experience that had been envisioned by Charles Moore, secretary to the Senate Park Commission, who recalled the group's directive "that the Memorial Bridge be a low structure on a line from the site of the Lincoln Memorial to the Arlington Mansion—a monumental rather than a traffic bridge, but a significant element in an extensive park scheme." Consisting of eight reinforced concrete arches covered in granite, plus a central bascule drawbridge span made of steel decorated to resemble stone, the bridge is an elongated cousin of Paris's many elegant classical spans across the Seine.

R2 Arlington National Cemetery

Arlington, Virginia
Established 1864

Tel: (703) 607-8000
www.arlingtoncemetery.mil

In 1864, the Union Army's quartermaster general, Montgomery C. Meigs, proposed that the federal government appropriate Robert E. Lee's family estate overlooking Washington and turn a portion of it into a cemetery. The first person buried there was actually a Confederate prisoner who died in a local hospital, but he was soon followed by thousands of Union soldiers. After the war, General Lee's heir, Custis Lee, claimed ownership of the land and successfully sued the federal government, which ultimately paid him $150,000 for title to the property. Today, Arlington Cemetery includes the graves of more than 300,000 war dead, high-ranking government officials, and other dignitaries (including Pierre Charles L'Enfant).

The cemetery, Arlington House, and the Lincoln Memorial, all linked by the Memorial Bridge, constitute one of the nation's great Beaux-Arts set pieces. Subsequent building in and around the cemetery has generally adhered to the Greco-Roman theme. The classically inspired Memorial Amphitheater is the site of major rituals, such as the annual Memorial Day ceremony. The Tomb of the Unknowns takes the form of a sarcophagus; its effective and restrained decoration is limited to three figures representing valor, victory, and peace.

President Kennedy is buried on a beautiful hillside beneath a slab of fieldstone from his beloved Cape Cod; he admired the site only days before he was assassinated in Dallas. Architect John Carl Warnecke, who had worked with the First Family to save Lafayette Square, discussed the treatment of the grave at length with Mrs. Kennedy; they eventually settled on a modest, landscapist approach that emphasizes the eternal flame. As Warnecke said, "The flame is the primary symbol at the grave, stronger than any sculpture or any structure that might be added to it." The president's brothers, Robert and Edward, his widow, Jacqueline Kennedy Onassis, and two children who died shortly after birth, are buried nearby.

One noteworthy new structure at Arlington is a maintenance facility at the southern end of the cemetery. Despite its mundane purpose, the building manifests an appropriate dignity through its high-quality materials, its segmented plan, and its modest but distinctive profile.

R2a John F. Kennedy's Grave

1966—JOHN CARL WARNECKE & ASSOCIATES

R2b Memorial Amphitheater

1920—CARRÈRE & HASTINGS
1992—Restoration: EINHORN YAFFEE PRESCOTT

R2c Tomb of the Unknowns

1921—LORIMER RICH; Sculptor: THOMAS HUDSON JONES

R2d Facility Maintenance Compound

1996—KRESSCOX ASSOCIATES

R3 Memorial Gate / Women in Military Service for America Memorial

1932—MCKIM, MEAD & WHITE
1997—Conversion: WEISS/MANFREDI ARCHITECTS; Preservation architects: OEHRLEIN & ASSOCIATES ARCHITECTS

The apse-like Memorial Gate was conceived by McKim, Mead & White as the terminus of the new axis defined by the Memorial Bridge and as the ceremonial entrance to the cemetery. Essentially an elaborate, concave retaining wall, the structure always fulfilled its urbanistic role majestically, but never really worked well as a gate.

In the 1980s, a new organization sought and received permission to create a memorial to women in military service, to be built behind and within the existing Memorial Gate structure. A subsequent design competition pro-

duced a spectacular winning entry by Weiss/Manfredi, which called for a series of simple glass spires, dubbed "the Candles," that would have served as skylights for the exhibition spaces by day and beacons of light by night. Although well conceived and beautifully presented, these bold gestures made a lot of people nervous, and sadly, they were eliminated from the final design. In the finished building, the exhibition space is lit by shallow, tilted skylights that are covered by an additional layer of thick glass panels, some of which are engraved with quotations. On a sunny day, the engraved words cast shadows on the white marble interior wall, sometimes clearly, at other times quite abstractly. Penetrating the arcing space is a series of staircases that are not accessible from inside—they connect the original plaza with an upper terrace affording views across the Memorial Bridge to the Lincoln Memorial.

R4 Arlington House

(Custis-Lee Mansion)

1804—North and south wings: GEORGE WASHINGTON PARKE CUSTIS, owner-builder
c. 1811—Alterations to north wing: ARCHITECT UNKNOWN
1818—Central section: GEORGE HADFIELD
1931—Restoration: L. M. LEISENRING
1953—Restoration: NATIONAL PARK SERVICE

One of the earliest American examples of Greek Revival architecture, Arlington House remains among the most impressive, largely due to its location. Its site overlooks Washington's monumental core, and conversely, the house is visible from many spots on the Mall and elsewhere in central D.C. It is in line with the Memorial Bridge, though not on axis with it—the bridge is oriented toward the west-southwest, while the house's portico faces due east.

Like the Capitol [see A1] and Tudor Place [see K41], Arlington House started out as two wings in want of a connector. George Washington Parke Custis, a grandson of Martha Washington and her first husband, Daniel Parke Custis, began the hilltop house as the seat of his 1,100-acre plantation. The wings, with their slightly recessed, arched windows,

were completed by 1804. At some point, Custis hired George Hadfield, who had worked on the Capitol and other prominent public buildings, to design the missing, central pavilion. Hadfield conceived the link as a single, temple-like form supported by eight enormous, unfluted Doric columns (including two behind the corner columns) and crowned by an unornamented pediment. Nearly 60 feet long and 23 feet deep, the portico is impeccably proportioned in itself yet dwarfs the rest of the house. When completed, the entire structure was stuccoed and painted to look as if it were made of marble blocks.

Robert E. Lee moved to Arlington when he married Custis's only surviving child, Mary Ann Randolph Custis, in 1831. According to the *Dictionary of American Biography,* Lee once wrote, "My affections and attachments are more strongly placed [at Arlington] than at any other place in the world." The couple and their eventual seven children lived in the house until the Civil War broke out. It was here that Lee decided to relinquish his U.S. Army commission and join the fight on the side of his home state. In 1955, Congress designated the house as a memorial to the Confederate general, who always inspired a degree of admiration even among those who fiercely opposed his cause. A major restoration of the property is under way at the time of this writing.

TOUR S

Other Places of Interest

This chapter presents a selection of architecturally significant buildings scattered around the District's less central neighborhoods, and, in the case of the first entry, a network of structures that spans the entire metropolitan area.

*In this engraving from c. 1910, the campus of Howard University and the McMillan Reservoir (*lower right*) are situated amid a pastoral landscape.*

S1 Metro System Stations

Throughout the City

1976 to present—HARRY WEESE ASSOCIATES
2002 to present—Exterior station canopies: LOURIE & CHENOWETH

To the typical American in the 1960s, the word *subway* would have evoked images of a Stygian netherworld entered at one's peril. Conscious of such overwhelmingly negative stereotypes, federal officials planning the new subway system for Washington, later named Metro, strongly advocated spending extra money to ensure that the system's stations were pleasant and inviting places. Even President Lyndon Johnson weighed in, sending a letter to the National Capital Transportation Agency in February 1966 directing the organization to "search worldwide for concepts and ideas that can be used to make the system attractive as well as useful. It should be designed so as to set an example for the Nation."

Chicago architect Harry Weese was hired to design the individual subway stations, and after a good deal of wrangling with design review authorities, by 1967 his firm had developed a prototype that featured a coffered concrete barrel vault sheltering passenger platforms that appeared to float within the space. It was a decade before the first of the airy stations based on this prototype opened, but when they finally did in 1976, they became instant icons of modern public transportation. The cleverest aspect of Weese's design is the combination of coffers and indirect lighting. Not only do the coffers make sense structurally—note how they grow shallower at the sides of the vault, where the forces acting on the tunnel are smaller—but when lit from below, they create a simple pattern of light and shadow that makes the scale of the space understandable and adds visual interest to what would otherwise be an undifferentiated expanse of concrete.

In 2001, the Washington Metropolitan Transit Authority conducted a competition for the design of a prototypical canopy to cover exterior escalators at many Metro stations, which have long been prone to breakdowns. The winning design was a vault of glass and stainless steel—recalling the form of the stations themselves—supported by slim steel struts. Canopies based on this prototype are gradually being built across the system.

S2 Hechinger/England Houses

2832 and 2838 Chain Bridge Road, NW

1952—THE ARCHITECTS COLLABORATIVE
1993—England House addition and renovation: WINTHROP FAULKNER & PARTNERS

This pair of houses was designed for John Hechinger, of the now-defunct Hechinger hardware store chain, and his sister (and their respective spouses). Built on a dramatically sloping site, the two houses are articulated as a series of simple, taut geometric forms exemplifying the design philosophy of Walter Gropius, the founder of the Bauhaus who led The Architects Collaborative at the time these projects were built.

The houses were designed and constructed during an extraordinary era in American residential architecture. Ludwig Mies van der Rohe's Farnsworth House, Philip Johnson's Glass House, and even The Architects Collaborative's own noteworthy enclave of houses at Six Moon Hill in Lexington, Massachusetts, were all built around the same time.

Perhaps inspired by such revolutionary works, the Hechingers and Englands commissioned what were arguably the first capital-M-Modern houses in Washington.

S3 Four Pavilions

2927 University Terrace, NW

1977—HUGH NEWELL JACOBSEN
2011—Renovation: RICHARD WILLIAMS ARCHITECTS

Local architect Hugh Newell Jacobsen became famous for his houses designed as assemblages of simple, gabled pavilions, but this is the only example of such a project in the District of Columbia. In this case, each pavilion is slightly offset from the next one, creating a serrated plan and making the house appear larger than it actually is. Jacobsen's trademark gutterless, eaveless roofs yield pure forms suggesting a child's archetypal drawing of a house.

S4 Cyrus & Myrtle Katzen Arts Center

Massachusetts Avenue at Ward Circle, NW

2005—EINHORN YAFFEE PRESCOTT

American University's Katzen Arts Center brought some much-needed architectural definition to Ward Circle, an otherwise undistinguished roundabout along this leafy stretch of Massachusetts Avenue. Occupying a long, skinny site and incorporating a number of

widely divergent functions, the building easily could have ended up as either a monotonous fortress or a mishmash of competing forms. Instead, the architects successfully used dynamic, curvilinear elements to break up the building's 660-foot length and to differentiate its myriad spaces. Although large expanses of the façades are windowless, the skin retains visual interest thanks to subtle variations in the color and pattern of the French limestone cladding.

In plan, the building looks a bit like a cubist painting of the human body, with the rounded "head," nearest the circle, housing the primary public exhibition space. In the "torso" are a recital hall, theater, and studio spaces, while the "legs" contain classrooms and other academic facilities for the university's visual and performing arts departments.

S5 Tenley-Friendship Library

4450 Wisconsin Avenue, NW

2011—Design architects / architects of record: FREELON; Associate architects: R. MCGHEE & ASSOCIATES

One of a series of innovative buildings commissioned by the D.C. Public Library in the early 2000s, the Tenley-Friendship branch is a dynamic composition of angular forms reflecting the irregular geometry of its polygonal site. In plan, the building is organized as two angled blocks separated by a skylit circulation zone, with book stacks and reading areas along the street and offices,

meeting rooms, and support spaces to the rear. The section facing Wisconsin Avenue has a transparent base sheltered by an overhang lined with angled louvers, which modulate sunlight coming into the library but also add a welcome vertical emphasis to the low-rise building. The apex of the oblique angle of the upper level directs visitors to the main entrance.

When the D.C. Public Library decided to demolish the bland, outmoded branch that previously stood on this site, city officials envisioned building a mixed-use complex here, with the library at the base and income-generating residential or commercial uses above. Some area residents were apoplectic, citing concerns about increased traffic and congestion, despite the fact that the site is across the street from a Metro station. Only the library portion was built, but at the request of the District government, the architects designed the building to accommodate an addition above should the development climate change in the future.

S6 Cityline at Tenley

Wisconsin Avenue and Albemarle Street, NW

1941—JOHN S. REDDEN AND JOHN G. RABEN
2005—Renovation and addition: SHALOM BARANES ASSOCIATES

A classic, Art Moderne former Sears store, with a swoopy canopy and soaring display window at the corner, now serves as the podium for a condominium apartment building with more than 200 units. The materials, fenestration patterns, and details of the new and old elements of the complex are dissimilar but aesthetically complementary. The striations of the aluminum panels on the apartment structure reinforce the characteristic, horizontal emphasis of the original building, while the new structure's broad, gentle arc plays off against the more acute curves of the Art Moderne base.

S7 Brown House

3005 Audubon Terrace, NW

1968—RICHARD NEUTRA
1993—Renovation and addition: CASS AND ASSOCIATES

Richard Neutra helped to define the "California style" of residential architecture in the mid-20th century, which, in turn, influenced domestic design across the country. Open floor plans, asymmetrical compositions of simple forms, and large expanses of glass blurring the distinction between indoors and outdoors yielded houses that epitomized the informality that became a hallmark of American domestic life.

Donald and Ann Brown commissioned Neutra to design what turned out to be his last single-family house. To understand his clients' needs and desires, the architect instructed them to keep a diary of their activities and take an inventory of all their possessions and even insisted on living with them for two weeks. Though often frustrated by Neutra's notoriously difficult personality, the Browns were thoroughly pleased with the house he designed for them, which came in exactly on budget.

The house retains a remarkably pure silhouette thanks in part to the lack of railings at the edges of the balconies—the Browns simply did not let their children out onto the balconies until they were old enough to avoid tumbling over the edge. A large new music room, added under the direction of architect Heather Cass, seamlessly extends the structural and spatial character of this classic house.

S8 Washington Theological Union

6896 Laurel Street, NW

Original buildings: DATES AND ARCHITECTS UNKNOWN
1996—Renovation and additions: KRESSCOX ASSOCIATES

This Roman Catholic seminary occupies an agglomeration of buildings that formerly served as the headquarters of the Seventh-Day Adventist Church. Early work on the renovation revealed a number of surprises related to the previous occupants' apocalyptic worldview, including nuclear fallout shelters filled with large supplies of vitamin C and aspirin. Moreover, what initially appeared to be four primary buildings turned out to be an incredibly complicated warren of countless conjoined structures. The Adventists presumably were not interested in long-range planning, and therefore built their headquarters on an incremental and haphazard basis.

The renovation architects enclosed the disused courtyard and turned it into the library, making it both the symbolic and physical core of the institution. A pergola was added along the eastern elevation to define the entrance. Finally, the entirely new Connelly Chapel of Holy Wisdom, connected to the main building by a glazed breezeway, was built at the southern end of the complex. With tall walls of buff brick and large clerestory windows separated by white aluminum-composite fins, the chapel has an almost industrial feel, which is augmented by its coincidental proximity to a brick smokestack. The interior is bright and neat, rendered in light-colored materials such as unstained maple. The ceiling of the sanctuary features a giant cross articulated by two pairs of steel beams and a smooth plane of acoustical plaster.

S9 St. Paul's Church

Rock Creek Cemetery
Rock Creek Church Road at Webster Street, NW

1775—ARCHITECT UNKNOWN
1810—Reconstruction: ARCHITECT UNKNOWN
1868—Renovation: ARCHITECT UNKNOWN
1922—Reconstruction: DELOS H. SMITH
2004—Restoration: ATELIER ARCHITECTS

The original chapel on this site, built around 1719, was the first church in what later became the District of Columbia. It was replaced in 1775; the replacement was then remodeled in 1868, but that version burned to the ground in 1921. The present one-story brick church, with its central entrance tower and projecting chancel, is a reconstruction incorporating surviving walls of the 1775 building.

S10 Rock Creek Cemetery / Adams Memorial ("Grief")

Rock Creek Cemetery
Rock Creek Church Road, NW

1890—Sculpture: AUGUSTUS SAINT-GAUDENS; Base: STANFORD WHITE

Henry Adams commissioned this heavily shrouded bronze as a memorial to his wife, Marian, after her suicide, and it almost immediately became one of the most revered works of art in Washington. Lorado Taft, who sculpted the Columbus Fountain near Union Station, said that to look on the figure's face was like "confronting eternity"; Augustus Saint-Gaudens himself felt the sculpture "beyond pain and beyond joy. It is the human soul face to face with the greatest of all mysteries." The figure sits on a rough stone with a simple bench in front, designed by the illustrious architect Stanford White.

S11 Armed Forces Retirement Home—Washington

(U.S. Soldiers' and Airmen's Home)
Rock Creek Church Road at Upshur Street, NW

1843—President Lincoln's Cottage: JOHN SKIRVING
1848, 1897, 1923—Additions and alterations to President Lincoln's Cottage: ARCHITECTS UNKNOWN
1857—Sherman Hall: BARTON S. ALEXANDER
1869—Addition and alterations to Sherman Hall: EDWARD CLARK
1912—Grant Building: BALDWIN AND PENNINGTON
2008—Restoration of President Lincoln's Cottage: HILLIER ARCHITECTURE

Lincoln slept here. Actually, several 19th-century presidents used what was then called the Soldiers' Home as a retreat from the White House, but Lincoln was especially fond of the place, and it is believed that he wrote the final draft of the Emancipation Proclamation in the cottage that is now named for him. Built in 1843 by banker George W. Riggs for his own use and soon expanded, that "cottage" is actually a rambling,

34-room house designed in the fashionably picturesque Carpenter Gothic style. In 1851, Riggs sold the house and surrounding land to the government, which was looking for a large tract on which to build an "asylum for old and disabled veterans." Lincoln named the house in honor of Major Robert Anderson, the Union commander at Fort Sumter when the first shots of the Civil War were fired, and it was later renamed for the president himself.

The Soldiers' Home was partially financed by General Winfield Scott, hero of the Mexican War, who donated a portion of the tribute paid to him by the Mexican government in exchange for sparing Mexico City. Several significant structures were soon built on the huge campus, including Sherman Hall, a neo-Romanesque castle with a tall, central clock tower. Also noteworthy is the Grant Building, an elegant, marble structure again in the Romanesque Revival style, which followed some 55 years later.

As of this writing the Armed Forces Retirement Home, as it is now known, is planning to tear down a major, mid-20th-century building and replace it with one that is more in scale with the historic structures nearby. Meanwhile, a plan to sell a portion of the vast property for a mixed-use development is pending.

S12 The Catholic University of America

620 Michigan Avenue, NE

1989—Edward M. Crough Center for Architectural Studies: JOHN V. YANIK ET AL.
1994—Columbus School of Law: FLORANCE EICHBAUM ESOCOFF KING ARCHITECTS
2003—Edward J. Pryzbyla University Center: BOHLIN CYWINSKI JACKSON

Washington, D.C., is home to the largest collection of Roman Catholic institutions and facilities outside of Rome, many of them concentrated in an area of the city's Northeast quadrant that is sometimes called the "Little Vatican." At the heart of the precinct is The Catholic University of America, which was founded by Pope Leo XIII in 1887 and is officially the national university of the American Catholic Church.

The campus includes several build-

ings of note, such as the School of Architecture and Planning, which occupies a renovated former gymnasium. The initial plan for the renovation was developed by students in the school under the direction of Professor John Yanik. Other prominent structures include the Columbus School of Law, a quietly contextual affair, and the new Pryzbyla Center, marked by a roughly 250-foot-long, undulating, glass-and-steel façade.

S13 Basilica of the National Shrine of the Immaculate Conception

400 Michigan Avenue, NE

1920–59—MAGINNIS AND WALSH (LATER MAGINNIS, WALSH AND KENNEDY); Associate architect (1920–32): FREDERICK V. MURPHY

Tel: (202) 526-8300
www.nationalshrine.com

Despite being the largest Roman Catholic church in the country, and one of the largest churches in the world, seating more than 6,000 people, this is technically not a cathedral. It is rather a shrine

dedicated to the Virgin Mary as patron saint of the United States. Designed and built over a period of 40 years, it is ostensibly a combination of the neo-Byzantine and neo-Romanesque styles, but the finished structure—particularly the interior—somehow conveys more than a whiff of 1950s Beverly Hills Moderne. The architects cited various rationales for the style of the church, one of which was a deliberate contrast with the Gothic-style National Cathedral across town.

The colorful dome and tall, slender carillon make the shrine one of the major landmarks on the Washington skyline. The main sanctuary, which was very loosely modeled after St. Mark's in Venice, features brightly colored mosaics and a succession of small chapels depicting the various incarnations of Mary. The basement houses an astonishing shop full of religious paraphernalia.

S14 Pope John Paul II Cultural Center

3900 Harewood Road, NE

2001—LEO A DALY

Tel: (202) 635-5400
www.jp2cc.org

The Pope John Paul II Cultural Center, designed to house exhibition galleries and an interfaith think tank, is a startlingly modern building that eschews trite symbolism and knee-jerk monumentality. It is impressive without being overbearing, dignified without being stuffy.

The building is a balanced but asymmetrical composition in both plan and elevation. The primary façade is enlivened by the visual interplay between two projecting forms—a stout cylinder containing the main entrance at ground level and a boardroom above, and a rather enigmatic, three-dimensional puzzle of planes and volumes enclosing a small chapel. Behind these foreground elements is the main body of the building, a long and solid bar offset by a wing-like, patinated copper roof, held aloft from the main structure by slender struts. The crowning touch is an attenuated, gold-leaf cross that engages a rectangular bay window before piercing the roof plane. Inside, the center affords visitors a number of rich spatial experiences, including a generously scaled bank of sloping walkways that connect the exhibition spaces on the three lowest levels.

The cultural center, which, curiously, was established and funded by the Archdiocese of Detroit, never attracted as many visitors as expected and has long struggled financially. As of this writing, the Knights of Columbus has just announced an agreement to purchase the center, with plans to expand its exhibitions and reinvigorate its educational programming.

S15 Franciscan Monastery of the Holy Land in America

1400 Quincy Street, NE

1899—Memorial Church of the Holy Sepulchre and Monastery: ARISTIDE LEONORI
1925—Ascension Chapel: JOHN JOSEPH EARLEY, BASED ON DRAWINGS BY P. RICCI
1926—Rosary Portico and Portiuncula Chapel: MURPHY & OLMSTED; Concrete artist: JOHN JOSEPH EARLEY
1942—Addition to monastery: A. HAMILTON WILSON
Various other renovations and additions: ARCHITECTS UNKNOWN

Tel: (202) 526-6800
www.myfranciscan.org

The Franciscan brothers who founded this monastery wanted nothing less than to create a "Holy Land in America." Their initial plan was to build a replica of Jerusalem's Church of the Holy Sepulchre on Staten Island, overlooking the entrance to New York Harbor. That project was never executed, but in 1897, they bought a 44-acre parcel of land in Northeast D.C.—a tract that, ironically, was known in the 17th century as "Cuckold's Delight"—and adjusted their plans to fit

the new site. Within just two years, they had conducted a successful fundraising campaign, hired Italian architect Aristide Leonori, and built an impressive church and monastery according to his design. Over the next three decades, the monastery gradually added a number of peripheral structures inspired by, or directly replicating, historic sites in Italy and the Middle East.

The centerpiece of the complex is the Memorial Church of the Holy Sepulchre, the design of which incorporates Byzantine, Romanesque, and even Renaissance elements (note, for instance, the Palladian window over the main entrance). The plan is in the shape of a modified Latin cross, with a tall nave and transept bracketed by four shorter, cubic elements nestled into the corners of the crossing. The exterior is relatively plain, in keeping with the Franciscan tenets of modesty and simplicity, but the sanctuary is surprisingly and spectacularly ornate, with vibrantly colored ceiling coffers, murals, and stained glass. At the center, beneath the dome, is an extraordinary baldacchino, with astonishingly slender posts supporting a delicate canopy.

Impressive though the church may be, some of the most significant architectural elements of the compound are the various artworks—including several full-scale structures—designed or executed by John Joseph Earley. Famed for his innovative concrete mosaics, Earley oversaw construction of the Ascension Chapel, which is a replica of the one erected by the Crusaders on Mount Olivet in Jerusalem. He also designed the mosaics in the Rosary Portico—the arcade that defines the church's forecourt—and the Portiuncula Chapel, which was copied from the small church in Assisi where St. Francis founded his eponymous order in 1209. To the south of the church is the Valley of the Shrines, featuring a series of grottos including more of Earley's characteristic mosaics.

S16 McMillan Sand Filtration Site

Michigan Avenue and North Capitol Street, NW

1905—LIEUTENANT COLONEL ALEXANDER M. MILLER; Landscape architect for park: FREDERICK LAW OLMSTED JR.

This former water filtration facility is now Washington's most intriguing ruin and surely one of the most popular sites for local architecture school projects, thanks to the irresistible challenge of figuring out how to incorporate the facility's strange remnants into some sort of new development. The District of Columbia bought the site from the federal government in 1987 and has announced plans for a major, mixed-use project that would preserve some of the property's historic elements.

S17 Howard University

607 Howard Place, NW

1867—Howard Hall: ARCHITECT UNKNOWN
1895—Andrew Rankin Memorial Chapel: ARCHITECT UNKNOWN
1939—Founders Library: ALBERT I. CASSELL; Principal designer: LOUIS E. FRY SR.
1996—Restoration of Howard Hall: OEHRLEIN & ASSOCIATES ARCHITECTS

Howard University is a private, historically black college that was chartered by the federal government in 1867. Its primary campus is just north of Florida Avenue on relatively high ground, affording excellent views over the city from several spots. The architecture of the university is predominantly Georgian or Colonial Revival, which might seem ironic, given the often-painful associations of colonialism for African Americans, but the result is a cohesive, dignified core campus reminiscent of numerous prestigious, northeastern colleges, which may have been a more important association for Howard's architects.

Founders Library is the most prominent building on campus by virtue of its location at one end of the main quadrangle and its 165-foot-tall clock tower. The building was modeled after Philadelphia's Independence Hall, and in this case, the principal designer of Founders Hall shed some light on the source of inspiration, saying that "since the Library was dedicated to liberty, there was no more appropriate design for Howard University's major building to emulate."

The exterior of the Gothic Revival Rankin Memorial Chapel is mostly understated, except for a bold, corner tower whose spire is bracketed with dormers that have their own spiky roofs. The adjacent entryway is marked by a broad, pointed arch. The interior has a dark wood ceiling supported by arches resting on dramatically projecting brackets.

Howard Hall, a tall, Second Empire mansion, is the oldest extant building on the campus. Built of hollow white bricks and later painted a succession of colors, it was the home of General Oliver Howard, a founder of the university and a commissioner of the Freedmen's Bureau. The university purchased the house in 1909 and, after years of neglect, it has now been fully restored.

S18 Watha T. Daniel / Shaw Library

1630 7th Street, NW

2010—DAVIS BRODY BOND AEDAS

The previous branch library on this site was a rough and rude concrete bunker, built in an era in which "urban" architecture often meant "defensive" architecture. The new building is everything its predecessor was not: open, light-filled, inviting, and environmentally sustainable to boot. Its most prominent feature is a perforated, corrugated aluminum screen suspended in front of the south façade, which reduces solar heat gain and helps to protect the library's holdings from the fading effects of direct sunlight. At night, it filters the artificial light emanating from inside, turning the building into a kind of civic lantern. Much of the rest of the building is covered in translucent Kalwall panels, which achieve similar but complementary effects. The library's sustainable credentials include a substantial reliance on recycled materials and a green roof.

S19 LeDroit Park

Florida and Rhode Island avenues between 2nd and 7th streets, NW

1873-77—JAMES MCGILL
2001—Multiple renovations and new houses: SORG AND ASSOCIATES
Various other buildings

Although it was originally built as an exclusively white neighborhood, LeDroit Park has long played a key role in the cultural and social life of historically black Howard University. The neighborhood was developed by Amzi L. Barber, one of the university's founders, who was white. In 1888, a group of African Americans, frustrated by having to walk around what was, in effect, a gated community, tore down part of the fence that surrounded it, and within a few years, the remaining fences and walls were dismantled and the area was integrated. It became a center of African American cultural life in the early 20th century, with residents including the poet Paul Lawrence Dunbar.

James McGill designed many of LeDroit Park's houses in the highly popular romantic styles of the period: Gothic Revival, Italianate, and Second Empire. The area remains largely intact, with some 50 of the original 64 dwellings still standing. The neighborhood was once marked by pastoral street names—Elm, Maple, and so on—that were later officially changed to fit the District's rational system of letters and numbers.

S20 Gallaudet University

7th Street and Florida Avenue, NE

1866—Master plan: OLMSTED, VAUX AND COMPANY
1868-81—Various buildings: FREDERICK C. WITHERS / VAUX, WITHERS AND COMPANY
1993—College Hall restoration: EINHORN YAFFEE PRESCOTT
1995—Kellogg Conference Center: EINHORN YAFFEE PRESCOTT
1999—Chapel Hall restoration: EINHORN YAFFEE PRESCOTT
2008—Sorenson Language and Communication Center: SMITHGROUP; Associate architects: KUHN RIDDLE ARCHITECTS
2010—Denison House renovation: AYERS SAINT GROSS

Gallaudet University was founded in 1864 as the Deaf Mute College, the first institution of higher learning for the deaf in America. Later named for Thomas Hopkins Gallaudet, a pioneering educator of the hearing-impaired, the university occupies a park-like setting removed from the bustle of the city. The campus plan by Frederick Law Olmsted and Calvert Vaux is a masterpiece of informality. While the buildings generally harmonize with each other and with the landscape, many also possess great individual character. Chapel Hall (Frederick C. Withers with Calvert Vaux), built of contrasting-colored stone and possibly the earliest Ruskinian Gothic college structure in America, and College Hall (Frederick C. Withers), built of brownstone and brick, both merit special attention.

Several recently constructed or renovated buildings on campus were influenced by the university's DeafSpace project, which encourages design that responds to the unique needs and culture of hearing-impaired people.

S21 Hecht Company Warehouse

1401 New York Avenue, NE

1937—ABBOTT, MERKT & CO.
1948, 1961—Additions: ABBOTT, MERKT & CO.
1992—Rehabilitation: ARCHITECT UNKNOWN

The finest work of streamlined, Art Moderne architecture in Washington, and one of the greatest such buildings anywhere in the United States, the Hecht Company Warehouse is a glistening layer cake of glazed brick and glass block. The ground floor, which originally incorporated large windows for displaying the department store chain's merchandise, is covered in glazed black bricks with jazzy, white accents. The upper levels consist of alternating bands of buff bricks and glass blocks, separated by thin black stripes. The glass block bands are interrupted by clear glass windows, which are aligned vertically and thus provide an understated but crucial balance to the building's insistent horizontality. On the fifth floor is another subtle trick: the Hecht Company's name is spelled out in glazed black bricks, which, in certain light conditions, are barely distinguishable from the surrounding glass blocks. Of course, the *pièce de résistance* is the multifaceted, glass block beacon that seemingly explodes from the top of the corner tower, which is difficult to explain as anything other than a magnificent gesture just for the fun of it.

Federated Department Stores, which bought the Hecht Company chain in 2005, soon sold the warehouse to a Pennsylvania-based developer who planned to restore it as part of a retail and commercial complex. As of this writing, it has been sold again to local developer Douglas Jemal, who has yet to announce specific plans for the site.

S22 Bureau of Alcohol, Tobacco, Firearms and Explosives (ATF) Headquarters

99 New York Avenue, NE

2008—SAFDIE ARCHITECTS; Associated architects: OPX

It was a safe bet that the new headquarters of the Bureau of Dangerous Stuff was unlikely to end up looking friendly and welcoming, and indeed, it does not. The architects' fundamental goal was to adhere to the incredibly strict security requirements imposed upon them by the General Services Administration, which manages federal office properties, while avoiding the eerie, peripheral dead zones and blank façades that are the common stigmata of high-security buildings. To achieve their goal, the architects placed the bulk of the secure spaces in an L-shaped structure aligning with, but set back from, N and 2nd streets, with a separate, curvilinear office bar in front of the main block and an atrium between the two. Along the south side of the site, the architects placed a trellis between the building and N Street to help animate the streetscape, which does not really work but is better than nothing. Along 2nd Street, the solution is more successful, involving a one-story retail wing that serves as a physical buffer to the main building. For the other two sides of the site, the security barrier takes the form of a curving, multi-story, concrete pergola surrounding a planted plaza that is accessible only from within the complex. The pergola is strange and forbidding now, but if, in some happier future, the garden might be opened to the public, one could imagine some inventive uses for the curious structure. With respect to the main building, one thing is a pity: the curtain wall on the curving block is quite interesting, with a serrated profile in section, but hardly anyone gets to see it up close.

S23 U.S. National Arboretum

24th and R streets, NE

1963—Administration building: DEIGERT & YERKES & ASSOCIATES
1976, 1978, 1980—Revisions: SASAKI ASSOCIATES INC.
1990—Corinthian column garden: RUSSELL PAGE, WITH EDAW INC.
1993—Bird garden and grove of state trees: HOH ASSOCIATES

www.usna.usda.gov

The National Arboretum comprises 446 hilly, green acres, incongruously adjacent to a gritty stretch of New York Avenue. Lobbying for an arboretum began at least as far back as 1901, and in 1927 Congress approved legislation to "establish and maintain a national arboretum for purposes of research and education concerning tree and plant life." Since then the institution has grown into one of the largest, most advanced of its kind in America.

The arboretum merits mention in this guidebook because it is now the site of nearly two dozen, 34-foot-tall sandstone Corinthian columns that were removed from the U.S. Capitol during expansions in the 1950s. The columns, designed by Benjamin Henry Latrobe and erected under the supervision of Charles Bulfinch, seemed, despite that pedigree, to be destined for some local landfill, until arboretum benefactor Ethel Garrett intervened and rescued them. After years of negotiations, the columns finally were taken out of storage and placed in the arboretum, and landscape architect Russell Page designed a setting for them on a knoll. Page died in 1985, but EDAW faithfully carried out his low-key plans: a small fountain adds gentle noise and movement to the composition and spills over to form a reflecting pool below.

S24 Langston Terrace Dwellings

Benning Road and 21st Street, NE

1938—HILYARD R. ROBINSON; Associated architect: PAUL WILLIAMS; Sculptor: DANIEL OLNEY
1962—Row house additions: LEROY BROWN

The first federally financed public housing project in the District of Columbia, Langston Terrace was built under the auspices of the Public Works Administration expressly for low-income African American families. The design by Hilyard Robinson, one of Washington's most prominent early African American architects, was heavily influenced by the famed Karl-Marx-Hof housing estate in Vienna, Austria, and other avant-garde projects that Robinson had visited while touring Europe. Although built on a very modest budget, the complex includes relatively elaborate sculptural elements, including bas-reliefs by Daniel Olney depicting "The Progress of the Negro Race." The development was named after John Mercer Langston, a former congressman who also served as acting president of Howard University.

S25 Frederick Douglass National Historic Site

(Cedar Hill)
1411 W Street, SE

1859—JOHN VAN HOOK
1878–93—Various additions: ARCHITECTS UNKNOWN
1922—Restoration: ARCHITECT UNKNOWN
1972, 2007—Restorations: NATIONAL PARK SERVICE

Tel: (202) 426-5961
www.nps.gov/frdo

Frederick Douglass, author, abolitionist, and editor, moved to this house in 1877 when he became U.S. marshal of the District of Columbia. He named the picturesque cottage to honor the cedar trees (most are now gone) that shaded the house. One evening in 1895, after returning from a women's rights meeting, Douglass suffered a heart attack and died in the house. His widow, Helen, successfully lobbied Congress to establish a nonprofit organization to care for Cedar Hill, and in 1903 the house was opened for public tours. The National Park Service acquired the property in 1962. The house has been faithfully preserved and thus provides an unusually vivid sense of domestic life in late 19th-century Washington.

S26 St. Elizabeths Hospital, West Campus

2700 Martin Luther King Jr., Avenue, SE

1853–74—Center Building: THOMAS U. WALTER
1899–1910—"Letter Buildings" and Hitchcock Hall: SHEPLEY, RUTAN AND COOLIDGE
1861–1979—Numerous other buildings: VARIOUS ARCHITECTS

Outraged by the shameful neglect of the nation's homeless and mentally ill during the mid-19th century, Dorothea Dix lobbied the federal government to improve the condition of the "many persons from various parts of the Union, whose minds are more or less erratic," and who "find their way to the metropolis of the country [and] ramble about . . . poorly clad and suffering for want of food and shelter." Congress heeded her pleas and approved funds for what was initially known as the Government Hospital for the Insane, but was later named St. Elizabeths (with no apostrophe). Working closely with the hospital's chief of staff, Dr. C. H. Nichol, architect Thomas U. Walter created the first building—a burly, red brick structure with a crenellated roof parapet and buttresses at key corners. Called the Center Building, it was serrated in plan to maximize access to natural light and air. Subsequent buildings include a series designed by the Boston firm of Shepley, Rutan and Coolidge around the turn of the 20th century in a neoclassical style that brings to mind collegiate campuses of the same era.

Over the years, thousands of men and women have been treated here. One of the most noted residents was the American-born poet Ezra Pound, who had lived in Italy for much of his life and was an ardent fascist. In the wake of Mussolini's execution in 1945, Pound was arrested by Italian partisans, turned over to American authorities, and later admitted to St. Elizabeths after he pled insanity in order to avoid a trial for treason. Released in 1958, Pound returned to Italy, declaring that "all America is an insane asylum."

The St. Elizabeths complex is divided into two major parts: the West Campus, which is owned by the federal government and includes the most historic buildings, and the East Campus, owned by the District of Columbia government. The East Campus is still in use as a mental hospital (and it is here that John Hinckley Jr., who tried to assassinate Ronald Reagan, still resides). The West Campus was gradually phased out of operations and was effectively abandoned by 2002.

At the time of this writing, the West Campus is being redeveloped to serve as the headquarters of the U.S. Department of Homeland Security. The project has sparked regret among preservationists that the hyper-secure complex will be inaccessible to the general public and hope among neighborhood activists that the influx of federal workers will generate economic activity in an area that could use it. The architects overseeing the renovations of the historic buildings and the design of new structures have taken pains to protect the fundamental character of the site, but it seems inevitable that the result will be a veritable fortress—a modern-day citadel with spectacular views across the city from which it is isolated.

Index

Credits

Photographs in this volume are by Alan Karchmer, except for those listed below. All illustrations are reproduced by permission.

© Peter Aaron / Esto. All rights reserved. E14, J7, O13a, S4
© Hoachlander Davis Photography, p. 15
© Wolfgang Hoyt / Esto. All rights reserved. J6, O12c
Nic Lehoux. Courtesy of Bing Thom Architects. C6
© Maxwell MacKenzie A20, B1, B5, B12, D1, G9, G20, G24, H10, I6, J11, J16, J17, K15, K22, M1, O12e, P17, R2d, S6
© Robert C. Lautman Photography, National Building Museum. A18, E1
Ezra Stoller © Esto. All rights reserved. D26

Andersson, Eve Astrid (www.eveandersson.com), p. 16; Andrade, Michael, E15, G17, G18; Architect of the Capitol, pp. ii–iii; Arthur Cotton Moore / Associates, K25; Baranes, Shalom, G19; Becker, Bryan, G6, I12, O7; The British Embassy and Ambassador Sir Robin Renwick, p. 255; CORE Group, PC, S3; Cott, George A., D2; Creamer, Robert, Q4; Cunningham, Dan, A2, G21, L23, M7; Davidson, D. Graham, K21; Dersin, Michael, G22, L17; Devrouax & Purnell, C14; Dumbarton Oaks, K43a; Esocoff, Philip A., C7; Feldblyum, Boris, A1b, A1c, A1d, A4, A6, A8, A9, A10, A13, A14, A15, A16, A17, A19, B10, B13, C3, C11, D4, D12, D13, D14, D15, D16, D18, D19, D24, E2, E3, E4, E5, E8, E12, E16, E18, E22, F1, F3, F11, F12, F16, G8, G10, G11, G12, G23, G25, G26, G27, G28, G29, H8, I3, I10, I13, I14, I15, I16, J1, J2, J8, J9, J12, J13, J14, J15, J18, K10, K17, K20, K23, K26, L1, L4, L6, L9, L10, L13, L14, L16, L18, L22, L25, M4, M6, M8, M9, M13, M14, M17, N1, N2, N5, N7, N8, O12f, O14, O16, P3, P6, P12, P13, P20, P23, P24, P26, P27, Q2, Q5, Q6, S2, S5, S12, S14, S21, S24; Fox, Debi, M11, M12, M15; Fred Sons Photography, L11; Greenhouse, Richard, C8; Gurney, Robert M., N12; Heine, Julia, K14; Highsmith, Carol M., F4, F17, G4, G14; Hoachlander, Anice, B8, F14, M16; Houlahan, Michael O., B4; Hursley, Tim, I19, S22; Jamison, Alex, L21, N11; Lautman, Robert C., D6, H14, S7, S16; Lebovich, Bill, O4a; Levine, Larry M., S1; Library of Congress, Prints and Photographs Division, pp. 3, 5-11, 17, 20, 21-22, 23 (top), 37, 47, 59, 77 (top, bottom left), 81, 97, 115, 133, 137 (top), 140 (bottom), 147, 173, 199, 219, 231, 241, 271, 277, 283; Loosle, Richard, maps A–R; Maryland Historical Society, p. 4; Miller, Jon, L2; National Building Museum, pp. 13, 85; O'Rourke, Ronald, o8, P4; Paine, Donald, A11; Patel, Prakash, E17, E20, G5, I18, L27, O12d; Paul Warchol Photography, O12b; Polidori, Robert, P25; Poyourow, Dan, J10; Quinn Evans Architects, H2; Rivera, Paúl, S18; Shalom Baranes Associates, F20, H11; Skidmore, Owings & Merrill, F13; Solomon, Ron, H7; Sorg, Nicole, M10; Suzane Reatig Architecture, E6; Wyner, Kenneth M., C15, E7, E9.

5/2016
32c